Children's Literature

Volume 5

j   WWC ✔   1 - 3
808.8
C536c
v.5
  Children's literature

Rochester Public Library
115 South Avenue
Dept. of Work with Children

ROCHESTER PUBLIC LIBRARY

Volume 5

Annual of
The Modern Language Association
Group on Children's Literature and
The Children's Literature
Association

Temple University Press
Philadelphia

j
808.8
C 536c
v.5

EDITOR-IN-CHIEF:
  FRANCELIA BUTLER

CO-EDITORS:
  BENNETT A. BROCKMAN and WILLIAM E. SHEIDLEY

BOOK REVIEW EDITOR:
  MERADITH TILBURY McMUNN

ADVISORY BOARD: Marilyn Apseloff, Martin Gardner, K. Narayan
  Kutty, Alison Lurie, William T. Moynihan, Peter F. Neumeyer,
  Thomas J. Roberts, William Rosen, Glenn W. Sadler

ASSISTANT TO THE EDITORS: Mark Boyer

SPECIAL CONSULTANTS: Charity Chang (Library), Anne Devereaux
  Jordan and Francis J. Molson (Children's Literature Association)

EDITORIAL ASSISTANTS: Carol Boardman, Ruth Maksvytis Howe,
  Bonnie Konowitch, Virginia Schaefer, David Tedone

Editorial correspondence should be addressed to:
  Editors, *Children's Literature*
  Department of English, U-25
  University of Connecticut
  Storrs, Connecticut 06268

Manuscripts submitted should conform to the second edition of the
  MLA Style Sheet. An original and one copy are requested.
  Manuscripts should be accompanied by a self-addressed envelope
  and postage.

Temple University Press, Philadelphia 19122
© 1976 by Francelia Butler. All rights reserved
Published 1976
Printed in the United States of America

International Standard Book Number: 0-87722-069-7 cloth; 0-87722-070-0
  paper
Library of Congress Catalog Card Number: 75-21550
Cover illustration by Jan Bakker

Contents

The Editor's High Chair   3

Articles

The Case for a Children's Literature   *Clifton Fadiman*   9
Change, Tradition, and Critical Styles
  in the Contemporary World of Children's
  Books   *Ravenna Helson*   22
For the Good of the Country:
  Cultural Values in American
  Juvenile Fiction, 1825–60   *Anne MacLeod*   40
Shaping the National Character
  The Origin and Development of the
  New England Primer   *Daniel A. Cohen*   52
  The McGuffey *Readers*   *Carol Kammen*   58
  The Story of a Bad Boy   *Ann Beattie*   63
The Utopia of *St. Nicholas*: The
  Present as Prologue   *Fred Erisman*   66
The Oddness of Oz   *Osmond Beckwith*   74
Jack London as a Children's Writer   *Susan Ward*   92
Skip Rope Rhymes as a Reflection
  of American Culture   *Francelia Butler* 104
The Real Secret of Superman's Identity   *Alvin Schwartz*   117
Six Characters in Search of the Family:
  The Novels of Paul Zindel   *James T. Henke*   130
Racism and Sexism in Children's
  Nonfiction   *Jim Haskins*   141
"The Nürnberg Stove" as an Artistic
  Fairy Tale   *Charity Chang*   148
Fact and Fiction in Natalie Savage
  Carlson's Autobiographical
  Stories: A Personal View   *Julie Carlson McAlpine*   157

THE INTERNATIONAL SCENE IN CHILDREN'S LITERATURE
Down with Heidi, Down with
  Struwwelpeter, Three Cheers for the
  Revolution: Towards a New Socialist
  Children's Literature in West Germany   *Jack Zipes*   162

W. W. C.

Some Features of the Modern Italian
  Literature for Young People   *Carla Poesio*   180
A List of the Juvenile Literature
  in the Hughes Public Library,
  Rugby, Tennessee   *Jan Bakker*   189

Reviews

Scholarship in New Disciplines   *Thomas J. Roberts*   239
History of Childhood   *Julius A. Elias*   247
Children's Literature as Historical
  Evidence   *Ruth Barnes Moynihan*   253
American History for Young People at
  Bicentennial   *Ruth Barnes Moynihan*   261
A Novel of Children's Liberation   *Virginia L. Wolf*   270
From Shakespeare to Brooklyn: New
  Trends in Children's Poetry   *Marilyn Apseloff*   273
Nonsense as Reality   *K. Narayan Kutty*   286
Six Fantasies: Theme and Style   *William H. Green*   288
Recent Science Fiction and Science
  Fantasy   *Craig Wallace Barrow*   294
Six Females: A Mixed Bookbag   *Rebecca Lukens*   298
Recent Biographies of Women for
  Young Readers   *Sheila M. Duram*   301
Isaac Bashevis Singer's Books for
  Young People   *Thomas P. Riggio*   304
Literature for and by Children:
  The Other Side of Elizabeth I's
  Character Never Before Revealed
  by Previous Historians   *Judy Rosen*   311

Varia

Of Note   *Rachel Fordyce*   315
Suggested Topics for Research   317
Contributors and Editors   320

Children's Literature

Volume 5

The Editor's High Chair

In this bicentennial year, I want to try to project what children's literature will be like one hundred years from now. I think that with the increased population and consequent social pressures as well as further technological developments which alienate man from himself, more reliance will have to be placed on simple, basic stories such as the old folktales and classics in fantasy which delight and sustain both adults and children.

My own view is reinforced by recently published essays by Isaac Bashevis Singer, Bruno Bettelheim, and P. L. Travers. In a recent issue of the *New York Times Book Review*, Mr. Singer writes in connection with a review of a newly reissued volume of old Russian fairy tales that "we must allow a place in the human spirit for things not limited by the laws of nature, a place where we can create our own laws." In *The New Yorker*, Bruno Bettelheim states that "nothing can be as enriching and satisfying to child and adult alike as the folk fairy tale":

> The fairy tale is future-oriented and guides the child—in terms he can understand in both his conscious and his unconscious mind —to relinquish his infantile wishes for dependency and achieve an independent existence, which the fairy tale helps him to perceive as more satisfying.

And in Volume 4 of *Children's Literature*, P. L. Travers wrote:

> If it is literature indeed, it can't help being all one river and you put into it, according to age, a small foot or a large one. When mine was a small foot, I seem to remember that I was grateful for books that did not speak to my childishness, books that treated me with respect, that spread out the story just as it was, Grimm's Fairy Tales, for instance, and left me to deal with it as I could.

The trend, then, seems to be towards a deeper study and awareness of the human content of the old tales. People are beginning to realize that much adult literature is not significantly different from children's literature, the difference being that adult literature embellishes and sometimes obscures the old themes—that it is more particular, less universal. The tales that satisfy are those that have endured for hundreds of years—religious stories, medieval folktales, fantasies. Miss

3

Travers also recalled recently how a young woman whom she knew slightly stopped her on the street and asked, "How can I learn to be a woman?" Miss Travers knew that the girl had had several lovers. "I cast about in my mind for some instructive book," Miss Travers writes in the *New York Times*, "and my good angel tapped me on the shoulder. 'Read Grimm's Fairy Tales,' I said, and left her open-mouthed and incredulous, standing on the corner."

Miss Travers could have asked her to read Jung or Freud, but instead she went directly to the source for all treatments of women, the all-inclusive world of the fairy tale. Of course, some of our current fantasies will prove to have this satisfying quality, as Mr. Singer suggests:

> It very well may be that a hundred years from now, Marxism, the theories of Freud and Jung, great parts of our modern sociology and psychology, and perhaps even medicine will be considered as nothing but folklore that our great-great-grandfathers and great-great-grandmothers once had told one another while they were flying primitive jet planes or watching old-fashioned television.

But of the continued need for the tales that have survived hundreds of years we can be reasonably sure. In Volume 2 of *Children's Literature*, Bennett Brockman stressed the importance to children and adults of medieval tales of innocence and experience, and in Volume 3, James Hillman, who gave the Terry lectures at Yale following such psychologists as Jung, Dewey, and Erich Fromm, urged children and adults to read Grimm's and other fairy tales.

Charity Chang surveys a literary fairy tale by Louise de la Ramée in this volume, and essays by Jack Zipes on German literature and Carla Poesio on Italian literature also reflect our continuing interest in international children's literature. But, as befits a 1976 issue, Volume 5 features essays on American children's literature from the colonial age to the present. We are especially pleased to be able to introduce the volume with an important essay by Clifton Fadiman, Senior Editor of *Cricket*, on the current state of children's literature. His essay is part of a larger work very close to Mr. Fadiman's heart, a study on which he has been engaged for a number of years. He has graciously given us a preview. Also, Ravenna Helson, a professor of psychology at the University of California at Berkeley, has elected to share with us the initial results of her findings on the criticism of children's literature conducted under a grant from the National Endowment for the Humanities—the first extensive attempt to look at the critics in this field.

Garland Publications has permitted us to reproduce three introductions from their series of 117 facsimiles of early children's books. Those selected are introductions to the *New England Primer*, the McGuffey *Readers*, and *The Story of a Bad Boy*.

Alvin Schwartz, for years a writer of *Superman* and other comics, now writing a volume on comics under a grant from the Canadian Commission on the Arts, has here an article which is part of that project. Jim Haskins, author of over thirty books, has contributed an article on racism and sexism in children's literature. Jan Bakker has contributed an extensive preliminary listing of the children's books on the shelves of the Thomas Y. Hughes Library in Rugby, Tennessee. This listing is important because it is the first exploration of a remarkable collection of children's books. Not an item has been added or taken away since the Victorian period. Other essays focus on mid-nineteenth-century American literature, while James Henke examines the ethos of today as it appears in Paul Zindel's works. Finally, Julie Carlson McAlpine offers a rare look at the autobiographical roots of two recent books from the privileged perspective of the author's daughter.

In the book review section, we continue our policy of emphasizing articles that examine major trends and issues in children's literature and the study of it. A notable exception is Judy Rosen's piece on a book written and illustrated by thirteen-year-olds—and reviewed by one.

Our next issue will feature a variety of psychological approaches to children's literature.

—*Francelia Butler*

Note: Several persons have wanted to know more about the origin of the pictures of Chinese Children at Play, as reproduced in Volume 4 of *Children's Literature*. These are from the private collection of T. C. Lai, author of books on Chinese folklore and Director of Extramural Studies at the Chinese University of Hong Kong. Professor Lai had them photographed especially for Volume 4.

Articles

The Case for a Children's Literature*

Clifton Fadiman

If a children's literature is to exist as "an intelligible field of study," in Arnold Toynbee's phrase, it must justify that existence on grounds beyond its contribution to mainstream literature. It must assert some qualified claim as a sovereign state, however small. Even if a cultural sirocco were instantaneously to dry up the mainstream, a children's literature would still have to show that it is identifiable as an entity.

On the surface the literature seems to need no defense. If it is but a by-product, what is the meaning of the avalanche of children's books that annually descends upon the bookstores? What shall we say of the thousands of children's book editors, authors, artists, anthologists, librarians, professors—even critics? Is there not a gigantic, nearly world-wide industry, working away to satisfy the child's demand for something to read—or at any rate the parents' demand for something to give the child to read? Can we not, like Samuel Johnson kicking the stone to refute Bishop Berkeley's theory of the non-existence of matter, merely point to the solid reality and say, "I refute it thus!"?

No, we must do a little better than that, just as Johnson should have known that kicks and phrases, however forcible, do not really dispose of idealism in episcopal gaiters. Let us therefore first glance briefly at the case against a children's literature.

The man-in-the-street puts it in simple terms: children's literature cannot amount to much because "it's kid stuff." The assumption here is that by nature the child is "inferior" to or less than the adult. His literature must be correspondingly inferior or less. Give the kid his comic, while I read grown-up books. But does not this amiable condescension shelter a certain insecurity? As racism is the opium of the inferior mind, as sexual chauvinism is the opium of the defective male, so child-patronage may be the opium of the immature adult. This book [the forthcoming study from which this essay is extracted], not surprisingly, admits that in certain ways the child is

*This extract from a longer essay entitled "A Meditation on Children and Their Literature" appears by the kind permission of Mr. Fadiman and Little, Brown and Company. All rights reserved. This material will be expanded in Mr. Fadiman's forthcoming book to be published by Little, Brown and Company.

patently inferior, but goes on to maintain that as an imaginative being—the being who does the reading—he is neither inferior nor superior to the adult. He must be viewed as the structural anthropologist views the "primitive"—with the same unsentimental respect, the same keen desire to penetrate his legitimate, complex symbol-system and idea-world.

There is, however, a more sophisticated case against a children's literature. Scholars have expressed it both negatively and positively.

Negatively the thing is done by omission. Literary historians leave out children's literature, as they might leave out the "literature" of pidgin-English. The English novelist Geoffrey Trease offers a key example. He refers to "Legouis and Cazamian's *History of English Literature*, in which no space is found, in 1378 pages, for any discussion of children's books and the only Thomas Hughes mentioned is not the immortal author of *Tom Brown's Schooldays*, but an obscure Elizabethan tragedian." Further examples are legion. Marc Slonim's authoritative *Modern Russian Literature from Chekhov to the Present* (1953) has no mention of Kornei Chukovsky as children's author. Hester R. Hoffman's *Reader's Adviser* (1964) finds space in its 1300 pages for a bibliography of Lithuanian literature, but not for Louisa May Alcott. C. Hugh Holman's *A Handbook to Literature* (1972) is alert to inform us about weighty literary matters from *abecedarius* to *zeugma*, but not about children's literature. That phenomenal compendium *Die Literaturen der Walt in ihrer mündlichen und schriftlichen Überlieferung*, edited by Wolfgang v. Einsiedel (1964), covers 130 assorted literatures, including the Malagasy, but from its 1400 pages you would never suspect that some writers have written for children. In Volume II of David Daiches' standard *A Critical History of English Literature* we find an otherwise excellent account of Kipling, but one from which we would never guess that he wrote masterpieces for children. While it is only fair to say that there do exist literary histories and reference manuals, notably those of recent years, that acknowledge children's books, the normal (and influential) stance of scholarship has been one of unconscious put-down by omission.

A few critics are more explicitly skeptical. In 1905 Benedetto Croce wrote: "The art of writing for children will never be a true art"; and again: "The splendid sun of pure art cannot be tolerated by the as yet feeble eye of the young." He argued also that the writer's ever-present consciousness of his child public inhibited his freedom and spontaneity.

In our time, too, there have been some thoughtful students to echo Croce's negative judgment. They claim that they cannot trace a sufficiently long tradition or identify an adequate number of masterworks. Robert Coles, for instance, who has himself done much to increase our understanding of the current juvenile literary scene, cannot find in the literature "style, sensibility, vision."

As long ago as 1896, the German educationist Heinrich Wolgast aroused a storm of controversy, echoes of which are still heard, merely by his statement that "creative children's literature must be a work of art." In 1969 the French scholar Isabelle Jan felt it necessary to begin her book with the question: "Does a children's literature exist?" Three years later, in a thoughtful article, "The Classics of French Children's Literature from 1860 to 1950," she gave a cautious answer to her question, confining the issue to her own country: "French children's literature . . . does not constitute a *literature* in the strict sense. Quite unlike English children's literature it has neither continuity nor tradition."

It is apparent that the esteem in which any vocation is held affects its development. If children's literature is not generally felt to be an identifiable art, important in its own right, potentially creative minds will not be drawn to it, and it will languish or become a mere article of commerce. It is, then, worthwhile attempting to outline briefly a case which will be amplified in the book to follow.

Apologists must at once concede that the children themselves couldn't care less. For them, books are to be read, not analyzed; enjoyed, not defended. They are only mildly curious as to who writes them, except insofar as a Richard Scarry, a Joan Walsh Anglund or a Maurice Sendak operates, like Wheaties, as a brand name. They do, of course, vigorously favor one book over another, but hardly on the basis of any rationale of values. Nor do they, unlike adults, show much interest in being up-to-date in their reading. The annual juvenile best-seller lists are loaded with titles first published a score of years ago. Children are proof against literary fads, literary gossip, and especially literary critics. For them books are no more literature than street play is physical exercise. The defense of their literary kingdom they cheerfully leave to their elders.

This elder rests that defense on the following grounds.

First comes the slippery concept we call tradition. A literature without a traceable history is hardly worthy of the name. If we relax our definition to the point of zero tension, children's literature may claim a foggy origin in St. Anselm's 11th-century *Elucidarium*, possibly the first book of general information for young students. That would take our "tradition" back about 900 years. But common sense tells us that the good saint is no true source. He no more begat Lewis Carroll than the 11th-century author of the *Ostromir Gospel* (often cited as the beginning of Russian literature) begat Dostoevsky.

Moving ahead a few hundred years we encounter an unidentifiable German who, between 1478 and 1483, issued *Der Seele Trost* ("The Soul's Consolation"), a religious tract explicitly addressed to children. Though valueless as literature, it may claim a little more legitimacy than the *Elucidarium*. One can view it as the *Urvater* of that long succession of moral tales that by this time should have turned children into paragons of virtue. If we reject *Der Seele Trost* we might accept as a point of origin Jörg Wickram's *Der jungen Knaben Spiegel* ("The Boy's Mirror"), perhaps the first "realistic" novel aimed at youth. Appearing in 1555, it would make children's literature date back over 400 years. And so we could proceed, making more and more plausible claims as we approach modern times, until we come to *A Little Book for Little Children*, by "T.W." The authority Percy Muir, dating it around 1712, considers it one of the first books designed for the entertainment of little ones. Push on a few years. In 1744 we meet John Newbery's publication *A Little Pretty Pocket Book*, from which English children's literature is conventionally dated. But at once we recall that Perrault's fairy tales appeared almost half a century prior to this; and from the head of Perrault French children's literature may be said to spring.

Perhaps it is fair to say, then, that our field of inquiry, strictly defined, is nearly 300 years old; less strictly, perhaps 500 years old. How many mainstream literatures can claim an equally venerable tradition?

Second comes the matter of masterpieces. Here we must admit that unfortunately one word must serve two somewhat different meanings. *Oedipus Rex* is a masterpiece. But so is *Mother Goose*. Both are true to human nature. Beyond that they have little in common. It will require further discussion to determine what makes a masterpiece in our field. At this point I assert dogmatically that in its 300-plus years of history the literature has produced first-order works of art in sufficient number to support our case. I can think of about fifty that merit discussion at length. Some are already classics in the simple sense that, enduring over the decades or centuries, they are still enjoyed by large numbers of children. Indeed, are they not more naturally "classical" than many mainstream classics? It takes the whole educational machinery of the French Republic to sell its boys and girls on Corneille. But Perrault, Jules Verne, even Madame de Ségur seem to survive by their own vitality. To the nuclear core of individual high-quality works we should add the total *oeuvre* of another fifty outstanding writers whose product as a whole is impressive but of whom we cannot so confidently assert that any single book stands out. Some of these are: Lucy Boston, Colette Vivier, E. Nesbit, Arthur Ransome, William Mayne, Eleanor Farjeon, René Guillot, Paul Berna, Tove Jansson, Gianni Rodari, Joan Aiken, Hans Baumann, José Maria Sanchez-Silva, Rosemary Sutcliff, David McCord, William Pène Du Bois, James Krüss, John Masefield, I. B. Singer, E. L. Konigsburg, Ruth Krauss, Kornei Chukovsky, Henri Bosco, Madame de Ségur, Ivan Southall.

In our view any literature worthy of the name also gains in health and variety through the nourishment supplied by writers of the second or third class, even by writers commonly scorned as purveyors of mass reading. Children's literature is rich in writers of ephemeral appeal and even richer in manufacturers of unabashed trade goods. But in a way this circumstance strengthens rather than weakens our case. The ladder theory of reading must not be swallowed whole. Yet it is true that children often normally work up from Enid Blyton or *Nancy Drew* to more challenging literature, whereas a *kitsch*-happy adult tends to stay *kitsch*-happy.

Third, our case rests also on the fact that, like science fiction, children's literature is a medium nicely adapted to the development of certain genres and themes to which mainstream media are less well suited. In "On Three Ways of Writing for Children" C. S. Lewis remarks that the only method he himself can use "consists in writing a children's story because a children's story is the best art form for something you have to say: just as a composer might write a Dead March not because there was a public funeral in view but because certain musical ideas that had occurred to him went best into that form." In the same essay, referring to E. Nesbit's Bastable trilogy, he speaks of the entire work as "a character study of Oswald, an unconsciously satiric self-portrait, which every intelligent child can fully appreciate"; and goes on to remark that "no child would sit down to read a character study *in any other form*" (italics supplied).

The major genre (perhaps nonsense verse is just as major) whose development is largely the work of children's literature is fantasy. Adult fantasies of a high order of course exist. But the form seems, for reasons we shall later examine, peculiarly suited to children;

and children seem peculiarly suited to the form. Consequently we can trace a long line of fantasies, growing constantly in expressiveness and intricacy. MacDonald, Carroll, Collodi, Baum, de la Mare, Barrie, Lagerlöf, Grahame, Aymé, Annie Schmidt, C. S. Lewis, Tolkien, Saint-Exupéry, Rodari, Juster, Hoban—these are a few of the many writers who have found children's fantasy well fitted to statements about human life that are conveyable in no other way. While a fairy tale for grownups sounds spurious, the fairy tale for children still has successful practitioners.

There are certain experiences we have all had which, though also handleable in adult fiction, seem to take on a higher authenticity in juvenile fiction. For example, moving. For the child, moving from one neighborhood to another may be as emotionally involving as a passionate love affair is to the adult. For the adult a new neighborhood is a problem in practical adjustment; for the child, who must find a fresh peer-group to sustain him, it can be another planet.

But it is not only minor themes, such as moving, or major genres, such as fantasy, to which children's literature throws open its portals. It also offers a natural home for certain symbols frequently held to be part of our unconscious, and universally present in myth.

Take the Cave. The Cave has an eerie, backward-transporting effect on us all, a sacral mix of awe, terror and fascination. Whether this is linked to racial recollection, to persistent memory of the womb, or to some still undiscovered kink in the psyche, we may never know. But we have all observed that the unnameable Cave-feeling is peculiarly marked in the child. With no real cave available, we will, out of a chair or a huddle of blankets, construct a reasonable facsimile. It is therefore not surprising to find in his literature a body of work ringing the changes on this "archetypal" symbol. It is no accident that Alice starts her dream life by falling through a hole in the ground; or that the most recallable episode in *Tom Sawyer* occurs in a cave. Richard Church's *Five Boys in a Cave*—an excellent suspense story—stands as the perfect type of a whole school of speleological literature, mainly for boys. France, a great land for caves, offers many examples. We can go back as far as 1864 to Jules Verne's *A Journey to the Center of the Earth*, which is really about a vast cavern. Indeed his masterpiece, *20,000 Leagues Under the Sea* (1870), may be read as a vision of a watery cave. Exactly a century later Norbert Casteret's *Dans la nuit des cavernes*, extremely popular with the young, continued to exploit the theme. One of the works of non-fiction that retains its appeal is Hans Baumann's *The Caves of the Great Hunters* (German publication 1961). This deals with caves and other prehistoric sites actually discovered by boys and girls—and in one case by a dog, an animal that long ago became a first-class citizen of the republic of childhood. There is, too, Sonnleitner's vast, curious *Die Höhlenkinder*, whose first part was published as long ago as 1918 and which, despite its almost archaic tone, refuses to die. Over 300,000 copies have been sold in the German edition and only a few years ago it was translated into English.

The Cave is but one of a group of themes, freighted with symbolic content, that find powerful development in children's literature. Related to its magical appeal is the child's affinity for the non-artificial, or for places man has abandoned to nature. A vast apparatus is needed to condition the human being to the fabricated, technological surround to which he now seems fated. But, until so conditioned, the child normally relates himself to a non-technological world, or its nearest approximation. "The literature of childhood," remark the Opies, "abounds with evidence that the peaks of a child's experience are not visits to a cinema, or even family outings to the sea, but occasions when he escapes into places that are disused and overgrown and silent." Dozens of children's writers know and feel this, foremost among them William Mayne. Only Samuel Beckett has made grown-up literature out of a dump. But in children's stories it is a familiar background, and it must be in part because such abandoned environments represent a grotesque triumph over the forces of "progress," forces the child must be *taught* to respect.

In short, any public defender of a children's literature will rest part of his case on the medium's high esthetic capacity to embody certain specific themes and symbolic structures, often more imaginatively than does the mainstream.

But the advocate must go beyond this. A body of writing ambitious to be called a literature may point to a tradition. It may claim to include a fair number of masterworks. It may make certain statements with marked effectiveness. But it must also demonstrate that it has both scope and the power to broaden that scope. A specialized, non-adaptive literature risks the fate of the dinosaur.

First, as to scope. Obviously children's literature cannot boast the range, amplitude, inclusiveness of general literature. General literature records human experience; and human experience, though not absolutely, is by and large a function of the flow of time. The child's book, though not limited to the reflection of his actual experience, is limited by what he can understand, however dimly; and understanding tends to enlarge with experience.

But we must not be too quick to pass from the dimensions of length and breadth to that of depth, and say that children's books can never be as "deep." The child's world is smaller than the grown-up's; but are we so sure that it is shallower? Measured by whose plumbline? Is it not safer to say that, until the child begins to merge into the adolescent, his mental world, though of course in many respects akin to that of his elders, in many others obeys its own private laws of motion? And if this is so, it might be juster to use one plumbline to measure the depth of his literature, and a somewhat different one for that of his elders. No one will deny the depth of Dostoyevsky's Grand Inquisitor episode. But who is to say that, to a sensitive child reader, William Mayne's *A Game of Dark* does not convey an equally profound intimation of the forces of evil? Here are six lines of a "song" called *Firefly*, by Elizabeth Madox Roberts. A seven-year-old child, who happened to be a genius, might have written it; and any seven-year-old child can read it with pleasure.

> A little light is going by,
> Is going up to see the sky,
> A little light with wings.
>
> I never could have thought of it,
> To have a little bug all lit
> And made to go on wings.

The child who feels all that these six lines convey (especially the fourth) is caught up in profound reflection on the very nature of creation. The esthetic experience is for the child no less rich than would be for the adult a reading of Eliot's *Four Quartets*. The scale differs, the "thickness" does not.

To return to the matter of scope: it is clear that traditionally the child's literature has been closed (nowadays there are narrow apertures) to certain broad areas of human experience: mature sexual relationships, economic warfare in its broadest aspects, and in general the whole problematic psychic universe that turns on the axletree of religion and philosophical speculation. That vast library generated by Unamuno's "tragic sense of life" is one that—though there are certain exceptions—is not micro-reflected in the child's books. Though again one must qualify, his is a literature of hope, of solutions, of open ends. To say that is to acknowledge the limits of its scope.

But if we turn to form rather than content, the judgment becomes a little less clear-cut. Children's literature contains no epic poems, not only because it developed long after the age of the epic but because its audience is ill-suited to the epic length. As for its lyric poetry, it includes several forms—nonsense verse, nursery rhymes, street rhymes, lullabies—in which the adult lyric tradition is comparatively defective. But in general its verse forms are simple and restricted as against the variety and complexity of mainstream verse. The literature contains little drama, whether in prose or verse, worth serious attention. It has so far evolved nothing closely resembling the traditional essay, although in an acute comment Jean Karl points to its remarkable powers of mutation: "Who would have dreamed that the familiar essay, no longer popular with adults, would suddenly be found in children's books, presenting all sorts of abstract ideas in picture-book form?" The reference here is to what is often called "concept books." A first-rate example is James Krüss's *3 × 3*, pictures by Eva Johanna Rubin, which is essentially a graphic expository essay on the abstract idea of three-ness.

But almost all the other major genres, whether of fact or fiction, are represented. Some, like the ABC book and the picture-book, are virtually (as would naturally be the case) unique to the literature. So, in the same way, are children's books written by children themselves: Daisy Ashford's *The Young Visiters* (1919), surely one of the dozen funniest books in English, or *The Far-Distant Oxus* by Katharine Hull and Pamela Whitlock, written when the authors were 14 and 15 respectively. Children's fiction can be so experimental as to be reactionary: Gillian Avery has written Victorian novels that are not parodies or pastiches, but interesting in themselves.

Most fictional forms one can think of are represented on the children's shelves. Some, such as the fairy tale, the fantasy, the fable, the animal story and the adventure yarn, can be found there in rich and highly developed profusion. The historical novel, especially in England, flourishes to a degree that makes it possible to hail Rosemary Sutcliff *tout court* as one of the best historical novelists using the language. Even the minor genre of the detective story is represented, long before Poe, in Mrs. Barbauld's *The Trail* (mid-1790's).

There are dozens of sub-genres and sub-sub-genres that are by nature given special prominence in children's literature: certain kinds of jokes and riddles; stories of toys and dolls, stuffed animals, animated objects; "bad boy" and "bad girl" stories; "career novels"; a whole school of chimney-sweep stories; children's puppet plays; "waif" novels; the school story; the vacation novel; and many others. We do not dispose of the matter when we say that these forms are simply a response to the child's natural interests, any more than we dispose of Proust when we say that his work is a response to the adult's interest in depth psychology. In both cases literature is enriched by the evolution of fresh vehicles for the imagination.

While no absolutely first-rate history or biography has been written for children, I would claim that the field has produced at least one masterly autobiography, on its own level as worthy of study as the *Confessions* of Rousseau or St. Augustine: Laura Ingalls Wilder's *Little House* series.

It is fair to say, then, that the scope of our literature, though it has its lacunae, is astonishingly broad. But it is not only broad. It has the capacity to broaden further, to invent or assimilate new forms, themes and attitudes, to devise original techniques of exposition and narration. The texts of Maurice Sendak are as "new" in their way as Joyce's *Ulysses* once was. So is the picture book itself, really a product of modern times, with its power to tell a story simultaneously in two mediums: Else Holmelund Minarik's *Little Bear* series illustrates this well. The all-picture book has evolved even more ingenious modulations: Mitsumasa Anno's dreamlike series of gravity-defying, non-Euclidean *Jeux de Construction* is only one startling example. The trick three-dimensional book (pop-ups, for example), though hardly part of literature, is nonetheless ingenious, satisfying, and a specific response to the child's desire to manipulate, change, construct.

Finally, as we shall see, contemporary children's literature has in the last decade or so found it possible to handle, even if not always successfully, a whole constellation of themes it was formerly denied: everything from drug addiction to homosexuality. (One anticipates with confidence the announcement of *The Boy's Own Handbook of Necrophilia.*)

The contemporary "teenage" or "young adult" novel has still to prove itself as art. Yet it bears witness to the flexibility of children's literature, its power to enlarge its range, to experiment with new forms and themes. Without such power its claim to be a "literature" would be vitiated. Indeed its receptivity is now of so high an order as to blur its boundaries. "Less is more," says Browning's Andrea del Sarto, a phrase Mies van der Rohe applied perhaps too rigorously. Yet it holds profound truth. Lately the human race has become aware of the fatality lying at the heart of unchecked growth. It is possible to argue that a similar fatality inheres in the unchecked growth of any art form. We may—the returns are far from all in—be witnessing such a wild cancerous proliferation in the body we are now exploring.

To complete our case for a children's literature I offer two last considerations, one turning on the matter of scholarship, the other on the matter of institutions. Both may be debater's points. I concede that they are less persuasive than the arguments already adduced. All they do is point to the probability of the literature's existence. In themselves they do not constitute firm evidence of its high quality or organic integrity.

A literature is the sum of its *original* communications, especially its better ones, more especially its best. It is hard for us to meditate upon a literature as an intelligible field of study until the non-original communicator, the theorist and historian, have worked upon it. Had Aristotle never lived, classical Greek literature would still rank supreme. Nonetheless the *Art of Poetry* helps us to perceive its topography and distinguish its boundaries. We are trying at the moment to establish such topography and boundaries for a children's literature. Now the specific identity of any art becomes more firmly established as it develops self-consciousness. Of that self-consciousness critics, scholars and historians are the expression.

It would seem that you cannot produce a theory without something to theorize about, nor a history without something to chronicle. Or is this always true? A. Merget's *Geschichte der deutschen Jugendliteratur* ("History of German Juvenile Literature") appeared in 1867, before the existence of any literature worthy of the name. But this striking example of German thoroughness does not completely undermine the feeling we have, when we see a signpost, that it is probably pointing to some place that is actually there.

Ten years ago, when I started this project, I thought all I had to do was read a few thousand original communications called children's books, think about them, and arrange my thoughts on paper. I knew, of course, that there were several standard histories which should probably be read too. But soon I became aware that there were almost (well, not quite) as many books *about* children's literature as there were books *of* children's literature, and that anyone

who wished to do more than merely rationalize a set of impressions
would have to become familiar with a learned corpus of astonishing
proportions.

In one of his few transparent lines of verse Mallarmé complains

*La chair est triste, hélas! et j'ai lu tous les livres.**

I can subscribe to neither half of the hexameter. Even after ten years'
sampling of the scholarly literature, my flesh remains moderately
cheerful; and it is a dead certainty that I have not read all the books.
No one could. Few disciplines of such modest dimensions have
evoked so much commentary as that associated with children's books
and reading. The children themselves would be dumbfounded, perhaps exploding into hilarious laughter, could they realize what alps
of research and theory have been reared since Perrault, his eye on
both young and old, first set down the tale of Little Red Riding-Hood.

I intend no mockery. The body of criticism and history is not only
formidable; it is valuable. It points up to the importance of what at
first might seem a minor field of investigation. Though some of it,
inevitably, is but dusty poking into the deservedly dead, and much
of it duplicative, yet as a whole it reflects a solid tradition, of acute
importance in the shaping of the minds and hearts of children.

There are few "developed" countries that have not produced a
scholarly literature. It is vast in the cases of the United States, Britain, most of Europe, including Soviet Russia, and Japan. While I
have not yet met with such material from Liberia, I have pored over
Paul Noesen's *Geschichte der Luxemburger Jugendliteratur*, keeping in mind that the population of Luxembourg, counting every child,
is 336,500.

True, the burden of our case rests on the original communications
rather than on the commentaries. But it is only fair to set against
such doubting Thomases as Coles and Croce the counterweight of a
host of creative writers and thoughtful scholars for whom a children's
literature is as much *there* as his mountain was for Mallory. Among
the creators of that literature who have defended its integrity are
James Krüss, Eleanor Cameron, Maurice Sendak, I. B. Singer,
J. R. R. Tolkien, C. S. Lewis, Kornei Chukovsky. Among the scholars who have analysed its properties, staked out its limits, and cele-
brated its charms are the Frenchman Paul Hazard, the Italian Enzo
Petrini, the Swiss Hans Cornioley, the Englishman Brian Alderson,

*The flesh is sad, alas, and all the books are read.

the Canadian Sheila Egoff, the Swede Eva von Zweigbergk, the Iberian Carmen Bravo-Villasante, the Netherlander J. Riemans-Reurslag, the Luxembourger Paul von Noesen, the Argentinian Dora Pastoriza de Etchebarna, the Mexican Blanca Lydia Trajo, the New Zealander Dorothy White, the Israeli Uriel Ofek, the Norwegian Jo Tenfjord . . . the catalogue, though not endless, is impressive.

The mere existence of institutions is, of course, no argument for the values they incorporate: the Mafia, one supposes, is as intricate and efficient an institution as one could well desire. Yet the complex world-network of children's libraries, book and record clubs, research centers, publishers, scholarly magazines, academies, book councils, "book weeks," prizes and awards, summer schools, writers' associations, radio and television programs (but switch on a red light here), illustration exhibits, book fairs—all this, while alloyed with commercialism, bureaucratization, cliqueishness, and a certain inappropriate solemnity, nevertheless demonstrates the existence of a large and lively world of children's literature.

Change, Tradition, and Critical Styles in the Contemporary World of Children's Books*

Ravenna Helson

"The arrival of *Harriet the Spy* with fanfare and announcements of approval of its 'realism' makes me wonder again why that word is invariably applied to stories about disagreeable people and situations," wrote Ruth Hill Viguers in the February 1965 issue of *Horn Book Magazine*. "Are there really no amiable children? No loyal friends? No parents who are fundamentally loving and understanding? I challenge the implication that New York City harbors only people who are abnormal, ill-adjusted, and egocentric." Mrs. Viguers went on to say that many adult readers would find the book sophisticated, funny, and penetrating. "Children, however, do not enjoy cynicism. I doubt its appeal to many of them. This is a very jaded view on which to open children's windows."

Harriet the Spy was not universally denounced. Other critics, also forthright and vigorous, acclaimed it as brilliant, new, and at long last something appropriate for modern children. For example, Ellen Rudin had written this in the *School Library Journal*, November 15, 1964:

> Harriet M. Welsh is not a lovable child, but she is one of the
> meatiest heroines in modern juvenile fiction. . . . This novel is . . .
> a children's book, surely, told at a level comprehensible to
> children, yet it is intensely written, involuted, rich in dramatic
> vignettes and in warm, breathing characters. Harriet suffers growth
> and change in the best tradition of literature's most anguished
> heroines. *Harriet the Spy* bursts with life. It is up to date, here and
> now, this minute, real. Get it into circulation, quick!

Louise Fitzhugh's *Harriet* became one of the early focal points in the upheaval that has gone on in the world of children's books over the last decade.

Who are these critics of children's literature? What are their beliefs about it, their values? Along what dimensions do they differ? Is there a "psychology" of the critic? Or perhaps several "psychologies"? How does change come into the children's book world? These are

*Presented at the Seminar on Children's Literature, Modern Language Association, San Francisco, December 26–29, 1975. The research was supported by a grant from the National Endowment for the Humanities.

complicated questions, but I have been studying some of them and can report my first findings.

A STUDY OF WRITINGS BY CRITICS

The Sample

The study began with a survey of English and American publications devoted to current children's literature. The project staff looked at books, journals, collections of articles, and discussions of children's books in major newspapers. Gradually, we compiled a set of articles written by men and women, all now living, who could be called important in the field or who had a strong point of view about children's literature and a sustained interest in it. The names of these writers were shown to consultants in library science, education, publishing, and literature, and suggestions for additions were solicited.

The sample now consists of articles by eighty "critics and gate-keepers." The term "gate-keeper" was taken from Kurt Lewin,[1] who used it in an interesting study of how housewives made grocery purchases during the shortages of World War II, especially the circumstances under which they decided to begin serving their families unfamiliar parts of meat such as hearts and kidneys. A parallel between this study and the incorporation of "realism" into the fare of children's books should not be pressed; nor will I go into Lewin's ideas except to suggest that his conceptualization of gate-keepers and "channels" does seem applicable to an analysis of the children's book world as a system and how changes come about in that system. Book editors or librarians who buy books for a city are good examples of gate-keepers; they may never write a review but they effectively determine which children's books become available for reading. On the other hand, a professor or a freelance journalist who writes critical articles and reviews about children's literature exercises a much more imponderable influence and may not be described so well as a gate-keeper. In this paper I shall refer to the authors of the eighty articles simply as "critics," using this term broadly to include all those whose participation in the discussion of current children's books includes exchanges in the form of written language.

Although our sample of articles is not representative of the "population" of critical writings in any precise way, several observations may be drawn reliably, I believe, from the demographic characteristics presented in Table 1. Departments of English are not contributing many articles. Writings by librarians are more prominent in the

United States than in England; in both countries women are strongly represented in this field. In England, men and women are about equally active as critics, but in the United States there is a heavy preponderance of women. All these facts have implications for the shape of criticism, though we will not discuss them now.

Table 1. Nationality, Sex, and Occupation of Contributors to the Sample of Writings on Children's Literature

Occupation	United States		Canada and England		Total
	Women	Men	Women	Men	
Librarians	12	3	6	2	23
Journalists and authors	7	4	4	6	21
Educationists	7	4	2	4	17
Book editors	7	1	3	2	13
Professors of English	2	2	1	1	6
Total	35	14	16	15	80

Measures and Analyses

The writings of the critics were analyzed by two rater-analysts, an experienced children's librarian and a graduate student in psychology, with some additional assistance from another children's librarian.[2] The rater-analysts described each article by rating the degree of emphasis on the following three sets of measures: (*a*) *themes*, such as concern with esthetics, interest in extending books to a wider circle of readers, analysis of books or problems in terms of sociological variables; (*b*) implicit *needs* of the critic such as the needs for achievement, aggression, order, and the expression of appreciation or of "caring"; and (*c*) *critical roles*, such as those of the challenger, upholder of standards, expert witness, door-opener, or bead-stringer.

After the ratings were averaged, analyses were undertaken to ascertain which measures tended to vary together. The cluster dimensions which emerged are reliable, and they account for most of the variation in the measures.

Results

The four clusters, shown in Table 2, begin to provide tentative answers to the questions raised at the outset by revealing patterns in the writings of the critics. The clusters may be considered as two

Table 2. Dimensions of Variation in Writings by Critics

Defining variables	Oblique factor coefficient
Cluster 1. Appreciation (reliability: .94)	
Appreciation (feeling and expressing the worth, beauty, or relatedness of things, nature, etc.)	.85
Contact with the spiritual, magical, miraculous or imaginative	.85
Concern with esthetics, with the form, style, beauty, delight, meanings and insights derived from a work or author	.81
Role of door-opener	.76
Role of recreator	.71
Exploration or discovery of ideas, relationships, implications	.67
Caring (sympathy, giving love or friendship to people, pets, etc.)	.67
Cluster 2. Elucidation (reliability: .89)	
Role of elucidator	.77
Order (obtained by laying out or sorting out the facts, or making useful distinctions or classifications)	.73
Order (obtained by trying to find the right pattern or perspective for things)	.69
Exploration or discovery of ideas, relationships, implications	.67
Role of sharer of ideas	.60
Concern with analysis of critical principles, or clarification of the intellectual process of evaluation and appreciation	.58
Role of structural analyst	.55
Concern with analysis of psychological processes and their effects	.55
Role of discerning critic	.46
Cluster 3. Challenge (reliability: .93)	
Role of challenger, dragon-slayer	.87
Aggression (negative criticism, attacks on opponents, etc., as well as emphasis on aggressive content in books under discussion)	.87
Role of skeptic	.85
Achievement (emphasis on winning a fight, making a point, making gains)	.84
Cluster 4. Upholder of standards (reliability: .83)	
Role of upholder of standards	.81
Concern with defense of literary values	.64
Appreciation (feeling and expressing the worth, beauty, or relatedness of things, nature, etc.)	.60
Concern with defense of traditional values	.60
Role of watch-dog, defender	.44

pairs. A first pair has to do with esthetic interests, one emphasizing *appreciation* and the other *elucidation*. The other pair of clusters describes two critical stances: an attitude of *challenge* and an attitude of *upholding literary and traditional values*.

Each article received four scores, one on each cluster. Figure 1 shows the distribution of scores for the eighty articles on the appre-

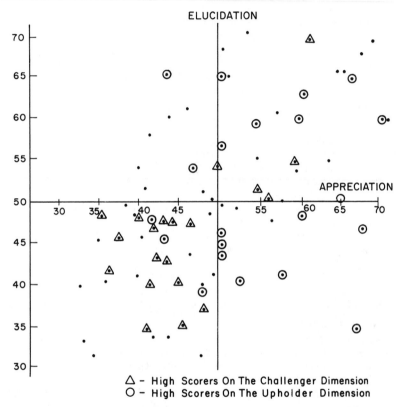

Figure 1. Distribution of Writings by Critics on the Elucidation and Appreciation Dimensions

ciation and elucidation dimensions. The second pair of clusters is represented by the use of triangles to show high scores on challenge and of circles to show high scores on upholding. One notices that the graph has been divided into quadrants, and that most of the articles high on challenge are in the lower left quadrant. When articles receive low scores on both elucidation and appreciation, they may almost always be found to treat either technical-professional or social topics; the articles high on challenge generally have to do with the latter.

Figure 1 may be regarded as a map showing areas where critics pursue their interests in characteristic ways. Even from the opening sentence or paragraph of an article, one can frequently predict where it will be located on the map. For example, if it starts off with a paradox, a germinal definition, or a statement of confusion, the essay will tend to be plotted in the "north." The author likes to set things up this way, one supposes, so that he will have ample scope for his elucidation.

> To be a critic—a literary critic—is almost, by definition, to be out on a limb. In addition to being in a precarious position, one never knows whether one will be top-heavy and crack the limb because of his weight or whether somebody will come along with a saw. Either way, the position is fraught with danger. Yet, since critics rush in where angels fear to tread, there must be some justification or explanation for their existence. [Paul Heins, "Out on a Limb with the Critics," *Horn Book*, 1970]

Or again:

> To give an account of how children respond to fiction is a near impossible task but it is perhaps less impossible than we sometimes think. [Nicholas Tucker, "How Children Respond to Fiction," *Children's Literature in Education*, 1972]

Critics who begin appreciating or caring right away generally belong in the east.

> This essay began some years ago when I reread the Oz books in order to begin writing an appreciation of them. [Roger Sale, "Child Reading and Man Reading: Oz, Babar, and Pooh," *Children's Literature: The Great Excluded*, 1972]

Here is a critic a little south of east:
> Here is a new book that is a new kind of book, and I like it very much. It is rather a job to tell you why because it has to be read aloud. You and I should be taking turns, chapter by chapter, laughing and seizing the book from each other. [Louise Seaman Bechtel, "Gertrude Stein for Children," *Horn Book*, 1939]

Critics to the south deal with appreciating too, but from southeast to southwest the context becomes more concrete, factual, or historical.

Books about the contributions of the American Indian to the
quality of life in this country have increased substantially during
the past few years. The following are a representative group of
recent books dealing with history, folklore, poetry, customs, and
fiction. [Jerome Cushman, "Walking a Mile in Their Moccasins,"
Los Angeles Times, July 7, 1974]

Or, the appreciation may become argumentative, whereupon the note
of upholding or challenging is amplified until it can be heard quite
clearly. The paragraph about the arrival of *Harriet the Spy* quoted at
the beginning of this paper will serve to illustrate both critical stances,
because occasionally a critic will uphold traditional values, as Viguers
did, by challenging a book or trend that is deemed inimical. Though
this review was not included in our sample, its fine rhetoric is characteristic of the dramatic scenery of the southeast, rather than the flat-
lands of the southwest, where the authors' modernity impels them to
more restraint.

Finally, the critics of the west are easy to tell because they start off
with a summary sentence or a direct statement of what they intend
to discuss.

This paper is designed as an analysis of the current reviewing of
children's books and is directed to a question pertinent to the
needs of the consumer: "What is the character and measure of *my*
access to current publication of children's literature via the sources
of critical evaluation? [Zena Sutherland, "Current Reviewing of
Children's Books," *Library Quarterly*, 1967].

Now I know that it is somewhat offensive to tear off introductory
sentences in this way, but the point is important: the critical orientations are strong and pervasive. Furthermore, as I have indicated in
Figure 2, they are readily interpretable in terms of classic esthetic
criteria. Jung's theory of the four functions is also appropriate; one
has only to write in "Thinking" beside "The True," "Intuition" beside "The Beautiful" (or "Complex"), "Feeling" beside "The Good,"
and "Sensation" beside "the Real."[3] The challenger and upholder
dimensions are somewhat more complicated to explain in terms of
Jungian theory, and this is probably not the place to try, but as
archetypal patterns of change and stability, they would seem important in any consideration of literary change.

One might complain that Figure 1 is a canopy of critical writings
suitable for discussion only by the Walrus and the Carpenter, that it
takes no account of differences in the responsibilities and goals of the

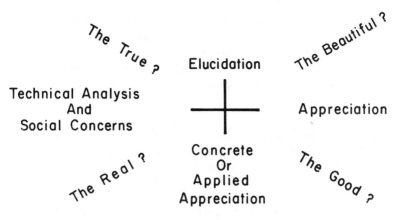

Figure 2. Interpretation of the Quadrants

very diverse professional groups who comprise the children's book world. Neither does it acknowledge that a critic's style might be expected to change with the task at hand. As for the second point, I know that critical styles vary to some extent. But the design of my study does assume that the general orientation tends to be stable. I certainly agree that the various groups involved with children's literature have different concerns, though I prefer to *use* this variability rather than eliminate it. Table 3 shows that the distribution of

Table 3. Distribution of Articles in the Quadrants by Occupation and Sex

Occupation and sex	High eluc.– low appr.	Low eluc.– high appr.		Low eluc.– high appr.	High appr.– high eluc.	Total
		Chal.	Non-chal.			
Librarians	3	3	7	5	5	23
Authors, journalists, and English professors	1	6	1	1	18	27
Educationists	4	4	5	1	3	17
Book editors	1	1	7	4	0	13
All men	2	5	7	1	15	29
All women	7	10	12	10	12	51

Note. Books in the low-low quadrant are subdivided according to whether they are high on the challenge cluster (scores of 55 or above) or not.

writings among the quadrants has a distinctive pattern for almost every occupational grouping, and also for the sexes. The versatility of librarians is almost as conspicuous as the insistence of authors, journalists, and teachers of literature upon writing articles which bring elucidation and appreciation together—if not that (or along with that), they write challenges.

PERSONALITY AND WORK STYLE OF CRITICS

With their writings and professional affiliations so diverse, one wonders whether critics as a group have anything in common. And whether or not they do, would it be possible to show that differences in personality and work style are associated with different critical orientations? To answer such questions, we asked the eighty authors of the writings included in the sample to participate in a study of critics and gate-keepers in children's literature. Five of the eighty had suffered incapacitating infirmities of old age. Of the remaining seventy-five, 77 percent have provided data for the study.

Comparisons of Authors and Critics

One approach to the question of whether critics have common personality characteristics would be to compare them with some other relevant group, such as authors. We were fortunate to have available data from a sample of authors of fantasy written for children.[4] Figure 3 shows profiles for critics and authors on the California Psychologi-

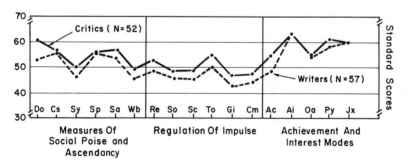

Figure 3. CPI Profiles of Critics and Authors

cal Inventory (CPI).[5] This instrument provides an overall picture of social functioning. The scales to the left assess extraversion, social poise, and ascendance. Those in the middle have to do with regulation of impulse, and those to the right are a mixture of scales assessing achievement and interest modes.

One notices some similarity between the two profiles. Both groups have their peak scores on Achievement via Independence (Ai), and both are higher on the left-hand measures of social poise and ascendance than on the center scales assessing regulation of impulse. However, the critics are more extraverted, they maintain a higher level of impulse control, and they score high on Achievement via Conformance (Ac). Eight scales show differences significant beyond the .05 level. These differences are what we would expect if the critic is to be conceptualized as actively mediating between the imaginative mind of the artist and the conventional requirements of society.

To test this construction, let us now compare the critics with a subgroup of writers, those whose work was rated highest in creativity.[6] These profiles are shown in Figure 4. Note that the differences

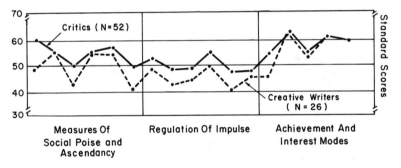

Figure 4. CPI Profiles of Critics and Most "Creative" Authors

are almost identical but increased in magnitude. One supposes that disagreements are quite likely between the ascendant, responsible, moderately conventional critic and the dissatisfied, stubborn, narcissistic, innovative author. Figure 4 might be showing us the profiles of Ruth Hill Viguers and *Harriet*'s author, Louise Fitzhugh.

Differences among Critics

A next question might be whether critics who take different positions about social change differ from each other. Indeed they do. Figure 5 compares personality profiles for women upholders and challengers, and Figure 6 does the same for men. Where the women challengers are more extraverted and ascendant than the upholders, these differ-

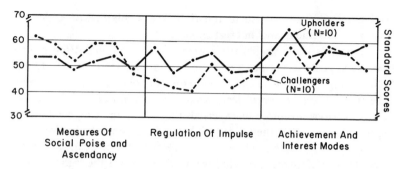

Figure 5. CPI Profiles of Women Upholders and Challengers

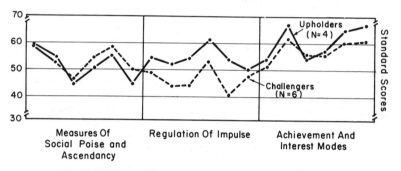

Figure 6. CPI Profiles of Men Upholders and Challengers

ences between the two groups of men are small. However, the most conspicuous feature of both graphs is the large difference between the profiles throughout the middle area, assessing regulation of impulse. For both men and women, upholders score high and challengers score low. Furthermore, both male and female upholders appear to be somewhat more intellectual (Ai) and higher on psychological femininity (Fe). The main difference between the challengers and the creative authors of fantasy (Figure 4) is that the challengers are more dominant and extraverted. They would seem to be *social* innovators.

The critics described their work style by rating a set of fifty-eight statements on a scale from one to five, where "five" meant that the item was very characteristic of the way they worked and "one" meant that it was not at all characteristic. It is thus possible to demonstrate that challengers and upholders differ in work style in ways congruent with the differences in personality as shown on the CPI profiles. Table 4 lists items placed highest by women challengers and upholders, and Table 5 those placed highest by male challengers and by "all other men," this latter group being employed because data were available from so few male upholders. All of the groups emphasize their high standards, but the differences in impulse control between the challengers and the comparison groups are evident in both tables. One notes also the pep and verve of the challenger women, the literary commitment of the upholder women, the openness of the male challenger to his inner complexity, and the firm self-direction of the comparison men.

The Superego in the Personality of the Critic

The findings that have been presented support the idea that the psychology of the critic has especially to do with regulation of impulse. If one thinks of the critic only as social parent or superego, one might

Table 4. Work Styles of Women Challengers and Upholders

Items placed highest, or significantly higher than by other group	Mean placement (5-point scale)
Challengers (N = 10)	
Has a lively curiosity, an inquiring mind, a desire to know and understand	4.4*
Enjoys using language accurately and expressively	4.0
Has high literary standards	4.0
Work is characterized by inventiveness or innovative applications of ideas	3.9†
Has a keen desire for earned recognition	3.8‡
Likes to stir up a little excitement or controversy	3.8†
Reacts quickly and generates many ideas	3.7‡
Upholders (N = 10)	
Enjoys using language accurately and expressively	4.4
Has high literary standards	4.2
Sensitive to sound patterns and rhythms	4.1†
Is interested in relations between literary form and content	3.9
Has a lively curiosity, an inquiring mind, a desire to know and understand	3.8
The sense of clarifying and sharing one's feelings or understanding is a major gratification in criticism	3.8
Seeks to preserve a core of cultural images and values through children's literature	3.6‡

*Difference between means of Challengers and Upholders significant at .10 level.
‡$p < .05$.
†$p < .01$.

Table 5. Work Styles of Male Challengers and Other Men

Items placed highest, or significantly higher than by other group	Mean placement (5-point scale)
Challengers (N = 6)	
Has high literary standards	4.2
Believes that values cannot be explained adequately in objective or scientific terms	4.0
Is easily distracted: tries to secure optimum conditions for concentration	3.8*
Has a keen desire for earned recognition	3.8
Feels deficient in knowledge of literary forms and devices, in familiarity with classics, theories of criticism, etc.	3.8†
Is aware of being a dual person: one part reacts and another judges	3.5‡
Other men (N = 18)	
Has high literary standards	4.3
Enjoys using language accurately and expressively	4.2
Productive; turns out a lot of work	4.0‡
Dislikes and avoids non-sequiturs and fuzzy generalities	4.0
Has a broad and balanced critical view	3.7‡

*Difference between means of Challengers and other male critics significant at .10 level.
‡$p < .05$.
†$p < .01$.

suppose that the important difference between challengers and upholders would be that the former had a social conscience, the latter a literary conscience. The findings do not support this hypothesis. An alternative construction would be that upholders are identified with social authority where challengers project their superego on to the "establishment" and then try to fight it or lessen its power. This line of thought is familiar from psycholanalytically oriented books such as J. C. Flugel's *Man, Morals and Society*, or from *The Authoritarian Personality* and the work it stimulated.

Here is a quotation from one rather extreme upholder who obviously has an identification with a stern superego:

As an academician I need to be critical of the work of others, both written and oral, and reviewing children's books is simply an extension of this. I tend, unreasonably so, to expect high standards, or standards similar to my own, from friends and acquaintances. After many years of study for my degree, I automatically analyze the content of books I read. For some years in fact I ceased to be able to read for pleasure at all, but this facility has returned.

He goes on to give examples of material in children's books which he has found offensive. They are usually instances of loss of control, sometimes loss of protection.

On the other hand, challengers can have an active superego too.

> My role as critic is particularly harmonious with the rest of my personality since I have always had a critical mind. . . . I tend to see flaws (and beauties) that others overlook. . . . No matter what the experience is, I am always thinking: does it work? is it successful? what makes that particular object beautiful? why do I like this so much? why was that film—which [others] loved—so flawed to me? . . . I do have a "tone of voice" as a critic, and sometimes I find it rather pompous. On the other hand, I use this same voice toward myself. . . . I do not have an image of myself as a critic, but the tone of voice is rather like the parent addressing the child. It can be too stern at times.

The books that this critic wants to survive are in the category of "rebellious realism"—which we might interpret to mean a rebellion against the stern superego.

There is obviously much more to be said on this subject of "super-ego psychology." I mean only to mention it, then, to emphasize that even among upholders and challengers, who may have the most vigilant superegos (though I am not sure this is true), there is a considerable range and variety in the patterning of the critical function with other aspects of personality. Attention to our elucidation and appreciation dimensions will help to make this point clear. Let us consider what two upholders, one an elucidator and one an appreciator, have to say about the way they work as critics. The elucidator says:

> I like to work in broad fields. It is not congenial to me to study a small area in great detail. I like to generalize and draw inferences, but I believe the generalizations and inferences must always arise out of the material, not the material be chosen or approached in such a way as to fit the generalization. I also like to *shape* things that are initially large and formless.

An appreciator has this to say:

> I give myself unreservedly to a book as I read it, as a child does, reacting to its qualities without any attempt at analysis. Consequently I apply no set criteria and make no notes. Only in "tranquility" afterwards do I begin to think about the book in any critical fashion, and at that stage I usually find that I have a clear impression of my reactions to it. I have related it to other work

of the same writer, and have placed it in the context of its time. By that time, too, my impressions and the words in which to express them have become inseparable.

The processes described by these two critics are similar, except that the elucidator derives more pleasure from "shaping" and "generalizing," the appreciator from "a wish to communicate enjoyment to others." This difference is manifest in the characteristic work of the two individuals.

Both critics are moderately high on impulse-control, as we have found upholders to be. The elucidator's pleasure in shaping seems productive and creative rather than compulsive, and one supposes that it is congruent with the masculine role. Perhaps it balances other of his interests that put more emphasis on sensitivity and feeling relationships. One might say that he is an upholder to maintain a balance in a complex and differentiated personality. The appreciator is an upholder, perhaps, out of loyalty to books loved in the past. As a child, he had access to only a few books, which he read over and over again. Although open to new impressions, his pleasure comes from a sort of esthetic nurturance, which means that he is more interested in continuing traditions than in breaking away from them.

Professional Roles and Reference Groups: The Social Psychology of the Critic

Creativity in a society depends on both the innovator and on the critic who recognizes the value of an innovation. Harold Lasswell said that critics (or judges, as he called them) tend to recognize (a) works the recognition of which will enhance their own position, and (b) works produced by others who have the same attitudes and values that they do themselves.[7]

Here again I can only illustrate how these ideas apply to the data obtained from the critics. Figure 7 compares the CPI profile of male critics who are professors with that of all other male critics. How socially powerful these professors are in comparison with the journalists, librarians, etc. who constitute the rest of the group! They are also highly intellectual, objective, and perceptive, to judge from their high scores on the right-hand scales. Where the two groups do *not* differ is on regulation of impulse. However, as one would expect, they do have different critical emphases. The professors are more inclined to think analytically, to "conceptualize processes" of various sorts, where the critics who are not professors are more concerned

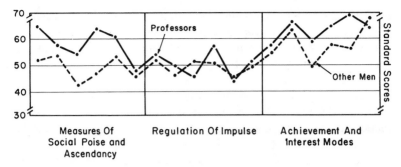

Figure 7. CPI Profiles of Male Professors and Other Male Critics

with "appreciating imaginatively what an author has created" and in evaluating literary achievement.

Academic people know very well the pressures on them which work to maintain this sort of difference in critical contribution, whether or not it is congenial to them personally. To "enhance their own positions," as Lasswell put it, they direct attention to certain kinds of books and to certain ways of treating literature that will win the "grudging admiration" of their colleagues. Nonetheless, Figure 7 shows that personality and job requirements tend to go together.

Of course, it is gross to think only in terms of whole professional groups. Small subgroups within a profession may exert influence altogether out of proportion to their size because they identify with a particular leader or a particular concern. They direct the interests, opportunities, and activities of critics, as the MLA Seminar in Children's Literature has been doing for several years.

The personality of the critic, his social roles, and his reference groups are interrelated in interesting ways, and these relationships change from one cultural context to another. Important changes in the world of children's books are not always achieved through encounters between challengers and upholders. In the United States in the 1920s they were brought about by a generation of "pioneers" —gate-keepers who built their own channels and their own gates. A comparison of critics of the 1920s and the 1960s is another topic we are continuing to pursue.

CONCLUSIONS

What, then can be "concluded" from this report of initial findings?

A systematic analysis of a sample of eighty writings by critics in England and America resulted in a "map" of criticism in the world of children's books. The main orientations on this map—elucidation, appreciation, challenge, upholding of standards—make contact with long-standing esthetic and psychological concepts. I believe that with some translation, perhaps, they would be applicable to literary and esthetic criticism generally.

Such a map is useful for many purposes. One of its uses here was to compare the style of contributions of critics in different professions related to children's books, but one might also compare critics of different "schools," of countries, or historical periods.

Secondly, the evidence shows that critics as a group have personality characteristics which distinguish them from authors in the same literary domain. The critics tend to be socially effective people, interested in the imaginative but responsive to social standards and concerns. The authors allow their imaginations and inner impulses to take precedence. From their "thorny paradise" they need the critics to mediate for them, just as the critics need the authors for their fruits. That there should be chronic tension between authors and critics is evident from their profiles.

Thirdly, the personality patterns of critics vary in ways which lead these men and women to perform different critical functions. Some are advocates for iconoclastic authors, and resemble them in personality. Others are more mindful of their roles as guardians of literary tradition, and their personalities differ accordingly. Change in the children's book world in the last fifteen years would seem to have come about through the innovativeness of a group of creative writers and challenger critics, met with the resistance, discrimination, and assimilation of upholders and their fellows.

Although the demonstration of systematic differences among critics is an important first step, there remains much in our data about the psychologies of critics, the processes of criticism, and the dynamics of literary change to be . . . elucidated? appreciated? systems-analyzed?

NOTES

1. Kurt Lewin, *Field Theory in Social Science* (New York: Harper, 1951), ch. 8.

2. I would like to thank Laurel Robinson, Valory Mitchell, and Susan Stanton for their services as rater-analysts, Suzanne Hildenbrand for research assistance, and Susan Hopkin for statistical analyses.

3. C. G. Jung, *Psychological Types*, in *Collected Works* (Princeton, N.J.: Princeton University Press, 1971), vol. 6.

4. Ravenna Helson, "The Heroic, the Comic, and the Tender: Patterns of Literary Fantasy and Their Authors," *Journal of Personality*, 41 (1973), 163–84.

5. Harrison G. Gough, *Manual for the California Psychological Inventory* (Palo Alto, Calif.: Consulting Psychologists Press, 1964).

6. Authors of fantasy rated medium in creativity are similar on the CPI to the authors rated highest. The largest differences in personality are those between these two groups and the authors rated lowest in creativity.

7. Harold D. Lasswell, "The Social Setting of Creativity," in H. H. Anderson, ed., *Creativity and Its Cultivation* (New York: Harper, 1959).

For the Good of the Country

Cultural Values in American Juvenile Fiction, 1825–60*

Anne MacLeod

An American fictional literature written for children and meant to cater—however cautiously—to children's tastes was a nineteenth-century creation. Though children's books had been available in America since the earliest settlements, they were almost without exception instructional literature of one kind or another, at least until the latter part of the eighteenth century.[1] Even after the Revolution, while there was a growing acceptance of fiction books for children, the American production of such literature was negligible; most non-school juvenile books were imported or pirated from Europe or England.

By the second quarter of the nineteenth century, however, American preoccupation with the future of the republic and with the children who would shape that future had brought about a fervent interest in all forms of literature for children, including fiction. And it was specifically American books for American children that were suddenly in demand. One author observed in 1825 that "the greater part of the juvenile books in the United States are foreign," and foreign books, however worthy, "give a wrong direction to the minds of the young, modelled as they are on a condition of life, and on prevailing sentiments, civil, moral and social . . . varying from those which American children should early be taught to cherish."[2] In the same vein, while paying her respects to such illustrious English authors of children's stories as Mrs. Barbauld and Maria Edgeworth, Lydia Maria Child described their work as "emphatically English." She herself, she promised in her first book for children, intended to portray "American scenes and American Characters."[3]

So nourished by national feeling, the flow of American juvenile books began about 1820–25, and swelled to a flood by the 1850s. By mid-century, there were hundreds of non-school books available in the United States written by American authors for American children. Samuel Goodrich, for whom the production of children's books had been bread and butter for over three decades, remarked in 1856:

---

*Presented at the first annual meeting of the Children's Literature Association, March, 1974. Some of the concepts in this essay are examined at greater length in the author's recently published *A Moral Tale: Children's Fiction and American Culture, 1820–1860* (*Archon Books*, Hamden, Conn.).

In casting my mind backward over the last thirty years—and comparing the past with the present . . . there is no point in which [advances] are more striking than in the books for children and youth. Let any one who wishes to comprehend this matter, go to . . . a juvenile bookstore . . . and behold the teeming shelves . . . and let him remember that nineteen twentieths of these works have come into existence within the last thirty years.[4]

Today, these early works of American juvenile fiction are largely forgotten. When noted by historians of children's literature, they have generally been damned as didactic, depressing, authoritarian, and sometimes morbid.[5] They have also been classified as literary failures, since not even one has survived to be read by children in the twentieth century.[6]

Certainly, the literary shortcomings of the juvenile fiction published before 1860 are undeniable. It *was* didactic, often narrow in scope and stilted in execution; most of all, it was tirelessly moralistic in purpose. Stories were designed, as the authors frankly said, to teach morals by example, much more than to provide children with entertainment. All writers of juvenile books subscribed to the view expressed by Jacob Abbott that the proper aim of fiction for children was "to present models of good conduct for imitation and bad examples to be shunned, to explain and enforce the highest principles of moral duty."[7]

Yet whatever they may lack as literature, stories written for children in any period provide an interesting, if sometimes oblique, source for the study of cultural history. In this early juvenile fiction, so firmly dedicated to didactic ends, many social and individual values were clearly presented, and very closely tied to contemporary beliefs about the requirements of a democratic nation. "The safety of the republic," wrote Catherine Sedgwick, "depends on the virtue of the people . . . and it is the business of the young, as well as of the old, to help on the cause of goodness."[8] Precisely because the juvenile literature of 1825–60 was dedicated to holding up the "highest principles of moral duty" to American youth, it is in many ways a better index to the conventional values of its society that a more imaginative creation might be. A fiction so committed to the advancement of American civilization through the moral education of its young put the accepted ideas of the time about childhood and its purposes, about society and its needs, clearly on display.

It remains to the twentieth-century reader, however, to compare the stated ideals of the juvenile books with the historical realities of the period for clues to that synthesis of the real and the ideal that lies at the base of the broad cultural outlook of any period. Since adults tend to project upon children both their hopes and their fears about the future, the value of children's fiction as social history exists on both the conscious and the unconscious levels. It is useful for what it has to say directly about the values the authors hoped to teach children, and it is equally interesting for what it suggests about the doubts and fears of its creators. In the inevitable gaps between the simplistic moral didacticism of the juvenile literature and the observed realities of the Jacksonian era, we may catch glimpses of both the optimism and the anxiety of early nineteenth-century American society.

What is in the books can be quickly summarized. The stories are much alike in structure, style, and approach, often rather closely modeled on their English predecessors in didactic fiction. Letitia Barbauld, Mrs. Sherwood, and Thomas Day, among others, all provided models for the American fiction; but it was Maria Edgeworth whose influence is most apparent. Her literary forms were the mold in which innumerable American copies were cast; her application of Rousseau's—and Richard Edgeworth's—theories of rational education of the young were faithfully reflected in hundreds of American stories for children.[9]

Settings in juvenile fiction were usually domestic, showing a child and his parents at home. Plots were simple and repetitious. One popular plot device, made familiar to Americans by Thomas Day's well-known *Sandford and Merton*, was contrast. Two characters carried these stories, one demonstrating ideal behavior, the other setting the "example to be shunned." Such tales were legion in the period and never subtle. Samuel Goodrich's story of two cousins, one trained to self-control and unselfishness, the other indulged in every wish, was quite representative. It ended with a typical address to the reader:

Thus you see that Edwin was now a spoiled child, while Edward was a good, kind and amiable boy. They were both good once, but Edwin had been indulged, and this indulgence had made him passionate, selfish and disagreeable. Edward, on the contrary, by being trained in the habit of giving up his wishes to another, had become even more gentle and generous. Thus you see, my little friends, that indulgence is bad for children, and being made to give up their wishes is good for them.[10]

Even more common were those narratives which revolved around a single young protagonist who was described as basically good (for the doctrine of natural depravity was all but dead by 1825), save for one or two glaring moral failings. Tales of this kind frequently opened with a bald statement of the dilemma: "There was once a little boy named Edmund. He was generally mindful and good-natured, but he had one fault . . ." or, "[Charles] was, in the main, desirous to do right, but he had one great fault. . . ."[11]

The story then placed the child in a situation in which he suffered more or less grievous consequences from his fault. If he was disobedient, he would surely fall through the ice he was told to stay off. If carelessness was his chief failing, he might well burn the house down. In one extreme example, a habitual tease plots to blow up his sister's chicken coop and instead blows up the gunpowder in his own face, disfiguring himself permanently and damaging his eyesight so that he is "obliged to wear spectacles the rest of his life." Such unhappy experiences showed the child the error of his ways and set him on the road to reformation, if they did not transform him instantly. As Miss Leslie noted briskly of her teasing culprit, "This sad accident entirely cured [George] of all his mischievous tricks."[12] It was in accord with the educational theories of most authors that the punishment for wrongdoing was nearly always a consequence of the child's own action, rather than something imposed by authority. And, though it was often improbably dramatic, the retribution was seldom really harsh.

It was the parents' role to guide the developing characters of their children, pointing out moral lapses where necessary. When Rollo sulks because rain has spoiled the family plans for a picnic, his father rebukes him gravely: "Rollo, did you know you were doing very wrong? You are committing a great many sins, all at once. . . . You are under the dominion of some of the worst of feelings; you are self-conceited, ungrateful, undutiful, unjust, selfish, and . . . even impious." Rollo (but five years old at the time) then retires to meditate upon his own behavior, and soon "saw his selfishness in a striking point of view."[13]

Rollo was fortunate in his parents, who always gave him such careful and detailed guidance. But if for some reason fictional parents neglected their duty to provide for a child's moral education, he might still learn for himself[14] or be properly instructed by some relative or friend of good character.[15] Even bad examples were frequently reformed by the influence of better-trained friends. Jack Halyard, a sturdy moralist at an early age, transforms Peter, who has "no manly ambition," from an idle, useless boy into an industrious and worthy lad. He accomplishes this (during a five-week visit) in part by "talking much and very sensibly," but most of all by setting an irresistibly good example before Peter's natural good sense.[16] The moral teaching in juvenile books was at once relentless and optimistic.

On the qualities that constituted ideal moral character, the consensus among authors of children's stories before 1860 was all but perfect. Everyone agreed that the ideal child was obedient and self-controlled above all else. "Children should never disobey their parents," warned Samuel Goodrich. "The number of children who die from the effects of disobedience to their parents is very large," agreed another author. Indeed, "the obedience of children to their parents is the basis of all government," according to Mrs. Sigourney, and therefore of legitimate concern to all. "There would be fewer mutinies and revolutions, if children were trained up in obedience," she added.[17] An ideal child was also kind, orderly, honest, punctual, and industrious, but these and other virtues were variously emphasized in juvenile books. The virtues dwelt upon in every tale were those of obedience and self-control.

The model adults in children's books were similarly rational and self-disciplined, especially in their role as parents. They knew that "the first step towards ruling others wisely, is to be able to rule one's own self."[18] Parental discipline was exacting, but it was neither emotional nor really authoritarian. "The only right way to govern anyone," wrote Maria McIntosh, "is by giving them confidence in your kindly feelings toward them—by love."[19] Physical punishment was almost always discouraged in the literature; the prescribed discipline was based on love and reason. Children who were "shut up or whipped," one author observed, had their "finer feelings . . . blunted, and their moral nature warped and deformed."[20] Even constant reproof was a mistake, according to Lydia Maria Child; "[it] may lead a child to conceal faults; but it seldom leads one to overcome them."[21]

In fact, child nurture was very much a cooperative effort between parents and children in the idealized homes of juvenile fiction. Children were expected to take as keen an interest in their own moral development as their mentors did; one distinguishing mark of an ideal child was his preoccupation with the state of his character. Jacob Abbott's Rollo is only the best-known example; similarly conscientious children were to be found throughout the literature.[22] As his active participation in his moral training indicated, the ideal child was expected to internalize moral standards thoroughly. The obedience every story praised was but a way-station along the road to self-control. An ideal child, "fortified by the wise counsels of his parents . . . felt strong within,"—and this was the real object of his upbringing.[23] The "true spirit of obedience," as authors often pointed out, led a child to behave rightly, with or without specific instructions.[24] The power of a noble person, Mrs. Follen observed, "arises from an inward strength that lasts long and shines most brightly in the darkest hours of trial."[25] It was clearly the aim of all the disciplinary methods recommended in juvenile fiction to develop in children such a strong and permanent inner direction.

A deep concern with inner character was the major theme of early children's literature. All the admirable people in the stories show high-minded scorn for shallow material values; happiness, they know, "does not depend on fine show, nor on bags of silver and gold."[26] All worthy models of behavior put character above possessions and kindness over worldly success. "I wish to have you good and happy, rather than fine," Mrs. Halyard told her daughter, and her sentiment was repeated in dozens of tales for the young throughout the period.[27] The greatest sin in juvenile fiction was selfishness—"There is no fault more unpardonable . . . nor any which . . . is more difficult to conquer"—and the stated goal of a good life was to live "for others."[28] Indeed, the only true contentment was to be found in a selfless dedication to the needs of others: "You can never be unhappy while you do everything that is in your power for others, without the hope of recompense."[29] The rewards of worldly success are short-lived and illusory, the stories always taught, but a satisfied conscience is a "true source of happiness."[30]

Socially, the juvenile fiction of 1825–60 was conservative, as children's literature generally is. The authors espoused few reform causes, and those few very cautiously, though the period was vivid with reform movements of every kind. They opted for stability in society, urging children to stay near home when they grew up, rather than pursue the will-of-the-wisp of success in far places. They especially feared the "insane craving for wealth" which lured young men to "the ends of the earth" or into the "maelstrom of city life."[31] Most writers of children's books, in fact, disliked cities, which they described as unwholesome and full of moral danger, and made their stories echo Jefferson's celebration of the farmer as independent, healthy, and content, the mainstay of the republic.[32] The farmer was "the possessor of true independence," thought Mrs. Sigourney, fortunate to be "sheltered from those riches and reverses, which in crowded cities await those who make haste to be rich."[33] Though the farmer's life held "much toil and exposure," remarked another writer, "yet few occupations seem so well suited to harmonize with our best feelings, or tend more to our preservation."[34] The answer to most problems in juvenile stories centered on hard work and self discipline; when these failed, Christian fortitude was recommended.[35] Very little in children's books before 1860 suggested that social institutions, governmental or otherwise, could be expanded or changed to deal with social problems. Even slavery, though it was occasionally deplored in the literature, was discussed in personal, rather than institutional, terms.[36]

In sum, then, the social and personal ideals presented in the children's fiction of Jacksonian America stressed order, stability, and individual morality. Materialism, ambition, and selfishness were strongly repudiated; cooperation was extolled.[37] Good character was generally portrayed as combining a highly sensitive conscience with an extraordinary level of self-control and a selfless dedication to the good of others. All of these moral goals the authors urged upon American children as indispensable not only for personal happiness, but for the survival of the American republic. As William Cardell wrote fervently, "The glory and efficacy of our institutions will soon rest with those who are growing up to succeed us. . . . They are the pivot of the moral world."[38]

Cardell, like other authors of this steadfastly didactic literature, presented his work as "true to nature . . . and the conditions of ordinary life."[39] Most writers of juvenile fiction before 1860 did the same. They strongly disavowed any imaginative aims, claiming that their efforts were directed toward giving young readers a true and accurate account of the real world.[40]

In fact, of course, even the briefest comparison of the moral and social ideals of the books with the actualities of the period reveals that children's fiction was a poor guide to the external realities of Jacksonian America. Jacksonian society was not stable and orderly, but turbulent, expansive, and full of tensions. The nation was growing, both physically and economically, at a breath-taking rate, and the headlong pace of change broke apart families, dissolved community ties, separated generations, and intensified such political and social problems as immigration, industrial growth, and, most inescapably, slavery.

Not cooperation but individual enterprise was the ruling spirit of the time. Jacksonian America offered opportunity to those who could and would reach out for it, and the American passion for "getting ahead" was vibrant. Selflessness as pure as that described in juvenile literature is perhaps an unobtainable goal at any time, but surely never more than in this scrambling, ambitious period. Every foreign visitor commented on how relentlessly Americans pursued the dollar; every social observer acknowledged that materialism was growing. Tocqueville saw democratic man driven by his ambition to a life of constant striving that yielded little emotional return. Americans as Tocqueville described them were neither rational nor serene but restless, lonely, and ultimately unsatisfied.[41]

Domestically, the images in most children's stories were no more accurate. It is seldom easy to determine from historical document the realities of a child's life in any period, but one truth about American children of the nineteenth century seems clear: they were *not* notably obedient. The many visitors who came to the United States in the first half of the century were very much interested in the domestic arrangements of this new republican society. They observed and judged—and they nearly always published their conclusions. Their comments on the matter of obedience were sharp and disillusioning. Far from being dedicated to perfect compliance with the wishes of their parents, American children, according to most visitors, were "precocious"—which meant willful, lacking in respect toward older people, even impudent. A friendly observer like Harriet Martineau called them "independent"; less kindly disposed visitors, like Frances Trollope and Captain Marryat, found them disobedient, unmannerly, and shockingly saucy toward their parents.[42]

The juvenile stories themselves contain evidence that these faults were not figments of foreign imagination. Rude or, as they were termed then, "forward" children were quite regularly deplored.[43] Everywhere in the literature, through the forests of admonition, one catches glimpses of real children displaying a vigorous independence of spirit, ignoring advice and authority, experimenting with strong liquor, shirking school lessons, playing with candles, skating on thin ice, swimming in swift rivers, growing up to join the army or sign onto sailing ships or pursue fortune in remote, untamed parts of the country. The children of the young republic were forever evading the safeguards and limitations their mentors wanted to throw about them. No doubt they had many virtues, but a reliable obedience to the wishes of anxious adults was not conspicuous among them. The model children of juvenile fiction were as remote from reality as the other idealizations in the literature.

Of course, there are always discrepancies between a society's stated ideals and its daily realities. But when the gap between the ideal and the real is very great, and when the rhetorical insistence upon the ideal is as strenuous as it was in the didactic literature of the Jacksonian period, then one begins to look for something more than the usual human slippage between intent and behavior.

What the children's stories of 1825–60 convey to a present-day reader is far less the literal reality of the time than the uneasiness many Americans felt about the future of their national life. It was not a time when it was common or popular for Americans to worry openly about the direction their society was taking. The prevailing mood was optimistic, patriotic, often bombastic. Citizens of a new republic were more inclined to celebrate the vigor and the progress of American life than to question where all the movement was going.

Yet there were doubts. The centrifugal force of expansion, the rapid and apparently ceaseless social changes—these produced an undercurrent of anxiety that can often be discerned below the surface optimism of the period.[44] A hortatory literature like that written for children before 1860 is perhaps especially revealing of the fears of its authors. Writers stressed the virtues they thought most threatened and warned against those faults they found most threatening. They idealized order because they saw order slipping away from American life.[45] They praised stability and leaned toward social conservatism because they were apprehensive about the ability of an increasingly democratic nation to maintain civil peace and social coherence.[46] Proud of their country, they were nevertheless fearful that the growing competitive spirit of American life would ultimately destroy all common kindliness and all community feeling, and so reduce society to a state of barbarous struggle for material success. "The greed of gain," wrote Catherine Sedgwick feelingly, "is the besetting sin of the most civilized, the best, and the most favored people of God's earth. My young friends, reform it, reform it altogether!"[47]

Because American society was increasingly free of the restraints of custom, because institutions were relatively weak and government a minimal influence on the affairs of individuals, most Americans believed that the quality of public life was highly dependent upon the moral behavior of individual citizens. Catherine Beecher expressed a conventional wisdom when she wrote that, "The success of democratic institutions . . . depends upon the intellectual and moral character of the mass of the people. If they are intelligent and virtuous, democracy is a blessing, but if they are ignorant and wicked, it is only a curse."[48]

And most Americans, certainly the authors of juvenile literature, were convinced that moral character had to be established early, before a child was corrupted by the competitiveness and the "greed of gain" they saw all around them, if the public weal was to be protected. "The positive influence of early and judicious instruction," said Cardell, "is the only safe dependence for public virtue."[49]

The children's books of the Jacksonian era were written to supply that "early and judicious instruction," with the good of the country in view. The enormous weight of the moral didacticism in the literature was not designed to oppress, nor to make children into automatons who would do the will of their elders without question. On the contrary, the authors believed that only early, firm moral training could make American children strong and independent, as they had to be to resist the dangerous undercurrents running just beneath the surface of a democratic society. Only the child who was by moral training "anchored to the rock of principle . . . [and] armed in the panoply of virtue" had the inner strength the authors were sure was needed to cope with the glorious, promising—and terrifying—freedom of American life.[50] It was the future of the republic that engaged the anxious attention of these early writers of juvenile fiction, and the future was then, as it always is, in the hands of children.

NOTES

1. See William Sloane, *Children's Books in England and America in the Seventeenth Century: A History and a Checklist* (New York: King's Crown Press, Columbia University, 1955), and Monica Kiefer, *American Children Through Their Books,* 1700–1835 (Philadelphia: University of Pennsylvania Press, 1948).

2. William Cardell, *The Story of Jack Halyard* (3rd ed.; Philadelphia: Uriah Hunt, 1825), p. x.

3. [Lydia Maria Child], *Evenings in New England* (Boston: Cummings, Hilliard, and Company, 1824), p. iii.

4. Samuel Goodrich, *Recollections of a Lifetime* (2 vols.; New York and Auburn: Miller, Orton and Mulligan, 1856), I, 174.

5. See Kiefer, *American Children Through Their Books,* and Cornelia Meigs et al., *A Critical History of Children's Literature* (rev. ed.; New York: Macmillan, 1969), especially Pt. 1.

6. Hawthorne's versions of the Greek Myths are an exception, but his few wholly original fictional tales for children have passed into obscurity with the rest.

7. Jacob Abbott, *Harper's Monthly Story Book,* Vol. I (New York: Harper and Brothers, 1854), pref.

8. Catherine Maria Sedgwick, *Boy of Mt. Rhigi* (Boston: Charles H. Peirce, 1848), pp. 5–7.

9. For a discussion of Maria Edgeworth's philosophy, see Gillian Avery, *Nineteenth Century Children* (London: Hodder and Stoughton, 1963), pp. 23–28.

10. Samuel Goodrich, *Short Stories for Long Nights* (Boston: Allen and Ticknor, 1834), p. 77.

11. *A Juvenile Keepsake*, ed. Clara Arnold (Boston: Phillips, Sampson, and Company, 1851), p. 23.

12. Eliza Leslie, *Stories for Adelaide* (Philadelphia: Henry F. Anners, 1843), pp. 48, 29.

13. Jacob Abbott, *The Rollo Philosophy* (Philadelphia: Hogan and Thompson, 1842), pp. 79, 86.

14. See, for example, *A Juvenile Keepsake*, pp. 106–10.

15. See *Laura's Impulses* (Philadelphia: American Sunday School Union, 1854).

16. Cardell, *Jack Halyard*, pp. 25–27, 97.

17. Samuel Goodrich, *Parley's Book of Fables* (Hartford: White, Dwier and Company, 1836), p. 18; *The Country Schoolhouse* (Philadelphia: American Sunday School Union, 1848), p. 27; Lydia Sigourney, *The Girl's Book* (New York: R. Carter and Brothers, 1851), pp. 45, 47.

18. Aunt Friendly, *Bound Out* (New York: Anson D. F. Randolph, 1859), p. 61.

19. Maria McIntosh, *Ellen Leslie* (New York: Dayton and Newman, 1842), p. 40.

20. *Belle and Lilly*, by "a New Pen" (Boston: Crosby, Nichols and Company, 1857), p. 30.

21. [Lydia Maria Child], *Emily Parker* (Boston: Bowles and Dearborn, 1827), p. 6.

22. For an extended example, see *Little Mary*, by "A Mother" (Boston: Waite, Peirce and Company, 1846).

23. *The Cooper's Son* (Boston: James French, 1846), pp. 13, 14.

24. Joseph Alden, *The State Prisoner* (New York: Lane and Tippett, 1848), p. 16.

25. Follen, *Twilight Stories*, p. 32.

26. William Cardell, *The Happy Family* (2nd ed.; Philadelphia: T. T. Ash, 1828), p. 12.

27. Cardell, *Jack Halyard*, p. 78.

28. Samuel Goodrich, *Parley's Magazine* (Boston: James Monroe and Company, 1842), p. 272.

29. *A Juvenile Keepsake*, p. 57.

30. *The Contrast* (Boston: Cottons and Barnard, 1832), p. 60. This theme was repeated in many stories. See, for example, Follen, *Twilight Stories*, p. 96, and Carleton Bruce, *Pleasure and Profit* (New York: Taylor and Gould, 1835), p. 13.

31. Louise C. Tuthill, *Get Money* (New York: Charles Scribner, 1858), p. 247. See also *Harry Winter* (New York: Mahlon Day, 1832), p. 5.

32. Child, *Evenings in New England*, p. 35.

33. Sigourney, *Girl's Book*, pp. 85, 86.

34. *The Child's Portfolio.* (New York: Mahlon Day, 1823), unpaged.

35. See Bruce, *Pleasure and Profit*, p. 195.

36. See Child, *Evenings in New England*, pp. 138–47, and Follen, *Twilight Stories*, pp. 15–22.

37. See, for example, Goodrich, *Parley's Book of Fables*, pp. 40, 54.

38. Cardell, *Jack Halyard*, pp. xi, xii.

39. Cardell, *Happy Family*, p. 10.

40. See *Father's Pictures of Family Influence* (Holliston, Mass.: David Heard, Jr., 1847), pref.

41. Alexis de Tocqueville, *Democracy in America*, ed. Phillips Bradley (New York: Knopf, 1945), II, 99.

42. For an overview of such commentary, see Richard L. Rapson, "The American Child as Seen by British Travellers," *American Quarterly*, 27, no. 3 (Fall 1965), 520–35.

43. See, for example, *The Juvenile Miscellany*, 2 (1832), 7; *Youth's Companion*, 20 (1846), 7; Sedgwick, *Boy of Mt. Rhigi*, p. 164.

44. The best discussion of this thesis is to be found in Marvin Meyers, *The Jacksonian Persuasion* (Stanford, Calif.: Stanford University Press, 1957).

45. See Sigourney, *Girl's Book*, p. 45.

46. See Sedgwick, *Love Token*, pp. 55, 56.

47. Sedgwick, *Boy of Mt. Rhigi*, p. 61.

48. Catherine E. Beecher, *A Treatise on Domestic Economy for the Use of Young Ladies at Home and at School* (rev. ed.; New York: Harper and Brothers, 1848), p. 36.

49. Cardell, *Jack Halyard*, p. xi.

50. *The Cooper's Son*, p. 111.

Shaping the National Character:
The *New England Primer*, the McGuffey *Readers*, and *The Story of a Bad Boy**

The Origin and Development of the New England Primer

Daniel A. Cohen

Perhaps no other book was as widely circulated among the children of early New England as the *New England Primer*. From the beginning of the eighteenth century, this little volume was a "stock" item in the bookshops and village general stores of that region, and untold thousands of copies were literally studied to pieces by children anxious (if not compelled) to learn to read, as one later observer put it, "that they might read the Bible."[1] In looking for the reasons behind its remarkable success, one must remember that the reading alternatives at that time, if a child was lucky enough to have any, generally ranged from the extremely dull to the downright grim. This, after all, was Puritan country, and there would have been no toleration among those pious and stiff-necked settlers for literary flights of fancy, even if directed toward the younger members of the congregation. Indeed, one basic cause of the *Primer*'s initial success was the complete ease with which it fit into the stern Puritan ethic of the New England community, and perhaps even with the equally austere New England landscape:

> Here was no easy road to knowledge and to salvation; but in prose as bare of beauty as the whitewash of their churches, in poetry as rough and stern as their storm torn coast, in pictures as crude and unfinished as their own glacial-smoothed boulders, between stiff oak covers, which symbolized the contents, the children were

*The following three essays are versions of introductions to volumes in the Garland Press series Classics of Children's Literature, 1621–1932, and appear here by kind permission of the authors and Garland Publishing, Inc., 545 Madison Ave., New York, N.Y. 10022.

led . . . to that happy state when, as expressed by Judge Sewall's child, they were afraid they "should goe to hell" and were "stirred up dreadfully to seek God."[2]

It has been estimated that in the period 1680–1830 between six and eight million copies of the *New England Primer* were printed.[3] There were hundreds of editions, issued in scores of locations (both in and out of New England), by numerous printers, publishers, and booksellers. There were many different versions of the *Primer*, and it was even occasionally put out under different titles. Yet of the millions of copies which were originally printed, remarkably few have survived the ravages of time and careless owners. For instance, the records of the Philadelphia publishing firm of Benjamin Franklin and David Hall show that between 1749 and 1766 they sold over 37,000 copies of the *Primer*; of these thousands of volumes, only a single copy is known to have survived.[4] Although the *Primer* almost certainly went through at least two printings by 1691, no complete copy of a seventeenth-century edition has yet come to light. The earliest extant *Primer* is believed to be an incomplete copy of a Boston edition of 1727, now in the collection of the New York Public Library.

Given the great rarity of all early editions of this work, it is not very surprising that the origins of the *New England Primer* remain something of a mystery. One person to whom several past investigators have assigned credit for the original compilation is the London printer, peddler of patent medicines, and fervent enemy of Catholicism, Benjamin Harris. Between 1673 and 1681, Harris printed tracts, broadsides, and even playing cards, many of them attacking the "evils" of popery. In 1679, and again in 1681, he issued tracts which offended the London authorities, and for the second offense, Harris was put in the pillory. After this experience, Harris temporarily stopped printing and in 1686, not long after the succession of the Catholic James II, moved to America.

In 1679, as part of his running campaign against the evils of Catholicism, Harris published a little book entitled *The Protestant Tutor*. This work was intended not only to instruct children how to "spel and read English," but also to display for the young reader "the errors and deceits of the Papists." Harris seems to have applied the bulk of his energies to the second task, and the result is a viciously anti-Catholic tract which describes in lurid detail both the alleged atrocities of popish conspirators and the allegedly low character of various pontiffs. Although the *Tutor* is addressed to children,

M R. J O H N R O G E R S , minifter of the gofpel in *London*, was the firft martyr in Queen M A R Y 's reign, and was burnt at *Smithfield, February* 14, 1554.—His wife with nine small children, and one at her breast following him to the ftake ; with which forrowful fight he was not in the leaft daunted, but with wonderful patience died courageoufly for the gofpel of J E S U S C H R I S T .

Page from the *New England Primer* (Hartford, Conn., 1849)

Harris even sinks to the bawdy in his zeal to discredit his sectarian archenemies. Yet the *Tutor* apparently struck a responsive chord with a British public restive under the rule of a king with Catholic leanings, as evidenced by its several reprintings during the following decade.[5] In 1685, a book with the same title was printed in Boston by Samuel Green, for the bookseller John Griffin, consisting of "A Catechism against Popery" and "Mr. Rogers' Verses," both of which appear in Harris's *Tutor*. There is no evidence, however, that this production met with any great success. Also, at about the same time, twenty copies of Harris's *Tutor* were shipped to a Boston bookseller.[6] Revised editions of the *Tutor* were printed at the beginning of the next century by Harris (who had by then returned to London), but in at least one of these editions the anti-Catholic propaganda had been somewhat attenuated.

Harris's *Protestant Tutor* has been considered by such authorities as Paul Leicester Ford and Charles Heartman to be the "legitimate predecessor" of the *New England Primer*.[7] Later investigators, however, have pointed out the underlying lack of similarity between the *Tutor*, as it was constituted in its early editions, and the *Primer*. While the former is basically a rather crude example of anti-Catholic propaganda, designed primarily to "Create in (the young) . . . an Abhorrence of Romish Idolatry," the latter is more legitimately a book of primary instruction (albeit religious) for young children. Even the specific similarities between the two works are, according to the later authorities, quite limited.[8]

The earliest known evidence relating to the origin of the *New England Primer* appears in the Stationer's Register of London, in the form of an entry by the little known and less than prolific London publisher Master John Gaine. The printing regulations of the time required the registration of all books prior to publication, and in the Register, under the date of October 5, 1683, Gaine entered a book entitled "the New England Primer or Milk for babes." Although there is no positive evidence that such a publication was ever actually issued by Gaine, the sixpence fee for registration would tend to make the entry of a spurious title unlikely. And in April 1685, Richard Chiswell, the London publisher, wrote the following passage in a letter to John Usher of Boston: "There is not one New England Primmer in London, if they will Take of Ten Grose and send over a book to print it by, they may be furnished, less than that Number will not Answer the Charge."[9]

The significance of this excerpt is obvious; if, as it appears, Chiswell was responding to a previous request for the *Primer* by Usher, then news at least of the existence of a *New England Primer* must have already reached Boston by 1685. Of course, there is no way of knowing positively whether the book requested by Usher was the one registered by Master Gaine a year or two before, or rather some other edition whose existence is as yet unknown. In any event, no copy of a *New England Primer* issued at that time by either John Gaine or some other publisher has come to light to help solve the mystery.

For the next clue concerning the origin of the *Primer*, we must return to the career of the ubiquitous Benjamin Harris. Harris, it may be recalled, had left England shortly after the succession of James II. He arrived in Boston in the autumn of 1686, and there became a successful bookseller. Over the next few years, Harris returned twice to London to obtain more books for resale in New England. Back in Boston by 1690, Harris published near the end of that year an almanac in which the following advertisement appears:

> There is now in the Press, and will suddenly be extant, a Second Impression of the *New England Primer enlarged*, to which is added, more *Directions for Spelling*: the *Prayer of K. Edward the 6th*, and *Verses made by Mr. Rogers the Martyr*. . . . Sold by Benjamin Harris, at the London Coffee-House in Boston.[10]

It can be surmised that Harris, sometime after his arrival in Boston in 1686, saw the possibility of publishing a primary reading book for the children of the region. Realizing, however, that the children of a New England, far removed from the popish plots of the Old, were not a suitable audience for his previously published *Protestant Tutor*, Harris decided to issue a different primer, which he first printed sometime between 1687 and 1690. It was the second impression of this new primer which was advertised in the almanac mentioned above. What connection, if any, there was between Harris's primer and the one(s?) registered by Gaine and referred to by Chiswell, is a question about which scholars can only speculate. Harris, by the way, returned to London in 1695. At the back of a book which he published there in 1701, appears an advertisement for books printed and sold by Harris. In this list appears *The New England Primer Enlarged; For the more easy attaining of English, To which is added Milk for Babes*. No copy of such an edition, one need hardly add, has survived.

As has already been mentioned, the earliest extant copy of the *New England Primer* is from a Boston edition of 1727. From this date forward, the work's history is much easier to trace, despite the relative sparsity of surviving copies. Between 1740 and 1760, a series of alterations and additions were made to the *Primer*: religious verses replaced secular ones in the rhymed alphabet, and several prayers and hymns were added. These changes, according to Paul Leicester Ford, constituted a further "evangelization of the *Primer*."[11] The American Revolution also caused some changes in content. Perhaps the most noticeable of these was the frequent insertion of the portrait of an American patriot (George Washington became the standard subject) in place of the picture of a British monarch, which had in some earlier editions served as the *Primer*'s frontispiece. In about 1790, another series of additions, taken from the British *Royal*

Primer, were made to new editions of the *Primer*. Woodcuts and rhymes were inserted portraying various animals, passages were included describing a "Good Boy" and "Bad Boy," and poems were added on "The Good Girl" and "The Naughty Girl." These secularizing changes did not, however, stop the gradual erosion of the *Primer*'s popularity among a public whose tastes were shifting toward less religious and more entertaining primers. Although it is true that more copies were printed during the period 1800–1830 than ever before, this was due more to the renown (and hence marketability) of the title than to the actual appeal of its contents. By the middle of the nineteenth century, the *Primer* had become as much an historical relic as an actual learning tool for young scholars; in about 1850 a facsimile of an eighteenth-century edition was issued and recommended "on account of its antiquity" as "an object of interesting and beneficial curiosity."[12] By 1897, the early bibliographer of the *Primer*, Paul Leicester Ford, could safely speculate that perhaps not a single child was still being taught by that "famous little manual."[13] The lengthy career of the *New England Primer* had clearly come to an end. And though its precise origins may well remain somewhat obscure, the eminent usefulness of its life can never be seriously doubted.

NOTES

1. Paul Leicester Ford, ed., *The New-England Primer: A History Of Its Origin And Development* (New York: Dodd, Mead, 1897), p. 4.

2. Ibid., pp. 1–2.

3. Charles F. Heartman, *The New-England Primer Issued Prior to 1830* (New York: Bowker, 1934), p. xxii.

4. P. L. Ford, pp. 19–20.

5. See Sister Mary Augustina Ray, "The Protestant Tutor," in United States Catholic Historical Society, *Historical Records and Studies*, XXX (New York, 1939), 87–88.

6. Worthington Chauncey Ford, *The Boston Book Market, 1679–1700* (Boston: The Club of Odd Volumes, 1917), pp. 35, 150.

7. P. L. Ford, p. 16; Heartman, p. xvii.

8. See Worthington Chauncey Ford, "The New England Primer," in *Bibliographical Essays: A Tribute to Wilberforce Eames* (Freeport, N.Y.: Books for Libraries, 1697; reprint), pp. 64–65; see also Frank Monaghen, "Benjamin Harris," in *The Colophon*, part 12, Dec. 1932.

9. Heartman, p. xv. See W. C. Ford, *Boston Book Market*, pp. 151–52, for full text of letter.

10. P. L. Ford, Plate V.

11. P. L. Ford, pp. 29–30, 46.

12. This statement is found in a "certificate" at the front of Ira Webster's reprint of a 1777 edition of the *Primer*, published in Hartford in about 1850.

13. P. L. Ford, p. 52.

The McGuffey Readers

Carol Kammen

The mid-1970s is an interesting point in time to re-examine William McGuffey's *First Eclectic Reader*. Most school districts long ago abandoned the *Readers*; but some are just now rediscovering them as part of a movement called "Back to Basics." Some contemporary educators believe that the *Eclectic Readers* promote good vocabulary skills, accurate orthography, and earlier reading comprehension than more modern—and perhaps less didactic—instructional books.

The *Readers* also promote certain cultural attitudes that the "Back to Basics" parents and schools seek. The *Readers* embody strong moral lessons that children absorbed as they read their way through, lesson by lesson. This, of course, was not accidental. The purpose of nineteenth-century American schools—be it an old, established New England town school, an elite Southern school, or a frontier common school—was to prepare citizens in character and proper principles. Noah Webster claimed in 1810 that his *American Spelling Book* would "instil into [children's] minds, with the first rudiments of language, some just ideas of religion, morals and domestic economy."[1] A textbook was expected to foster those virtues that were valued by a pious, middle-class society; and the authors of textbooks took their charge most seriously. Many authors believed that the texts they wrote were responsible for the creation of that most elusive quality—a national character.

The first American readers were published during the 1780s, and almost every other year for the next twenty years another new title would appear. Most of those readers, and indeed the accompanying geographies, spellers, and math books, were produced by teachers and scholars from New England. In 1849 George W. Bethune wrote that "nearly all of our teachers, with the authors of our school books, and a very large proportion of our preachers, as well as our editors . . . come from, or receive their education in New England."[2]

But this was not true of William Holmes McGuffey. He was born in western Pennsylvania, in Washington County, in the year 1800. His parents had been raised in the county by immigrant Scots and Irish pioneers. When William was three, the McGuffey family pushed

West into the fertile Western Reserve and settled in a section of Ohio known as Trumbull County. The city of Youngstown was nearby— a village then.

William's mother, Anna Holmes McGuffey, was better educated than her husband and it was she who taught William to read and cipher. He in turn taught his younger brothers and sisters. When a common school was established nearby, William attended. He soon outgrew it, however, and was sent to live and study with the Reverend Wick in Youngstown. Before William was fourteen years old, he had been hired as a common school teacher for a cluster of twenty-three families in Calcutta, Ohio. He held school for a four-month term, taught forty-eight children of various ages, and received a salary of $46.00.

Though now qualified as a teacher, William aspired to further education for himself. He went to the Old Stone Academy in Greensburg, Pennsylvania, where he lived with the Presbyterian minister and worked as a janitor for the Church in order to cover his four-dollar-a-term school bill. McGuffey went on to Washington College in Washington, Pennsylvania, where he studied the standard academic fare of the day, Greek and Latin.

Again McGuffey turned to teaching, and again he gave it up to return to the matter of his own education. This time he enrolled in Miami University at Oxford, Ohio. The president of the school, the Reverend Robert Hamilton Bishop, was so impressed by his new student that he offered McGuffey a professorship in the Greek and Latin languages.

McGuffey remained at Miami University as a professor until 1836. There he met and married Miss Harriet Spinning. And, to his home in Miami, William called his younger brother Alexander to live and study with him.

The white frame house on Spring Street in Oxford that McGuffey bought for his bride Harriet was soon enlarged by a brick addition to house their growing family. It was here that McGuffey tried out his educational system on neighborhood children who gathered in class when summoned by a shrill whistle. These classes, taught by both William and his wife, concentrated on reading, mathematics, and spelling. This building now houses the McGuffey Museum, an interesting memorial to the man and to his works.

The publishers Truman and Smith of Cincinnati had issued several textbooks geared to children in the midwest. In 1833 they sought out McGuffey to produce an eclectic reader, that is, a book containing readings from various sources.

In 1836, just as McGuffey resigned his professorship at Miami University to assume the presidency of Cincinnati College, McGuffey's *First* and *Second Eclectic Readers* were published. The *Third* and *Fourth Readers* were issued in 1837, and the *Fifth* in 1844. Alexander McGuffey produced a companion speller in 1846, and the *Sixth Reader* was printed in 1857. After that the *Readers* underwent numerous printings and some revisions; some 125,000,000 copies were sold throughout the nineteenth century.

The *Readers* were designed for common schools, and were ungraded. That is, the stages designated in the titles bore no relationship to a student's status in school, or to any other graded series of texts. The *Third Reader* was not designed for the third grade, nor was it equal to Cobbs' *Third Reader*, or to any other. It was simply the third most difficult reader in its own series.

In an era when teachers were poorly or, at best, inadequately trained to cope with students of differing ages and abilities, textbooks were of the greatest importance. The most common method of instruction was for the teacher to require letter-perfect memorization. The student was expected to display his knowledge by recitation. McGuffey's *Readers* provided passages of suitable length to be memorized and of appropriate content to reinforce the values of the expanding midwestern middle class. The *Readers* ultimately became the dominant textbook throughout the Western Reserve, the Mississippi Valley, and in the Old South.

A McGuffey student learned that individual enterprise was expected of everyone:

> "For when a man resolves to do his work himself,
> you may depend upon it, that it will be done."
>
> *(Second Reader)*

Truthfulness was extolled:

> The truth itself is not believed,
> From one who often has deceived.
>
> *(Third Reader)*

Abstinence was a virtue:

> "My child will not be a drunkard!" Cheering thought! How it swells the heart with emotions too big for utterance!
>
> *(Fifth Reader)*

Illustration by H. F. Farny for selection LXXVI, "Rivermouth Theater" from *The Story of a Bad Boy* by Thomas Bailey Aldrich, in McGuffey's *Fourth Eclectic Reader* (1879)

Self-indulgence was frowned upon:

> Thus, he would never take the pains
> To seek the prize that labor gains,
>   Until the time had passed;
> For, all his life, he dreaded still
> The silly bugbear of *up hill*,
>   And died a dunce at last.
>
> *(Fourth Reader)*

Promptness and industry were expected:

As Amy went home, she thought of what her teacher had often told her—"Do your task at once; then think about it," for "one doer is worth a hundred dreamers."

(Third Reader)

About Honesty:

Let no little boy or girl ever take things without leave. This is stealing; and they who steal are thieves.

(Second Reader)

Even the animals in McGuffey's were careful and clean:

[Fido] took care, however, not to be troublesome, by leaping on
him with dirty paws, nor would he follow him into the parlor,
unless he was asked.

(Second Reader)

And religion was the bulwark of life:

> I am cheerful, young man, Father William replied;
> Let the cause your attention engage;
> In the days of my youth I remembered my God!
> And he hath not forgotten my age.

(Second Reader)

Selections in the *Eclectic Readers* were culled from a variety of
poets and prose writers popular during the nineteenth century. There
are only a few selections that dip into the wisdom of the past; and
foreign writers are infrequently represented. Goldsmith and Wordsworth are two of the few who do appear. There are selections from
the works of Henry W. Longfellow, Thomas Bailey Aldrich, Nathaniel Hawthorne, Charles G. Eastman, John Greenleaf Whittier, Sara
Josepha Hale, and William Cullen Bryant. The *Readers* emphasize
a homogeneous America, and suggest a society uncomplicated by
minorities; blacks and Native Americans are almost nonexistent.

The Eclectic Series gained great popularity, and in 1845 William
McGuffey was appointed to the Chair of Moral Philosophy at the
University of Virginia. He remained there until his death in 1873.
His *Readers*, which sold for approximately 7 cents apiece, or 1 dollar
a dozen, were still selling in 1920. In 1946 The American Book
Company again published the series, updated with new illustrations.

Much has been written about McGuffey's *Eclectic Readers*. Hamlin Garland credited them with awakening his literary interests;[3]
Herbert Quick said that the *Readers* "constitute the most influential
volumes ever published in America."[4] Mark Sullivan surveyed Mc-
Guffey's influence and estimated that at least half the school children
of America, from 1836 to 1900, drew inspiration from the *Readers*.[5]
And Hugh Fullerton wrote in the *Saturday Evening Post* in 1927
that "except the Bible, no other book or set of books has influenced
the American mind so much."[6]

NOTES

1. Noah Webster Jr., *American Spelling Book* (Boston, 1810), quoted in
Ruth Elson, *Guardians of Tradition*, Lincoln, Neb.: University of Nebraska
Press, 1964, p. 1.

2. George W. Bethune, "The Claim of our Country on Its Literary Men" (Cambridge, Mass., 1849), quoted in Elson, p. 7.

3. Hamlin Garland, *Son of the Middle Border* (New York: Macmillan, 1917), p. 112.

4. Herbert Quick, *One Man's Life* (Indianapolis, Ind.: Bobbs Merrill, 1925), p. 156.

5. Mark Sullivan, *Our Times* (New York: Scribners, 1927), II, 18.

6. Hugh Fullerton, "That Guy McGuffey," *Saturday Evening Post*, Nov. 26, 1927, pp. 14–16.

The Story of a Bad Boy

Ann Beattie

The Story of a Bad Boy is to a great extent autobiographical. Thomas Bailey Aldrich certainly did not need to look far to find a name for his hero, Tom Bailey. Portsmouth, New Hampshire, where Aldrich grew up, appears in the novel as Rivermouth. When Aldrich's father died in 1852, his plans for college were put aside and, like Tom, he went to work.

Aldrich's bad boy is like others that Leslie Fiedler has described in *Love and Death in the American Novel*: "The Good Bad Boy is, of course, America's vision of itself, crude and unruly in his beginnings, but endowed by his creator with an instinctive sense of what is right." Americans have always accepted, if not actually encouraged and worshipped, "badness" in young men. Somehow, this is healthy, charming. When Tom describes himself early in the novel as "really . . . not a cherub," the reader can sit back and smile contentedly; who wants to hear about a good boy?

But this boy is surprisingly good, especially considering the kind of world he moves in. Tom, who is devoted to his horse, Gypsy, must lose her to a traveling circus; he has been separated from his parents and is never again to see his father, who dies during a cholera epidemic; his best friend, Binny Wallace, floats away to his death as Tom and some other boys stand helplessly on shore. Surely these are not events conducive to good spirits, yet Tom Bailey does not dwell on any of them, and the general mood of the novel—and of its main character—ranges from cheerful to ebullient. In part, this may be explained in terms of perspective: Tom Bailey writes the book as an adult, and adults, in America, learn to overlook the bad (how else can we explore new frontiers?) just as little boys learn not to cry. Children are often told that their childhood is the happiest part of their lives, and this seems to be what Tom Bailey believes, even in spite of some strong evidence to the contrary, as he recounts the story from an adult's perspective.

The issue of perspective might also, in part, explain why Mark Twain's *Tom Sawyer*, written only seven years later, has so far outdistanced its predecessor, becoming an American classic while Aldrich's novel is, at best, a minor one. When Aldrich's Tom tells us "I am, or rather I was," a bad boy we feel obliged to share the mature perspective of the author. In *Tom Sawyer*, we can wallow without embarrassment in the "badness" we love. But even if the narrator's mature perspective tempers a little our having fun, Aldrich's book captivates us all the same with its vivid details and fast pace. This effect takes hold because, unlike Captain Nutter's sister, Miss Abigail, a true victim of classical conditioning who can smell tobacco burning in an unlit pipe, Tom's responses are immediate and honest. And, like his creator, Tom has an artist's sensitivity: pictures, images, and brief, significant moments capture his attention. He loves the wallpaper patterned with birds in his bedroom because it is beautiful; "that no such bird existed didn't detract," he tells us. On his way to Rivermouth for the first time, he is fascinated by a "shaggy yellow dog" and "two boys fighting behind a red barn." Like William Carlos Williams' "The Red Wheel Barrow," which suggests so much, the colors and arrangements of this scene remain fixed in memory. He is fascinated by Sailor Ben's tattoo of a mermaid because the man is the embodiment of art, and Tom has the perceptions of an artist; he even appreciates the aesthetics of a sign reading "Root Beer/Sold Here." In his imagination, snow falling on the garden gate transforms the posts into "stately Turks." Sailor Ben may believe that "we don't larn nothin' by experience," but certainly Tom would not agree: his own proper moral code pays off and his heightened awareness transforms the commonplace into the unusual. What we should learn from experience is how to cope better; it is significant that Sailor Ben is pessimistic because he left his bride to set sail, as he agreed to do when drunk. Tom believes in accepting reality. When Captain Nutter cannot read to Tom the letter announcing Tom's father's death, Tom takes the letter from him and reads it himself. He accepts that he cannot go to Harvard and takes a job with an uncle. It is very fitting that the society he belongs to with other boys is called the Centipedes —a centipede moves slowly, with its legs on the ground. While his imagination might temporarily transport him, he remains true to the Puritan ethic of diligence and common sense.

Certainly a child reading the book today would realize that this is not the way things are. But like Tom's nostalgia for the past as he rummages through the attic at the Nutter House, there is something fascinating, and even important, about *The Story of a Bad Boy*. Speaking of Kitty, who was separated from Sailor Ben shortly after their marriage, Tom says, "Happy are they that have no history." Kitty's history is sad, but ours is not. The vision of the American past presented in the book is a pleasant one—there is no social criticism, and the veneer of well-being is seductive. When the inhabitants of Rivermouth run in every direction after Tom and his friends sneak out during the night to set off the cannons, it seems very refreshing that they are not diving into bomb shelters; when the boys perform *Hamlet*, and when Tom reads Goethe, it is delightful that they are not sprawled in front of a television. Just as there is respect for Dame Jocelyn, confined indoors for fourteen years and out of touch with the times, we should have a fond feeling for *The Story of a Bad Boy* and for what Aldrich has attempted to do. "The old ways and the old times were good enough for her." This novel, written more than a hundred years ago, has its own charm and deserves to be treated kindly. It contains the thoughts of a gentleman, gently stated.

The Utopia of St. Nicholas

The Present as Prologue*

Fred Erisman

When the publishers of *Scribner's Monthly* launched *St. Nicholas Magazine* in November 1873, their aim was clear. The newcomer, edited by Mary Mapes Dodge, was to be the qualitative equivalent of the adult magazine, conveying and reinforcing the values of its upper-middle-class readers. The two were to be "harmonious companions in the family, and the helpers of each other in the work of instruction, culture and entertainment."[1] This aim remained remarkably constant throughout the magazine's history. As late as 1923, it was restated thus:

> [*St. Nicholas*] builds character; it fosters true manliness and womanliness through the doctrine of labor, courage, fortitude, self-respect, and the golden rule.
>
> It keeps pace with the world and the important things that are going forward in it.
>
> It prepares boys and girls for life as it is, and stimulates ambition for a life of usefulness and service to mankind.[2]

These are clearly extensions of the original goal. They are also something more.

In its goals lies much of the importance of *St. Nicholas*. The magazine consistently presents to its readers the basic ideals of middle-class America—a clear-cut sense of right and wrong, a regard for the Puritan work ethic, and a sense of personal responsibility. In doing so, it implies that these values are desirable and worthy of perpetuation. At the same time, however, it also presents a divided society, one split between the ideal world of middle-class values and the somewhat less than ideal world of reality. In a random sampling of those issues of *St. Nicholas* published between 1890 and 1910, both sides of this split appear. Throughout the years immediately prior to World War I, the magazine transmits, in its nonfiction, a sense of the technological competence necessary to prosper in an urban, mechanized world, even as it presents, in its fiction, the professed values of the middle-class world of the American dream. Taken together, the two groups of literature make up a singularly utopian body of

---

*A paper presented at the first annual conference of the Children's Literature Association, at Storrs, Conn., March 1974.

writing, as they equip young readers to survive in—and to improve —the world in which they find themselves.

The nonfiction of *St. Nicholas* poses and answers three didactic questions: "What is the world like?" "How does the world operate?" and "How can I best get along in the world?" The first of these is dealt with by descriptive articles embracing topics from matter-of-fact travel accounts to discussions of significant world events. Typical of these are Theodore Roosevelt's "Hero Tales of American History" (May–October 1895), Annie C. Kuiper's "Queen Wilhelmina's Lessons" (October 1903), and Bertha Runkle's "Child Life in China and Japan" (January 1905).

Two themes emerge from these articles: that the well-rounded person must have a general understanding of the world and its history, and that the individual can benefit from the examples of others. The examples, however, are inevitably couched in ideal terms. William Abbatt, citing Captain James Lawrence's dying injunction, "Don't give up the ship," goes on to suggest that persistence and optimism are qualities applicable to all facets of life: "[These words] are a good motto in every trouble of life. Don't give up the ship— don't despair, lose heart, surrender, but take courage, and, like General Grant, 'Fight it out on this line if it takes all summer.' "[3] What the individual learns from history are the lessons of courage, industry, and fortitude. If he patterns himself upon these lessons, he will find himself attuned to the world in which he lives.

The second question, the "how" of the world, is answered by a host of scientific and technological articles. Representative of this group are Lieutenant John M. Ellicott's history of explosives (July 1896); Tudor Jenks's "Mirrors of Air" (January 1897), on mirages; and George Ethelbert Walsh's "What a Lump of Coal Could Do" (October 1904). These articles, without exception, stress the importance of general knowledge in its own right, and man's ability to mold nature to his will through technology. Thus, Walsh's essay concludes: "The harnessing of the waves and wind for generating electric power, or the focusing of the sun's rays on a boiler . . . are but further illustrations of man's efforts to cast his burden of hard labor upon forces which are all around us, if we but know how to release and employ them. When some of the potential power of a pound of coal was first released and harnessed . . . a vital step in the progress of humanity and civilization was taken."[4] The message is plain: precise knowledge of the world and the harnessing of its knowledge are among the keys to success.

The final question, "How can I best get along in the world?" is the subject of numerous practical articles, presenting to the reader of *St. Nicholas* his environment, the organization and operation of his culture, and assorted skills and accomplishments likely to be of use to him. Among these are Ernest Ingersoll's discussion of city-planning, "Reasoning Out a Metropolis" (January 1898); Cleveland Moffett's several articles on "Careers of Danger and Daring" (1901); and H. Irving Hancock's two-part article on jiu-jitsu, "Japanese Athletics for American Boys" (January–February 1904).

Despite all this practicality, though, professed American ideals appear, quietly but explicitly. Cleveland Moffett, after describing several technical and dangerous occupations, drives home the lesson: "These every-day heroes . . . may give us a bit of their spirit for our own lives, the brave and patient spirit that will keep us unflinchingly at the hard thing (whatever it be) until we have conquered it. And perhaps we too may feel impelled to cultivate . . . the habit of courage."[5] Even if the life is that of the twentieth century, the ideals are those of an earlier, simpler America—courage, patience, and unquenchable fortitude.

Throughout the nonfiction of *St. Nicholas*, one finds a sense of learning about reality. Facts abound, presented without apology, to be appreciated for themselves. Beneath these facts, however, lies a humane, conservative world somewhat at odds with the practical world of reality. These worlds, the editors seem to say, exist concurrently; the ideals of the American dream are at least partially compatible with the facts of a technological society. Despite this compatibility, though, a division is clear. Bound by facts, the authors at times have to struggle to reconcile their ideal view with the real society of which they write. Significantly, no such struggle appears in the fiction. Here the authors, unfettered by the need to assimilate cold facts, are free to portray the ideal world.

In its way, the fiction of *St. Nicholas* is as unabashedly didactic as the nonfiction. Its primary purpose, to be sure, is entertainment. But even as it provides quality entertainment, the fiction also supplies cultural ideals, standards, and models to assist the young reader in directing his life. It reinforces at every turning the child's sense of his place and role in a middle-class world. Whatever the type of story being presented, the plot line is paralleled by a strong current of cultural indoctrination.

"A player passing the ball to another on the run" by C. M. Relyea, from Anita L. Corbert, "Intercollegiate Basket-Ball for Women," *St. Nicholas*, 26 (Jan. 1899), 249

The first major class of fiction, that of fantasy and science fiction, is a mixed group. Like the nonfictional works, many of these stories glorify technical competence, as in Clement Fezandie's "Through the Earth" (January–April 1898), telling of a tunnel to the Antipodes. Others, however, move into the imaginative realm of fantasy and the supernatural. Regardless of the subject matter, though, the stories stress the familiar values of obedience, industry, and contentment, implying that these are the traits that make their imagined worlds attractive. Thus, for example, a boy who suddenly acquires magical powers finds that they bring him only grief. He surrenders them without regret, remarking afterward that "since then I have never longed for anything that comes without effort—for whatever is worth having is worth working for."[6]

The second notable class of fiction, historical fiction, although somewhat restricted by its basis of fact, advances the same cultural attitudes. The stories are of a familiar type: a young person, aged between ten and eighteen, comes into contact with notable events or persons, and learns something of himself, his times, and the world. Typical are Roberta Nelson's "The Field of the Cloth of Gold" (January 1899), Annah Robinson Watson's "Eleanor's Colonel" (July 1900), and Gensai Murai's " 'Kibun Daizin,' or From Shark Boy to Merchant Prince" (July–November 1904). The lessons taught by the stories, like the stories themselves, are familiar. Adherence to duty, for example, is highly regarded, as is self-reliance, in all its forms. Thus, the editors, introducing the story of a seventeenth-century Japanese boy, remark: "The shrewdness and dauntless ambition of the young hero of this story will commend him to the admiration of American boys."[7] Though the stories exist primarily to entertain, they obviously also teach, stressing the attitudes and ways of behavior professed by turn-of-the-century America.

The largest class of fiction in *St. Nicholas* is that dealing with ordinary persons under ordinary conditions, such as Carolyn Wells's "The Story of Betty" (January–October 1899), or Frances Courtenay Baylor's "In the Cavalry" (July 1903). In every case, the stories, through the actions and attitudes of a sympathetic central character, provide an example for the reader to follow. Ralph Cruger, for example, a city-bred sixteen-year-old, grows in wisdom under the guidance of his country cousin, Harry:

Each day was marked by some new experience, some new thing learned, some step forward toward manliness and self-reliance and

"Betty clasped her arms tightly around a lamp-post, thus anchoring herself" by R. B. Birch, from Carolyn Wells, "The Story of Betty," *St. Nicholas*, 26 (April 1899), 473

self-control, frankness, and truth. Ralph, under the tutelage of Harry's constant example, had learned . . . to know that a quick hand and ready brain and fearlessness were things of steady value, and to have driven into him, so deeply that they were never uprooted, the old, old lessons that success comes only through repeated failure, and that he is thrice brave and thrice a conqueror who conquers self. He had good stuff in him, this boy, and the semi-rough life brought it out.[8]

The lessons of *St. Nicholas* are "the old, old lessons": they stress the importance of duty, industry, thrift, and self-reliance, arguing in the process that these are the major virtues. In doing so, the magazine perpetuates qualities that one of its authors admits are old; it presents them, however, not as museum pieces, but as viable standards, as valid in an urban setting as in a rural one, as valid in the twentieth century as in the eighteenth. In doing so, it creates a tantalizingly utopian situation.

Karl Mannheim, in *Ideology and Utopia* (1929), speaks of two kinds of "situationally transcendent ideas," which illuminate the utopianism of *St. Nicholas*. Ideologies, says Mannheim, are the ideas that, although never achieving realization, are the ones usually cited as the rules and values by which the society claims to live.[9] Utopias, on the other hand, are those ideas that can potentially change the existing order: "When they pass over into conduct, [they] tend to shatter . . . the order of things prevailing at the time."[10] Ideologies, in short, tend to preserve the status quo; utopias tend to change it. This tension between ideology and utopia appears quite clearly in *St. Nicholas*.

The years during which the magazine was in its prime were years of social and technological change, in which the American individual was asked to reconcile an increasingly impersonal, mechanized society with a system of values based upon individuality and open, decent personal relations. This change, however, is not apparent in the magazine. If one takes the contents of *St. Nicholas* at face value, one finds that they present a society in which man and machine live in harmony, a culture in which the comforts of the industrial era are complemented by the ideals of an earlier America. It is an interesting society, and an appealing one, but it is not the one in which the young readers of the magazine would find themselves as adults.

If *St. Nicholas*, despite its own professions, does not truly prepare its readers for "life as it is," it does equip them to change that life. Although the ideologies of middle-class America permeate the magazine, they are presented as workable ideals; the contrast between the real and the ideal is absent. Lacking a sense of this contrast, but finding in life that the contrast exists (as would be inevitable for these children, who would come to maturity in the years following World War I), the child, as adult, might reasonably be expected to set out to change his life. The change, presumably, would be one enabling him to practice those ideals in the context of modern life. If effected, the change would indeed tend to shatter the prevailing order of things.

In its presentation of the compatibility of the modern world and traditional values, *St. Nicholas* is, in the best sense of the word, utopian. Implicitly and vaguely dissatisfied with the shifting present, it looks to the future, recognizing that change must come about through the individual. Recognizing further that the children of the present are the adults of the future, it presents to its readers the ideals of the past in the context of the present, giving them the means with which to change the future.

NOTES

1. "St. Nicholas," *Scribner's Monthly*, 7 (November 1873), 115.
2. "Fifty Years of St. Nicholas," *St. Nicholas*, 51 (November 1923), 20. A thoughtful account of the magazine's history and stature appears in Florence Stanley Sturges, "The *St. Nicholas* Years," in *The Hewins Lectures, 1947–1962*, ed. Siri Andrews (Boston: Horn Book, 1963), pp. 267–95.
3. William Abbatt, "The Chesapeake Mill," *St. Nicholas*, 24 (July 1897), 730.
4. George Ethelbert Walsh, "What a Lump of Coal Could Do," *St. Nicholas*, 31 (October 1904), 1120.
5. Cleveland Moffett, "The Locomotive Engineer," *St. Nicholas*, 28 (October 1901), 1068.
6. Tudor Jenks, "A Magician for One Day," *St. Nicholas*, 24 (October 1897), 1016.
7. Gensai Murai, " 'Kibun Daizin,' or From Shark-Boy to Merchant Prince," *St. Nicholas*, 31 (July 1904), 777.
8. H. S. Canfield, "The Boys of the Rincon Ranch," *St. Nicholas*, 29 (April 1902), 525.
9. Karl Mannheim, *Ideology and Utopia*, trans. Louis Wirth and Edward Shils (1929; reprinted New York: Harvest-Harcourt, Brace, n.d.), pp. 194–95.
10. Mannheim, p. 192.

The Oddness of Oz*

Osmond Beckwith

TWENTY YEARS AFTER

In 1950, a father wanting to read to a young daughter, I bought with other "children's classics" *The Wonderful Wizard of Oz* by L. Frank Baum. Later, drawn by curiosity, I also bought most of the remaining Oz titles *by* Baum (for this series so popular with children had not been allowed to die with the author's death in 1919). In my own childhood I had known Baum only from his *Ozma of Oz*, a book I seem to remember having found in our school library: odd if true, for schools consistently denied shelf space to Oz as to most ephemeral or "fad" books which children read to the exclusion of anything else.

In my fatherly reading and re-reading I discovered—if what seemed so obvious could be a discovery—the material for an article on the unconscious in children's literature like that of an earlier study by an English novelist on *Elsie Dinsmore*. (If now known only to specialists, in their day the "Elsie books" were a juvenile series as frantically popular and endlessly extended as Oz. Of all such series, Oz seems the only one to please successive younger generations.)

I researched Baum in the New York Public Library, discovering nothing about Oz of the kind I feared; more oddly, since Dorothy, the Scarecrow, the Tin Woodman and the Cowardly Lion were apparently firmly fixed in American public imagination, almost nothing in print about their creator. Of the few brief adult Oz-appreciations then extant, the best and longest—itself brief enough—was still the earliest, that of American editor and anthologist Edward Wagenknecht in a 1929 chapbook.

I intended my Baum article for *Neurotica* (1948–51), a little magazine edited by G. Legman, author also of the magazine's most sensational and influential article, "The Psychopathology of the Comics," also in its way a study of children's literature. It was Legman who made the rather mortifying suggestion that my interest in

---

*A part of this essay appeared in a different form in *Kulchur* and is printed here with permission.

Baum was a name-fatality: "Oz," that is, because of Osmond or
"Ozzie." (For whatever such name-fatalities may be worth, my
daughter's as well is a variant of Dorothy.)

Later Legman told me, "If you're going to write about Baum
there's a man you ought to meet." And so to Oz I owe my introduction to Martin Gardner, who needs no introduction as a writer and
critic of children's literature. Among his numerous avocations at
that time, he was, I think, contributing editor of *Humpty Dumpty's
Magazine.*

My Baum knowledge shrank when faced with Martin Gardner's,
his collection of Oziana and rarer Baum titles, his friendships and
correspondence with other Oz-buffs. Martin prophesied truly that
the forthcoming expiration of the *Wonderful Wizard*'s copyright (in
1956) would spark new interest in Baum. In anticipation he was
then trying to place his own Baum-biography, "The Royal Historian
of Oz," with a large-circulation magazine such as the *Ladies Home
Journal.* He showed me the manuscript, which I examined nervously,
expecting on every page to find myself anticipated. But to my relief
it was straightforward biography in his usual lucid style.

In turn I showed my manuscript, which Mrs. Gardner began reading. Then and later its first two sentences ran: "*The Wonderful
Wizard of Oz,* America's most popular juvenile fantasy, originally
appeared in 1900, a little more than ten years after the death of
Louisa May Alcott. Like Miss Alcott, Oz-author L. Frank Baum
made his appeal especially to young girls." At which point Mrs.
Gardner stopped reading and demanded immediately, "Martin, is
that true?" "I'm afraid it is," he replied. In our subsequent discussion
I don't remember that we read any more of my manuscript.

Time passed. "The Royal Historian" did not appear in a magazine
of large circulation, but in two 1955 issues of the *Magazine of Fantasy & Science Fiction. Neurotica* was long defunct before I finished
the thirty-second revision (a conservative estimate) of my article.
That saw print finally (1961) in *Kulchur,* another little magazine, as
"The Oddness of Oz."

Twenty years later Baum needs much less introduction than my
article gave him. Beside Martin Gardner's, he has been the subject
of another full-length biography and several respectful critical articles, while the *Wonderful Wizard* has reached publishing apotheosis
in a 1973 coffee-table-sized *annotated* edition. Yet it is still question-
able whether all this later research has better answered my article's
theme-question: What made (makes) Oz so popular?

Explanations of Oz's vitality are generally in terms of the books' "native" or "indigenous" subject matter—which is merely to repeat Edward Wagenknecht's earlier definition of Oz as "the first distinctive attempt to construct a fairyland out of American materials." Wagenknecht had even insisted that only an American—in a country overrun with mechanical influences—could have conceived the robots and automata which are so characteristic a part of Ozian fantasy.

Creating robots and automata would seem automatically to place Baum as a forerunner in the United States' growing concern with science-fiction and scientific fantasy (a concern as great today as twenty years ago). Yet, to an unprejudiced adult, re-reading the Oz books will disclose little likeness to modern science-fiction. Rather the resemblance is to those English Christmas pantomimes in which the role of "principal boy" is traditionally played by a girl (in Oz, however, the principal boy always wears skirts). The question of the indigenous quality of the books deserves to be taken up in more detail.

THE ODDNESS OF OZ

There are strong similarities between *The Wonderful Wizard of Oz*, the prototype of the series, and another more universally acknowledged children's classic: Lewis Carroll's *Alice in Wonderland* (published in 1865, when Baum was nine).

Both *Alice* and the *Wonderful Wizard* are fables of innocence and experience. Both have as "hero" a little girl. Both are packed as full as puddings of unconscious distortions and symbolizations. The differences between them, including basic differences in literary ability, are biographical or, if you like, indigenous.

Carroll's Alice drops down the rabbit hole unharmed and unharming; she even replaces the crockery examined on her way, so as not to hurt anybody, but Baum's Dorothy enters Oz with a death, her cyclone-carried house killing an old woman. Though an atmosphere of delicacy, of social contretemps, embarrassing situations, tiffs, and misunderstandings accompanies Alice throughout her long dream—which is always identified as a dream—the only situation that seems likely to become serious is ended by her awakening. It is quite different with Dorothy. Her adventures not only include attacks by mythical beasts but by lions, wolves, bees, monkeys, and creatures who snap their heads like hammers. She is overcome by poison gas, and almost by chapter threatened with death in various forms.

Dorothy and the
Cowardly Lion, from
The Wonderful Wizard
of Oz

The motivating force in both books is a search, but while Alice
looks for the lovely garden she has glimpsed in her first hour in
Wonderland, Dorothy, surrounded by all the beauty of a fairy kingdom, only wants to go home. Alice travels alone; Dorothy makes
friends, but what sort of friends?—a straw-stuffed scarecrow, a woodchopper who having chopped himself to bits is now completely artificial, and a lion afraid of his own roar (three different ways of
writing eunuch). Searching for the wonderful wizard who is to heal
them, and give each his heart's desire, the friends reach the Emerald
City of Oz, but must be blinkered in order to enter. Aloof and terrifying, the Wizard refuses his help unless Dorothy kills off still another old woman, the powerful witch of whom he lives in constant
fear. In attempting this exploit, the Scarecrow is eviscerated, the Tin
Man scrapped, the Lion captured, and the girl enslaved.

Carroll tells his tale by puns, parodies, and witty transubstantia-
tions of harsh reality. The word "death," if I am not mistaken, occurs
only once in his entire book. But Baum's approach throughout is
literal and matter-of-fact. He doesn't suggest that his horrors might
not exist; he spares no detail to increase their vividness. The climac-

tic episode of the first half of his book is Dorothy's "melting" of the
Wicked Witch, who, in Baum's words, "fell down in a brown, melted,
shapeless mass and began to spread over the clean boards of the
kitchen floor. Seeing that she had really melted away to nothing,
Dorothy drew another bucket of water and threw it over the mess.
She then swept it all out the door."

The story resumes as Dorothy's revivified friends return to claim
the Wizard's promise. But the Wizard proves a fraud, an old balloon-
ascensionist in Oz by accident, like Dorothy. For the three citizens
of fairyland he is able to improvise placebos, not for the human
being. He constructs a balloon, but bungles the take-off and leaves
Dorothy behind, so the travelers renew their journey, this time to
the palace of Glinda the Good Witch of the South, eternally young
and beautiful. From her Dorothy learns that a pair of magic slippers
—loot of that first accident with the cyclone—has been on her feet
all the time. She wishes herself home, following a distribution of
thrones: to the Scarecrow the missing Wizard's, to the Tin Woodman
the melted Witch's, and to the Lion (who in a side excursion has
knocked off the technical claimant) that of Beasts.

The Marvelous Land of Oz, Baum's second Oz book, offers no
points of comparison with Carroll's sequel but is a fable of sex warfare, in which a palace revolt led by a strong-minded girl calling
herself General Jinjur unseats King Scarecrow. It is more than a
revolt, it is a revolution. As a "sad-looking man with a bushy beard,
who wore an apron and was wheeling a baby-carriage," informs the
Scarecrow: "Since you went away the women have been running
things to suit themselves. I'm glad you have decided to come back
and restore order, for doing housework and minding the children is
wearing out the strength of every man in the Emerald City."

Most of the book's action is taken up, not so much by the Scarecrow's efforts to regain the throne as by his difficulties, aided by the
Tin Woodman and other newly introduced manikins, in keeping out
of harm's way. Tip, a boy brought up by the old witch Mombi, is
the creator, thanks to the old woman's Powder of Life, of such con-
traptions as Jack Pumpkinhead, the Saw-Horse, and the "Gump."
The Woggle-Bug, a ridiculous pedant, completes the party. These
half-crippled makeshifts stumble through a series of flights and escapes, appealing finally to Glinda. The sorceress has her own army
of young girls, which recaptures Oz and throws Jinjur into chains.
Glinda overpowers the hag Mombi, who admits that the real heir to
the throne of Oz, the missing princess Ozma, was committed to her

care years ago and transformed by her *into a boy*! (Italics in the original.) All eyes turn to the boy Tip. Glinda orders Mombi to reverse her incantations, with this result:

> From the couch arose the form of a young girl, fresh and beautiful as a May morning. . . . [She] cast one look into Glinda's bright face, which glowed with pleasure and satisfaction, and then turned upon the others. Speaking the words with sweet diffidence, she said:
> "I hope none of you will care less for me than you did before. I'm just the same Tip, you know; only— only—"
> "Only you're different!" said the Pumpkinhead; and everyone thought it was the wisest speech he had ever made.

Ozma of Oz, third in the series, reintroduces Dorothy, washed ashore in a floating chicken coop with a talking yellow hen, on the beach of the land of Ev (perhaps Eve?). The hen insists her name is Bill, though Dorothy prefers to call her Billina. Ev turns out to be the familiar Baum matriarchal fairyland, its temporary ruler the Princess Langwidere, who has thirty different heads, one for each day of the month.

Apotheosis of Billina, from *Ozma of Oz*

Ev's late king has sold his wife and children to the Nome King before committing suicide. Dorothy rescues his faithful servant, Tik-Tok; he (Baum's automatons are always male) rescues her from the terrifying Wheelers, although his clockwork fails when it is a question of braving Langwidere, who has insisted on an exchange of heads with Dorothy. Coming to rescue the Queen of Ev, Ozma with her army of twenty-six officers and one private (this is not an efficient girl-army like Glinda's or Jinjur's) crosses the burning desert which separates Ev from Oz. Dorothy and Ozma love each other immediately. Dorothy frees Billina from Langwidere's hen-yard after watching her lick the rooster.

Ozma's expedition enters the underground Nome Kingdom by passing between the legs of a mechanical colossus. The Nome King, a fat and smiling villain, has transformed the Evians into bric-a-brac which he invites the Ozians to identify; if they guess wrong they become bric-a-brac themselves. All fail except Dorothy, until Billina, nesting under the throne, overhears the King's secret codes and disenchants everyone. The King summons his army, but, blinded and poisoned by two of Billina's eggs smashed in his face, he is unable to prevent the theft of his magic belt and the loss of all his prisoners.

The fourth book is the first to introduce a boy—that is, a boy who stays boy. Whether or not he is responsible, *Dorothy and the Wizard in Oz* is one of the most gloomy and depressing of the series. Most of the action takes place underground, and a steady succession of horrible characterizations express the most implacable hatred of anything fertile or human.

Dorothy and her companion Zeb (for which read Zed) are dropped by an earthquake into the kingdom of the Mangaboos (three syllables of fright, disgust, and horror), who are vegetables, reproducing asexually from a parent tree. The Wizard appears and slices up the Mangoboos' magician for disputing authority with him. Dorothy picks the Mangaboo Princess to restore, as usual, woman's rule.

This princess not remaining friendly, the earth people with their cat and horse are driven into the Black Pit. Beyond, in open country, they meet a normal family of two children with father and mother, but *invisible*: seemingly endurable in this form. They have a bloody encounter with invisible Bears, and take to the hole in the mountain again. Passing the Braided Man, who sells an appropriate brand of Baum comic-relief, they climb to the land of the Wooden Gargoyles. Earth, grass, leaves are wooden; nothing grows or flows; and the Wooden Gargoyles never speak; they hate sound. Inevitably the earth people are captured, and escape death only by stealing the Gargoyles' detachable wings. After touching a match to this firetrap, they plunge into another hole in the mountain, which seems, like Dante's Malebolge, to grow up through the middle of the earth.

Again they fall into a worse danger, the den of the Dragonettes. Since the half-grown monsters cannot eat them, having been secured by a careful mother before going out on her hunting, they engage in a "whimsical" conversation parodying the reactions of well-educated and dutiful children of a mother who happens to be a dragon.

Rescued through Ozma's magic intervention, the party is transported to Oz, and the remainder of the book is devoted to the humiliation of Jim, the flesh-and-blood Cab-Horse, by the mechanical Saw-Horse; and a trial for murder of Eureka, the cat, whose continual threats to eat one of the Wizard's pet piglets have furnished a cannibalistic commentary to the action.

These first four books contain the meat of Baum's message. The later stories merely dilute and conventionalize this strong original flavor.

In these books Baum has found a surprising number of ways to vary his message; or, as a psychoanalyst might say, his neurosis has found a variety of outlets. In the analyst's terminology again, everything is "over-determined." Nothing is ever simply demonstrated once.

Very particularly in the *Wonderful Wizard of Oz*, the most artistic as it is the most honest of the series—for only there are we occasionally allowed to glimpse the pathos of his condition—has Baum set out, almost as a real artist might, to personalize all his anxieties.

He is by autobiographical definition Dorothy, an innocent child, who through no fault of her own (but very luckily, nevertheless) kills her mother as she is born. It is all for the best, everyone assures her, but still she is guiltily anxious to get out of a world where such things happen. She goes to look for her father, who can, perhaps, *send her back*. Her innocence is complemented and balanced by the innocence of the Scarecrow (Baum again), who has just been born and is therefore of the same age as Dorothy. A love affair is indicated, and of course Dorothy does love the Scarecrow best of all, but after all he is only a man stuffed with straw, an intellectual who only wants brains. As might be expected, the Scarecrow is never of any use to Dorothy in physical difficulties: he gives good advice, but is always getting knocked over or punched flat when the fighting begins. So the Woodchopper is required. He has *once* been a real man who has loved a woman, but an older woman has been jealous—not of him, but of his beloved who lives with her, in just what relationship is not explained—and by magic the Woodchopper's axe has repeatedly slipped until he is cut to pieces, a friendly tinsmith supplying prosthesis. The Woodman still loves until his heart is cut through; but then he ceases to love. He means to ask Oz for a heart and afterward to return and ask the girl to marry him, when he can love her again. (He forgets all about this, incidentally, after he gets the heart, but maybe that is because it is really a heart that Oz gives him. The Woodman is a very delicate person and would be unlikely to call things by their proper names.)

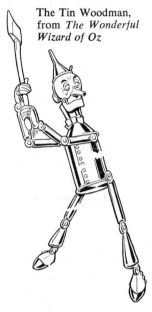

The Tin Woodman, from *The Wonderful Wizard of Oz*

There is a great deal of fine characterization in the Woodman, who of course is Baum again at a more advanced stage. He is depressed, weeps easily, avoids stepping on insects and hurting people's feelings, and is pathetically grateful for Dorothy's ministrations. He is of tin—the ridiculous metal. The terrible "chopper who chops off your head" is armed with a gleaming axe which he uses for nothing except to cut down trees (until later—Baum's characterizations do not hold very long). He is a nightmare de-glamorized. All good so far.

The Lion is Baum again in man's conventional sexual role. What is the point of being king of beasts, he seems to be saying, and come roaring out of the forest, if I am full of inward doubts and fears and can be stopped by a slap on the nose? What is the use of a thick beard and big teeth and loud voice, if they cannot even get me a mate (as they apparently have not)? Better if I turned into a little dog and ran at this girl's heels—because that's what I want to do, if the truth were known. And so another nightmare is tamed.

It should not pass unnoticed that Baum, while satisfying himself, has also satisfied the canons of conventional romance by surrounding his heroine not only with protectors but with guardians. What was usually accomplished by relationship or senescence—and the nineteenth century made great play with uncles and grandfathers—he accomplishes by emasculation, not only once but three times.

However the attitude so far (and Baum is one-third through his book) is not unhealthy. Three objects of greater fear to a child than a Lion, a Scarecrow, and a Chopper (who is also a Cripple) could not easily be named, and yet Baum has kept them all gentle and touching. He has pumped them full of himself, and since he is a harmless and pathetic fellow, he is saying in substance to the child, "And so are your fears!"

But he has gone as far as he can go on that line. Ten pages after the fake-Lion he introduces the Kalidahs, terrifying invented animals. The childish reader invariably trembles at this point, puzzling the adult, to whom the Kalidahs do not seem that terrible. But the child is right. There are other terrors in the world, then, besides "men," he feels; the Kalidahs are *real*. They are all the more real because they are made up. There is no chance of their ever turning back into Daddy. We are in the world of nightmare, of fever dreams, where a pet grows the "body of a bear and the head of a tiger."

Baum is now definitely committed to a tale of adventure, and little more healthy can occur. The Emerald City ought by right to be a vast fake, since its people are compelled to wear green glasses, but actually it is a fake-fake and the emeralds are real. The Wizard plays out all over again the Baum "appearances": he is a Head, a beautiful Lady, and a horrible Beast. His ultimate exposure is long deferred. For the story he is a father-figure, who instead of being tender or loving, or even weak and pathetic, is suspicious and implacable. Instead of consoling and comforting his daughter, he ridicules her fears, and tells her she can only win his love by killing again. Even in the conventional story-book sense the Wizard is a horrible man. He insists that the witch is evil, but admits she has never harmed him; it is only because she *might* that he wishes Dorothy to kill her; he is too cowardly to do so himself. He is Baal or Moloch, immolating children to placate the elements; and this aspect of his character is suggested by his fourth appearance, as a flaming ball of fire.

No one could ever possibly like the Wizard after this self-indictment; and yet his subsequent devaluation is only used to humanize him, even to justify him: fear makes us do anything! "I think you are a very bad man," Dorothy says. "Oh no, my dear," he replies, safely complaisant now that his archenemy is liquidated, "I'm really a very good man; but I'm a very bad Wizard, I must admit." Dorothy is not quite reassured. When he satisfies her friends, however (which is not very hard to do), she allows herself to be appeased. Poor Dorothy! Her history is that of a gradual reconciliation.

Glinda, the Good Witch, must not be taken as a mother-symbol. The mothers are all ugly old women, who get it in the neck de-

servedly. Glinda is eternally young and eternally beautiful. She has
never married; she could hardly be a mother! Glinda, in boarding-
school terminology, is Dorothy's *ideal*. There is no man good enough
for her. To emphasize this point, a long story is told about an earlier
sorceress, possibly one of Glinda's remote ancestresses, and her diffi-

The Wizard as an
enormous head, from
*The Wonderful
Wizard of Oz*

culties in choosing a husband. True love, in Oz, is love between girls,
when one is a little older than the other, innocent, sterile, and un-
competitive. Glinda thinks only of what Dorothy wants. She puts
only one kiss on her forehead. She assists Dorothy's friends, who in
her presence uneasily remember their rags, their scars, their crude
beastliness. Kindliness repays adoration, for Glinda. The sixth form
puts the third form on to the ropes, and all ends happily at Prize-
Day.

Oz revenges as many old injuries as it invents fantastic fulfill-
ments: the chief resentment apparently, next to having been brought
into the world in the wrong form, is for having been brought into

the world at all. Though "mothers" are worse than "fathers" in the Oz world, both are preferably extinct altogether. In no other American children's books, even Horatio Alger's, do there seem to be so many orphans. No human Oz-star in our four-book canon ever has both parents at once. Only the supers have a normal and usually comic family life. The animals fare no better: there are no records of the parentage of the Cowardly Lion, the Hungry Tiger, or Jim the Cab-Horse. Eureka the cat is a foundling. Billina is presumably immaculately hatched and brought up by a farmer boy who (to make the double point) never knew until too late whether she was a hen or a rooster. But the horrible Dragonettes have a horrible mother.

Baum's fondness for automata and magically created beings can be safely attributed to this same rejection or exclusion of natural begetting. Only the Tin Woodman, whom we already know to be the most honest and touching of the Ozian creatures, is allowed mention of a real father and mother, though both are long dead. The Scarecrow is the contrivance of two farmers (male), and Tik-Tok the invention of two inventors (male). Tip by himself, while still male, gives life to the Gump and the Saw-Horse, but these are very lumpish productions, almost stillbirths; it would seem, in Oz as in the real world, that two progenitors are really necessary. Mombi and Tip's creation of Jack Pumpkinhead seems to be an uglified travesty of birth (as Tip's later transformation is a sweetened travesty of emasculation). After the boy has laboriously worked to make his man, the old woman comes along and sprinkles it with the powder of life, quickening it for her own nefarious purposes. And even this powder she had originally stolen from a male magician. The solemn Jack Pumpkinhead insists on addressing Tip as "Father"; and since Tip is a little boy who is really a little girl, the confusions and insults appear deliberately multiplied.

The drama of decapitation (in the psychoanalytic vocabulary, decapitation and castration are synonymous) is played over and over and again as entr'acte. The Tin Woodman, who has once chopped off his own head, chops off the head of a hunting Wildcat. Oz first appears as an enormous Head, hairless, armless, and legless. The Lion kills his opponent, the spider-monster, by striking off its head. The Scarecrow twists the necks of the Crows. The Scarecrow's head is also removable (he tells Oz: "You are quite welcome to take my head off, as long as it will be a better one when you put it on again"); and this is only one of a selection of demountable, retractable, and replaceable heads that culminate in Langwidere's gallery of thirty.

The Hammer-Heads use their heads like battering rams; the Scoodlers use theirs as missiles. The Gump is all head. Jack Pumpkinhead deserves his name: he is in continual fear lest his head rot off. And so on. The conversations about decapitation recall that other humorous work, *The Mikado*.

Billina the hen is Oz's final topsy-turvy insult to injury. On the surface a "sensible" young female, she will have nothing to do with love, which like the suffragettes of Jinjur's army she sees only as masculine presumption ("Do you think I'd let that speckled villain

Tiktok swears allegiance, from *Ozma of Oz*

of a rooster lord it over *me*?"). She lays eggs and has, apparently, hatched them, but she never mentions the offspring of this incubation; the barnyard role of the mother-hen is not for her. She speaks of "thirteen" as a suitable clutch to illustrate, presumably, her real feelings about this unlucky necessity. Laying to her is a sanitary habit ("I feel better since I laid my morning egg"), and she is only concerned with the freshness (infertility) of her product. She connives in the use of her eggs as poisonous weapons, in fact suggests it. Though she frees the Queenmother of Ev and her children, it is not out of maternal concern; she derides the Queen's anxiety and tells her sarcastically, "Don't worry. Just at present they [the lifeless children] are out of mischief and perfectly safe, for they can't even wiggle. Come with me, if you please, and I'll show you how pretty they look." Billina's reward, "a beautiful necklace of pearls and sapphires," is, like Ozma's new clothes, the typical material reward of the spoilt-child gold-digger—and should be contrasted with the merely appetitive fudge and chocolates awarded Jinjur and her suffragettes.

Sociologically viewed, the Oz myth as Baum created it can be considered a vast transvaluation of juvenile romantic values. Boys' adventures become girls' adventures; girls' humiliations become boys' humiliations; boys' affairs with older boys become girls' affairs with older girls; and the mother is the villain instead of the father. It is a transvaluation because the values remain the same: traveling, fighting, and killing achieve the rewards, and the punishments are subordination and domesticity. (It should be remembered that the Wicked Witch "tortures" Dorothy by making her do housework!) The arena is no longer the social one of Louisa May Alcott but the transvestite one of a boy-turned-girl. Baum has kissed his elbow; Tip has put on women's clothes; but it is only to breed more girls-turned-boys. (In this connection it may not be insignificant to note that the *L.* in L. Frank Baum stood for "Lyman.") A determination to expunge the "man" from his name might seem to explain this amputation of his signature, so important to a writer. But both his name's syllables would have quickly grown hateful to a young fantasist continually addressed as "LIE MAN!"

Baum's frantic popularity with young girl readers really requires no further explanation. This audience, if not completely understanding, could appreciate his idolization of an immature and impubescent femininity. The combination of innocence with authority that produced all these girlish brows wrinkling over problems of finance and policy, these girlish arms driving chariots of state or extended imperiously, these girlish feet in the silver of safety or the satin of luxury, had the attraction, to them, of a mirror of Narcissus.

What young boy readers saw in Oz is not so clear, though clearly it was not the image of themselves they found in boys' books. But the boys Oz did strike were struck deep (all or most of the adults who find Oz unforgettable seem to be men). In psychoanalytic language, the boyish girls of Oz are *phallic*, and thus deeply reassuring to boys (or men) with castration anxieties. The reassurance is against their unconscious fear that girlish girls are what they seem to be, castrated boys.

CODA

Apart from Oz, many of Baum's other fantasies offer examples of his obsession for those who care to look. Even *Father Goose, His Book* (of which more later), Baum's first big "hit" as a children's author, has a title whose obvious commercial transposition (a father goose is a gander) also hints at a transposition of traditional authority-roles. *The Enchanted Island of Yew* (published a year before *The Marvelous Land of Oz*) has a fairy heroine who—reversing Tip's sex-change—becomes a knight. The idea of ambivalent (interchangeable) sex is further emphasized in that book by the chapter on Twi land, where everything exists in double form. *John Dough and the Cherub* was Baum's try at purely equivocal sex: Chick the Cherub is an incubator baby, and his or her sex is never disclosed. The "Trot" books, *The Sea Fairies* and *Sky Island* (which Baum hoped would replace Oz), star another boyish little girl and her crippled (one-legged) male companion, with more queens and feminine warfare.

Of all Baum's unconscious embodiments, in or out of Oz, Billina the hen must be the one most based on actual experience. Baum had begun breeding and raising chickens in adolescence, a hobby—his family was wealthy—he still took seriously enough at the age of thirty to treat technically in his first published book, *The Book of the Hamburgs*. The previous portrait of Billina is too brief, chiefly because psychoanalytically she is an embarrassment of riches. Almost everything she does cries out for interpretation.

Note that Billina comes to her audience already equipped with the fascination young children find in domestic fowl such as chickens (or geese). They lay eggs, and from these fascinating eggs hatch apparently sexless, or sexually identical, babies. With admirable simplicity, as children see it, both eggs and droppings emerge from the mother fowl's single body opening or *cloaca*. Kept ignorant of the reproductive purpose of the second female opening in humans, young children commonly surmise that they too were born through the human *cloaca* or anus, like eggs. This belief is forgotten or repressed with growing knowledge but retains much unconscious strength.

Poultry-breeders must also consciously recognize—what many adult human males often resist recognizing—that male fowl do the work of fatherhood without a penis or intromittant organ. This characteristic in itself could explain young Baum's engrossing interest in chickens as well as his later over-determination, after the success of *Father Goose, His Book*, to decorate his newly purchased house everywhere, on porch, walls, furniture, even to the extent of a specially made stained-glass living room window, with pictured geese.

Throughout the book which should be named after her, Billina is characterized by her regular laying. She is indifferently casual about the results, inviting Dorothy for example to eat her first egg (though indignantly rejecting Dorothy's "cannibalistic" suggestion that she

eat it herself) and assenting silently when the Hungry Tiger is offered her second. Baum the poultry-fancier knows these eggs are
infertile and takes pains to excuse Billina's indifference by telling
us so through Billina's beak. But his point is beyond his childish
readers, to whom Billina's eggs are her *babies*. (Consciously Baum
may not know this, but his unconscious creature the Tiger knows,
and four times in one speech warns us that it is babies, "fat babies,"
who are in danger.)

The Hungry Tiger, by the way, has a previous record: another
Oz-critic has already seen in his hangup between appetite and conscience the psychoanalytic concept of id and superego. Alas, this
admission only conceals a deeper admission which is not made. The
Tiger, a traditional glutton, is also a eunuch. Like the Cowardly
Lion, with whom he has everything in common (both are now slaves,
happily yoked to Ozma's chariot), he has resigned completely his
too-demanding masculine role in the jungle. (Indeed, conceptually
the Tiger is just another and weaker form of the Lion, as Tik-Tok
is another and weaker form of the Tin Woodman.)

To return to Billina: while no eggs or babies actually suffer before
the final climactic sacrifice (but in a good cause!) of her two egg-
babies at once smashed on the Nome King's face, it is Billina's hard-
headed acceptance of the risk that intensifies—for childish readers;
adults hardly notice—the growing suspense as to when heaven's
wrath (perhaps the mechanical giant's retributive hammer?) will fall
on this unnatural mother.

Eggs or no eggs, Billina is a hen, and therefore a mother. But not
a good mother. (Noticeable throughout the book is her repeated
morning "kut, kut, ka-daw!" coming in place of the "cock-a-doodle-
do!" which is never heard. Quite literally and as the proverb says,
Billina is a "crowing hen." But her feminist scorn of frivolous male
animals—the two Ozians, with ribbons tied to their tails—or her
rooster-licking revenge on bossy brothers and fathers, should not
disguise that she is also a living reminder that mothers are hens.)
To know she is a bad mother it is not even necessary to hear her
mock a good mother (the Queen of Ev), though it helps. Since there
is no other in this Oz book, Billina herself must be the mother-villain
—as in a very real sense she is.

She is not only a bad mother but a bad child. Couched under the
king's throne (hens more naturally roost somewhere higher, but let
it pass), she is the primal guilty eavesdropper on the parents' secrets.
(Everything is there, even to being awakened from sleep by their

noise! The Nome King's nagging Chief Steward takes the part of wife.)

In her next-morning's bargaining with the King, Billina uses as counter her latest casual egg—for which, contrarily, the King shows the most frightened respect. In his womanless underground world women's alarming fertility is "poisonous," unsafe except as lifeless ornament (explaining his transformation of the Queen of Ev). His anxious fib about "surface" things should not deceive us: of the thirty-odd surface creatures invading the King's domain, only one has this quality he fears.

Billina is now revealed as the book's heroine, to the joy and confusion of the youthful reader. Joy because of the coming comeuppance of that wicked *man*, the King; confusion because this is going to be done, and can only be done, by a *mother*. (Mothers don't *do* these things in Oz. There is also here a very deep and troubling confusion between good and evil, which the childish reader—and probably also the author—feels but cannot resolve, and so must put out of mind by violent action.)

Billina must necessarily change her identification-role, which she does, aptly enough, in the transformation scene, where for the first time she acts alone and we see only through her eyes. She turns now into the girlish *ideal* (Glinda the Good again), though this time more down-to-earth: the swaggering, scoffing (but kindly) older girl, whom the younger girl watches with frightened awe as she breaks all of Mama's rules unharmed.

This scene also supplies the point, which few children—or mothers —will miss, of the Queen of Ev turned into a footstool. But the kindly transformations are not the climax of the book, which is of course the King's humiliation. In that violent hurly-burly the child reader is completely satisfied, put beyond good and evil. The chapter ends in a complete denial of fertility-value, with eggs being created wholesale and scattered by the hundreds on the ground.

Billina's portrait has been objected to on the ground that she appears in the fifth book, *The Road to Oz*, with baby chicks. Giving a whimsical answer to a whimsical objection, the explanation might be that in the interim she has matured, met the rooster of her dreams, married and settled down. But no father chicken is brought on the scene and Billina retains enough maternal indifference to announce she has given all her chicks the same name. We adults, who know what happens when a cock and a hen appear to be fighting, might consider these chicks the natural result of Billina's "fight" with the

Evian rooster in Langwidere's hen-yard. But the right answer is that Billina's character is no more consistent than any other Ozian's from book to book.

As to the overall span of Oz books: not only their internal evidence but the demands of the commercial "series" they became (demands with which Baum was thoroughly familiar from his other potboiling work) must contradict the sentimental idea that Oz was extended as a planned Utopia, coherent legend, or "labor of love." As a recognized brand-name, Oz was continued for MONEY. The plain evidence is that Baum was reluctant to go on repeating himself. Though not carrying his reluctance as far as Arthur Conan Doyle, for example—who grew to detest the very mention of *his* unconscious creation—Baum did announce in his fifth book and confirm in his sixth that he had had it with Oz. (Making our four-book canon even more reasonable.) But Baum was a gentle, unaggressive man, in debt, the support of his family, a semi-invalid during his last years, and he can hardly be blamed for doing what so many other more healthy (and wealthy) writers do as a way of life.

Jack London as a Children's Writer

Susan Ward

Jack London is best known as the author of *The Call of the Wild* and *The Sea-Wolf*, a handful of short stories about the Yukon and the South Seas, and *Martin Eden*, the fictional "biography" of a struggling young writer. Yet London wrote children's stories as well as stories for adults. Between 1899 and 1907 he wrote twenty-one stories for the children's magazines; these stories make up the second largest group of works directed toward a single audience in the London canon.

London came to write stories for children because he was looking for a market early in his career and the children's magazines offered him one. In late 1898, when he was just beginning to send out work for publication, London sent a story to *The Youth's Companion*. The story was rejected, but in September of 1899 the *Companion* published his "The King of Mazy May," and London's career as a children's writer began. Over the next eight years, he wrote sixteen more stories for the *Companion*, two stories and a novel for *St. Nicholas*, and one short story for *Holiday Magazine for Children*. The children's stories form a cohesive unit in the midst of other literary activities. Because they occur early in his career and because they are the first of many efforts he made to write for specialized audiences, they are important to any study of Jack London's literary career.

London's correspondence indicates that between 1899 and 1907 he definitely tailored or shaped stories for the children's fiction market. In early 1900, he wrote to Anna Strunsky: "Shall now amend a boy's story for the *Youth's Companion* which they have accepted on condition that I change certain things."[1] He changed them, and the story, "Dutch Courage," was published in the November 29 issue of the magazine. The same year, he wrote to Cloudsley Johns that he had "sold *Youth's Companion* a four thousand word story ["The Lost Poacher"] which they say is the best I have yet sent them."[2] In 1902 in a letter to George Brett, his publisher at Macmillan, he mentioned both the Fish Patrol stories "which I had nearly completed for *Youth's Companion* before I went to England last summer" and a juvenile serial "written a good while before for *St. Nicholas*."[3] These letters suggest that London was aware of the conventions which governed fiction and that he knew he had to conform to those rules if he wished his children's stories to be published. His own attitude toward his children's stories was less than flattering. As early as 1899, he wrote to Johns of his "luck" with the *Companion* stories. In the same letter he noted pragmatically: "Though such work won't live, it at least brings the ready cash."[4]

London's ability to appeal to different segments of the American reading public is one of the keys to his success. His children's stories are an apt illustration of this ability. The stories reflect the most popular conventions of the children's fiction of the day and vary them enough to have been thought "original," but they never stepped outside the conventions further than the market would have permitted. The best of them added something, a "Jack London touch," to the children's fiction of the period. But London was wise enough not to allow that touch to become too strong. To do so would have been to write himself out of the conservative children's fiction market.

Let us, then, examine London's children's stories in relation to the stories of other children's writers of the period and in relation to statements by editors and authors which helped to shape the conventions governing the children's fiction market. The children's authors and editors whose statements appear here include some of the best-known and most important literary figures of the period; the stories on which I have based my general remarks are part of a sample extracted from the pages of *The Youth's Companion* and *St. Nicholas*, the two magazines in which London published almost all his children's stories. By working with these materials, I hope to indicate both how London conformed to the dictates of the children's fiction market and how he rose above them. Though such a discussion may portray London as a bit of a literary shark, it also suggests his uncanny ability to understand and respond to the likes and dislikes of this special segment of the American reading public.

Turn-of-the-century children's fiction differed in purpose from children's literature written earlier in the century in that its authors and editors saw entertainment as an important function. Mary Mapes Dodge, editor of *St. Nicholas Magazine*, signaled this attitude when she wrote:

> A child's magazine is its pleasure-ground. Grown people go to their periodicals for relaxation, it is true; but they also go for information, for suggestion, and for today's fashion in literature. . . . But with children the case is different. They take up their weekly or monthly because they wish to, and if they don't like it

they throw it down again. Most children of the present civilization attend school. Their little heads are strained and taxed with the day's lessons. They do not want to be bothered nor amended nor taught nor petted. They just want to have their own way over their own magazine.[5]

Mrs. Dodge was not the only important literary figure who had begun to express this view. Horatio Alger, one of the most popular children's authors of the period, noted that "a story should be interesting" since "a young reader will not tolerate dullness";[6] Frank Lee Farnell, an editor for *Frank Leslie's Pleasant Hours for Boys and Girls*, wrote in 1896 about ways to interest children;[7] the editors of *The Youth's Companion* regularly mailed a leaflet of literary policies to would-be contributors which announced that "stories must not fail to entertain from beginning to end."[8] Mrs. Dodge reflected, if she did not stimulate, an important stride forward. From about the 1870s, when *St. Nicholas* was successfully launched, the pleasure-ground theory of children's literature became acceptable in publishing circles.

In turn-of-the-century children's fiction, both character and plot were designed to appeal to as well as to instruct child readers. Horatio Alger, in cautioning future writers on selection of characters, mentioned a children's author "whose hero talked like a preacher and was a perfect prig" and who "seemed to have none of the imperfections of boyhood, and none of the qualities that make boys attractive."[9] This was not the kind of hero to incorporate into children's stories of the period. The heroes and heroines of turn-of-the-century children's fiction were almost always good children, but they were children with small faults as well as virtues. The creator of the "prig" hero, as Alger pointed out, wrote only one book for children.

Jack London followed this prescription. The heroes of "Dutch Courage," for example, carry a bottle of whiskey when they scale Half Dome to rescue a trapped climber, and the hero of *The Cruise of the Dazzler* sets events in motion by running away from home. When Joe Bronson, the hero of *The Cruise of the Dazzler*, expresses his scorn for "good little boys in white collars, with collars always clean and hair always combed, who like to stay in at recess and be petted by the teacher," he more or less expresses London's attitude toward the "prig" heroes of children's fiction.

London's boy heroes are also attractive for possessing qualities which the age considered heroic. They are physically capable (Alf Davis, the young sailor in "In Yeddo Bay," swims a mile to board his ship anchored off Yokahama); they are clever (Keesh in "Keesh, the Bear Hunter" devises a way to trap meat animals without weaponry to the amazement of everyone in his tribe); they are masters of their environments (Walt Masters in "The King of Mazy May" stops claim jumpers because he is able to drive sled dogs fast and skillfully enough to beat them to the claim recorder's office). In an age in which Theodore Roosevelt was the national hero, conservation and the out-of-doors a leading national issue, and education and self-improvement national preoccupations, these qualities could hardly fail to make London's characters attractive to children. In fact, London's children were unusually heroic, and this represents one way in which London outdid the conventions of the children's fiction of the period.

Plots in turn-of-the-century children's fiction were to be interesting, move quickly, and end happily. Frank Lee Farnell advised that "stories should have plenty of incident and movement in them";[10] Horatio Alger noted that "it should not be forgotten that boys like adventure";[11] and the editors of *The Youth's Companion* stated that all stories should have "a well-devised plot, and at least one strong incident" with the additions of "movement" and "dramatic effectiveness."[12] *The Companion's* editors also stated the happy-ending rule succinctly in their policy pamphlet. "In stories of pathos," the pamphlet read, "we beg our contributors to turn their art toward brightened ending. *The Companion* wishes to convey cheer; final impressions of death or calamity are not desired."[13] In the face of these prescriptions, it would have been sheer folly to have attempted either a slow-moving story or a story with an unhappy ending.

London met the demand for incident and movement naturally; action was a major ingredient in all of his stories. In "Yellow Handkerchief," the first of the Fish Patrol stories, the narrator sails his sloop around a fleet of Chinese junks illegally fishing for shrimp, captures one by dropping a patrolman on board to subdue the crew, himself boards and captures a second, sets sail back to port with four Chinese prisoners, quells a near mutiny when his rebellious assistant joins forces with the Chinese, and delivers his prisoners safely to the proper officials. London's second technique for emphasizing action is also in evidence in his children's stories. As early as 1899, he began his practice of incorporating a race, a fight, or some other action-centered incident into a story and describing it detail by detail until it became the story's central event. "The King of Mazy

May," published in *The Youth's Companion* in November 1899, in which Walt Master's race by dogsled is the central event, is one children's story which utilizes this technique.

The quality of incident in London's children stories also relates to the action principle. Usual children's stories of the period did not contain adventures that involved such life-and-death matters as steering a sailing vessel through a storm or hunting bear to ward off starvation. But London's did, and this factor undoubtedly contributed to their popularity. Both the quality of incident in London's children's stories and London's practice of including a series of action incidents in a single story were techniques not much in evidence in other children's fiction of the period. These practices, then, may be regarded as real contributions to the genre as well as ploys adopted by London to make his children's stories popular.

London adhered to the happy-ending rule in all but one of his children's stories. The exception, "A Northland Miracle," was published in *The Youth's Companion* ten years after his death and was very probably not written specifically for that magazine. Two children's stories which have analogues in London's adult fiction, however, indicate that he followed the rule consciously in an effort to place stories in children's magazines. In an early version of "To Build a Fire" which appeared in *The Youth's Companion* in 1902, the main character is saved when his matches catch fire, and in "The 'Fuzziness' of Hookla Heen," which appeared in the *Companion* later that same year, a white boy raised by Indians is reunited with his real father. In a later version of "To Build a Fire" which appeared in *The Century Magazine* the main character dies, and in "Li-Wan, the Fair," a story which deals with the same motif as "Hookla Heen" and which was published in *The Atlantic Monthly*, the main character is not reunited with her native people. That London rewrote both stories and changed the endings suggests that he wrote the first versions to satisfy some prescription he did not believe in: the existence of the happy-ending rule, together with the fact that both stories were published originally in children's magazines, makes it likely that the early versions were written to satisfy the demands of the children's market. At least in the case of "To Build a Fire," London's correspondence bears out this supposition. In 1908, writing about the original version of the story, he noted: "A long, long time ago I wrote a story for boys which I sold to *The Youth's Companion*. It was purely juvenile in treatment." Later in the letter he remarked that he determined to rewrite the story because he had treated the motif in the first version "for boys merely."[14] Although there is no proof that he had written "Hookla Heen" for boys merely, the existence of "Li-Wan," with its similar plot and strikingly different ending, suggests that the earlier story was also a juvenile version which London later rewrote for adults.

A second important characteristic of turn-of-the-century children's magazine fiction was the degree to which it sought to inform readers about the outside world. During this period in which travel became easier, improvements in communication linked distant neighbors, and the invention of photojournalism stimulated an interest in faraway places, regionalism was an important trend in juvenile as well as adult fiction. The seventies and eighties saw the travelogue story book becoming a popular literary form for children, and both *The Youth's Companion* and *St. Nicholas* responded to this interest by running articles on faraway places, printing letters from readers in distant lands, and featuring stories with foreign or interesting regional settings.[15] In a sample of stories from these two magazines, thirteen depend for at least a part of their interest on a regional setting, including China, Germany, ancient Greece, Ireland, Paris, fifteenth-century Venice, the lumbering country of northern Wisconsin, and a mining camp in the Rockies. In addition, writers sought to inform children about the professions they might eventually follow. Such stories make up a second important group in the sample. One boy-hero wishes to become a civil engineer; others are railroad dispatchers, marine postmen, doctors, and mule team drivers.

London responded to both interests. For the most part, he wrote about professions and places he knew. Three of his early children's stories, "The Lost Poacher," "Chris Farrington, Able Seaman," and "In Yeddo Bay" borrowed from his own experiences as a sailor, and *Tales of the Fish Patrol* to some extent reflected his short career with the San Francisco Bay Patrol. The three sea stories convey scattered impressions of what life aboard a sailing vessel might be like, and the Fish Patrol stories gave a fair picture of the life and duties of a patrolman in the San Francisco Bay area. All these stories depend on London's ability to render details of the day-to-day business of the major characters.

The regional stories London wrote for the children's magazines are all about the Yukon. They fulfill the informative function by describing physical details of the setting and in some instances by describing details of activities which the setting prescribes. In "Chased by the Trail" readers learn what it is like to canoe before an ice jam;

in "The King of Mazy May" they learn what it is like to race by dogsled across the frozen tundra; in "To Build a Fire" they learn some of the ways in which a man might cope with frostbite. In some instances, the stories inform the readers about details of life in a different culture. "The Story of Keesh," for example, implies something about the tribal life of certain northern Indians, and "The 'Fuzziness' of Hookla Heen" imparts the knowledge that white children were sometimes raised by Indians. In these stories, London began some of the practices which were to make him one of the best regional writers of the period. The sense of immediacy he created by the use of detailed description and occasional lapses into the present tense and the successful integration of setting and plot he began to work toward in the children's stories were techniques he brought to perfection in later regional works, and they placed his work above that of other children's writers in the field.

The Yukon was a timely subject in the late nineties. Gold had been discovered there in 1896, and in 1897 *McClure's*, *Cosmopolitan*, and *Forum* all ran articles on the Northland, with other magazines following suit during the ensuing year. Magazine readers were eager to read about the territory, and children were as interested as their parents. While London was not the first to write about the North for children, he was the first to do so consistently. His first-hand knowledge of the territory and his special ability to work with physical detail combined to make his regional stories successful on the children's magazine fiction market.

Education was the third area in which London had to deal with set convention when he wrote children's stories. Turn-of-the-century children's fiction, like almost all children's fiction before it, had education as a primary aim. In this period, however, the didactic impulse had become less obtrusive, and was not allowed to override the entertainment principle. Mary Mapes Dodge, writing about didacticism in children's magazines, noted: "Doubtless a great deal of instruction and good moral teaching may be inculcated in the pages of a magazine but it must be by hints dropped incidentally here and there."[16] And Kate Douglas Wiggin, a popular children's author of the period, cautioned: "If we dictate too absolutely, we *en*velope instead of *de*veloping [the reader's] mind, and weaken his own power of choice."[17] How to teach as well as what to teach became important in the closing year of the century, as children's authors began to seek subtler means of teaching than their predecessors had employed.

One of the more obvious ways was through choice and manipulation of plots. According to R. Gordon Kelly in a recent survey of children's periodical fiction of the nineteenth century, the plot of the child who saves the day and the plot of the child who learns a lesson were the two most popular children's plots of the period.[18] The plot of the good child who attracts attention or reforms others by example was a third popular form. All of these taught by example. Readers were encouraged to emulate the behavior of the characters in the first and third and to avoid the behavior of the character in the second. Though the "lessons" were not always stated outwardly by the authors, the didacticism was difficult to overlook, particularly when we compare these stories to examples of contemporary children's fiction.

Most of London's children's stories are constructed around the child-who-saves-the-day formula. Gus La Fee and Hazard Van Dorn in "Dutch Courage" rescue a rock climber trapped atop Half Dome; Jerry in "The Banks of Sacramento" saves two people caught in a swaying cable car hundreds of feet above the riverbed; the narrator of *Tales of the Fish Patrol* helps to enforce justice in every story in the series. These stories "teach" by encouraging boys to imitate the qualities of physical and moral courage and mental cleverness embodied in the main characters. Perhaps because he was more interested in heroism than in penitence or simple goodness, London constructed most of his children's stories around this plot. He used the lesson formula only rarely and then in combination with a heroism subplot; the introduction of the heroism motif in such stories forces us to admire even those heroes who learn something as the result of a foolish action. In *The Cruise of the Dazzler*, for example, Joe Bronson learns that it is rash to quit one's studies and leave home at the age of fifteen, but this lesson is undercut by the fact that Joe rescues a stolen safe and is able to return it to its owner at the same time that he is admitting his hasty judgment. The reader must admire Joe at the same time he recognizes the truth of the lesson he has learned. This double reaction is evoked by any of the children's stories London constructed around the lesson-plus-heroism plot.

Turn-of-the-century children's stories also sought to instill particular virtues in children. Mary Mapes Dodge, whose editorial policy announced that her magazine would seek "to foster a love of country, home, nature, truth, beauty, and sincerity," and Horatio Alger, who listed "honesty, industry, frugality, and a worthy ambi-

tion" as virtues to be enforced through the medium of a story, give
an indication of some of the qualities the age regarded as essential.[19]
London's children embodied all of these qualities. He sometimes
allowed his adult heroes to do without a prescribed virtue, but never
his children. His hesitancy was a tacit acknowledgement of the strin-
gent censorship applied to the children's literature of the period.

As we might expect, the censors exercised strong control over the
children's magazines. L. Felix Ranlett, a staff member at *The Youth's
Companion*, recalled some universally acknowledged censorship rules
when he wrote:

> Characters in stories or articles might not play cards. They might
> not even mention liquor. Swearing was not for them. They might
> not smoke, at least they might not smoke cigarettes, though I seem
> to remember that a pipe—"a black foul one"—would occasionally
> be allowed to a villain. Violent crime was out, though, of course,
> James Willard Schultz's Indians were straight shooters with
> firearms and skullduggery of sorts to make a story go. Love-
> making was merely hinted at, not enacted in the infrequent story
> where it could not be dispensed with. Sex was unheard of. . . .[20]

London respected all these taboos. No one smokes in London's
children's stories. Alcohol is introduced only to be thrown out, as
in "Dutch Courage," when Gus learns that whiskey does not contain
nerve, or to prove villainy, as in *The Cruise of the Dazzler*, when
French Pete's face is lit by a "vicious flush" after a third glass of wine.
Although Ranlett's recollections imply the absence of girl characters
a bit too strongly for the sum total of children's stories of the period,
London's stories conform with the implication. There are practically
no girls in London's children's fiction, and, when they are present,
they are relegated to minor roles.

Besides reinforcing allegiances to proper ways of behavior, censorship strove to break allegiances to a form of writing which had become popular around the middle of the nineteenth century and
which parents, teachers, and the more established literary figures
wished to combat. The offensive form was most manifest in the
"story papers" printed on pulp paper and bound in yellow covers
which were available at every newsstand. They usually contained
speeches, poems, dialogues, stories, and the stories were usually adventure stories about hunters, Indians, pirates, outlaws, and other
unsavory characters. According to William Graham Sumner, writing
in 1878, these publications were either "intensely stupid" or "spiced
to the highest degree with sensation," and they carried the added

offense of being written "almost entirely in slang."[21] The values most frequently objected to were the brutality and violence they seemed to sanction and the view that a life of physical action was synonymous with a life of romantic adventure. Sumner spoke for most who objected to story–paper values when he wrote, "These papers poison boys' minds with views of life which are so base and false as to destroy all manliness and all chances of true success."[22] And Kate Douglas Wiggin voiced the fear of those concerned with the stylistic influence of the story papers when she noted: "Mothers sometimes forget that children cannot read slipshod, awkward, redundant prose, and sing-song vapid verse, for ten or twelve years, and then take kindly to the best things afterward."[23] Combatting the story papers, then, was another way in which children's authors strove to educate their readers.

The editors of the children's magazines sought to carry out this aim by featuring stories with values directly opposed to story–paper values and, occasionally, by featuring stories which dealt directly with the bad effects of reading the yellow-covered periodicals. *St. Nicholas* printed such a story in the November 1884 issue; whether or not the story provided direct inspiration for Jack London as the editors of the magazine later maintained, it dealt with a theme which London was to use in two of his children's stories.[24] In the 1884 *St. Nicholas* story, a boy who learns from the story papers to prize adventure runs away with his brother's yacht and becomes involved in a variety of mischievous pranks before he is recaptured. Two of London's early children's stories, "To Repel Boarders" and *The Cruise of the Dazzler*, involved major characters who run away to sea because they are seeking a more romantic and adventurous life and who come to regret their decisions.[25]

The style with which parents, teachers, and editors sought to combat story–paper slang was as grammatically correct and as historically accurate as possible. Ranlett wrote of *The Youth's Companion* style sheet: "It used the Merriam Webster dictionaries as its authority for spelling; . . . *The King's English* by H. W. and F. G. Fowler, and *The Principles of Rhetoric* by Adam Sherman Hill were its guides to English usage."[26] Ranlett also recorded some examples of *The Companion's* grammatic accuracy: "The word 'practically' in its colloquial sense of 'to all intensive purposes' was forbidden. 'Virtually' was prescribed in its stead. 'Obtain' was used when the meaning was 'to get' and 'secure' was, quite properly, forbidden in that sense." London followed these standards carefully in his children's stories.

His descriptive style is impeccable, and when a character in a children's story speaks ungrammatically he is either speaking in dialect or has been described beforehand as uneducated. Since London did not follow this rule quite so strictly in his adult fiction, we can conclude that his attention to style was another attempt to conform to the strict standards set for the children's literature of the day.

Education was one area in which London did not try to achieve anything out of the ordinary in his children's stories. The stories upheld the proper virtues, outlawed improper subjects, illustrated proper grammar and behavior, and instilled respect for the proper kind of literature. Though London failed to rise above the conventions in this area, he did so with good reason. The establishment was stricter on this count than on any other. Without the proper lessons, it is doubtful that his children's stories would have been published.

Jack London was a successful children's writer. The sheer number of his stories which were published in popular children's magazines during his lifetime confirms this; the fact that his work continues to be reissued for children of today substantiates his claim to success in the field. That he conformed to and often capitalized on what he recognized to be popular conventions of the genre is true, but in his ability to render setting vividly and to create interesting and admirable child characters and fast-moving, action-packed plots he often rose above the conventions to forge new techniques which would be utilized by future children's writers. London's willingness to conform played a large part in making him successful. And the market's willingness to accept his flights beyond conformity gave many children interesting and well-written stories in an age when reading was becoming an integral part of the fabric of American life.

NOTES

1. Jack London, letter to Anna Strunsky, Feb. 13, 1900, in *Letters from Jack London*, ed. King Hendricks and Irving Shepard (New York: The Odyssey Press, 1965), pp. 91–92.

2. Jack London, letter to Cloudsley Johns, Mar. 1, 1900, *Letters*, pp. 95–98.

3. Jack London, letter to George P. Brett, Nov. 21, 1902, *Letters*, pp. 138–43.

4. Jack London, letter to Cloudsley Johns, Sept. 26, 1899, *Letters*, pp. 58–59.

5. [Mary Mapes Dodge], "Children's Magazines," *Scribner's Monthly*, 6 (1873), 352–54.

6. Horatio Alger, "Writing Stories for Boys," *The Writer*, 9 no. 3 (Mar. 1896), 36–37.

7. "Editorial Talks with Contributors," *The Writer*, 9, no. 3 (Mar. 1896), 143–45.

8. Ray Stannard Baker, American Chronicle (New York, 1945), pp. 70–71. Baker, who received one of the leaflets with a rejection letter, discusses its contents in his autobiography.

9. Alger, p. 37.

10. [Farnell], "Editorial Talks with Contributors," p. 145.

11. Alger, p. 37.

12. Quoted in Baker, p. 70.

13. Quoted in Baker, p. 71.

14. Jack London, letter to R. W. Gilder, Dec. 22, 1908, *Letters*, pp. 273–74. The relationship between the two versions of "To Build a Fire" is further explored in Earle Labor and King Hendricks' "Jack London's Twice-Told Tale," *Studies in Short Fiction*, 4 (Summer 1967), 334–47.

15. See Virginia Haviland, "The Travelogue Storybook in the Nineteenth Century," in *The Hewins Lectures, 1947–1962*, ed. Siri Andrews (Boston: The Horn Book, 1963), pp. 25–63, and Raymond Kilgour, *Estes and Lauriat, A History, 1872–1898* (Ann Arbor: Raymond Kilgour, 1951), pp. 87–130, for discussions of the development and influence of this form.

16. Dodge, "Children's Magazines," p. 354.

17. Kate Douglas Wiggin, "What Shall Children Read?" *Cosmopolitan*, 7 (1889), 355–60.

18. See R. Gordon Kelly, *Mother Was a Lady: Self and Society in Selected American Periodicals, 1865–1890* (Contributions to American Studies, no. 12; Westport, Conn.: Greenwood Press, 1974). My own research bears out Kelly's conclusions, though I would add a third category as noted in the text.

19. See Horatio Alger, p. 37, and Mary Mapes Dodge quoted in Florence Stanley Sturges, "The *St. Nicholas* Years," in *Hewins Lectures*, pp. 267–95. In addition, Kelly lists fortitude, temperance, prudence, justice, liberality, and courtesy as the virtues children's magazine fiction of the period prescribed.

20. L. Felix Ranlett, "The Youth's Companion as Recalled by a Staff Member," in *Hewins Lectures*, pp. 85–104.

21. William Graham Sumner, "What Our Boys Are Reading," *Scribner's Monthly*, 15 (1878), 681–85.

22. Sumner, p. 685.

23. Wiggin, p. 359.

24. See William Webster Ellsworth, *A Golden Age of Authors: A Publisher's Recollection* (Cambridge, Mass.: Houghton Mifflin, 1919), pp. 97–98; Harold French, "The Cruises of Boy-Pirate Jack: What A *Saint Nicholas* Story Did for Jack London," *Saint Nicholas*, 44 (1917), 848–50; and Alic B. Howard, *Mary Mapes Dodge of Saint Nicholas* (New York: Messner, 1943), pp. 18–90.

25. See French, "The Cruises of Boy-Pirate Jack," for a comparison of London's two stories with the Moonraker piece.

26. Ranlett, pp. 93–94.

Skip Rope Rhymes as a Reflection of American Culture*

Francelia Butler

The summer before the collapse of South Viet Nam, I spent several weeks there collecting folk rhymes at schools and orphanages. One rhyme was particularly popular on playgrounds:

> Let's go sightseeing in Long Thanh [Hanoi][1]
> Which has in all thirty-six streets:
> Basket Street, Silver Street, Hemp-Cloth Street,
> Sail Street, Tin Street, Slipper Street, Tray Street,
> Horse's Tail Street, Pipe Street, Shoe Street,
> Eel Pot Street, Long Bamboo Hurdle Street, Rattan Street,
> Musical Instrument Street. . . .
>
> We enjoy what we've seen.
> The streets of Long Thanh are prettiest of all.
> They stretch in a mesh, like a chessboard.
> Back home, we miss them greatly,
> So we praise them warmly here.
>
> *Translated by Doan Quoc Sy, Saigon*

This rhyme clearly shows the deep inner yearning for unity on the part of the Vietnamese people. It occurred to me then that if the politicians would listen to the children instead of to each other, they might more accurately predict the course of history.

Curiously, however, neither this rhyme nor other foreign folk rhymes used for skipping have the violent confrontations often found in American rhymes. Oriental rhymes furnish the clearest contrast. Japanese rhymes, for instance, tend to be more placid, as I discovered last year in Tokyo, where I arranged to see an exhibition of children skipping rope on the playground of a large school, the elementary division of Toho-Gakuen College. I was astonished to see that the children each held a bit of paper and were reading the chants. When I asked why they did not know the chants from memory, the teachers were astonished: "Surely," they said, "in an advanced country like yours, children no longer employ anything so quaint as skip-rope chants!" When I told them that indeed children still chanted and on almost every playground, they seemed to doubt me. I then

*Address given at the Children's Literature Convention, Piedmont College, Demorest, Georgia, June 6, 1975.

realized that in trying to imitate Western culture, they have abandoned their own rhymes, while not yet assimilating ours. They read
and skipped to such old rhymes as this, revived for their foreign
visitor:

> One crow sings caw caw caw
> Two chickens sing cocicoco cocicoco
> Fishes are swimming
> Grandfather with white hair.

In the People's Republic of China, the rhymes often appear to be
tests of skill, like this one:

> Little ball
> Banana swim
> Cauliflowers
> one by one
> one five six
> one five seven
> one eight one nine
> twenty seven
> two five six
> two five seven
> two eight two nine
> thirty seven . . .

In Malasia, a number of children's folk rhymes appeared to be in the
nature of charms, to help toward self-realization. This one, which I
picked up in Penang, is for swinging (skipping is generally done
without chants there):

> If I swing high
> And touch the rooftop
> Before my teeth grow
> I can read a book.
>
> If I swing high
> And touch the tree top
> I can buy a new dress
> From a Chinese shop.[2]

Proper boys and girls in Thailand can go out to play together by
making the excuse that they want to do a kind of skip-rope dance
descended from the bamboo dance. A doubled rope is held at each
end and shifted unexpectedly. The fun comes in anticipating the
movements of the rope holders. One rhyme goes:

> Beautiful girls
> Beautiful hearts of girls.
> We dare not go to sleep
> Girls command the sounds of birds
> With us, making music
> In a land of happiness and gaiety.

The significance lies in the romantic innuendoes and in the skill of the performers. Some of this meaning is also in a rhyme from Laos:

> Scattered and gleaming on the hillside
> Like the full moon
> Are sampots perfect and innumerable
> Sampots of every color
> Some are even yellow.

(Sampots are the squares of cloth men knot about their waists. Yellow is a royal color. The sampots have been washed and spread out on the hillside to dry.) And:

> Adorned with egrets and with mother-of-pearl inlaid
> The palaces shine like golden stars
> Roofed in with massive gold instead of thatch
> The queen is named Canda
> Graceful as any drawing.

By way of contrast to these gentle rhymes, here is a typical American chant, jumped by a disgruntled babysitter fearful of future assignments:

> Fudge, fudge
> Call the judge
> Mama's got a baby.
> Ain't no girl
> Ain't no boy
> Just a plain old baby.
> Wrap it up in tissue paper
> Put it on the elevator
> First floor—miss!
> Second floor—miss!
> Third floor—kick it out the door!

Here we have a commencement—a statement of the situation, a suggestion of conflict, a carrying or motivating force as the elevator rises, and a violent conclusion. At least some of these elements are found in many American rhymes, which tend to be mini-dramas:

> Johnnie over the ocean
> Johnnie over the sea
> Johnnie broke a milk bottle
> And blamed it on me.
>> I told Ma
>> Ma told Pa
>> Johnnie got a lickin'
>> Ha! Ha! Ha!

So much for sibling rivalry. Then there are rhymes dealing with unpleasant teachers:

> The Devil flew from North to South
>> With Miss Hooker in his mouth
> And when he found she was a fool
>> He dropped her on the Cherrydale School.

The adult world is satirized:

> My mama and your mama lives across the way
> Every night they have a fight and this is what they say:
>> Acca-bacca-soda-cracker
>> Acca-bacca-boo
>> Acca-bacca-soda-cracker
>> Out goes you!

External dangers are dramatized in this old Scottish rhyme turned into something typically American:

> Last night, the night before
> A lemon and a pickle come a knockin' at my door.
> When I come down to let them in,
> They hit me over the head with a roller pin.

Authority figures are dealt with:

> I won't go to Macy's any more, more, more.
> There's a big fat policeman at the door, door, door.
> He took me by the collar and made me pay a dollar,
> So I won't go to Macy's any more, more, more.

Not infrequently, children go through a stage of petty thievery. Some of them get caught. Similar rhymes have to do with Wanamaker's and Marshall Field's.

The hypocrisy of political figures is considered:

>> George Washington never told a lie
>> But he ran around the corner
>> And stole a cherry pie!

Political chants often contain a note of protest, and protest frequently tends to be bawdy—something that has been true ever since the English rhyme of the Renaissance period, "I had a little nut tree." This skip-rope rhyme is from Harlem:

> Abraham Lincoln was a good old soul
>   He washed his face in the toilet bowl
> He jumped out the window with his dick in his hand,
>   And said, " 'Scuse me, ladies, I'm Superman!"

Children vigorously take up characters in movies, comics, the news, and history and create small "happenings" about them:

> Marilyn Monroe
> Broke her toe
> Riding on a buffalo
> On the way to Mexico.

Children understand that something has happened to the great sex symbol, Marilyn Monroe, and equate it with an almost archaic animal: the buffalo. Sir Charles Chaplin's virility is suggested in this one:

> Charlie Chaplin
> Went to France
> To teach the girlies
> How to dance.
>   Heel, toe, around we go!
>   Heel, toe, around we go!
>   And keep the kettle boiling!

Sometimes, Donald Duck is substituted for Charlie Chaplin, and in bawdy versions, the obvious four-letter word is substituted for "dance."

Something bad happened to Hitler:

> In 1944
> Hitler went to war
> He lost his socks in the middle of the docks
> In 1944.

An ancient skip-rope rhyme is entering the northeastern United States through Canada. The earliest contemporary version was collected in 1974 by Angela Tietolman of Montreal who obtained it from a ninety-year old Frenchman. Though he associated it with the Napoleonic Wars, actually it is much earlier. It refers to La Palice, Grand Marshal of the French army, who was killed at Pavie in 1525.[3] The original rhyme went:

> Monsieur de La Palice est mort,
>   Mort devant Pavie;
> Un quart d'heure avant sa mort,
>   Il était encore en vie.

Later another stanza was added:

> Il c'est fait faire un habit
>   De quatre ou cinq planches
> Le tailleur qui lui a fait
>   Il n'avait pas mis de manches.

Originally, the rhyme was flattering to the Marshal, who fought up to a quarter of an hour before his death. Later, the rhyme became distorted, so that now it goes, in English translation:

> Mr. Policeman is dead.
>   Dead before Paris.
> A quarter-hour before he died,
>   He was still alive.
> They made him a suit
>   Of four or five boards.
> The tailor who made it
>   Forgot to make the sleeves.

The prints from the British Museum which illustrate Leslie Daiken's *Children's Games throughout the Year* (London: B. T. Batsford, Ltd., 1949) suggest that adults skipped rope in early periods of history. But, though scraps of skip-rope rhymes, such as "All in together, girls/No mind the weather, girls" may have classical sources, no skip-rope rhyme has been tracked earlier than the seventeenth century. Under "Ludi," the *Dictionnaire des Antiquités Grecques et Romaines* prints an ancient statue of a Greek maiden swinging a rope of vines over her head. There is no evidence that she chanted as she skipped, and there are countries in Europe and Asia now where children skip without chanting.

The first rhymes chanted by American skippers were lyrical verses descending from English sources. Since children are traditionalists, these rhymes, passed from child to child, still linger alongside their rough, native counterparts. Here is one of the English rhymes with an interesting history:

> On the hilltop stands a lady
> Who she is I do not know
> All she wears is gold and silver
> And she needs a nice young man. . . .

I first heard the rhyme in 1945 on the playground of a black school
at Ball's Hill, Virginia, near Falls Church, where it was preserved
by the black culture. The rhyme is from an old English ballad, "O
no John," of which there are many versions in Cecil Sharp's collection. Originally, it had to do with seduction involving adultery. The
late Arthur Kyle Davis, an eminent folklorist at the University of
Virginia, discovered that the colonial patriot, John Randolph of
Roanoke, knew some of the lines in his early childhood, and in 1822,
in middle life, wrote to a friend asking for the rest. It had been taught
him, he recalled, "by a mulatto servant girl." The rhyme can be
found in New England, the Midwest, and the far West.

This rhyme, also of English origin, was skipped in the early nineteenth century in Schodack, now Castleton-on-Hudson, New York:

> Intry mintry cutry corn
> Appleseed and apple thorn
> Wire, briar, limber lock
> Twelve geese in a flock
> One flew East and one flew West
> And one flew over the cuckoo's nest.

One begins to see the American touch in this mid-nineteenth-century
rhyme:

> I love my papa, that I do
> And mama says she loves him, too
> But papa says he fears some day
> With some bad man I'll run away.

Toward the end of the century, we get this one, recorded by William
Wells Newell (*Games and Songs of American Children* [New York:
Harper & Bros., New York, 1883]):

> By the old Levitical law
>   I marry this Indian to this squaw
> By the point of my jack-knife,
>   I pronounce you man and wife.

A variant of the rhyme also was recorded in Virginia. Already we
see the violence and drama which characterize so many American
rhymes. Two children jump together under the rope in a ritualistic
marriage. As sexual beings in the inhibited Victorian period, they
can ease their consciences by pretending they were forced into marriage at knife point. Newell, himself, collecting in the nineteenth

century, suggests a more pious interpretation which seems irrelevant
to the rhyme's obvious meaning. Newell explains it as meaning, "If
I break this vow, may I perish by the edge of the sword."

Published in 1801, Joseph Strutt's book *Glig-Gamena Angel-Deod*,
or *Sports and Pastimes of the People of England* indicates that boys
were once the jumpers. As everyone knows, the sport now is mainly
the province of girls. Various conjectures have been made as to why
this is so, the most frequent one being that it is a gentle sport and
could be indulged in by young ladies without even showing the ankles.

Cover of *Stories for All
Seasons* (New York:
McLoughlin Bros.,
1892)

But girls do have a way of appropriating the practices traditionally
assigned to boys. Histories of perfume reveal, for instance, that per-
fumes were once worn by men only. With diminishing distinctions in
sex roles, however, boys are reentering the game, as scenes on many
playgrounds now reveal. In any event, the unique character of American rhymes, their bold confrontations with problems, is a late nine-
teenth- and early twentieth-century phenomenon. My conjecture is

that the nature of the rhymes attests to the American conviction that
problems can be solved if one goes about them in a forthright way:

> Nine o'clock is striking
> Mother, may I go out?
> All the boys are calling
> Just to take me out.
> One will give me coffee
> One will give me cake
> One will give me fifty cents
> To kiss him at the gate.
>
> I don't want your coffee
> I don't want your cake.
> I don't want your fifty cents
> To kiss you at the gate.
>
> I'd rather wash the dishes
> I'd rather scrub the floor
> I'd rather kiss the iceman
> Behind the ice box door.

Of course, if one fails to perform the skipping ritual properly, it
can be fatal:

> Little Miss Pink
> Dressed in blue
> Died last night
> At quarter past two.
> Before she died
> She told me this:
> When I jump rope
> I always miss.

With school integration, rhymes of black and white students are now
traded cross-culturally. But black rhymes in America are also characterized by their vigor and drama. They often have a choral quality:

> O Donna died. O how she die?
> Died like this! (gesture) O, she died like this!
> Where she live? O, where she live?
> Down aroun' the corner in Tennessee.
> Hands up! Too chay too chay too chay too
> Hands down! Too chay too chay too chay too.

Or this example, from southeastern Washington, D.C.:

> Went down town to alligator roun'
> Sat on the fence and the fence broke down.
> Alligator caught me by the seat of the pants
> And made me do the hoola dance.

A good cross section of black rhymes may be found in Jean Alexander's *Jump Clap and Sing*, a publication of the Children's Area Festival of American Folklife, Washington, D.C., 1974.

The rhymes that "catch on" in the States from outside must fit into this dramatic cultural pattern. One rhyme has been given to me by students from the Virgin Islands, Jamaica, and most recently, by a student, Donna Andrade, who collected it in the schoolyard of Harding High School, Bridgeport, Connecticut, where, she was told, it had been around since the 1950s. The rhyme comes from black students there. Since it depends for its effect on the double meanings of words at the ends of lines, it recalls similar use of word ambiguities in the Renaissance, such as those employed by Matthew Merrygreek in the mid-sixteenth-century play, *Ralph Roister Doister*. The rhyme chanted now goes:

> Miss Lucy had a steamboat, the steamboat had a bell,
> Miss Lucy went to heaven, the steamboat went to hel-
> Lo operator, give me number nine
> If you disconnect me,
> I'll kick up your behin-
> The refrigerator there's a piece of glass,
> Susie fell upon it and broke her little as-
> Me no more questions, tell me no more lies.
> Boys are in the bathroom, zipping down flies-
> Are in the country, bees are in the park,
> Boys and girls are kissing in the dark, dark, dark!

The trend seems toward making rhymes more openly sexual. When I used to skip the following rhyme in the 1920s, it went:

> Cinderella
> Dressed in yella
> Went downstairs
> To meet her fella.

Now on my block I hear it this way:

> Cinderella
> Dressed in yella

> Went downstairs
>   To kiss her fella.
>   She made a mistake
>   And kissed a snake!

Many extremely bawdy skip-rope rhymes can be found, too. Most
of them protest sexual inhibitions and seem to stem from the feeling
that adults hypocritically deny their own sexuality and demand a
standard of sexual conduct from youth that they do not maintain
themselves. A collection of bawdy rhymes is that of Joseph C. Hick-
erson and Alan Dundes, "Mother Goose Vice Verse," *Journal of
American Folklore*, 75 no. 295 (Jan.–May 1962), pp. 250, 252.[4]

In literary accounts of skipping, the magical quality of the ritual
has been recognized by Frances Hodgson Burnett in *The Secret
Garden* and by the American novelist Ellen Glasgow in her short
story, "The Shadowy Third." But literary skip-rope rhymes do not
show the cultural differences suggested by their oral counterparts.
Professor David Sonstroem found a skip-rope rhyme by Alfred Lord
Tennyson, printed in 1842 but omitted in all editions after 1850. It
depicts a girl of marriageable age skipping rope—and indeed, as indicated earlier, adults once skipped. The rhyme is:

> Sure never yet was antelope
>   Could skip so lightly by.
> Stand off, or else my skipping-rope
>   Will hit you in the eye.
> How lightly whirls the skipping-rope!
>   How fairy-like you fly!
> Go, get you gone, you muse and mope—
>   I hate that silly sigh.
> Nay, dearest, teach me how to hope,
>   Or tell me how to die.
> There, take it, take my skipping-rope,
>   And hang yourself thereby.

Tennyson's ditty does not have the poignant impact of the following
poem by Elias Lieberman, published in *The Saturday Evening Post*,
August 23, 1958:

> There is a chant that goes with skipping rope,
>   A nonsense rhyme as playful as a breeze
> That shakes the rain from trees, a lilting hope,
>   Designed of fantasies.

> *All in together*
> *The sheep's in the meadow*

These jingles of her skipping ritual
  Are runes to ward off sorrow. They must hold
When fallen leaves will mold against a wall
  And winter winds grow bold.

> *The cow's in the clover*
> *All jump over.*

The slack rope swings
  And through its looping arc
A child who sings
  Has leaped beyond the dark.

American commercial firms have sometimes employed skip-rope rhymes in advertisements. For instance, a pink pig, already conscious of a weight problem, skips rope in *Rexall Nursery Rhymes*, distributed by that drug company in 1905. Entitled "Teaching a Pig How to Skip Rope," the rhyme is:

Illustration from *Rexall Nursery Rhymes* (1905), one of a collection of early advertising booklets in Special Collections, University of Connecticut Library

Teaching the Pig How to Play Skipping Rope.

"This Pig's too stout," said Captain R.
"Her fat is quite distressing;
"But I do hope a Skipping Rope
"To her will be a blessing.
" 'Twill help to shape her shaking sides
"And make her light and airy—
"An hour a day of such smart play—
"She'll dance like any fairy."

If the maxim is true that the essence of charm is being unconscious of having it, then perhaps it is a mistake to point out that we have a unique culture in our skipping rhymes. But even up to the present time, we have had to undergo so many criticisms for our lack of culture that perhaps a little awareness of our national aptitudes will buoy our spirits. Once when I was speaking on skip-rope rhymes at a folklore convention in Nashville, Tennessee, some young fellow came up to me and drawled, "I declare, I didn't know we had a culture, but I'm mighty glad to hear it." There are other Americans like him who want to think of their country as something more than an amorphous cultural blob somewhere between Europe and the Orient.

Alexis de Tocqueville, who in his *Democracy in America* (1835) showed amazing prophetic perception of the American cultural temper, prophesied that literature in America would evolve to satisfy those who "require strong and rapid emotions, startling passages, truths or errors brilliant enough to rouse them up and plunge them at once, as if by violence, into the midst of the subject." He was a keen observer, interested in the nature of things, who traveled extensively in the United States, sleeping in the huts of pioneers. Possibly he heard some American skip-rope rhymes like "I marry this Indian to this squaw by the point of my jack knife."

NOTES

1. Ancient name for Hanoi. Long Thanh is a short reference to Thang Long Thanh, as Hanoi was called during the Ly Dynasty (1009–1225).

2. To be able to buy a dress from the shop of the monied people, the Chinese, means, "Some day, with the help of this magic ritual, I will have money."

3. See "La Palice" in *Grand Larousse encyclopédique*, p. 602, column 2.

4. Of general rhymes, not bawdy, the best collection is *Jump-Rope Rhymes: A Dictionary*, ed. Roger D. Abrahams, published for the American Folklore Society by the University of Texas Press (Austin and London, 1969).

The Real Secret of Superman's Identity

Alvin Schwartz

For about sixteen years, from the beginning of the forties to the mid-fifties, I suffered a peculiar kind of occupational thralldom. But I wasn't entirely aware of it. In fairy tales and legends, there are numerous stories of humans bound into the service of trolls, giants, witches and other demonic and supra-human entities. But in today's rational world, we are scarcely likely to recognize or give credence to such creatures. Consequently, when we are, in a very direct sense, taken over by such a being, we either tend to reduce it to mere psychology[1] or deny that it's happening altogether.

In my case, as well as that of all my co-workers, we chose the path of denial. It simply never would have occurred to us that we were, to put it bluntly, "being directed." For myself, I thought I was doing nothing more remarkable than making a living by inventing and writing the adventures of a meteorically rising star of popular fiction known as Superman. With sometimes desperate regularity, I used to turn out ten-week stretches of syndicated newspaper continuity as well as respectable quantities of intricately plotted comic book stories featuring the Man of Steel.

Apart from the support of a very competent group of editors with whom many of the finer involutions of plot were frequently shaped, I was under the impression that, occupationally, I was a free agent. I was also under the impression that I'd worked my way to the "seventh level" of my occupational hierarchy because, before I got to Superman, I had catalogued the adventures of a lot of other "union suit" characters as we used to call them in the trade. These included Green Lantern, The Flash, Green Arrow, Captain Marvel, Mr. Terrific, Aquaman, then Batman, until finally I was certified to direct the destinies of the most distinguished of them all in the sense that the others were at best secondary elaborations.

I was not to understand until long afterwards, however, that it wasn't I, or any of the other writers or the editors, or even the originators, Siegel and Shuster, who directed Superman's destinies. Superman directed his own destinies. All of us were merely his pawns. But the realization seems to be, long after the fact, mine alone.

The first stage of awareness came one day in 1948 when the *New Yorker* sent a reporter by the name of Spencer Klaw to my home.

My first book had just been published and the *Times* had referred
to it as "perhaps the first conscious existentialist novel in America."
Mr. Klaw wanted to know how I managed to write both Superman
and philosophical novels. "How," he asked, "do you manage to keep
the two things apart?"

My explanation had a certain spontaneous simplicity. I professed
that I had two differently colored workrooms separated by a phone
booth. In changing from one type of writing to the other, I just passed
through the phone booth and switched suits. That story never made
the *New Yorker* and I lost whatever publicity for my novel the
interview might have produced because I hadn't the strength of character to resist improvising that phone booth transformation story.
Actually, Mr. Klaw had posed a question that proved to be catalytic.
"How *did* I manage to keep the two things apart?"

As I saw it up to that particular moment, my *modus operandi* as
a novelist was precisely the reverse of that of the anonymous biographer of Superman. In the former role, I consciously let the characters take over and lead me. In short, I allowed subliminal or unconscious elements to operate. With Superman, there was a conscious
effort to control the character, to mold him to the demands of the
plot. But Klaw's question made me reconsider. After he had gone, I
began to examine what I really might have told him had I not been
overwhelmed by my sudden uprush of levity. And then, unaccount-
ably, I found myself confronting the memory of a previous summer
when I happened to be gazing out the window of a cottage I had
rented in Provincetown. I had been in the throes of working out one
of those ten-week newspaper continuities which, of all the forms of
literary contrivance, is perhaps the most difficult since it involves—
(1) The invention of a cliff-hanger at the end of every three panels,
without interrupting the general story line, (2) The use of dialogue
which, while remaining natural, must also be able to recapitulate the
story for readers who may have missed previous episodes, and (3)
The pruning down of dialogue in order not to crowd out the pictures
while keeping in mind the artist's capacity to carry out the visual
requirements of the script. All this—apart from the special qualities
of a character like Superman about whose activities I was to discover
some wholly unsuspected features long after I had severed my occupational connection with him.

In any case, while I was wrestling with my story and the various
constraints under which it had to proceed, my wandering gaze happened to discover about a hundred yards from the house, a group

of children dressed in an assortment of improvised capes, very definitely of the Superman variety, engaged in play that consisted unmistakably of a mimicry of flight and of superstrength. My immediate association with the recollection of this particular scene following Mr. Klaw's visit was the rather revealing phrase, "oral tradition." At the same time, I had the first uneasy intimation that my relationship with Superman was something much more complex than a means of working my way through Grub Street in order to write "serious" novels.

As I mulled over those two words, "oral tradition," I realized they had something to do with story or plot. The more I considered it, the more it struck me that plot, in relation to the oral tradition, went considerably beyond the specification of the antipodes of a communication accompanied by its ultimate resolution, as for example, in that familiar schema: "Boy meets girl; boy gets girl; boy loses girl." Plot has to do with fiction *par excellence*. It is the way we structure truth and make it intelligible which no mere record of empirical or haphazard events—so called "realism"—can accomplish. Even in science, as we use it to organize reality, we *hypothesize*. That is, we take the indiscriminate record and bind it into the unity of a story.

I'd like to underscore this point by referring to one of my own Superman continuities in which a student has written a physics term paper citing Superman's extra-physical powers. For this, he receives a failing grade. When he goes to the professor to complain, he brings with him a copy of the *Daily Planet* with headlines announcing that Superman has traveled faster than the speed of light. "So you see," the student says, waving the newspaper at his physics professor. "It's true. Superman does have extra-physical powers." To which the professor stonily replies: "In science, we're not interested in truth. For truth, go to the metaphysics department."

Before the scientific hypothesis came along with its dependence on stored data and libraries and a written language, we structured the truths of our world in both physical and psychological terms by means of myths, legends, and fairy tales. The transmission of these fictional forms from one generation to the next was by word of mouth. And one of the things we've observed even today among tribal remnants lacking a written language is the way in which this oral inheritance has developed ritual accretions of music, rhythm, dance and other patterns of group acting out. But when we examine the collected and printed forms of our oral tradition, we note how much of it, fairy tales in particular, has been relegated to the role of children's literature. This tends to be especially the case where the rational function (as information, as science, as technology) has taken over. The fact is, of course, that fairy tales were never originally intended for children. But with universal literacy, children are the only ones left among whom the oral transmission of culture is still active for the simple reason that reading is not an innate capacity. Nor should we ignore the fact that fairy tales, owing to the kind of archetypal characters that people them, lend themselves particularly to the kind of acting out developmentally associated with childhood. Children, like primitives and others who are still, by virtue of education or psychic development, in a less individuated state, have a need to hear the same stories over and over again, a need that readily accommodates itself to the kinetic and participational modes of the oral tradition.

So in recalling those youngsters disporting in their Superman costumes that previous summer, it also occurred to me that Superman too was not originally written for children, yet somehow it had been taken over by them for the same reason that they had adopted fairy tales. I was to discover, bit by bit, that Superman was as much an archetype[2] as many of his legendary predecessors and shared with them both a certain healing magic and a certain autonomy.

The Superman strip first emerged out of the world of pulp fiction at a time when that world was being transposed from the purely printed word into the graphic form of the comic strip. Jerry Siegel, who wrote the original scripts, and Joe Shuster, who was responsible for the visual conception of Superman, after much effort, finally succeeded in peddling the rights to a comic book publisher almost all of whose editors had come originally from Leo Margolie's world of Thrilling Wonder, Thrilling Detective, Thrilling Adventure—that is, the standard fare of science fiction, detective, and adventure magazines whose varied story appeal did not happen to include children. Unlike many comic strips that have had a long history marked by a moderately ascending curve of popularity, Superman achieved a meteoric rise in a relatively brief period. But it peaked out within a period of about a decade, a meagre span compared to the longevity of appeal of many of our leading North American comic strips. At the same time, Superman spawned a host of secondary elaborations, "union suit" characters which in one modality or another tended to duplicate various extrinsic features of the Man of Steel without quite achieving his archetypal verisimilitude.

Batman, for example, has none of the telluric features of Superman, but is rather an ordinary human in disguise, whose antecedents
are to be found among such pulp heroes as the Phantom Detective
or the Shadow—products of cultural hero fantasies, conscious deri-
vations, rather than the type of spontaneous projection that Superman appears to be. This is why it was possible to parody the character of Batman directly as was done in the recent ciné-camp series
that enjoyed a brief season on television a few years ago. Superman
may be ignored or forgotten for reasons that I will elaborate below,
but where he appears, he tends to retain his intrinsic character. And
while Superman, like any other folkloric image, may become a subject and even a target for humor, within the strip itself, he can never
become, as did Batman, a parody of himself. The differences between
Superman and his "union suit" derivatives go deeper than that, however, as the following exegetical treatment of Superman's "secret"
identity suggests.

> Clark Kent, mild-mannered reporter for the Daily Planet, is
> walking along when, suddenly, his super-hearing picks up the
> sounds of a robbery in progress. He steps into a nearby phone-
> booth. An instant later and the Man of Steel streaks toward the
> scene of the crime. . . .

In the spate of recent books and articles on comics, I've not noted
anywhere a sense of the significance of this familiar transformation
scene. In switching from Clark to Superman, the comic strip hero is
not donning a disguise but, in fact, stepping out of one. This is because Superman is the reality; Clark Kent is the disguise.[3] To take
this a step further, Superman is a hidden reality; his visible aspect,
with the aid of his costume, is a highly colorful one, pointing precisely
to his hiddenness.

Hiddenness in this special sense is a symbolic property since a
symbol is one of the habiliments of value, and value is one of those
ineffabilities that can only be made visible by its clothing. To put this
seemingly paradoxical concept another way, there is that which we
call "value" and which has no value unless it rests finally and absolutely in itself. That is, there is no "value" without a highest value
and all other values derive from it hierarchically.[4] This is a basic
tenet of contemporary axiology, the science of value. But it has nowhere been more perfectly expressed than in the Tao Teh Ching:

There is something formless yet complete
That existed before heaven and earth.
    How still! How empty!
Dependent on nothing, unchanging,
All pervading, unfailing
One may think of it as the mother of all things under heaven.
I do not know its name.
But I call it Tao.
If I had to give it a name, I would call it great.

                           (Chapter XXV)

We put thirty spokes together and call it a wheel;
But it is on the space where there is nothing that the utility
    of the wheel depends.
We turn clay to make a vessel;
But it is on the space where there is nothing that the utility
    of the vessel depends.
We pierce doors and windows to make a house;
And it is on these spaces where there is nothing that the
    utility of the house depends.
Therefore just as we take advantage of what is, we should
    recognize the utility of what is not.

                           (Chapter XI)[5]

By interpreting these chapters from the Tao as "descriptions" of
the ultimate reality, then I think we can justifiably construe Chapter
XI as referring to the act of finitizing reality which, in itself, is invisible (i.e., "not this, not that"), by clothing it in a vessel, a house,
a wheel. Or, viewing the whole matter within the context of Superman's colorfulness, it might be worth noting that in the architectural
symbolism of the cathedral, the ineffable white light of the divine is
colored and made apparent by the stained glass windows that adorn
these numinous Gothic temples. We should keep in mind too that
the word "color" is related to the Latin, *celare*, which also means
to hide, in the sense of *cover* or *clothe*.[6] Accordingly, we must make
a distinction with respect to Superman. In his dormant or non-active,
invisible, or "mild-mannered" phase, Superman is Clark Kent. In his
active, otherworldly, or, if you like, avatar phase, he is made visible
or *incarnate* by his colorful costume. Apart from that costume, he
is largely colorless, pure essence rather than personality—and this is
the case even apart from his role as Clark Kent, which is, at best, a
simulacrum of colorlessness. It plays a part in the story, if you will,
but it is not the essential colorlessness I refer to here. This notion

will become clearer as we proceed with a more detailed analysis of Superman's Clark Kent persona.

Clark Kent, as we have already seen, is one of the aspects of Superman. As a reporter, standing at the center of the newspaper world of information and facts (how appropriately the newspaper is called The Daily Planet!), he symbolizes only a single higher function of Superman—the rational mind. In that role, he is the conforming, self-conscious mass man, completely anonymous, the split-off rational portion of that manifestation of wholeness which appears only at moments of crisis, embracing not only the mind but the imagination by its capacity for flight, by its otherworldliness, its irresistible power, its avatar role as it responds to threatening and extreme situations. Like the archetypal hero of many a myth, Superman broke into a particular segment of history, his moment of *kairos*, like an irrigation, a vivifying force arising out of what Carl Jung has described for us as the collective unconscious. And in the same way that Jung has treated the mythic tale as a "healing fiction," so too the adventures of Superman provide this type of "fiction par excellence"—a representation of reality from beyond the surface of the everyday; the Hidden, colorfully made manifest. But it is precisely by means of the "fiction," that is, the plot or story, that healing takes place.

To those of us with a secure share in the literate world of technology and information, who possess, in consequence, a variety of life options, there is no crisis and no healing irruption of the sort that Superman is capable of providing. But there are those who like children were much closer to the oral tradition when Superman first appeared. It was, it may be recalled, the height of the Great Depression. There were blacks, Chicanos, Puerto Ricans and, around the world, masses of semi-literate ghetto inhabitants, minorities, persons displaced by the devastating urbanization of rural cultures, who, in one way or another, were excluded; who, like children, had not attained that level of differentiated functioning that separated them from the oral tradition. And then too there were even those of us who maintained a firm grip on the rational until consciousness and rationality were shattered by World War II. This produced, to my mind, one of the most persuasive pieces of evidence that Superman had a certain healing quality for those who had no external choices. For during the war, fifty percent of the circulation of Superman went to the armed forces. And no one, regardless of his pre-war status was more lacking in choice than a conscript soldier in the midst of a war. At the end of hostilities, when the conscript armies disbanded, Superman's circulation dropped severely. As ethnocentrism developed a new pride and new options among blacks, Chicanos, Puerto Ricans, and other ghetto minorities during the fifties and sixties, Superman's circulation dropped further still.

What remains is now largely a children's market, not enough to sustain Superman at his previous meteoric level, but sufficient to keep him around for a while longer at a fairly steady rate.[7] Children, of necessity, cannot escape from the kind of story-awareness that belongs to the oral mode. It is, in fact, one of the requirements of healthy psychic growth.

In referring earlier to the architectural symbolism of the cathedral and its stained glass windows, I did not mean that symbols of this order are "invented," unless, of course, the word is used in the sense of "discover." A symbol, as an image or representation of something unknown, is very different from a sign whose meaning relates exclusively to known entities. Accordingly, a symbol acts as a means of release and transformation of psychic energy. I think this is what we mean when we speak of something as alive. The cathedrals were not "invented" as we normally tend to use that word. Their inherent principles and symbolism were discovered, step by step, by the anonymous artists and craftsmen who dedicated themselves to their construction over a considerable period of their lives. It is why the best examples of medieval Gothic seem to convey to the sensitive observer the impression of an actual living presence.

It may seem a long way from the medieval cathedral to Superman, but allowing for appropriate differences of scale, the living quality of Superman was gradually demonstrated for me by his autonomous functioning, which further served to underscore his archetypal character.[8] That is to say, as writers and editors, working on Superman, we thought we were, in effect, manufacturing the character. In actuality, we did no more than "discover" Superman.

For example, there were various rationalizations we used to explain why Superman had to keep his identity secret. These were to the effect that evil men could get hold of Lois Lane and use her as a hostage to force Superman to act for them. Or that somehow, if it were known that Superman was Clark Kent, Superman would be unable to live a "normal" life. In no case did any of our reasons make sense, especially when measured against the extremes to which Superman would go to keep his identity hidden. For example, when

Clark is caught in a "death-trap" with Lois, he is unable to become Superman and rescue her until he has first surreptitiously sucked all the air out of the room so that Lois loses consciousness long enough for him to become Superman without her discovering it. Naturally, the problem of keeping that identity secret was thoroughly mined for stories. I myself was responsible for a number of variations of that particular plot constraint, including one called "Superman's Search for Clark Kent," in which Superman, suffering from amnesia, does not know that Clark is his other identity and, consequently, when Clark is reported missing, sets out to try to find him, coming on one trail after another that seems mysteriously to lead back to himself. An interesting comic strip simulacrum of the process of individuation!

But the point is that these rationalizations for maintaining a secret identity had little to do with the real reasons, which lay in the nature of the character himself—his capacity for asserting his autonomy. If, as I have proposed here, Superman represented an archetypal intrusion from the unconscious, then for that reason alone there was a need for a separation of the realms. The promiscuous mixing of conscious and unconscious contents makes for psychological chaos and the character would have lost much of his numinous power and remarkable influence since he would then have been completely lacking in what E. F. Edinger has predicated of any genuine symbol —"a subjective dynamism which exerts a powerful attraction and fascination on the individual."[9] So, in a sense, the character himself determined the conditions under which he was to operate, not the authors and editors.

It might also be worth noting that Superman, taken by himself, was like many heroes of his type, dull. Far more interesting were the Superman villains who, it should be remembered, had many things in common with Jung's description of the Shadow archetype.[10] I refer particularly to such characters as the Prankster, the Toyman, Luthor, and certainly that fifth dimensional imp, Mr. Mxyztplk, whom Superman could only overcome by tricking him into saying his name backwards, a strategy reminiscent of Goethe's Faust trapping Mephistopheles by the special use of a pentogram.

The question as to why a hero such as Superman should be dull raises a similar question often posed in connection with Milton's *Paradise Lost*, in which many have insisted that Satan rather than God is the real hero, since he is so much more fully realized as a character. The late C. S. Lewis has suggested that this is merely because we are incapable of fully realizing someone so much more perfect than ourselves. I don't think this is quite the case. Without the villains, there is no story, no plot, no "healing fiction." The problem of the separation and the need to reunify the opposites, the drama of the differentiated functions, imagination and rationality, consciousness and unconsciousness, struggling toward equilibrium, toward a self-regulating balance, is the important thing. Drama is never about wholeness. Wholeness is another state of being. It is unmanifest, withdrawn into itself. *The cosmic dance goes on in costume.*

Consider too that the Superman villains, like those in Batman and other comic strips of this type, are *un*wholesome precisely because they are specialists—not whole men. And it is out of their very lack of wholeness, that is to say, out of the conflict engendered by their fragmented or split-off personalities, that the drama develops and realization of sorts arises. James Hillman, Director of the Jung Institute at Zurich, appropriately observes:

> From my perspective as depth psychologist, I see that those who have a connection with story are in better shape and have a better prognosis than those to whom story must be introduced. . . . To have story-awareness is *per se* psychologically therapeutic. It is good for soul. . . . To have had story of any sort in childhood— and here I mean oral story . . . puts a person into a basic recognition and familiarity with the legitimate reality of story *per se*. . . . My practice shows me that the more attuned and experienced is the imaginative side of personality, the less threatening the irrational, the less necessity for repression, and therefore the less actual pathology acted out in literal daily events.[11]

And so with the Superman villains, their unwholesomeness depotentiated into a kind of dramatic humor by the healing magic of story. I introduced these comments on what we call "union suit" characters by suggesting that I was in thrall to an archetype. In fact, we all of us are. But not all of us have become conscious of it. There were several of us who wrote and edited and worked on the various Superman comic books, daily and Sunday newspaper continuities, and none of us, at the time, were in any way aware of what might be called the logic of the unconscious that compelled us to set up certain conditions for Superman's way of operating which, instead, we explained by means of the rationalizations I have described above. But in spite of our illusion of conscious control, Superman functioned with an autonomy real enough to have made his way into folklore.

Strip for "Hi & Lois" by Dik Browne, © King Features Syndicate, Inc.; used by permission

As folklore, and as a secondary reflection of his true archetypal presence, it is hardly surprising to discover him turning up in so allusive a form and in so odd a place—as another comic strip.

NOTES

1. When we speak of reducing a thing to psychology, the reference is usually and properly to the more widely accepted reductive approach in that so-called science. Analytical psychology is an altogether different matter, a

fact that will hopefully find abundant support in the sections that follow.

2. See note 8 below.

3. While the New York cartoonist, Jules Feiffer, has made the same distinction between Superman and Clark Kent in *The Great Comic Book Heroes* (New York, 1965), he then goes on to explain the whole thing as being interesting because it was "junk"—insisting, rather archly, that people simply like "junk." In other words, Feiffer applies a non-term as though it were an explanation. This kind of trivialization falls far short of the need to draw any kind of significant conclusion from the fact that Superman is the reality and Clark the disguise. Why mention it at all unless it has some operational value in enabling us to apply the distinction to the way in which Superman differs from the other "union suit" characters who are just as much "junk" in Feiffer's sense, whether their true identity is embodied in uniform or out of uniform. In fact, the distinction is interesting precisely to the extent that it leads us directly to the notion of hiddenness as an attribute of the symbol.

4. This, of course, is the role played formerly by the "gold standard" in the world monetary system.

5. The quotations are from Arthur Waley's *The Way and Its Power* (London, 1934) with slight changes made by R. F. C. Hull, Jung's English translator, to accord with Richard Wilhelm's translation into German on which Jung relied. I am responsible for one minor change in the second-last line of verse xxv. I cannot accept the word "meaning" as derived from Wilhelm, this being too specific for a concept that I would regard as necessarily apophatic. I therefore prefer to stay with the original Tao.

6. See Merriam Webster, 1945 ed.: color n. (ME., fr. OF. color, colour, fr. L. color; akin to L. *celare* to conceal. See HELL.) In addition, the conceptual kinship is strikingly obvious. Color conceals and hides; it also makes visible. Adam's fig-leaf, similarly, conceals his nakedness and reveals his shame. Symbols generally, even stained glass windows, can become opaque, as symbols. Then they only succeed in concealing what they were meant to reveal.

7. There is, of course, a certain climate of nostalgia that seems to be producing a distinct secondary peak. But nostalgia is an altogether different story from that set forth here.

8. There is a tendency to confuse the notion of *archetypes* with something that I have heard referred to as *archetypicality*, which is merely a grandiose redundancy. Neither, on the other hand, can the appearance of an archetype such as Superman be properly described, as suggested by some who have heard me lecture on the subject, as "a bursting forth of the sacred." The term *archetype* as used in analytical psychology is a peculiarly difficult one. Perhaps the following quotation from Jung's paper "The Psychology of the Child Archetype" (*Psyche & Symbol* [New York: Anchor, 1958]) would be helpful: ". . . the archetype is an element of our psychic structure and thus a vital and necessary component in our psychic economy. It represents or personifies certain instinctive data of the dark, primitive psyche, the real but invisible *roots of consciousness. . . .*"

This means, too, that archetype precedes ego, or—as in Superman's case— the reality, Superman, precedes Clark Kent. And further, that Superman's "colorful" costume points precisely to his archetypal hiddenness. Clark, as I suggest above, is the superficial or temporal ego-accretion in the sense of his being at the center of the rational world of information—the newspaper. At the bottom of page 23 (op. cit.) Jung comments significantly: "There is no 'rational' substitute for the archetype any more than there is for the cerebellum or the kidneys."

It may be of some further help to consider an explanation by Jolande Jacobi, a long-time associate of Jung, who says of archetypes: "They possess no material existence; they are a sort of *éternels incréés* (Jung sometimes uses this Bergsonian term for them), which must first be endowed with solidity and clarity, clothed as it were by the conscious mind, before they can appear as 'material reality,' as an 'image,' and, in a manner of speaking, be 'born' " (Jacobi: *Complex/Archetype/Symbol in the Psychology of C. G. Jung*, trans. Ralph Manheim [Bollingen Series LVII, Princeton University Press, 1959], p. 52). And again, from Jung: "Not for a moment can we succumb to the illusion that an archetype can be finally explained and disposed of. Even the best attempts at explanation are only more or less successful translations into another metaphorical language" ("The Child Archetype," *Collected Works*, par. 271).

Some additional insight into the concept can be gleaned from Charles Norris Cochrane's analysis of the concept of *arché* deriving its essential intelligibility within classical and early Christian culture as being outside time, as a beginning only in the sense of "eternal beginning" or foundation—somewhat in the way Santayana says of God and the Unseen world, according to Platonic doctrine, they "can precede, create, attract and survive their earthly emanations" (C. N. Cochrane, *Christianity and Classical Culture* [Oxford, 1944]). Finally, it would not be inappropriate to consider Goethe's inspired vision of "The Mothers" in the second part of *Faust* for what is perhaps the most powerful metaphoric illumination of the concept of archetypes ever to find expression in a modern western language.

9. E. F. Edinger, *Ego and Archetype* (New York: G. P. Putnam's Sons, 1972).

10. *Aion: Contributions to the Symbolism of the Self* (Collected Works of C. G. Jung, Part II, Vol. 9; New York: Bollingen, 1958).

11. James Hillman, "A Note on Story," in *Children's Literature*, 3 (1974), 9–11, p. 9.

Six Characters in Search of the Family

The Novels of Paul Zindel*

James T. Henke

Since the appearance of *The Pigman* in 1968, the novels of Paul Zindel have been the objects of a good deal of contradictory discussion and evaluation. These works, *The Pigman, My Darling, My Hamburger,* and *I Never Loved Your Mind,* have been hailed as delightfully humorous, refreshingly honest attempts to deal with a number of the classic themes of modern literature. On the other hand, they have been condemned, with equal fervor, as squalid pieces of trash, as slick "con jobs," and as simple-minded hack work.[1]

Obviously, the resolution of such controversy, if indeed any resolution is possible, is an undertaking far too ambitious for a single essay. Therefore, in this discussion my goals will be much more modest. First, I will sketch one thematic approach to Zindel's novels and then attempt a brief evaluation of the literary worth of each. In so doing, I anticipate that, rather than providing a resolution, this discussion will intensify the Zindel debate.

In any case, for the moment we will put aside the problem of the literary quality of Zindel's novels and turn instead to the ideas contained in those novels. Better yet, we will focus upon one idea that, with varying degrees of clarity, informs all three of the author's books. The tracing of this major theme may possibly prove rewarding regardless of the merits of the works themselves. So, let us turn first to *The Pigman.*

The hero of Zindel's first novel is John Conlan, sixteen years old, a bright, imaginative, rebellious high school sophomore. The heroine is Lorraine Jensen, sixteen years old, a bright, somewhat less imaginative, and somewhat less rebellious high school classmate. John and Lorraine are friends, and the novel is their collaboration on a first-person, reflective account of their experiences with Mr. Pignati, the Pigman.

By page eleven of the book the reader has been introduced to the respective parents of the protagonists. John's father, whom he calls the "Bore," is a reformed alcoholic and a thorough-going materialist,

---

*Versions of this essay have been presented at Youngstown State University's first annual Children's Literature Workshop (Nov. 1974) and at the seventeenth annual meeting of the Midwest Modern Language Association (Nov. 1975).

a preoccupied commodities broker who cheats on his income tax. John's mother is a compulsive housekeeper who will not allow the boy to use her spotless living room. Lorraine is a bit better off. She has only one parent, a divorced mother, a private nurse who specializes in terminal cancer cases so that she can sell the dying patient to the highest-bidding mortuary. The reader can easily understand, then, why both John and Lorraine are lonely and why, as Beverly Haley and Kenneth Donelson note in a recent article, they attempt to escape the loveless reality of their existences by guzzling beer and playing mischievous games.[2] That is, until they meet the Pigman.

Angelo Pignati, the third major character of the novel, is a sixtyish widower who is attempting to escape his own unfaceable reality: he cannot admit to himself that his wife is dead. Rather, he insists upon pretending that she is visiting a sister in California. Obviously, like the children, he lives a life without love; like the children, he yearns for something, for someone.

When these three meet quite by accident, their lives are changed, but not in the way critics generally assume. For instance, Haley and Donelson write: "Then they [the children] find a substitute parent in Mr. Pignati, a childless widower, who becomes the parent neither has ever known, as they become the children he has never had."[3] Although close, this is not quite on the mark. None of Zindel's heroes and heroines is seeking a surrogate parent. Quite to the contrary, all of Zindel's paired protagonists (and the reader encounters these boy-girl teams in all three novels) have rejected the subordinate role of child and are seeking to assume for themselves the dominant identity of parent. In other words, what they attempt to do is in various ways to create their own families in order to successfully fulfill the role of parent, a role at which their own parents have failed so miserably.

Thus, in *The Pigman* John and Lorraine are not searching for a substitute father. Without the remotest awareness on their part, they are searching for a surrogate child, and Mr. Angelo Pignati, the aging widower, becomes that child.

Indeed, the thing about the old man that first strikes John and Lorraine is his childlike openness and his youthful enthusiasm for fun and games. Five minutes after they first meet, he offers to teach the children a memory game. "Do you know the secret of how to memorize ten items?" he asks eagerly. John remarks: "I looked at him, and I had to bite my tongue because I was going to burst out laughing. He looked just like a great big kid—so happy we were there" (p. 41).[4] Lest the reader miss the significance of the Pigman's incongruous youthfulness, then, Zindel helpfully allows John to underline that significance for him. And just to make doubly certain that he recognizes Mr. Pignati's symbolic role, when with a great deal of pride the Pigman successfully demonstrates his skill at the memory game, Zindel once again allows John to note: "Then he said the items, starting with girl and working back to cockroach, and I swear he looked just like a great big baby that had just made a super-duper mud pie" (p. 42).

Certainly, the reader must view John's evaluation of Mr. Pignati's character and conduct with some suspicion. The trustworthiness of the solitary, first-person narrator must always be suspect. Lorraine, however, shares some of the narrating duties in this novel. Though somewhat less imaginative than John, she seems the more sensitive of the two and her evaluation reinforces his.

Note her account of a "family" shopping spree. No sooner do the three enter the department store than Mr. Pignati, the avid zoo fan, pleads, "Can we look at the pet shop?" Like the much-put-upon father, John groans, but Lorraine, scowling at John, and humoring the Pigman, assures him, "Of course we can" (p. 85). A bit later, the role she is playing is clarified for the reader. The three are in the sporting goods department, and Mr. Pignati wants to buy them all roller skates. Lorraine, shocked at the extravagance, shows her displeasure. But Mr. Pignati wheedles, "Please let me get them." The girl remembers that the old man had been "practically asking for my permission" (p. 87).

Here she is clearly the surrogate mother and the old widower her child, and although she never seems completely to grasp this psychological reality, she is at least partially aware of it. Later, just before the Pigman's first heart attack, she reflects on the significance of her and John's relationship with the old fellow: "The longer he knew us, the more of a kid he became. It was cute in a way" (p. 108).

But it is not really cute; it is tragic. Mr. Pignati's regression indirectly costs him his life. While he is in the hospital, John and Lorraine take over his house and, *sans* sex, act out the role of man and wife. They masquerade in adult clothes, enjoy a candlelight dinner, and even throw a cocktail party. The fantasy is shattered, however; for at the party John gets drunk, the guests become unruly, and Mr. Pignati's cherished collection of pig figurines is smashed—just as Mr. Pignati returns home unexpectedly from the hospital.

The Pigman forgives John and Lorraine. He forgives them as only the adoring child can forgive those parents who have inexplicably caused him pain. Yet they know and the reader knows that their betrayal is partially responsible for the death of their surrogate son. The following day, Pignati is stricken by a second, and this time fatal, heart attack.

In Zindel's next novel, the theme of adolescent aspirations to parenthood is once again traceable, but, perhaps because *My Darling, My Hamburger* concerns two teenage couples instead of one, the idea is less central than in *Pigman*. In *My Darling*, the story focuses as much upon the maturation of Maggie and Denis as upon the young lovers Sean and Liz. Moreover, in this second book the author seems to get tangled in a rather superficial examination of such fashionable topics as teenage premarital sex, illicit pregnancy, and abortion, and in so doing partially to slight the theme he first introduced in *The Pigman*. Nevertheless, the idea is there and merits examination. But we will shorten that examination by ignoring the stories of Maggie and Denis and by noting that, for the parents of Sean and Liz, Zindel once again creates stereotypically "bad" parents, not unlike those which appear in *The Pigman*.

In this second book, then, the reader again encounters a teenage couple attempting to escape the harshness of their respective family lives by creating a third family in which they assume the parental roles. Now, however, the protagonists are older and are no longer content to "beget" surrogate children. Sean and Liz, high school seniors, become lovers and soon Liz becomes pregnant.

Like John and Lorraine in *The Pigman*, these young people also botch their new parental roles. With a premeditation lacking in John and Lorraine, they kill the life that they have created. Sean, who had promised to marry Liz, reneges under pressure from his father and the girl gets an abortion.

What is interesting here is not the love story itself, but the elaboration upon a Zindel stance not fully developed in *Pigman*. In *My Darling* the author suggests the reason why these adolescents fail in their prematurely assumed parental roles is that contemporary society is so brutal and so sterile itself that it deliberately seeks to corrupt the greatest parental duty, which is not simply to create life, but to cherish it.

Indeed, in this book Zindel goes even further. Contemporary society corrupts Sean and Liz by forcing them to sacrifice the life they have created. In Sean's essay "The Circus of Horrors," which he writes for an English honors seminar and which is inserted toward the end of the novel, it becomes clear that society has forced the children to murder their baby. Sean describes a circus performance in which a naked boy and girl, standing on a huge wagon, are pulled into a large tent to confront a savagely howling audience. With them they have a baby. To the delight of the mob, the ringmaster, assisted by a male acrobat and female witch, forces the young couple to submit the baby to a guillotine. Obviously, the mob is society, and the male acrobat and female witch represent parents.

Now surely, the sensitive reader must see that this is, in part, Sean's attempt to shift guilt. Yet Zindel's third-person narrator never clearly points out this fact. Thus, the reader is justified in interpreting Sean's unconscious rationalization as Zindel's conscious condemnation.

That Zindel does indeed share with his adolescents their view of contemporary society becomes even more apparent in his last novel, *I Never Loved Your Mind*. In this first-person narration by Dewey Daniels, the seventeen-year-old high school dropout, the family, which in the earlier novels stood as the chief symbol of a sterile society, has all but disappeared. On one occasion when Dewey asks Yvette Goethals, the heroine of the book, why she does not live with her parents, she responds: "Because they're bastards. My mother's a dumb one. My father's a mean one" (p. 29). But this is virtually the only time they are mentioned. To Yvette, they seem to be merely a part of the general corruption and brutality of society, a society for which her own neighborhood becomes a kind of malignant biopsy sample blighted by such as a crooked judge, a cheating doctor, a thieving cop, and a host of other parasites. As Yvette herself says, "practically every house has some type of lousy, sneaky, illegal, bloodsucking scrounger in it" (p. 62). Nor, indeed, do Dewey's parents play a more prominent role in the story. As with Yvette's, the reader never sees them, but Dewey does say: "My folks happen to be plain, nice, detached, insignificant people, and nobody has the right to pin any rap on them" (p. 33). Rather than parents, then, in this last novel, the principal symbol of a degenerate society is the hospital in which both Dewey and Yvette work, a hospital steered by a vacuously authoritarian administrator, staffed by indifferent nurses, and stocked with deformed or dying patients.

In the midst of this pain and despair, Dewey discovers Yvette, another high school dropout. The girl, who once waged a futile battle with bulldozers to save a plot of woods in her old neighborhood, becomes a symbol of new life. In fact, Yvette Goethals appears to be a twentieth-century, adolescent reincarnation of the Greek goddess Demeter, the Earth Mother and Goddess of Grain. Consider that throughout the narrative, Dewey, with what appears to be unconscious intuition, speaks of her in such a way as to link her with all things natural. For instance, when he first meets her, she appears to him to "look like an owl with a thyroid condition" (p. 3). On their first date Yvette wears a huge, furry mouton coat which, Dewey tells the reader, makes her look like a grizzly bear, a "wolf-woman" (p. 46), and a "koala cub" (p. 58). When she runs and the wind catches the coat, she reminds him of a pterodactyl, spreading its wings (p. 59). At the end of this first date, he walks her to Clove Lakes Park, but she will not allow him to take her home. As Dewey describes it: "She just took off into the brush, like a bear at Yellowstone National Park . . ." (p. 67). Probably, she is headed for her house on "Van Pelt" street. This house Dewey will later see and will describe as being surrounded by "landscaping that resembled an acre of overfertilized rain forest" (p. 75).

Even more than the narrator's intuitive descriptions, however, the actual events of the story suggest that Yvette is a twentieth-century version of the Earth Mother, who, in addition to her role as fertility goddess, is also a goddess of rebirth. That Zindel does indeed intend to endow the girl symbolically with the Goddess' power of rejuvenation is apparent in the fact that Dewey first actually meets his love in the autopsy room, as he awakens from a fainting spell to see her bending over him. The symbolic significance of this episode is underscored some eight chapters later when Dewey describes his thoughts and emotions on the morning after he and Yvette have made love: "When I woke up in my own room on Saturday morning, I felt like I had just been born. . . . I kept myself in a luxurious somnolent state, trying to relive everything all over again. . . . I remembered her gently nursing me back to health in the autopsy room" (p. 91).

This, then, is symbolic rebirth, but before complete rebirth Dewey had had to ply his Demeter with "sacrificial offerings." When he first courts Yvette, he gives her flowers and candy. However, she tells him that instead of these she would prefer bags of seed, especially wheat and barley (both grains are traditionally associated with Demeter). Moreover, on the night they make love, Dewey brings her a fifty pound bag of Burpee radish seed.

Nevertheless, even though he thinks himself born anew, the goddess ultimately rejects him. Although she loves him, she feels that he has been corrupted by society, and she flees with the Electric Lovin' Stallions, a rock music group with whom she has been living.

Now, Dewey and the reader discover the literal reason for the girl's bizarre taste in gifts: she and the Stallions are leaving in a horse-drawn covered wagon for New Mexico, there to establish a commune.

Does Dewey follow? Zindel does not tell the reader. He lets him see only that Dewey has indeed undergone a rebirth of sorts. In the final pages of the novel, having learned the address of Yvette's commune, the hero resigns his position at the hospital and closes his story: "I don't really know what I'm going to do. . . . I'm not going to give civilization a kick in the behind, because I might need an appendectomy sometime. But I'm going to do something, and I have a strange feeling it's going to be phantasmagorically different" (pp. 134–35).

Zindel's final novel, then, presents a mythically translated and exalted treatment of the theme of the adolescent aspiration for parenthood. After all, while John and Lorraine become surrogate parents and while Sean and Liz almost become real parents, Dewey may have the chance to embrace the family of the Earth Mother. And because, as Yvette has told him several times, her relationship with the Stallions is platonic, if the hero is accepted as being worthy of the honor, he will become the goddess' consort and patriarch of the communal family.

But Zindel may be hinting at much more here. Should the Earth Goddess mate, the result would be a general rebirth of nature. Thus, the author may be telling the reader that from the zest for life, from the compassion for nature of such young people as Dewey and Yvette a new order is possible. Such vital young parents may beget not just children, but a whole new world.

The question is whether or not one must turn his back on contemporary society to create this world. Here, perhaps, Zindel's attitude toward contemporary society may soften. Although Yvette has fled, Dewey has resolved not to do so completely. He is not, as he says, "going to kick civilization in the behind." Maybe this is just a cowardly evasion on Dewey's part. Or maybe Zindel is saying that society can be rejuvenated and purified by the union of the hero, who will not forsake it, and the goddess: the one representing the rebirth of civilized humanity's love for nature, the other representing the lifegiving forces of nature itself.

Is this a Pollyannic interpretation of Zindel's meaning? Perhaps. But before we dismiss it, we ought to remember that in the hospital, that symbol of a dying society, both Dewey and Yvette worked in the inhalation section. Their jobs were to resuscitate patients with oxygen, literally to revive them by providing a breath of fresh air. We ought to remember, too, that when Yvette leaves the hospital and heads for the covered wagon that will take her to a new world, Dewey tries to stop her. In the struggle, her mouton coat flaps open, and Dewey sees that the girl has strapped a "Byrd" machine to her waist. At first, this detail may seem insignificant, since Yvette previously has pilfered medical supplies from the hospital. Still, on second thought, we must wonder: after all, the function of a Byrd machine is to resuscitate patients dying of asphyxiation. In other words, literally and symbolically Yvette has the means to revive and restore life; all that remains now is for Dewey to have the courage to go after her and teach her how to use it.

This, then, is a sketch of the treatment of one of Zindel's themes, an overview which we can use as background for a rough evaluation of the author's individual works. So, let us return to *The Pigman*.

Paul Zindel's first novel is rich in provocatively suggestive metaphor and symbol, only a small part of which is noted in our previous discussion. For instance, Mr. Pignati's beloved zoo is a symbol of the plight of modern man in our impersonal society. Each of us, so Zindel says, lives in his own cage of indifference, boredom, or self-absorption. As do the creatures in the zoo, we may live in close proximity, but we do not live together. At the zoo, Mr. Pignati delights in tossing peanuts to Bobo the gorilla, and John delights in teasing Bobo by attempting to "speak" like an ape. Both acts, one pathetic, the other comic, are symbolic of modern man's need to communicate with someone, something, anything. Lorraine suggests yet another symbolic significance of the zoo. Both she and John have cut classes and she is waiting for him at the sea lion pool. She broods over the indifferent, unimaginative way a zoo keeper feeds the sea lions: "I mean, if you're going to feed sea lions you're not supposed to plop the food into the tank. You can tell by the expressions on their faces that the sea lions are saying things like 'Don't dump the fish in!' 'Pick the fish up one by one and throw them into the air so we can chase after them.' 'Throw the fish in different parts of the tank!' 'Let's have fun!' 'Make a game out of it!' " (p. 54). This may be simply a comment on man's inhumanity to the animals. But is it not far more likely that the character's observations are a metaphoric indictment of what the author considers to be the stifling sterility of our modern schools?

In *The Pigman* even stereotypes are functional. Although John's and Lorraine's parents may remind the reader a bit of Cinderella's stepmother, the author puts their stereotypical nature to good use as a yardstick against which to measure the final actions of their children. Consider, for instance, the drunken cocktail party which wrecks Mr. Pignati's house. Inadvertently, without malice, John and Lorraine betray the trust of their "child." Surely, the reader is meant to compare their selfish thoughtlessness with that of their own parents. They have failed their "child," as they themselves have been failed. Thus, the stereotyped parents stand as an indictment of the actions of their children, while at the same time the stereotype of the "bad" parent is given greater depth by those actions, which suggest that John's and Lorraine's parents abuse their children, not out of brutality, but out of thoughtlessness. Finally, the rigid parental stereotypes, when compared with the protagonists' final contrition, serve to emphasize John and Lorraine's moral superiority: they are capable of moral growth; their parents are not.

About Zindel's second novel, *My Darling, My Hamburger*, I wish I could be as enthusiastic. This appears to have been a hastily written book whose stereotypical characters and actions manifest little of the functional utility of those in *Pigman*. With minimal injustice, the love story of this novel can be summarized as follows: Liz, the most beautiful girl in the senior class, and Sean, the handsomest boy, have an affair which culminates in an illicit pregnancy. The pregnancy is aborted in an operation arranged by a slimy hospital technician. Liz's future, rich in promise, is destroyed; Sean's is forever blighted by his sense of guilt for having rejected Liz. Moreover, in this story the reader also encounters parents whose wickedness is as unmotivated as is that of Cinderella's stepmother. In fact, Liz's father, a particularly vicious and insensitive type, is really her stepfather, *à la* Cinderella. The story reads like a mushy episode from *Peyton Place*.

Still, *My Darling, My Hamburger* does have interest as a transitional link between *The Pigman* and *I Never Loved Your Mind*. Indeed, *My Darling* could prove very useful in the classroom. Paired with *The Pigman*, for instance, it could be used to demonstrate to young readers the limitations of slick, pat literature, and at the same time, to demonstrate the provocative richness of the other work.

Finally, Zindel's last novel, *I Never Loved Your Mind*, is both his most ambitious and his most difficult. The craftsmanship here is painstaking, but it is often obscured by the narrator Dewey's cloyingly fatuous prose style, perhaps best described by his own favorite adjective "puerile." Nevertheless, Zindel clearly intends the style to be functionally suggestive. The overused technique of alliteration, the often-inappropriate diction, and the generally inflated rhetoric suggest both the immaturity of Dewey's intellect and the fact that he does possess a vigorous, perceptive intellect capable of growth.[5] In one sense, we should see Dewey as an embodiment of the intellect, of the mind paired with but at the same time contrasted to the unbridled spirit of the flesh, Yvette Goethals.

The danger with this novel is that because Zindel chooses to tell the story through the limited, first-person narration of a hero who does not yet understand either his own or Yvette's role, the inexperienced reader may confuse the story's meaning and accept the girl's flight from society as the intelligent way to deal with evil. But this is not Zindel's meaning. The phoniness of the Loveland commune, to which Zindel devotes an entire chapter, and Yvette's illiteracy, evidenced in the note which Zindel inserts toward the close of the story, suggest both her own very limited intelligence and the impossibility of realizing the pastoral dream. This impossibility is further emphasized by the plight of Irene. In the hospital Irene, eighty years old and dying of emphysema, writes a poem entitled "Let's Go Back." But just as she cannot return to childhood, so neither can society return to an agrarian Eden.

As her covered wagon pulls away from the hospital gate, Yvette screams at Dewey: "I never loved your mind." Certainly. The business of the Earth Goddess is not the intellect, but the spirit and the flesh. Zindel seems to be telling his youthful readers that only by a combination of common-sense intelligence (one that appreciates the virtue of civilization represented by the appendectomy Dewey may some day need) and passionate spirit can society be saved.

The final evaluation, then? Paul Zindel is a fine craftsman, a genuine literary artist. Whether, as many have questioned, his novels are appropriate for the adolescent audience, I will leave to others to decide. I am certain of one thing, however: I will not be the last critic to attend to those novels.

NOTES

1. For a sample of this discussion, see, among others, review of *The Pigman* in *Best Seller*, 28 (Nov. 1, 1968), 327; D. F., review of *The Pigman* in *Horn Book*, 45 (Feb. 1969), 61; E. M. Graves, review of *My Darling, My Hamburger* in *Commonweal*, 91 (Nov. 21, 1969), 257; Margot Hentoff, review of *I Never Loved Your Mind* in *New York Review of Books*, 15 (Dec. 17, 1970), 11; Josh Greenfield, review of *I Never Loved Your Mind* in *New York Times Book Review*, pt. 2 (May 24, 1974), p. 14.

2. Beverly A. Haley and Kenneth L. Donelson, "Pigs and Hamburgers, Cadavers and Gamma Rays: Paul Zindel's Adolescents," *Elementary English*, 51, no. 7 (Oct. 1974), 941–45.

3. Haley, p. 943.

4. Quotations from Zindel's novels are taken from *The Pigman* (1968; rpt. New York: Dell, 1970), *I Never Loved Your Mind* (1970; rpt. New York: Bantam, 1972).

5. For an interesting treatment of Dewey's style, see Lou Willett Stanek, "The Junior Novel: A Stylistic Study," *Elementary English*, 51, no. 7 (Oct. 1974), 947–53. Stanek notes that Dewey's language is not "authentic teen-age speech" and suggests that this lack of authenticity may be due to the fact that Zindel is using the style to parody other writers such as Salinger.

Racism and Sexism in Children's Nonfiction*

Jim Haskins

A lot of time and paper have been devoted to the subjects of racism and sexism. However, in almost every instance, the time and paper have been devoted only to the area of fiction. Dorothy Broderick, in her *Image of the Black in Children's Fiction*, for example, says much that can be applied to nonfiction, but her primary concern is clearly fiction. Most of the articles that deal with sexism in children's literature in Diane Gersoni-stavn's *Sexism and Youth* also focus on fiction. The same can be said of articles devoted to other minorities in America: the primary concern is fiction.

As a writer of nonfiction, with a special interest in biography, I am concerned with the lack of attention given to racism and sexism in nonfiction. It could be argued that things have improved and undoubtedly will continue to improve in coming years; but that is a cop-out. The point is that enough time has passed already for us to expect substantial progress; yet this progress has not occurred. Racist and sexist books are still being published, kept in print, and stocked by libraries and bookstores. No individual or group can be blamed, but changes are not going to happen until someone takes a stand for them and sticks to it. There undoubtedly will be cries of censorship and denial of children's rights when this stand is taken, but we cannot remain forever in this state of limbo.

Perhaps the limited attention being paid to nonfiction grows out of the belief that factual material presents less opportunity for racism and sexism. Yet the biographer or nonfiction writer is not immune from subjective involvement with a subject. I know when I research the life of a subject, I get totally caught up in his or her time period and daily life. As Judith Thompson and Gloria Woodard state in their article "Black Perspective in Books for Children," appearing in *The Black American in Books for Children*, I try to illuminate the black experience through history and biography. My being black has nothing to do with my approach. I am required, as a former slave commented to Julius Lester, to "wear the shoe" of the subject.

Racism and sexism occur in nonfiction through omission rather than commission. There are exceptions, of course—but they are less

*A transcription of an address delivered at the University of Connecticut, April 24, 1975.

likely to be accepted by publishers. Margaret O. Hyde's *Your Brain*, published by McGraw Hill in 1964, serves as a good example of this "sin of omission." The brain is a "colorless" subject—Jensen and Shockley notwithstanding—yet only whites appear in the book's illustrations. Another book, concerning a child's first encounter with a hospital, remains admirably nonsexist throughout the text. However, the illustrations depict only female nurses and male doctors.

Publishers continue to turn out books which purport to represent humanity, but which actually deal only with men. A book about prehistoric mankind for instance will confine itself to a discussion of the first men in the world, when it is obvious that women have contributed a great deal to humanity's growth and development. Such books are not overtly racist or sexist. Hyde never says that black people lack brains, and the "great men of the world" books do not state that there are no great women. Simply by omitting references to other races and sexes, however, they imply and foster these attitudes. The next time you examine a nonfiction children's book, check to see if it includes a mixture of races and if the girls are as actively involved as the boys in scientific experiments, arts and crafts, and sports.

Children themselves are becoming more conscious of these omissions and inequities. I heard recently about two third-grade girls who approached a children's librarian because they were furious about a book entitled *Better Football for Boys*. They enjoyed the sport and played it often. The librarian, sharing their opinion, gave them the publisher's address and they immediately wrote a letter of complaint. I don't know whether they ever received a reply. The point is that they felt strongly enough to take action against an author and a publishing house.

Lothrop, Lee and Shepard, the Juvenile Division of William Morrow and Company, filled a great void with their series "What She Can Be," covering such occupations as veterinarian, lawyer, and architect. Too many girls felt that teaching, secretarial work, and motherhood were their only options. It is unfortunate however that the series couldn't have been "What They Can Be" and that a mixture of races doesn't appear in the books.

Research shows that children develop racist and sexist attitudes before they enter kindergarten. Numerous studies document firmly held opinions among preschoolers of what is appropriate for boys and girls. When asked, "Who drives the car?" most children will answer, "Daddy." This holds true even for children who have seen their mothers drive more frequently than their fathers. Since it's been proven fairly conclusively that sexual differentiation doesn't exist at birth, it's true—as the song says—that "you've got to be carefully taught."

The same song begins "you've got to be taught to hate and fear." Research also demonstrates that white children acquire negative attitudes toward black Americans before they enter kindergarten. Mary Ellen Goodman documents the awareness of racial differences in children between the ages of three and five. Trager and Yarrow have found that whites in kindergarten and in first and second grades were antagonistic toward blacks. A look at recent history makes this understandable. Augusta Baker, in her "Guidelines for Black Books: An Open Letter to Juvenile Editors," wrote that when she was working at the Countee Cullen Branch of the New York Public Library in 1937 and 1938, most of the black children using the library were aware only of Frederick Douglass, Booker T. Washington, and George Washington Carver among great black people. They marveled when they were introduced to Phillis Wheatley and Robert Smalls. She states rightly that: "If black children were so ignorant of their heritage and history, then why expect white children to know?"

The same is true of the awareness of women's contributions through history. If little girls know only about Betsy Ross and Madame Curie, how can little boys know of others? In talking with Shirley Chisholm, my biography of whom will soon be published, I learned how important it had been for her to discover Harriet Tubman, Susan B. Anthony, and, later, Mary McLeod Bethune. They provided a basis for her own hopes to be somebody one day. Had she not been an avid reader and library-goer, she might not have discovered these women until long after her concrete attitudes toward herself had been formed.

Fortunately there are a few valuable books available to those who look for them. In 1947 Shirley Graham's *There Was Once a Slave* introduced Frederick Douglass to thousands of Americans for the first time, and won an award for the best book combating intolerance in America. Ms. Graham followed this book with her biographies of Phillis Wheatley, Benjamin Banneker, George Washington Carver, Booker T. Washington, and Jean Baptiste de Sable. With these books one should contrast Elizabeth Yates' 1951 Newbery Award-winning *Amos Fortune, Free Man*. Throughout this book Amos Fortune says, "No, I'm not ready for freedom, don't give it to me yet." With this attitude in mind, I agree with Dorothy Sterling that the book shouldn't appear on the reading lists of ghetto schools.

After the Supreme Court's decision on school integration, publishers jumped on the bandwagon, bringing out such titles as Langston Hughes' *Famous American Negroes*, Gwendolyn Brooks' *Bronzeville Boys and Girls*, and Dorothy Sterling's *Freedom Train: The Story of Harriet Tubman*. They soon realized, however, that the Court's decision had little impact on the field of children's literature, and retreated to their safe little shells. Dorothy Sterling wrote in *Soul of Learning*, excerpted in *The Black American in Books for Children*, about the problems she faced trying to get her *Captain of the Planter* published. The book was a biography of Robert Smalls and told of Negro disenfranchisement and the birth of Jim Crow.

In 1965 Nancy Larrick wrote *The All-White World of Children's Books*, which greatly altered public opinion regarding the scope of racism in children's literature. She opened her article with a question asked by a five-year-old black girl in a New York nursery school as she looked through a picture book: "Why are they always white children?" A good question—particularly when in 1965 black children comprised 65 percent of the schoolchildren in New York City Public Schools, 53 percent in Cleveland, 56 percent in St. Louis, and 70 percent in the District of Columbia. Some 6,340,000 nonwhite students attended class across the country. Ms. Larrick's main concern was for the 39,600,000 white children learning from their books that they were the "kingfish" of the world— when on a world basis they were actually a minority.

> As recently as 1967, John Oliver Killens wrote:
> The American Negro remains a cultural non-entity as far as books, television, movies and Broadway are concerned. It is as if twenty million Americans do not exist. A Negro schoolchild can go into school and look into his schoolbooks and children's books and come home and watch television and go to an occasional movie and follow this routine from day to day, month to month and year to year and hardly ever see a reflection of himself.

In 1968, when the Kerner report pointed out the facts of racism and prejudice in America, the publishing industry suddenly regained its interest in mass-producing books by and about blacks. Ample federal money for schools and libraries via LSCA funds kept this movement alive longer than the first. Now that the economic crunch is on, however, belts have to be tightened and concern for representative books has waned.

Fortunately this movement had a far-reaching impact and sparked other concerns such as the treatment of Mexican-Americans, Native Americans, Puerto Ricans, and most recently Asian-Americans in juvenile literature. There are a few articles on this subject: Tony DeGerez's "Three Times Lonely; The Plight of the Mexican Child in the American Southwest," in *Horn Book* (Feb. 1970); Mary Gloyne Byler's "The Image of American Indians Projected by Non-Indian Writers" in *SLJ* (Feb. 1974); "Asian Images—A Message to the Media" in *Bridge Magazine* (April 1974). These groups, however, have not enjoyed the same coverage as anti-black, racism, and sexism groups. Mary Gloyne Byler's article is perhaps the most pertinent to my topic. She points out that unlike most minority groups in America, the Indians have been "represented" in thousands of books since frontier days. The difficulty of separating fact from fiction seems unimportant—as does the fact that these books portray images of Indians held by non-Indians. Ms. Byler concludes that there are too many books about American Indians—featuring painted, whooping, befeathered Indians closing in on peaceful white settlements. Too many books portray the childlike Indian saved by white benevolence and give expert advice on what is "best" for the Indian people. In other words, these books create a fantasy image of the American Indian which serves only to sustain the belief that these barbaric people deserved to lose their lands. What else can be expected when one publishing house willingly publishes such a book, originally brought out in Austria, by a German-born author, educated in Munich, who lives in Bavaria and raises riding ponies!

Ms. Byler feels that only American Indians can tell non-Indians what it is to be Indian. There is no longer any need for non-Indians to "interpret" American Indians for the American public. The same has been said of whites writing about blacks—even of white critics evaluating the work of a black author, but I'm not sure I wholly agree.

I do agree that stereotypes of American Indians should be withdrawn and forgotten. But being Indian does not in itself guarantee someone greater competence in writing about Indians than an outstanding black or white writer who researches the subject thoroughly and writes the total picture. Byler feels that publishers should seek out Indian writers. I agree not only that they should seek out writers for house-engendered projects, but also that they should be constantly receptive to the books of Indian writers. Their chief consideration however must remain a well-written, balanced, and accurate account.

We are now halfway through the 1970s, and still we discuss racism and sexism over and over again. But there is no real action. Some changes occur in the publishing and literary worlds, but frequently backsliding wipes out all positive achievements. Too often we are so pleased that February is Black History Month that we forget that most students never read books by and about blacks during the other eleven months.

In her article "High John Has Risen Again," in *Horn Book* (April 1975), Virginia Hamilton describes how busy she is each February. She also discusses her surprise in learning that many of the students with whom she works and to whom she lectures wouldn't consider reading a black-oriented book on their own. She protests, as I do, the location of Black English in black study departments rather than in English departments. The same problem exists with history. Go into any library and ask for a book on black history. The librarian will go automatically to the 326 shelves where these books are classified. Ask for a book on American history, however, and the librarian will take you straight to the 970 shelves.

It is a subtle distinction, but one which encourages children, teachers, and other adults to isolate the study of blacks and other minorities from the mainstream of American history.

Books about blacks in the armed forces, whether in the Civil War or World Wars I and II are similarly separated. How many knew of Crispus Attucks before the advent of Black History Week? How many teachers and librarians over twenty-five knew anything about Chief Joseph before Xerox's TV special "I Will Fight No More Forever?"

A librarian friend of mine once shocked her supervisor by asking who Benjamin Banneker was, after visiting a Bedford-Stuyvesant school of that name in 1968. She wasn't stupid—she had majored in American history. But in all her years of schooling she had never encountered any other famous blacks than George Washington Carver, Booker T. Washington, and Frederick Douglass.

Fortunately once she discovered this gap in her education, she began to do some independent study in the area. How many others never see this gap or realize the need to fill it? Some must be in publishing—whether as writers, editors, illustrators, or proofreaders.

It has only recently been acknowledged that America's proud melting-pot includes only Europeans. Blacks, Asian-Americans, Mexican-Americans, Native Americans and Puerto Ricans have known this for years. More Americans now recognize the history books do not give them the whole story. S. Carl Hirsch pointed this out in his book, *The Riddle of Racism*, and frightened many who realized that he wrote for children.

Gradually more books are dealing with this educational void. In his *Album of Reconstruction*, William Katz discusses the myths surrounding the Reconstruction period—myths making heroes of the Ku Klux Klan, exaggerating the failures while forgetting the contributions of the public school system, women's rights, and tax laws. There are now biographies of Fidel Castro and his hatred of America, Mao-Tse-Tung, Malcolm X, Jesse Jackson, Fanny Kemble, Abby Kelley Foster, and Frances Wright. There are also praiseworthy series such as Crowell's "Women of America," "Crowell's Biographies," and Franklin Watts' "Picture Life of ——."

But we are celebrating our two hundredth birthday. Why are we only now introducing our children to the truths of American history? Will these truths grow and root out earlier falsehoods, or will they wither and fall back? Look over the recent titles of various publishers and the reactions of reviewers with special concern for racism and sexism. We have good reason to worry.

Virginia Hamilton states:

We need good literature for young people that will bring characters and the past and the present to life through uncontrived situations. I don't care whether this is accomplished through so-called street language or an oneirocritic's nightmares.

She also says:

Our present experience is not one and the same with the oppression of slave time. While we are not wholly free, neither are we totally captured. For never before has black creative intelligence coincided so opportunely with the development of black pride, the advancement of political cultural awareness, independence, and style to affect black art. My assumption . . . is that non-white literature, defined through its diversity, is as American as white.

Her thoughts apply to any American minority—racial or sexual. The same sentiment echoes in Langston Hughes' poetry:

I, too, sing America, I am the darker brother.
(America never was America to me.)

Perhaps someday this second line will no longer reflect the feelings of America's many minorities.

"The Nürnberg Stove" as an Artistic Fairy Tale

Charity Chang

In the 1920s, almost every school child in America knew the story of the Nürnberg stove—mainly because it was one of the Little Blue Books series widely distributed at a nickel apiece. It is an artistic fairy tale, or fantasy, in which Ouida, one of the most prolific and controversial writers of the nineteenth century, intermingles personal elements with those of universal meaning. This appealing tale, rich in motif and meaning, first appeared in 1882 in *Bimbi*, the best-known and perhaps the most successful of Ouida's three collections for children.[1] Described by its author as "the best children's book since *Alice in Wonderland*,"[2] *Bimbi* is a collection of nine stories, each provocative enough for a separate study. The present essay takes up "The Nürnberg Stove," which is, in some respects at least, the most fascinating and complex of the nine.

An artistic fairy tale is the conscious creation of a conscious creator. It is a fantasy with fairy-tale elements. In her creation of "The Nürnberg Stove," Ouida has used the familiar motives of a dangerous journey and the achievement of a near-impossible goal to convey her own personal vision of the relationships of people to themselves and to each other. The stove itself is simply a stage prop, a main ornament if you will, around which Ouida invents detail about a very sensitive young boy and his response to the problems and pressures of life. Little August's fantasy world during his maturation is not radically unlike that of children in any era, or even of adults, for that matter, so if Ouida has done her work well she will bring her protagonist after his long imaginary journey back to the real world and to himself. We shall see.

Let us for a moment consider *Bimbi*, the collection of stories containing "The Nürnberg Stove." Why did Ouida write and publish the stories in *Bimbi*? The answer is twofold. First of all, although she did not normally like children, Ouida made an exception in the case of Bertie Danyell, whose artist mother had done a rather flattering portrait of her. The bond between Bertie and Ouida was undoubtedly genuine, since it was for Bertie that she first invented the charming tales later published in *Bimbi*. Secondly, Ouida, who until her death was possessed of a streak of vanity, was determined to dedicate the published work to a child—no less than the little Italian crown prince who later was to become ex-King Victor Emmanuel III. The copy of *Bimbi* which the little prince received was bound in white vellum and bore a copy of his monogram.

But to return to "The Nürnberg Stove"—why did Ouida write this unusual tale? The answer no doubt lies in the story itself. What then are its themes and what are its meanings? To find answers to these questions one must consider both the story and, to a certain extent, the childhood and personality of its author.

Louise de La Ramée (1839–1908), by preference called Ouida, was herself a fanciful child who continued to live, even in adult life, more "in her fancies than in anything around her" (Bigland, p. 25). She possessed

> an intense feeling for natural beauty, for landscapes, for all things
> that exist out of doors, for wind, for sun and rain. Only a deeply
> introspective child would, as she sometimes had been known to do,
> have brought home from a country walk a stone picked up off
> the road, saying that it was a poor neglected and unloved thing.
> And this she would treat as though it were alive, talking to it,
> endowing it with feelings and treating it as though it had an
> individuality. (Ffrench, p. 11)

And so it is with little August, the protagonist of "The Nürnberg Stove." He, too, is a fanciful child and, like Ouida, introspective— always "thinking, thinking, thinking" (*Bimbi*, p. 20). Surely he treats the Nürnberg stove as if it has feelings (*Bimbi*, p. 16):

> Oh, dear Hirschvogel! you are almost as great and good as the
> sun! No; you are greater and better, I think, because he goes away
> nobody knows where all these long, dark, cold hours, and does
> not care how people die for want of him; but you—you are always
> ready: just a bit of wood to feed you, and you will make a
> summer for us all the winter through!
> The grand old stove seemed to smile through all its irridescent
> surface at the praises of the child. No doubt the stove, though it
> had known three centuries and more, had known very little
> gratitude.

At the time of the story, August Strehla is a small boy of nine years—the fifth of ten children who live with their widowed father in the little town of Hall, Austria. The eldest child, Dorothea, is seventeen; the youngest, Ermingilda, three. Ermingilda's birth cost the Strehla children the life of their mother. The father, a good but weak man, works at the salt furnaces. Discouraged after the death of his

wife, he drinks too much and is otherwise incapable of assuming
the full responsibilities of father and head of the household. Even
so, the children are happy, have enough food, and receive tender
care from the capable and loving Dorothea. The Strehla home,
though sparsely furnished, is clean and warm—warmed in winter by
Hirschvogel, the pride of all the children. Hirschvogel, is, in fact,
the Nürnberg stove, made in 1532 by the greatest potter of Nürnberg, Augustin Hirschvogel. Dug up by grandfather Strehla out of
some ruins where he was building, the stove has warmed three generations of the Strehla family. August is obsessed with the beauty
and majesty of the handsome stove, which had once, no doubt, belonged to royalty.

A full eight feet tall, the stove has the statue of a king at each
corner.

> The body of the stove itself was divided into panels, which had
> all the Ages of Man painted on them in polychrome; the borders

Frontispiece for Louise
de la Ramée, *The
Nürnberg Stove* (Boston:
L. C. Page and
Company, 1897)

of the panels had roses and holly and laurel and other foliage, and German mottoes in black letter of odd Old-World moralizing, such as the old Teutons, and the Dutch after them, love to have on their chimney-places and their drinking-cups, their dishes and flagons. The whole was burnished with gilding in many parts . . . a very grand thing. (*Bimbi*, pp. 16–17)

The Strehla children gather nightly in winter months around the great stove and listen as the nine-year-old August weaves magic stories about men and kings. All the children regard the stove as a living creature, and August, a dreamer of dreams, dreams of the day when he will be a man and make lovely things such as the potter Hirschvogel had done. Further, he will build himself a house in Innspruck and place the beloved stove in a beautiful room in his own house. But alas for the gossamer threads of which dreams are made! Imagine his shock and hurt at hearing his father announce abruptly one evening that he has sold the beautiful stove. To little August, to sell the stove is to sell the life, the joy, the sun, the comfort of all the Strehla family. He pleads, but the father is unrelenting. The stove will go to Munich tomorrow.

It is not difficult to guess that August will find a way to go with the stove, and go with it he does, an incredible journey for a nine-year-old hidden in the belly of the great stove. Safe inside, cold, frightened, and conscience-smitten over the worry his leaving home will cause Dorothea, August takes comfort in the thought that God and Hirschvogel will take care of him. After a day, a night, and another half-day the train carrying the stove with little August inside arrives in Munich. The stove, with August still inside it, is safely unloaded and carted by truck to a small, dark curiosity-shop in the Marienplatz. Here August spends the night, again inside the stove. His night is relieved by dreams through which he imagines the genuine art objects of the curiosity-shop talking with animation about the merits of the genuine versus the imitative, or counterfeit, or worthless bric-a-brac also present in the shop.

The eight or more pages describing the night scene in the curiosity-shop serve as an example of the author's intermixing personal elements with those of universal importance. These pages do not advance the story artistically and could be deleted without any real loss. Their deletion would, in fact, tighten and improve "The Nürnberg Stove." At any rate, after his night of dreaming, August awakens next morning with a wonderful sense of happiness and security about

him. He does not mind so much the next journey. He and the stove
are carried from the curiosity-shop and placed once more on a train,
which carries them southward to Würm-See, from which a boat carries them to Berg. They are unloaded and for a mile and a half
carried by porters to the royal castle of Berg, where the king himself,
opening the brass door of the stove, discovers August.

The scene which follows is a grand one. When August is discovered
in the stove by the king, he is terrified, springs out of the body of the
stove, and falls at the feet of the king. Some of the king's courtiers
seize August but the king speaks kindly: "Poor little child! he is very
young. Let him go; let him speak to me." August does speak, pleads
to stay with Hirschvogel, and tells the king that he wishes to become
a painter like the maker of the Nürnberg stove. The king bids August
stay, promises that he shall be taught to be a painter, and assures
him that, if he does well and bravely, he shall have the coveted stove.
The story ends, but not before revealing that the Strehla family has
been given another stove. August remains with the king, where he is
"a happy scholar and promises to be a great man" (*Bimbi*, p. 74).

In some ways, "The Nürnberg Stove" is a realistic story, no matter
how romantic, exaggerated, and impossible its events may be. However, in a long letter published in *The Times* in 1883 under the head-
ing of "Romance and Realism," Ouida herself gave an apologia, of
sorts, for her lusher novels and—if the reader cares to make such
an interpretation—an explanation for all her writing up to that time:

> I have, I believe, been accused of writing "fairy-stories"; but is
> not life itself very often a fairy-story, if too often, alas! one in
> which the evil genius preponderates and the wishing-cup is
> foolishly used by the unwise? . . . To many of us—to myself, I
> confess, among the number—the world seems a marvellous union
> of tragedy and comedy, which run side by side like twin children:
> like a "web of Tyrian looms" with the gold threads crossing and
> recrossing on the dusky purple of its intricate meshes. . . . I do not
> object to realism in fiction; what I object to is the limitation of
> realism in fiction to what is commonplace, tedious, and bald—
> is the habit, in a word, of insisting that the potato is real and that
> the passion-flower is not. . . . I cannot suppose that my own
> experiences can be wholly exceptional ones, yet I have known very
> handsome people, I have also known some very wicked ones, and
> I have also known many circumstances so romantic that were
> they described in fiction they would be ridiculed as exaggerated
> and impossible. (Bigland, pp. 169–70)

Is not "The Nürnberg Stove" one such fiction? The realist would say so. Yet neither the realist nor the severest critic can invalidate the meaning and value of this hauntingly beautiful story.[3] It is a carefully crafted, artistic fairy tale in which the true subject is the human condition and through which Ouida seeks to portray the real meaning of human existence.

"The Nürnberg Stove" is a story with many themes and several levels of meaning. Marie von Franz states that "the fairy tale is its own best explanation; that is, its meaning is contained in the totality of its motifs connected by the thread of the story."[4] Julius Heuscher feels that "if one had to select any central theme occurring in the majority of fairy tales, it would probably be that of development . . . of a spiritually self-aware individual."[5] Does, then, "The Nürnberg Stove" contain the central theme of the development of a spiritually self-aware individual, and does it contain other motifs which are connected by the thread of the story?

The idea of growing up physically is one of the basic themes in children's literature, as is the conflict between parents and children, and between good and evil. These themes are all present in "The Nürnberg Stove." When good triumphs, the result is spiritual self-awareness and growth. In the process of growing "each individual in his own development is challenged to come to terms, not only with the surrounding physical world, not only with his fellow human beings, but also with his own instinctual drives" (Heuscher, p. 53). The epochs of human evolution are, according to Heuscher, a progressive feeling of loss of unity with spiritual origins, a growing awareness of individual identity in the course of contact with the physical world, and eventual synthesis on a higher plane (Heuscher, pp. 106–7).

Does August Strehla of "The Nürnberg Stove" experience these epochs of evolution? The story itself indicates that he does. It can be argued, of course, that spiritual self-awareness is unlikely to be present in one so young as August, that one cannot have had sufficient contact with the material world to gain any real awareness of one's own identity by the age of nine, and that one is even less likely to feel any loss of identity with spiritual origins while still so young. There appears to be enough evidence in "The Nürnberg Stove" to refute such an argument. In the first place, August's spiritual origins go back to his mother's womb, which furnishes a cocoon, of sorts, for his embryonic soul. Since "The Nürnberg Stove" tells us that August's mother is dead, it may be further surmised that August

Strehla experiences the ultimate in loss of unity with his spiritual origins upon the death of his mother.

Meanwhile, the young August, again unaware of the individuation process at work within him, is developing his own spiritual cocoon which, in its own way, assists him, in the course of his growing contacts with the material world, to gain—even if only still partially in the unconscious—an awareness of his own identity. The story itself provides some specific instances. We notice, for example, August's resolve when in summer he was "high upon the alps with his cattle, with the stillness and the sky around him . . . that he would live for greater things" (*Bimbi*, p. 19). And whether he is at the time conscious of asserting self-identity, certainly he does so when he challenges his father's selling of the Nürnberg stove:

> August sprang to his feet and threw his hair back off his face; the blood rushed into his cheeks, making them scarlet; his great soft eyes flamed alight with furious passion. "You dare not!" he cried, aloud, "you dare not sell it, I say! It is not yours alone; it is ours ————." (*Bimbi*, p. 28)

When the dealer who has purchased it comes to claim the stove, "August sprang erect, his fists doubled, his eyes blazing. 'You shall never touch it!' he screamed; 'you shall never touch it!' " (*Bimbi*, p. 28) August's eventual maturation is achieved through his journey in the stove, which serves as a mother image, the belly of the stove being the womb to which August regresses. The stove both imprisons and saves him. In it he is lonely and isolated, but protected for growth and new life possibilities:

> He curled himself up . . . and being safe inside his dear Hirschvogel and intensely cold, he went fast asleep. . . . When he did awake . . . he was in absolute darkness; and for awhile he was sorely frightened, and trembled terribly . . . but August was brave, and he had a firm belief that God and Hirschvogel would take care of him. The master-potter of Nürnberg was always present to his mind, a kindly, benign, and gracious spirit, dwelling manifestly in that porcelain tower whereof he had been the maker. (*Bimbi*, pp. 38–40)

Many thoughts occur to August while he is within the belly of the stove, and it cannot be denied that his thoughts reflect his child-like fears. Sometimes he even "sobbed in a quiet, heartbroken fashion, thinking of them all at home . . . but it never occurred to him to try and go back" (*Bimbi*, p. 39). Whether his thoughts are child-like or man-like, conscious or unconscious, does not matter. What does matter is that August is incubating to full individuation and self-realization. He is taking a strange winter's journey to eventual synthesis on a higher plane.

An artistic fairy tale ordinarily says something about things as they are, but it must also say something of things as they should be. Ouida comments effectively upon things as they are in "The Nürnberg Stove" through her use of archetypes, a device used by many tellers of tales. In "The Nürnberg Stove" the king is an archetypal Christ figure who discovers ultimately that August's father has been cheated by two dishonest traders, archetypal sinners, who pay two hundred florins for Hirschvogel; the traders in turn sell the stove for two thousand ducats to the king's trusted counsellor in art matters. The counsellor serves as Judas, betraying the king by pretending he has paid eleven thousand ducats for the stove. Both king and counsellor suffer, and the sinners are made to compensate August's father. The king in essence tells them "Go and sin no more," although his actual words to the two traders are: "You are great rogues. Be thankful you are not more greatly punished" (*Bimbi*, p. 73).

The conflict between good and evil has been presented and resolved without sermonizing in "The Nürnberg Stove." The conflict between August and his father has been effectively shown and satisfactorily resolved, and August's own individuation has been conveyed through a tantalizing story characterized by excitement and wonder. Like many other good fairy tales, this artistic creation of Ouida has a happy ending. Both hero and reader are left with the feeling that courage, justice, and love do work after all.

NOTES

1. Louise de la Ramée, "The Nürnberg Stove," *Bimbi: Stories for Children* (London: Chatto & Windus, 1882), pp. 9–75; hereafter cited as *Bimbi* in the text. *Bimbi* was one of three collections of stories for children written by Ouida. Ten years earlier she published *A Dog of Flanders and Other Stories* (London, 1872), a collection read and loved by both John Ruskin and Cardinal Manning (Eileen Bigland, *Ouida, the Passionate Victorian* [New York: Duell, Sloan and Pierce, 1951], p. 76; hereafter cited as Bigland in the text).

2. Yvonne Ffrench, *Ouida: A Study in Ostentation* (New York and London: D. Appleton-Century, 1938), p. 96. Hereafter cited as Ffrench in the text.

3. Carl Van Vechten makes an interesting suggestion in *Excavations* (New York: Knopf, 1926), p. 64: "Indubitably, a new edition of Ouida, on good paper, handsomely printed and bound, with prefaces by a few of her more illustrious admirers, would do much to dispel the current illusion which has it that in reading Ouida one is descending to the depths of English literature. I suspect, indeed, that if Ouida were suitably printed and bound she would

begin to rank not very much below Dickens and Thackeray and considerably above the turgid George Eliot" (Dec. 29, 1921).

4. Marie Louise von Franz, *An Introduction to the Interpretation of Fairy Tales* (New York: Spring Publications, 1970), Section I, p. 7.

5. Julius E. Heuscher, *A Psychiatric Study of Fairy Tales: Their Origins, Meaning, and Usefulness* (Springfield, Ill.: Thomas, 1963), pp. 106–7; hereafter cited as Heuscher in the text.

Fact and Fiction in Natalie Savage Carlson's Autobiographical Stories

A Personal View

Julie Carlson McAlpine

When I was sick in bed as a child, I was treated to nearly an hour of my mother's undivided attention before it was time for me to go to sleep each night. The choice of entertainment was always mine. Usually I would ask my mother, Natalie Savage Carlson, to "tell me about when you were a little girl, Mama." She often reminisced about life at "Shady Grove" and her Visitation Convent boarding school days. It was almost worth being sick to hear about stunt riding on circus horses, and I even felt as if I were the one who rescued her pet doves.

Many years of publishing successful juvenile books about foreign places like Paris and sometimes fantastic characters like the bear Alphonse went by before my mother decided to draw on her own childhood for *The Half Sisters* (New York: Harper, 1970). It closes with the heroine Luvvy leaving the home nest to go to boarding school with her older half sisters. The inconclusive ending almost demanded its sequel, *Luvvy and the Girls* (New York: Harper, 1971). This is how my mother explains what finally inspired her to draw on her own background instead of seeking out new places and plots for her stories:

> Years ago when my editor at Harpers suggested that I write a book based on my childhood, I was completely uninterested. It was much more interesting to visit a colorful, out-of-the-way place and to write about the children I found there. Then, on a trip south, I made a detour to see what Time had done to "Shady Grove," my childhood home in Maryland. The large farmhouse showed a half-century of neglect. Black tar-paper covered the two wings, the green shutters were gone and so were many of the old trees whose shade had given the farm its name. The nearby village of Weverton was being scooped out for a freeway. The Chesapeake and Ohio Canal was only a weed-grown ditch with one of the wooden locks rotting into the ground. The railroad tracks that followed the canal were rusted. There was no trace of the blockhouses which had sheltered poor squatters. No one I contacted in Brunswick, the nearest "big town," knew that horse tournaments had once been held there. I was filled with nostalgia. If only I could bring back that beautiful, rugged region of western Maryland as it had been in the old days! I could and I did. I

wrote *The Half Sisters* and *Luvvy and the Girls* so a way of life gone forever wouldn't be forgotten.

While the books provide an authentic picture of childhood in the colorful locale of Weverton, Maryland, during the early twenties, certain departures from strict factual reporting have necessarily taken place. For example, when my mother supplied the illustrator with snapshots of "Shady Grove" and Frederick Visitation Academy, he drew accurate backgrounds. But since she had no family pictures of that period to give him, Thomas di Grazia created a curly-haired family with a very Italian-looking Papa. My mother observes: "I have noticed that artists prefer to give their own pictorial interpretation to the characters I create." Although members of the Savage family may chuckle over their unaccustomed curls, readers, in any case, like artists, probably imagine the physical appearance of characters for themselves, no matter what they may look like in the mind of an author. Some changes from autobiographical fact, however, my mother introduced with a definite purpose in view.

Luvvy's struggle in *The Half Sisters* is the aspiration of an eleven-year-old girl going on twelve to be grown up. Although she is the oldest of Papa's brood of children by his second wife, she does not wish to be associated with them. Rather, she desperately desires to be accepted by her older half sisters and to join them at boarding school. Actually, by constantly nagging her parents, my mother gained permission to go away to boarding school at the tender age of five. Her acceptance by the Girls was not achieved, as in the story, through the death of her younger sister and her subsequent maturation, but happened as it does to most of us: when young adulthood is reached, brothers and sisters forget about relative ages. This was a key change for my mother in fictionalizing her childhood experiences. By keeping the story within a brief time period, she built a strong plot of related, intertwining events, focused on the universally recognizable theme of pre-adolescent longing to grow up.

My mother and her sisters had been somewhat isolated on the farm, which may account for their clannishness. It also makes plausible Luvvy's difficulty in relating with children of her own age outside the family. Although in reality my mother enjoyed meeting new people and was not shy, she made this Luvvy's big problem to overcome in boarding school. The consequence of this change is to bind the gradual loosening of dependence on the family into the book's central theme by making it a stage in growth to adulthood. Many juvenile readers of our time may not identify with overdependence on the family, but they do know what it is to want and need friends.

The dominant character traits of my mother's sisters are accurately portrayed in the two works. The eldest is the proud family beauty, while the next in line is neat and proper. The youngest half sister has a strong temper, and my mother comes through as sensitive, creative, and strong-willed. Ruling over all is Papa, a domineering father with a mischievous sense of humor. His impact is tempered by cheerful Mama, who smiles more than she frowns and who treats all the children equally. But my mother changed the first names of the characters to show that much about them has been fictionalized. One younger sister was eliminated—or rather combined with another to form a composite. Too many characters can be as distracting to an author as to a reader. No child has yet asked why Luvvy is not named Natalie.

Somewhat surprisingly, my mother made her fictionalized Papa go to church. He actually belonged to no religion, but she felt it wouldn't look right to have the family attending church without him. One doubts that the modern reader would have noted the omission or have been concerned about it. Similarly, Papa's tool-manufacturing business was not Mr. Savage's, but was borrowed from a family friend, since my mother thought a whiskey distillery did not belong in a book for children. Given the current fashions in juvenile fiction, the change was probably unnecessary. My mother suggests, however, that without it readers might have blamed the handyman Sam's alcoholism on Papa's business.

There really was an intemperate Sam, but he was not fired when Luvvy's favorite horse escaped from the pasture and was struck by a train during one of his "toots." To this day my mother cannot remember what final straw caused his dismissal. She used the horse incident to tighten her plot: Luvvy has to deal with the loss of her favorite horse and the kind handyman as a prelude to her sister's death.

Before her illness and subsequent death, Maudie the tagalong is once grudgingly accepted by Luvvy because she helps rescue the wild doves and assists at the funeral of one of them. Maudie asks if the dove will go to heaven. When Luvvy replies that birds don't have souls, Maudie rejoins, "I'll give her a little piece of mine." It was I who said that as a child when my cat Little Mew was to be put to sleep by the veterinarian. My mother says it has always impressed her. Maybe these words of Maudie impress the reader, revealing something of her character in preparation for the later scene when the child herself dies.

The real sister's death was caused by a fall on roller skates instead of a colt's kick; the change makes for more direct involvement of the protagonist Luvvy. Also, Mama was not in fact pregnant at that time with the long-awaited boy; he had already been born. The expectation of the baby adds the excitement and compensation of new life to the first book, while the impact of his birth is reserved for the next volume, where it has greater fictional usefulness. A poor girl's thoughtfulness of baby Clay, for example, moves Luvvy while she is at boarding school; this same girl eventually becomes her best friend.

Real-life Mama did in fact take to her bed in grief over her daughter's death, but it was the family doctor, not the oldest of the Girls, who lured her out of seclusion. Giving the fictional half sister this task made her decision to join the Sisters of Charity much more believeable. Though she actually entered the cloistered Visitation Sisters, my mother transformed her into a Sister of Charity because working with the poor and sick is a more popular idea now than teaching in a fashionable boarding school. Thus young readers are able more easily to perceive the value of the sacrifice.

Many readers laugh when Luvvy forces a proposal of marriage for the oldest sister. This incident is fiction, but one can see why my mother put it in. Besides, she was inspired by her own daughter, who did this to an aunt. When my mother was twelve, the year was 1918 and she lived in California. "I wanted to avoid a World War I background with its complications for Alec," she explains. She even tied up the loose end by providing the next sister for him after the first breaks off the engagement. Avoiding California also enabled her to take advantage of Weverton local color with its supersitions and customs, as when she derived some comedy from having the disagreeable cook call the contaminated milk "hoptoad milk." One of the important features of the setting is the canal. My mother invented her spectator's part in the canal-boat picnic incident in order to describe it, putting the youngest half sister closer to Luvvy and adding one more disappointment for her.

Fewer changes were consciously made in *Luvvy and the Girls* than in *The Half Sisters*. The incident of speaking pig latin instead of French in the refectory is invented, however, my mother having felt that readers would find this humorous and interesting. "Actually," she says, "we didn't talk at all during the French meals." Visiting the School for the Deaf was second-hand material from an older half sister, included for its inherent interest and to show today's children some of the unusual aspects of convent-school life in former times. When Luvvy is selected to recite at the commencement exercises, she reflects, "Ah, the glory of it! But oh, the pain!" Luvvy has purloined one of my own favorite expressions, again because it impressed my mother as true and apt.

Finally, the telescoping of an autobiographical time-scheme into the condensed span of the fiction required some adaptation—and offered some fortunate opportunities. Mother was not writing stories at the academy when she was only five years old. But she was busily turning out romances and tragedies at age twelve, a titiliating consideration for the aspiring authors among her young readers. And Agatha, the charity-student orphan, was really an older girl, not a member of five-year-old Natalie's group. But how often in real life friendship with the homely, nonconformist child is overlooked in favor of the more attractive and glittering one! It seems especially meaningful, therefore, that Agatha's devotion and humor finally help Luvvy become less bound to her family and more involved with the family of man.

Most of the changes my mother made in these stories from the pure recollections she used to regale me with at bedtime have served to tighten their plots, strengthen their thematic implications, and increase the pleasure they bring to young readers—all without falsifying the real life they reflect. A ten-year-old girl who has read many of my mother's books loves *The Half Sisters* and *Luvvy and the Girls* the best. Sara Scott wrote, "They're interesting and exciting. I'd like to go to a boarding school. The convent really seems nice. I know pig latin too; I don't know French though. I love the names Agatha and Amy. I like the part where Luvvy leans over the railing and had to sit on the penance bench and when Betsy ate a pickle in the street and the lady caught her. Commencement week would be fun too." For this reader, who probably represents many, Natalie Savage Carlson has indeed recaptured an era and a way of life.

The International Scene
in Children's Literature

Down with Heidi, Down with Struwwelpeter,
Three Cheers for the Revolution
Towards a New Socialist Children's Literature in West Germany

Jack Zipes

Ever since the rise of the student movement in West Germany during the late 1960s, there has been a growing interest in socialist children's literature. Radical students quickly recognized that the struggle against arbitrary authority as a manifestation of monopoly capitalism would be a long one and that the power of authority not only lay in the control of the government and economic process but was also deeply rooted in the control over child rearing and the education system.[1] In fact, a large segment of the New Left soon sought to recover its links to the rich socialist tradition of the 1920s to gain a better perspective on the present. Students and professors alike turned to studying psychology (Wilhelm Reich, Vera Schmidt, Max Adler, Siegfried Bernfeld) and progressive pedagogy (Makarenko, Otto Rühle, Edwin Hoernle, Otto Kanitz) in order to locate stages where critical and creative thinking might be instilled which would lead to the development of socialist individuals—that is, people who would grow to become masters of their own destiny and history in a morally and socially responsible manner. The formation of socialist daycare centers, women's groups, youth centers, and university workshops led to the production of significant new studies about children's education and culture.[2] Most important, it brought about the production of new materials which could be used to further socialist education.

The progress in children's education has been remarkable. Not only have there been innovative research studies exploring child psychology, literature, theater, play, and schooling, all of which have led to the development of concrete forms of emancipatory cooperation, but the new fiction that has risen has begun to alter and challenge the more conservative children's books which have dominated the market. Since the upsurge of an expressly *socialist* children's literature is almost unique among Western capitalist countries, it is important that we take note of it, for the transformation of children's literature in West Germany can open possibilities for a richer children's literature in America. Certainly it will call our traditional views into question. Since it is extremely difficult to give a complete historical picture of the far-reaching changes in West German children's literature, I shall limit myself to a discussion of three major points: (1) the socialist critique of the classics, particularly *Heidi* and *Struwwelpeter*; (2) the production of new anti-authoritarian and socialist books by three different, representative publishing houses, Basis, Weismann, and Rowohlt; (3) the prospects for a new socialist children's literature.

The Socialist Critique of Classical German Children's Literature

The term "classical" is a difficult one to define, especially when discussing children's literature, since children do not determine what books they want to read, nor are they encouraged to evaluate and produce them. Classical children's books are essentially those standard works which have been selected by adults in part of a historical socialization process, and therefore they correspond greatly to the aesthetic tastes and moral standards of a particular adult world. For the most part, they convey a distinct image of the world to children and foster the ideological hegemony of ruling-class interests. Looked at from a historical-materialist point of view, classical children's books are vital instruments in the formation of class consciousness, aesthetic sensibility, and character structure.

It is clear that not every classical children's book serves repressive ends. Nor is there a conscious plan to produce books which nullify the potential for creativity and critical thinking in children. Every children's book must be looked at historically to determine its real aesthetic and ideological value. Here many factors must be taken into consideration. Generally speaking, a book for children should aim to render a clear and interesting picture of an epoch or topic with all its contradictions and speak to children's problems truthfully so that they can learn to master these problems and develop their own identity. The communicative function of the language and images should help the child improve his or her learning ability and creative potential. Restricted codes and closed reference systems should be avoided. Each new book should try to incorporate the most recent pedagogical and psychological discoveries about education and so-

ciety in order to increase the emancipatory value of the book. By
this I mean that the structure and contents of a children's book
should be geared, no matter how fantastic the subject matter and
style, toward helping children understand how to work together to
free their own individual talents and to overcome obstacles which
may be preventing their free development. In this respect the entire
question of book production and the reception of a book must be
reconsidered to include the participation of children in the entire
process. Ultimately, if this is done, the term classical will take on
another, more authentic meaning.

No doubt, some classical books deserve their status because they
were written to speak, and continue to speak, to children's *real* needs.
Most have unfortunately retained classical status because they are
still useful in the indoctrination of children to the standards of a
ruling class and also serve the market needs of the book industry.
It is from this historical-materialist perspective, then, one which
corresponds to the socialist critique of the New Left in West Germany,[3] that I shall be using the term classical, and here the two
books *Struwwelpeter* and *Heidi* are perfect models of the classical
German children's book. Not only have all children in German-
speaking countries from the late nineteenth century to the present
been predominantly influenced by these two books, but children in
America as well.

Struwwelpeter was written in 1844 by the physician Heinrich Hoffmann, who could not find an appropriate book for his three-year-old
son and decided to write his own, based on stories he used to tell
his young patients to prevent them from becoming disruptive and
getting upset.[4] Soon after the book was published in 1845, it grew
in popularity. Up through 1974 there have been over six hundred
different German editions and numerous translations, not to mention
the hundreds of imitations and parodies. There is hardly a German
adult or child who does not know that Struwwelpeter is everything
one is not supposed to become, the model of the disobedient child
who never cuts his fingernails and lets his hair grow wild—in short,
a barbarian. The rhymed, illustrated stories which follow our introduction to him present a composite picture of Struwwelpeter: evil
Peter, who tortures animals and people with a whip, and who is
finally bitten by a dog and put to bed; little Pauline, who plays with
matches and burns herself to death; three boys who make fun of a
Negro and are then dipped in black ink as punishment by a stern
adult; the wild hunter, who loses his rifle and is shot by a rabbit;

Konrad the thumb-sucker, who has his thumbs cut off because he persists in sucking; Kaspar, who wastes away to nothing because he refuses to eat his soup; Phillip, who is smothered by a tablecloth because he will not sit still at the table; Robert, who goes out into a storm and is carried away forever by a huge wind; Hans, who never watches where he walks and almost drowns while walking near a pond. All the stories are written to frighten the young reader, and the illustrations are correspondingly gruesome and terrifying. (Adults generally find them comical.) Only one of the stories involves a little girl. As always, the assumption is made that little girls are more docile and obedient than little boys, who are terrors. Hoffmann's picture of what a little boy is and how he should be treated is an accurate reflection of the general *Biedermeier* (Victorian) attitude toward children: "Little children are to be seen, not heard," and if they are heard, they are to be punished severely.

The danger of *Struwwelpeter* and its imitations stems from the fact that it can be easily comprehended by children from age two on and has indeed stamped the consciousness of German children for generations.[5] To a great extent, it reflects a peculiar hostility to children (what Germans call *Kinderfeindlichkeit*)[6] which has been a disturbing element in the history of German civilization. *Struwwelpeter* glorifies obedience to arbitrary authority, and in each example the children are summarily punished by the adult world. No clear-cut reasons are given for the behavior or the punishment; discipline is elevated above curiosity and creativity. It is not by chance, then, that this book has retained its bestseller, classical status to the present. Whether it will be superseded by the most recent parody, *Der Anti-Struwwelpeter* by Friedrich Karl Waechter, will depend on the general development of the new socialist children's literature.[7]

Heidi, Lehr- und Wanderjahre was written by the Swiss author Johanna Spyri in 1880.[8] Again, we are dealing with a classic that has gone through hundreds of editions and translations and has had an international effect difficult to measure. In addition, there have been several film versions. In 1937, Shirley Temple played Heidi in a sentimental Hollywood production. The other films were made in 1951 (Swiss), 1965 (Austrian), and 1967 (German-American, with Michael Redgrave and Maximilian Schell). There have also been records, an opera, and an American musical based on the book. Like *Struwwelpeter*, *Heidi* is a conservative product of the nineteenth century which has been kept very much alive in the twentieth. Spyri, a devout Christian, projects a vision of a harmonious world which can only be held together by Judeo-Christian ethics and God himself. Briefly, her story concerns a five-year-old orphan, Heidi, who is sent to live on top of a Swiss mountain with her grandfather, a social outcast. After three years, her aunt, who works in Frankfurt, comes to fetch her so that she can become a companion to a rich little girl who is crippled. Both the aunt and the rest of the Swiss village think it will be better for Heidi, for they have a low opinion of the grandfather and feel that Heidi needs to be educated. For the grandfather, who has come to love Heidi deeply, this is a devastating blow, and he becomes more of a misanthrope. In Frankfurt, Heidi turns a wealthy bourgeois household upside down with her natural ways, which are contrasted with the artificial and decadent ways of the city people. Nevertheless, she endears herself to the grandmother, Klara the cripple, the businessman father, and their servants. Only the governess and teacher cannot grasp her "wild" ways. Eventually, Heidi becomes homesick for the mountains, and Klara's grandmother tells her to have faith in God, who will always help her. Indeed, as Heidi begins to wane, God interferes in the person of the doctor, who advises the businessman to return Heidi to the grandfather. When Heidi is sent back to the mountains, the grandfather is ecstatic and becomes convinced that it was an act of God which brought about the return of his granddaughter. In this sense, Heidi is God's deputy and reconciles the grandfather to the rest of the community.

Although there are abridged versions for younger children, *Heidi* was essentially written for the child ten and over. Quite opposite to *Struwwelpeter*, it concerns the experiences of a little girl, who is made into some kind of an extraordinary angel, a nature child with holy innocence, incapable of doing evil, gentle, loving, and kind. At first, she does not comprehend the world, but as she grows, everything is explained to her according to the accepted social and religious norms of the day. Here it is important to see the pedagogical purpose of the narrative and its dependence on the traditional *Bildungsroman*. Heidi learns that the world is static and directed by God. Although she is disturbed that her grandfather and relatives are poor and must struggle merely to subsist, the grandmother in Frankfurt brings her to believe that God wants it that way and that material poverty is insignificant when one considers the real meaning of richness: to be rich means *possessing* faith in God and behaving like a good Christian—that is, making sacrifices to benefit the wealthy and looking forward to paradise in the world hereafter. While the simple, pious community of the Swiss village is contrasted with the false, brutal life in the city, Spyri does nothing to explain the real contradictions between city and country. The hard life in the Swiss mountains becomes idyllic. There the people are pure and closer to God. The world of Switzerland caters to the escapist tendencies of readers who might seek release from the perplexing, difficult conditions of urban life. Heidi, too, is a figure of the infantile, regressive fantasy which desires a lost innocence that never was. Since *natural* equals *Christian* in this book, there is no way in which children can comprehend what really is a natural or socially conditioned drive.[9] Nevertheless, Heidi, like Struwwelpeter, has taken on a classical existence that has become more lifelike than that of real Heidis, and she continues to serve as a (dubious) model for young readers. In both instances, the classical stature of the books is closely linked to their commodity value.

ANTI-AUTHORITARIAN AND SOCIALIST CHILDREN'S LITERATURE

It is in opposition to classical books like *Struwwelpeter* and *Heidi* and in keeping with broad socialist goals that books like Waechter's *Der Anti-Struwwelpeter*[10] have come into existence. Since the recent production of anti-authoritarian and socialist children's literature depends heavily on the policies of collectives and publishing firms, three typical organizations and their products will serve as examples to illustrate the general tendencies in this field. The three are Basis, Weismann, and Rowohlt.

Basis Verlag, like Oberbaum and Das rote Kinderbuch,[11] developed from a collective which worked in daycare and youth centers during the late 1960s and has continued this work, largely in Berlin. The members of Basis are socialists, who see their task as preparing the *base* for a new socialist society. Their main emphasis is on the production of books for children between the ages of four and twelve, although they have also produced a comic book and photographic story for apprentices who work in factories.[12] To date, they have published over fourteen books for children, all of which tend to deal with the contemporary scene and social conditions in a realistic manner. In 1973 they also began publishing a complementary series of theoretical studies which either demonstrate how to use their own children's books or deal with general problems such as the ideological contents of pictures and illustrations and the real meaning of comic book heroes.[13]

The Basis books for children were developed at a time when the anti-authoritarian phase of the New Left was coming to an end in

West Germany—that is, the phase when arbitrary authority was defied for the sake of defying authority. Though there are some anti-authoritarian elements in Basis books, their main goal is to demonstrate how working collectively can lead to a greater sense of oneself and the world and to the resolution of problems confronting children in their everyday lives. Six of the works written between 1970 and 1974 will give an example of the aims and production methods of the Basis Verlag: *Die Geschichte von der Verjagung und Ausstopfung des Königs* (The Story about How the King Was Chased Out and Stuffed); *Zwei Korken für Schlienz* (Two Corks for Schlienz); *Krach auf Kohls Spielplatz* (Trouble at Kohl's Playground); *Die Kleine Ratte kriegt es raus* (The Little Rat Gets to the Bottom of Things); *Krokodil* (Crocodile); and *Die Krügelsteiner und die Räuber* (The People of Krügelstein and the Robbers).

Die Geschichte von der Verjagung und Ausstopfung des Königs is introduced by a statement telling how the book was produced: "Karin wrote the story for you. Then we called up our friends and asked them if they would like to dress up and play a knight, poet, king, or bear. And when they all said yes, then we acted out the entire story, and Ute photographed us. Dieter and Reiner printed the pictures and the story, and in the end, the bookbinders made the book into a real book."[14] The statement also says that Mome painted the bear into the pictures and asks the readers to send in their comments. The story concerns two poets who want to write a book for children but really don't know children all that well. Both think up traditional stories: one deals with a bear who is big and strong and goes fishing, and the other, with a loyal knight who departs to fight for his king. The two stories come together as the bear meets the knight in the woods. They decide to go play with the children in the local neighborhood (set in the present) instead of fishing and fighting. The poets become angry that their heroes have abandoned their traditional roles and story-lines and go searching for them. They come across some knights who, sent by the king to fight against the peasants, have been soundly defeated. The poets complain that this normally does not happen in stories, but the knights argue that something is wrong with the usual stories since the peasants had never harmed them—that is, until the king had sent them to destroy the peasants. They all decide to turn against the king, and with the help of the bear, the loyal knight, and the children, they capture the king, stuff him, and set him up as a monument in a park as a warning to all monarchs. The country then belongs to everyone and is renamed country of the knights, peasants, poets, bears, and children. Here the traditional manner of telling fairy tales which glorify feudalism is criticized in a novel way. The subtle use of photographs and comics adds to the Brechtian estrangement effect, which prompts children to think critically and creatively throughout the story. The main difficulty with the narrative is that the social message and aesthetic innovations are perhaps too complex for a child to understand alone.

In the second edition of *Zwei Korken für Schlienz*, the collective states that changes were made in keeping with the criticism of children. This story uses only photographs and combines elements from well-known folktales to illustrate housing problems in the city. Four young people (all in their twenties) decide to live together: Schlienz, who can smell extraordinarily well; Minzl, who can hear long distances; Gorch, who can run faster than cars; and Atta, who is tremendously strong. They rent an apartment, and the landlord tries to cheat them. However, they are too smart for him, and ultimately they set up a collective household which runs smoothly until the landlord raises the rent arbitrarily. The four decide to organize the tenants in the entire building to fight and protest the hike in rent, and they use their extraordinary talents to unite the tenants and take over the building. However, since the people come from different classes (a teacher, bank clerk, metal worker, insurance inspector, and railroad worker) and have different interests, the landlord is able to play upon the divisiveness in the coalition and, with the help of the police, defeat the strike. Schlienz, Minzl, Gorch, and Atta are arrested. Nevertheless, while in prison, they reconsider their strategy and make plans so that they can be successful the next time they try to organize the tenants. The book closes with a series of newspaper articles about landlords cheating tenants. The photographs in this story combine humor with accurate depictions of housing conditions. The remarkable talents of the heroes are not so fantastic that they might lead children to have unreal expectations of their own powers. The fact that the four heroes (two men and two women) do not succeed shows to what extent the authors clearly understand the stage of the social struggle within the cities. Here the emphasis is not so much on gaining a victory but on creating a sense of need for collective action.

A similar story for somewhat older children, *Die Kleine Ratte kriegt es raus*, deals with Renate Müller, about ten, who does not understand why her father, a sanitation worker, earns less than

Doctor Gruschwitz, the father of a friend, nor why she and her family must live in such cramped quarters compared to the huge apartment of the Gruschwitzes. When she goes on a quest to find out the answers, information about salaries, work conditions, rents, and social classes is conveyed to her and, of course, to the readers. This information is incorporated into the story through questions, comics, photographs, and charts. After numerous adventures, Renate and two friends come across two young factory workers who spend time with them to clarify everything and who explain that the social contradictions can only be overcome by workers who learn to trust one another and cooperate to take over the means of production. Only through this type of action will the social disparities that confront Renate during the day be eliminated.

Krach auf Kohls Spielplatz is for three-year-olds. Andrea is troubled by Theo Kohl, who controls the playground because his father is rich and owns the construction company which employs most of the parents living in the housing settlement and neighborhood. Theo manages to bribe Joachim, the strongest boy, with candy to act as "law enforcer"—that is, until Andrea and the other children get together and unite to defeat Theo and Joachim and set up mutually beneficial rules of play. Though the book is instructive in pointing out the link between a bully and the possession of money, the language and pictures of the story are so devoid of imagination that the message will have only a minimal effect upon young readers.

This is not the case with *Krokodil*, written for and by five-year-olds. The book is a sort of documentary children's story, for it is based on a newspaper article about seven African children, who save one of their comrades with their bare hands from being devoured by a crocodile. When the article was read to children in a preschool class and then discussed, the children reacted positively to the manner in which the African children united to protect their friend from the crocodile at the risk of their own lives. At one point the teacher introduced the idea of doing a picture book about this story together. The children were skeptical since they knew nothing about book production, but the teacher explained how books were put together and encouraged the children so that they realized it was possible to make their own book. After the children drew pictures and helped compose a text, they selected which pictures were to appear as illustrations. The result: a unique book, with startling, colorful, and concrete pictures about collective action which reinforces not only the concept of solidarity but displays as well how the collective skills of children can be practically put to use to develop their own awareness of socially responsible action.

Die Krügelsteiner und die Räuber, written by Jochen Unbehauen for six-year-olds, develops this theme in an amusing tale with colorful illustrations by Günther Schwartz that correspond to each dramatic situation and are edifying at the same time. Krügelstein is a tiny village tucked away in the mountains and inhabited by three families who make pottery and sell their wares once a week in a town in order to support themselves. For the three children of the families, Franz, Alois, and Maria, Krügelstein is boring, at least until three robbers arrive to terrorize the village. Since there is no money to steal, the robbers decide to force the Krügelsteiners to produce more pottery so that there will be a surplus to provide them with money and luxuries. However, the robbers soon realize that they will have to organize production differently and build machines if the Krügelsteiners are to increase their productivity. They invent new ways to improve production and distribution, and the Krügelsteiners learn a great deal and triple their output. Yet, they are not happy because all the profits go to the robbers, who use their weapons to intimidate the villagers. Finally, the children, who are also forced to labor in a manner which they dislike, devise a plan to capture the robbers. They succeed, and instead of sending the robbers to jail, the Krügelsteiners teach the robbers how to make pottery and begin to take advantage of the new socialized means of production which will enable them to share and enjoy their work in such a way that their living conditions in general will be improved. The remarkable feature of this story is that it explains the aspects of robbery stemming from capitalist production in a concrete, humorous manner without becoming heavily theoretical. Not only does the critique of the robbers' capitalist exploitative methods stem naturally from the forced working conditions of the Krügelsteiners, but the positive gains of socialized production brought about by the robbers are also shown to be necessary for the Krügelsteiners' welfare. When these socialized means of production are taken over by the Krügelsteiners collectively, they become more liberated and happy. The clear descriptions and explicit language of the narrative enhance the emancipatory value of this story, which is geared toward enabling young readers to understand the work process as a form of liberation.

Generally speaking, Basis books are directly related to the actual class struggles in West Germany. The major figures are from the working class, and the contents of the stories are, broadly speaking, of utmost concern to the underprivileged in society and lead to developing class consciousness. Some of the stories tend to be too didactic as if the significance of the message itself were enough to strike the imagination of children. Obviously, this is a failing which Basis of late has been attempting to rectify. For the most part, the language of the books is vigorous and blunt; colloquialisms and curses are used because children are accustomed to hearing them in their surroundings—used to explain their surroundings. The authors do not talk down to the children. They employ a great deal of irony in the depictions, and the techniques of photography, comics, and montage dialectically enhance the communicability of the theory. The books are children's books in that the production is geared to a child's standpoint and in that children often participate in the production. At the same time, the books also transcend the category of "children" or "childish," for adults can learn and enjoy in producing and reading them.

The books of Weismann Verlag[15] also point in this direction. A socialist collective which is not as active as the Basis Verlag in day-care and youth centers, the Weismann group has published over ten books, mainly by teenagers. The Weismann books are not as directly concerned with immediate German social problems. One book, *Herr Bertolt Brecht sagt* (Mr. Bertolt Brecht Says, 1970), is a collection of anecdotes, stories, and poems by Brecht. Another book, *Kinderstreik in Santa Nicola* (The Children's Strike in Santa Nicola, 1970) by Günter Feustel, deals with the exploitation of Italian children in the farm region of Sicily. *Russische Kindheit* (Russian Childhood, 1972) by Arkadi Gaidar, a well-known author of children's books, is an autobiographical account of his experiences as a boy during the Russian Revolution. *Eltern Spielen, Kinder Lernen* (Parents Play, Children Learn, 1972) by Wolfram Frommlet, Hans Mayhofer, and Wolfgang Zacharias is a handbook mainly for adults about how to start community groups which want to create better play conditions for children. *Wir sind zornig und böse* (We Are Angry and Mad, 1972), edited by Nadine Lange, contains reports by black children about slum conditions in the United States.

In general, the Weismann Verlag is more concerned with explaining social issues to teenagers and explicating socialist theories. The following three books are most typical of their general policy: *Kinderbuch für kommende Revolutionäre* (A Children's Book for Future Revolutionaries, 1970) by Ernst Herhaus; *Wie eine Meinung in einem Kopf entsteht* (How Opinions Originate in Your Head,

1971) by E. A. Rauter; *Von einem der auszog und das Fürchten lernte* (About Someone Who Went Out and Learned about Fearing, 1970) by Günter Wallraff.

Herhaus' book begins with a story about Poppie Hollenarsch, young daughter of an old-time Communist, who has become a drunkard and a cynic because the times are against him. Consequently, Poppie is neglected and flounders. She decides that the only way to survive in a capitalist society is by selling oneself. So, she becomes a prostitute. At one point she meets a radical who takes a sincere interest in her and promises to explain to her what enlightenment means and why she is a victim of capitalism. The stories and anecdotes which follow are written in a blunt, crass manner and deal with the author's attempts to write a children's book while at the same time indirectly answering Poppie's questions by showing how children themselves must think dialectically and enlighten themselves about social conditions so that they will acquire the skills and knowledge to change the social system.

Rauter is even more theoretical in his book. His major thesis is that individuals are made in schools, that is, through education which consists of the home, movies, television, theater, radio, newspapers, books, and posters. Just as an object is made by an instrument, so is an individual, and the instrument which makes him/her is information. Consequently, whoever controls the instruments of information is able to control mankind's consciousness and action. Using concrete examples, Rauter explains how the media and schools produce conformists and nonthinkers. With each point he makes, he draws closer to his conclusion that we all must turn the education process around so that we can control our lives and prevent further production of passive, perverse human beings.

Günter Walraff's book is the most explicit example of how one can actually bring about changes in West German society. Wallraff is a type of Ralph Nader, with the exception that Wallraff has dealt with exposing the sordid conditions in factories and business firms by working in them. Over the past seven years (often with the help of pseudonyms and disguises) he has held jobs in different plants and firms throughout West Germany and has revealed the exploitative methods of capitalists. His book is a report about his activities which begins with a description in diary form of how he was maltreated by the army as a conscientious objector and how he then worked at different factories, wrote for newspapers, and was subjected to harassment by big industry and the government. The book closes with an account of how workers took over a glass factory in Immenhausen, prevented it from going bankrupt, and now run it collectively—a model for workers' control.

All three of these Weismann books are noteworthy for the respect they pay teenagers. Words are not minced. These books are written in a clear, intelligible language which makes the theory and connections drawn to the social realities comprehensible for young readers. Sparse illustrations, generally photographic montages, are used effectively to reveal existing contradictions in society. All Weismann books lay great emphasis on authenticity and documentation. Many are limited in their appeal to a young progressive intelligentsia because of their abstract quality, but their socialist perspective and edifying aspect provide a basis within the material itself for readers of all social classes to understand the theoretical arguments. In this sense, the difficulty presented by the Weismann publications lies not so much in the books themselves as in the educational system which restricts the use of such books in the classroom.

Due to the efforts of Weismann, Basis, Oberbaum, Das rote Kinderbuch, März, Luchterhand, Melzer, and several other smaller publishing houses, some of the larger liberal firms such as Ellermann[16] and Kindler[17] have included anti-authoritarian or socialist books in their lists of children's books. Most notably, Rowohlt Verlag, one of the largest and best houses in West Germany, has started a series called Rotfuchs (Red Fox) under the general editorship of Uwe Wandrey. The series began in April 1972, and well over sixty inexpensive paperbacks with superb artwork and photography have been published since then. Most of the authors are already well known in West Germany. It is to Wandrey's credit that he has encouraged authors and artists who normally work for the adult world only to concern themselves with children's needs. The general policy of Rotfuchs is one of cultural pluralism. That is, the series contains books which range in their critique of society from mildly reformist to socialist. The age groups addressed are anywhere from five to fourteen. Some of the books are limited in their appeal to a distinct age group, whereas others cut across age and social class differences. Here are brief summaries of seven books which will convey an impression of the spectrum of this series.

Angela Hopf's *Die grosse Elefanten Olympiade* (The Great Elephant Olympics, 1972, ages 5–8) is a critique of the do-or-die achievement ethos of sports, especially the Olympics. With amusing, unusual illustrations of elephants competing against one another,

Hopf brings out in her narrative how sports can be fun. Friedrich Karl Waechter's *Tischlein deck dich und Knüppel aus dem Sack* (Table, Be Covered, and Stick, Out of the Sack, 1972, ages 6–11) is a remarkable modern version of the Grimms' fairy tale. Here a young man invents a table cloth and a magic stick which are expropriated by a factory owner in order to intimidate the workers and hold them in his power. However, the young inventor joins with his fellow-workers, who had participated in the development of the inventions, to foil the owner's plot. In the end, they take charge of the factory and their own lives. Here, too, the illustrations are pertinent, subtle, and comical. Waechter has also illustrated a selection of the Grimms' fairy tales, *Der kluge Knecht* (The Smart Knave, 1972, ages 5–9) with an important afterword by Wandrey about the social content of fairy tales. Rüdiger Stoye's book *Der Dieb XY* (The Thief XY, 1972, ages 7–12) involves a boy who decides to hunt for the thief XY after watching a television program which actually exists in West Germany and posts rewards for the capture of criminals. After he mistakenly paints XY on people whom he suspects to be criminal, the young boy is severely punished by his parents. Consequently, he decides to run away, and he comes across a mysterious stranger in the woods who helps and comforts him. The stranger turns out to be the wanted thief, with whom the boy decides to live until both are captured by the police. Here the illustrations are stark and photogenic. There is no preaching, but the boy learns that there is another side to criminality than that which he views on television. Günter Herburger's *Helmut in der Stadt* (Helmut in the City, 1972, ages 6–10) is about a young boy who is supposed to look after his sister while his parents work. He has a quarrel with her, and she disappears. Helmut goes looking for her and winds up by exploring the entire city, which becomes his playground. After several hours of seeing different aspects of city life, Helmut returns home only to find that his sister had been hiding in the cellar. Both promise not to upset their parents by telling what happened during the day. The story is filled with photos of Helmut in the city that depict social and work conditions. Helmut is pictured neither as cute nor heroic, but rather curious and alert. He responds to an emergency situation with remarkable calm and understanding. Hellmuth Costard's *Herberts Reise ins Land der Uhren* (Herbert's Journey to the Country of the Clocks, 1974, ages 5–8) is filled with lively illustrations picturing Herbert in situations where he learns how compulsive and murderous people become under the pressure of time. In this sense the journey is beneficial because Herbert (and the young reader as well) realizes that time cannot be allowed to control his life. *"Mein Vater ist aber stärker!"* ("My Father's Stronger than Yours!" 1974, ages 6–10) is a collection of sketches, stories, and anecdotes by students of the school of education in Hamburg, based on their practice teaching in youth homes and schools. The main intent of the stories is to demonstrate how children learn through conflict and that serious conflicts dominate their lives, which are not as rosy as most children's books portray or adults think. This theme is continued in Heike Hornschuh's *Ich bin 13* (I'm 13, 1974, ages 12 and up) recorded by Simone Bergmann, with photographs of Heike, her family, and friends. Here a young girl gives a candid account of her life and views of family, sex, society, the role of women, and her possibilities for a career. The remarkable feature of this narrative is that it offsets most of the clichés about young girls, for Heike shows herself to be extremely conscious of the underprivileged role she has as female, and her efforts to overcome the obstacles which hinder her full development are by any measure exemplary.

The advantage of the left-liberal policy of the Rotfuchs series is also its disadvantage. The Rotfuchs books speak to many different audiences and propose various alternatives to the existing social system. Some indicate revolution, some reform. Some see change coming about by developing the creative and cognitive faculties of children while others seek to raise class consciousness. The mode of portrayal ranges from the parable, fable, and surreal to the realistic and documentary. The language is generally high German, although slang is used. Dialects are avoided. All classes of children are lumped together, and no overall didactic goal can be ascertained, except to say that the series wants to teach critical thinking. This is its disadvantage since many of the books in the series contradict one another and are at odds in their fundamental educational goals. Without a clear-cut policy, the books will be consumed indiscriminately by children who will learn to tolerate different views but not really learn how to think critically in a social context and historical manner.

PROSPECTS FOR A NEW SOCIALIST CHILDREN'S LITERATURE

There can be no doubt that the new socialist children's books are changing the style and contents of children's books published by the more liberal and conservative firms. The socialist books have been especially influential in several ways. They use plain, everyday language which corresponds to that most familiar to both children and adults. It is intelligible and clear but not childish and simplistic, and it serves to enhance the learning ability of the readers, not to compensate for inadequate education. Story-lines address themselves to actual problems in present-day Germany. Boys and girls are treated as equals, and traditional role-playing is brought into question. The heroes and the heroines are the collective. Emphasis is placed on struggle and solidarity. The perspective of the story is a general socialist one. The resolution of problems is not made easy, for there is no happy end. Photographs and comics are used in unique ways to convey a clear picture of social conditions and contradictions. The art work is subtle and fosters original thinking and appreciation. Socialist theory helps clarify the social disparities encountered by children in concrete situations. The production of the books is geared to the reception by children. An earnest attempt is made by the producers either to involve children in the production process or to write books which pertain to the interests of children and stimulate class consciousness and solidarity.[18]

For the most part, socialist children's literature pays a great deal of attention to the production of books in relation to pedagogical praxis. As Dieter Richter has noted,[19] the books serve to bring together adults and children and to promote a common critical and creative activity. These books are not to be consumed and forgotten, but to be discussed and used as tools for the development of each participant's full abilities. Some of the contributions and innovations made by socialist children's literature are not new, and some will be appropriated by the more conservative literature. Nevertheless, the socialist children's literature is forcing producers of children's literature in general to grow up and respect the intelligence of children and deal with their problems in earnest instead of writing the usual condescending, unreal, and trivial stories. Here the positive effect of socialist children's literature is clear. But will it survive?

Aside from the fact that fewer and fewer people read in West Germany, the socialist children's literature tends to appeal mainly to children of the progressive intelligentsia, or, in other words, the children of the producers. This dilemma can only be solved as more contact with educational institutions and the working classes is established. As Beate Scheunemann points out, socialist children's literature can only become effective if it is part of practical agitation, which means class struggle at the schools.[20] Here it appears that socialist children's literature will have to wage a long battle before it is accepted as part of the general school program. The reason for this, as Oskar Negt and Alexander Kluge have remarked, is that:

> the public sphere of children like the public sphere of the proletariat has the tendency to include the totality of society. It does not allow itself to be organized in small groups. When children attempt to organize for themselves and herein regulate their lives, it cannot be their intention to pay for their freedom of space by completely withdrawing from reality and withdrawing from the adult world, which is the prime link to the source of all objects together and to the children. Therefore, the public sphere of children cannot be brought about without a material public sphere which connects the parents, and without public spheres of children at all levels and in all classes of society which are able to be brought into contact with one another. . . . Self-organization and self-regulation of children will be just as vehemently disputed by all kinds of authoritarian interests as is the self-organization of the proletariat. Whoever thinks that the public sphere of children is a grotesque idea will have difficulty conceiving what the public sphere of the proletariat really is.[21]

Negt and Kluge argue that the public sphere has historically become dominated and institutionalized mainly by the bourgeoisie, and there is no sector of public education, communication, assembly, production, or distribution which does not serve the interests of this ruling class. For society to become truly free, democratic, and socialist, they assert that a proletarian public sphere must be created so that people will become aware of their own genuine material needs and desires and the ways to fulfill these needs and desires. This means an intrusion into the bourgeois public sphere. In this regard, a children's literature which truly speaks to the material needs and desires of children, whether it be expressly socialist or democratic, must by necessity contradict and challenge the bourgeois public sphere. By earnestly attempting to establish a children's viewpoint—a public sphere of children—it immediately aligns itself with proletarian interests (i.e., the interests of the majority of the people) seeking to push for social democratic changes.

The question is whether the children's public sphere can actually emerge and make itself felt, which is a question of organization and distribution. Concomitantly there is a problem of co-optation, whereby the bourgeois public sphere appropriates the new forms developed in behalf of children (and the proletariat). To be more precise, most of the books produced by Basis and Weismann are handled by radical bookstores or are sold through the mail.[22] The standard bookstores do not distribute them, nor are they awarded prizes by the established children's book committees.[23] This again limits the audience for socialist children's literature to the initiates. The real success of socialist children's literature will depend ultimately on who controls the market for children's books. Though the immediate prospects for socialist children's literature are not rosy, a struggle has commenced which suggests that the days of the "classics" are numbered and that literature for children will make more sense and be more lively. This struggle will not be settled overnight, and the new socialist children's literature reflects this. In this respect, its ultimate worth will depend on how we in the West (not only in West Germany) value the future we glimpse in the eyes of our children.

NOTES

1. See my article, "Educating, Miseducating, and Re-educating Children: Attempts to Desocialize the Capitalist Socialization Process," *New German Critique*, 1 (Winter 1973), 142–59.

2. There has been such a prodigious output of noteworthy studies that it would take a small pamphlet to list them all. Some of the more important ones are: Johannes Beck et al., *Erziehung in der Klassengesellschaft* (Munich, 1970); Claus Biegert and Diethard Wies, *Kinder sind kein Eigentum* (Munich, 1973); Jörg Claus, Wolfgang Heckman, and Julia Schmitt-Ott, *Spiel in Vorschulalter* (Frankfurt/M, 1973); Wilfried Gottschalk, Marina Neumann-Schönwetter, Gunther Soukup, *Sozialisationsforschung* (Frankfurt/M, 1971); Freerk Huisken, *Zur Kritik bürgerlicher Didaktik und Bildungsökonomie* (Munich, 1972); Hellmut Lessing and Manfred Liebel, *Jugend in der Klassengesellschaft* (Munich, 1974), and Hartmut Titze, *Die Politisierung der Erziehung* (Frankfurt/M, 1973).

3. For the most recent criticism by the New Left, see the special issues of *Kursbuch*, vol. 34 (Dec. 1973) and *Kürbiskern*, vol. 1 (1974) as well as *Die heimlichen Erzieher: Kinderbücher und politisches Lernen*, ed. Dieter Richter and Jochen Vogt (Reinbek, 1974).

4. For a complete picture of the historical background, see Helmut Müller, "*Der Struwwelpeter*—Der langanhaltende Erfolg und das wandlungsreiche Leben eines deutschen Bilderbuches," *Klassische Kinder- und Jugendbücher*, ed. Klaus Doderer (Weinheim, 1970), pp. 55–97.

5. Cf. Otto F. Gmelin, *Böses kommt aus Kinderbücher* (Munich, 1972), pp. 29–40, and Elke und Jochen Vogt, " 'Und höre nur, wie bös er war,' Randbemerkungen zu einem Klassiker für Kinder," *Die heimlichen Erzieher*, pp. 11–30.

6. A recent issue of the prominent journal *Vorgänge* was devoted entirely to this problem. See "Kinderfeindlichkeit oder: Die Chancen einer wehrlosen Minderheit," *Vorgänge*, vol. 7 (1974).

7. Darmstadt, 1973. Waechter's book transforms all the stories into their opposites. It is more than a simple parody in that it incorporates emancipatory features into a critique of authoritarian behavior.

8. For a good analysis of this novel, see Ingrid and Klaus Doderer, "Johanna Spyris *Heidi*—Fragwürdige Tugendwelt in verklärter Wirklichkeit," *Klassische Kinder- und Jugendbücher*, pp. 121–34.

9. *Ibid.*, p. 130.

10. See note 5 above.

11. See Birgit Dankert, "Die antiautoritäre Kinder- und Jugendliteratur," *Jugendliteratur in einer veränderten Welt*, ed. Karl Ernst Maier (Bad Heilbrunn, 1972), pp. 75–84.

12. The title of the comic book is *Lehrlingsfront 1*, and the photographic story, *Liebe Mutter, mir geht es gut.*

13. See Hartwig Denkwerth, *Verordnete Illusionen* (Berlin, 1974), which deals with pictures and illusions used in schools; Dagmar von Doetinchem and Klaus Hartung, *Zum Thema Gewalt in Superhelden-Comics* (Berlin, 1974), which studies the portrayal of power and force in comics; and Dieter Richter and Johannes Merkel, *Märchen, Phantasie und soziales Lernen* (Berlin, 1974), which deals with the imagination and learning how to read fairy tales.

14. Berlin, 1971, p. 1.

15. Weismann has recently joined with Raith Verlag of Munich, a progressive firm which has concentrated on publishing books dealing with psychology and education.

16. Ellermann has published one of the pioneer books in the anti-authoritarian tradition, Elisabeth Borcher's *Das rote Haus in einer kleinen Stadt*.

17. Kindler has issued an anti-authoritarian story, *Ein Roter Zug will fliegen* by Ivan Steiger, and some important studies about children and children's literature by Otto F. Gmelin and Monika Sperr.

18. For an excellent study about the concept of solidarity in children's literature, see Wolfgang Grebe, *Erziehung zur Solidarität* (2nd rev. ed.; Wiesbaden, 1973).

19. See "Kinderbuch und politische Erziehung—Zum Verständnis der neuen linken Kinderliteratur," *Asthetik und Kommunikation*, 5–6 (February 1972), 31–2. Richter's essay is the best one on the subject of radical children's literature. He has also edited a most significant collection of essays dealing with socialist children's literature, *Das politische Kinderbuch* (Darmstadt, 1973).

20. "Kind und Buch," *Kursbuch*, 34 (December 1973), 79–102.

21. *Öffentlichkeit und Erfahrung: Zur Organisationanalyse von bürferlicher und proletarischer Öffentlichkeit* (Frankfurt/M, 1973), pp. 466–67.

22. Weismann has cooperated with several industrial unions which distribute books like Wallraff's *Von einem der auszog und das Fürchten lernte* to young workers.

23. See Wolfram Frommlet, "Jugendbuchforschung in der BRD," *Kürbiskern*, 1 (1974), 74–88.

Some Features of the Modern Italian Literature for Young People

Carla Poesio

Among the main features of contemporary Italian children's literature one may note the continuous presence of antinomies and conflicts typical of mankind at large. This also characterized the literature of earlier periods, but with a substantial difference in presentation. Though such conflicts, which are so difficult to solve or overcome, may be considered an educational liability rather than as an asset in books for children, deeper analysis will show them in another light, for they provide an effective way to build up a dialogue, a possibility of communication. An evaluation of differences and conflicts existing between individuals or social and ethnic groups can be made, in fact, not to any discriminatory purpose, but with a view to acquiring in depth some data which will enable any reader to define for himself the terms of the different problems—and maybe solve them. Of course to understand does not mean to consent, to accept does not mean to approve. Differences, antinomies, conflicts *do* remain, in great part. However, the way to any form of dialogue passes through the knowledge of differences. The problem is, in our field, how to choose the tools (that is, the narrative language) which will let young people seize and know these differences, not in a traumatic way or, still worse, in a sweetened form, but in a dynamic, constructive process.

Italian children's literature from its inception (about the second half of the last century) is an exhaustive fresco of differences of all kinds: economic, social, ethnic, psychological, philosophical; they reflect the historical situation of a country which reached its unity as a state in a slow and gradual movement from 1848 onward. But the achievement of this unity has not cancelled, not even to this day, the unpleasant consequences of the previous situation, the frictions and contrasting attitudes connected with it.

I will omit here the outstanding titles and the well-known writers of the period before the first World War—Collodi with *Le Avventure di Pinocchio* (Pinocchio's Adventures), De Amicis with *Cuore* (Heart), Vamba with *Il giornalino di Gianburrasca* (Gianburrasca's Diary), and Salgari, Nuccio, Capuana. These are the milestones of our literature for young people, where I could easily underline the presence of the great differences I mentioned above.

It pays to compare the aims of past writers with contemporary ones as regards the depiction of the world around them and around their heroes, in every country's literature. As concerns the Italian, here are the main questions: How do contemporary writers introduce to young readers the conflicts and antinomies typical of our time? What conflicts do they choose to show? Do they lead the reader to the solution of problems or do they not? In the best books the main point is the provocative strength of their statements, which do not suggest a solution but rather stir up the reader to look for it, to weigh its necessity, to shape a personal proposal. In other words, the problem is, for the writer, how to induce his reader to meditation and, afterward, to participation and engagement.

In the best books of the past (the ones mentioned above and some more of the period from 1918 to 1945) situations were communicated to the reader without the aim of stirring up in him anything more than sympathy. On the contrary, in the authors writing after 1945 which I will mention here, we find a more provocative expression and an invitation to initiative (sometimes even an initiative of rebellion, of revolt) as if the writers themselves would admit that young people better than adults are able to change a world which is on the way to dehumanization.

Let me show this by some examples. I shall begin with Renee Reggiani. She has had the merit of bringing into books for young people the problems deriving from the differences between the North and South of Italy. The South, for historical reasons, is far less developed than the North, mainly from an economic point of view, but the economic situation has its consequences and effects also in other fields. Renee Reggiani underlines the violent frictions, the stereotypes, the misunderstanding arising from such a situation. In her two novels *Quando i sogni non hanno soldi* (When Dreams Haven't Any Money; Milano: Fabbri), and *Il treno del sole* (Sun Train; Milano: Garzanti), children and adults migrating from the South in search of a job of bearable conditions meet with people of the North who welcome them with a rather hostile attitude and often exasperating differences of behavior, of ideas, problems, and so on. However, even if social structures do not offer the possibility of spiritual meeting between a man and another man, still individuals must look for such a meeting by just exploring in discussion or meditation the reasons for whatever differences divide (or seem to divide) human beings from one another. That is why in Reggiani's books the frictions generally elicit a possibility of dialogue. There is always a point, a moment which permits the starting of the dialogue, the precious moment when people begin to communicate, to open up to each other. Of course, the dramatization of such a moment is the fulcrum of narrative invention in this writer; it may be preceded by suspense, by pathos, by a deep inward crisis of the hero, or by significant events. All these elements will be arranged in such a way as to involve the reader not only in the plot, but in its ground motives, in its implicit meaning, in its essential aims. That is a matter of artistic creation: of course the author is neither a preacher nor an essayist; her work is essentially an artistic product. It will have eloquence, persuasion, but, above all, it will have artistic qualities. Another of Reggiani's novels, *Carla degli scavi* (Carla of the Excavations; Milano: Garzanti), is a clear example of that. Here we find two very different persons: Carla, a modern-minded girl living in Milan, who looks down on anybody who does not live in the modern and dynamic spirit of her industrial town, and her uncle, a typical Neapolitan scholar, who resents the superficiality he attributes to modern youth as well as anything which might disturb his carefully planned everyday life. When Carla's parents send their daughter to Naples to spend some months at her uncle's house, cold war begins between the two. Yet a point of balance appears: a common interest of both is the archaeological excavations of Stabia, a Roman town which, like Pompei, was buried by a volcanic eruption in 82 A.D. The passionate chronicle of this discovery, due to the studies of Carla's uncle (and based on true, nonfictional events), and the many hostilities and difficulties he must endure in his scholarly pursuit of a gradual reconstruction of the life of ancient times allow the two characters to deepen their mutual knowledge. They can find each other and then go their separate ways, but mutually enriched.

In the best novel by this writer, *Domani dopodomani* (Tomorrow, the Day after Tomorrow; Firenze: Vallecchi), we have as a background a little isolated village on a hill in a rather depressed Italian area. Here a dramatic fight takes place between culture, education, and logic (represented by a young teacher) and tradition (represented more or less by all the village's inhabitants), a tradition still admitting witchcraft, ignorance, passivity. At a certain moment we sense the coming victory of the new times over such a tradition. So we follow this thin thread through dramatic events and alternatives full of suspense till—not *the end*, because no end can solve such a situation in *deus ex machina* fashion—but till a new balance of facts appears, full of promises which may or may not actually be kept.

Gianni Rodari, the best known of our contemporary writers, was awarded the H. C. Andersen Prize in 1970. He employs humor and fancy to point out some of the oppositions which cause conflicts and wars: poor and rich; people of good will and people of bad will; oppressive people and peaceful people; exploiters and exploited. He believes in children as the ones who are not overwhelmed by prejudices, stereotypes, and ideologies which would prevent them from building a better world.

In his book *La torta in cielo* (The Cake in the Sky; Torino: Einaudi), a strange space ship lands in the outskirts of Rome. Authorities, army, police, are in fighting trim. Only children escape such a hostile attitude; they approach the space ship and discover . . . it is an enormous cake! They taste it, or better, they eat it up, until they discover, well hidden inside, a scientist full of shame for what has happened to him. In fact he was to prepare an atomic bomb, but, by an incredible mistake in the mixture of the different elements, his bomb became a cake. A great blow to the prestige of a scientist, indeed! But when he sees the enthusiasm of the Roman children for his cake he makes up his mind: he will always prepare cakes instead of bombs.

Marcello Argilli shows us how fancy can vitally oppose the coldness of our mechanical civilization, which increasingly discourages any human value, any aptitude for personal choice and engagement. Argilli's heroes are machines, but they undergo a process of anthropomorphization. As heroes of the plots, they assume a new role, the one that human beings seem to have forgotten; they appear in fact full of sympathy, generosity, and dignity. In the collection of tales, *Fiabe dei nostri tempi* (Fairy Tales of Our Time; Napoli: Morano), we find some significant examples of the "transfer" of magic in the world of machines. Here we have the submarine which falls in love with the whale and gives up his military life in order to enjoy freedom in the wonderful depth of the sea; the slot machine which chooses to distribute food also to poor people lacking money; the typewriter which refuses to write what is wrong and contrary to human dignity.

For adults Argilli proposes another type of opposition: the one existing between father and children, adults and young people. His problematic book *Ciao Andrea* (Goodbye, Andrew; Milano: Mondadori) introduces the difficult relation between parents and children into a plot where symbol and reality harmonize in a fascinating way. A journalist welcomes in his home as a son Andrea, a teenage boy, coming from no one knows where. After a short time the boy flies away, but then comes back; flies away again and comes back once more. The journalist accepts this "difficult" son and does not let him feel the weight of gratitude or of any obligation. It remains a mystery, for him too, where the boy has been, where he comes from. Andrea claims to have been among the Jewish prisoners in the lagers, then among farmers in Vietnam; sometimes he asserts he has shared the life of Arab children in Algeria under the French, or the hard labor of poor young workers in the sulphur mines of Sicily. Lies, only lies, obviously, because the data of space and time so glaringly contrast with reality; yet Andrea's reports have many elements of truth and appear quite irrefutable. He represents something, obviously—maybe the suffering of children all over the world. The alternatives of his life with the journalist and his milieu are full of clashes and yet they develop on the line of "fair play." Andrea learns what it means to be a son, but the journalist himself learns how to be a father. To be a father means, according to the writer and his heroes, "to wish for one's son the freedom that all men must have."

Quite similar to this difficult relationship between parents and children is another form of conflict: the boy or the young man on one side and on the other the world of adults, a world which often appears hostile, a world where it is difficult to grow up. We might even label some books as "novels reflecting the *labor* of growing up."

Such "labor" is the dominant feeling in *Marco in Sicilia* (Marco in Sicily; Firenze: Vallecchi), by Luciana Martini. This writer has resumed, from her point of view, the theme treated by Renee Reggiani—that is, the deep difference separating the North and South of Italy—but she denies for the present any possibility of deep human union, because of the indifference or the bad will of men, who preach the ideal of collaboration and mutual understanding, but really do very little to transform their preaching into reality. Their attitude insinuates doubt and confusion into the simple and frail vision of the world that children build up gradually inside themselves. The hero of Martini's novel, Marco, is the son of an engineer who has temporarily left Milan to work in Sicily for an oil refinery. There are new experiences for the whole family in this country quite unknown to them, but especially for Marco, who becomes the friend of a poor Sicilian boy extremely different from him in social condition, family, customs, way of life. Friendship ignores limitations when it is sincere, and North and South seem to join in the two boys. But only for a short time. As a matter of fact, a wall remains between them and will show its cruel solidity in dramatic circumstances. When Marco looks for a logical explanation for such a situation and asks his father about it, he can only get a vague answer: "You see, the world cannot be changed. . . ." Marco revolts against these words and, when his family leaves the island forever, he promises to himself to come back when he is an adult. Will Marco really come back? The uncertainty in which Luciana Martini leaves her reader, her courage in denouncing some very hard human conditions, and the discrepancy between utopia and reality are among the strongest stimuli for promoting personal initiative in her young readers.

The denunciation of a dramatic situation is present also in *Addio al pianeta Terra* (Goodbye Earth!; Milano: Bompiani), by the same writer. Here a terrible atomic war is carrying our planet to complete destruction. The leitmotif is the anguish, the distress, the fear increasing in every page while Teo (the young hero of the novel) with his mother and father are looking for an escape in underground shelters, together with an enormous crowd coming from everywhere. But even in the shelters people will only delay death. By their own hands men have done away with every possibility of survival. At the end of the plot, where the scattering and disintegration of every social structure is dramatically shown as a sort of general regression of mankind, Teo and a few others leave Earth in a space ship. He has lost his mother and father; he has lost everything, as have the other people with him. Will they have the possibility of building up a new world elsewhere? The book finishes with this mark of interrogation, midway between a past full of faults and ruin and a future unknown and uncertain. There is no happy ending, no definite solution to the problem, only some possibilities of choice for the time being and a desperate appeal to the sense of responsibility of every human being. A deep antinomy again: on one side the desire for a human equilibrium we are unable to reach, on the other side the advancing of a merciless technological civilization we are unable to control.

We can find such antinomies (though differently expressed) in the last three writers I shall mention: Calvino, Arpino, and Libenzi. The social problem takes new dimensions in them, so that we can really speak of a new literary trend. The writer no longer deals with class differences, distribution of wealth, and discrimination. He points out the alteration of human life owed to consumerism, to the invasion of cement buildings and machines, to the destruction of nature. On one side he posits the desire, the longing of man for a type of life in accordance to nature; on the other the so-called *progress* which squeezes us as in an iron vise.

This is what happens in *Marcovaldo* by Italo Calvino, published by Einaudi in Turin. Marcovaldo is a pathetic character (very close to the Charlie Chaplin of the silent films), a sort of errand boy of a big firm with a poor salary and a large family to support. He keeps in his heart a longing for the countryside, for life outdoors, for open spaces far from overcrowded buildings. He pursues the realization of this desire through many disappointments and misadventures which Calvino narrates in a humorous and grotesque way. Marcovaldo never loses his good temper (as Charlot didn't) or his hope and his poetic sensitiveness, which few men nowadays possess.

The same atmosphere characterizes *Rafe e Micropiede* by Giovanni Arpino (Torino: Einaudi). Rafe is a boy from a poor district of Rome who leaves his home in search of a place where one "can live better." He is accompanied by Micropiede, an electronic tortoise, who leads him to a lot of places where modern civilization has created and settled everything with absolute perfection. But such coldness, such mechanical perfection dominate everywhere that Rafe comes back to his poor home and understands that *there* is the place where "one can live better."

A similar conception culminates in one of Arpino's tales from the collection *Assalto al treno* (Assault on the Train; Torino: Einaudi). We find there the aspect of a city of the future whose inhabitants are human only from the waist upwards; from the waist downwards they are part of the motor cars which they can't abandon any more.

This opposition between humanity in a genuine sense and mechanization exacerbating itself more and more becomes the theme of *Il pianeta dei matti* (The Planet of the Fools; Milan: Garzanti) by Ermanno Libenzi. The planet of the fools is the Earth in the year 2000; Libenzi in fact introduces some aspects of our near future in a humorous mood often jumping into satire and grotesque. Let us judge from one of its episodes:

The number of motor cars in the year 2000 is so great that, one day, they can't move any more. In the streets one can see a carpet of immobilized cars; people, in order to walk, just jump from a roof of one to the roof of another. To remedy such a situation, authorities decide to build a new roadway above this carpet of cars, covering them with a casting of cement: the ground floors of the buildings will be remade on the tops of the buildings themselves. But such a remedy does not last long and a new roadway has to be built on the previous one, and still another, after a short time, at such a rhythm as to change continually the city's face. Great is the enthusiasm of firms producing cars because they can launch on the market a new type of much inferior quality, called "take and throw it away!" (a hymn to consumerism) and great too is the enthusiasm of common people, who think that the new city, so much higher, will have the best climate of all. There is another category of fools rejoicing; that is the people of culture who are persuaded to prepare the best chances for the archaeologists of the future: what imposing, wonderful material will they have at their disposal! But one morning a citizen wakes up with two wheels instead of two legs. Every possible remedy is requested from doctors everywhere, but there is nothing to be done. And after all, in a short time the man discovers that "two wheels are better than two legs." In the meantime the same thing happens to some other citizens. This is the end of the era of Homo Sapiens. A new one, the era of "Rotaurus" (the Man with Wheel) has begun. Wheels, not brain or feelings. Robot, not man. This Rotaurus, opposed to Homo Sapiens, is very near to the "half man" by Arpino I have quoted before. It is the same opposition which deeply involves the reader, especially the young reader, the one who has to make his choice.

A List of the Juvenile Literature in the Hughes Public Library, Rugby, Tennessee*

Jan Bakker

Rugby was a late nineteenth-century English settlement or colony, as the settlers preferred to call it, in the untouched Tennessee woods. Thomas Hughes, English philanthropist, social and moral reformer, and author of *Tom Brown's Schooldays*, was its spiritual and intellectual mentor. Rugby was to provide a place for indigent Englishmen, some of whom were the younger sons of the gentry whose prospects at home were slight. The colony was supposed to be a second chance, the old American dream of a new beginning.

The Hughes Public Library in what remains of Rugby is a quiet, clapboard building in the trees, white with green shutters over the great windows in either wall and a ventilator-cupola in the peak of its roof. Outside and in, it looks today as it did when it opened in October of 1882. Its collection of about 7,000 volumes, largely publisher's reprints, acquired between 1880 and 1889 is unique. It is a period library, frozen in time, virtually unchanged since the end of the nineteenth century. It has been administered by a Library Board of local citizens that has functioned continuously since the demise of the Rugby colony in the 1890s. This protection, the decline in the use of the library, and its remote location on the Cumberland Plateau of northeastern Tennessee are responsible for the preservation of this period collection.

Among these volumes—"one of the best representative collections of Victorian literature in America"[1]—are something over a thousand juvenile books. For the most part, these reflect the concerns of the time for moral and religious teaching, for character building through

---

*Copyright © Rugby Restoration Association, 1976.

1. Brian L. Stagg, Executive Director of the Rugby Restoration Association, makes this statement about the library in his booklet, *The Distant Eden: Tennessee's Rugby Colony* (Knoxville: Paylor Publications, 1973), pp. 6, 24. Particular thanks must be given Mr. Stagg for the permission he obtained for me to use the Hughes Public Library freely. Certain information about the history of the library and Hughes's philosophy of it was gotten from Douglas Kirke Gordon's unpublished University of Tennessee dissertation (1974), "The Thomas Hughes Free Public Library, Rugby, Tennessee: A History and Partial Bibliography." Special thanks, too, must be given Jeff Lovingood of Concord, Tennessee, who helped me make my list of the juvenile books. And thanks to Marvin Bailey for bibliographical advice.

books such as the Proverb Stories for Boys and Girls, the Rollo Series and other tales of Jacob Abbott, or stories by T. S. Arthur. But there is much literature for entertainment in the children's section, too. There are the fairy tales of Hans Christian Andersen and the Brothers Grimm. There are adventure stories by R. M. Ballantyne and W. H. G. Kingston. There is even one volume of the nonsense of Edward Lear, and one volume each of *Alice's Adventures in Wonderland* and *Through the Looking-Glass.* Among the otherwise well-preserved books in the three shelf-sections of the juvenile literature, the large picture, story, and verse collections in the *Chatterbox* series show the most serious wear—covers and pages missing, worn out on their shelf.

At their organizational meeting in October 1880, the Rugby colonists planned a library. Hughes felt that civilization and culture for the settlement would come after hard work tilling the soil. Civilization and culture would start with a good library, whose holdings would be designed to build intellect and character. But he believed in work first, leisure afterwards. His idea was for the library named after him to be a repository of serious literature rather than escapist, diverting fiction. It was to be open to all the citizens. Hughes's concern for the library reflected the Victorian attitude toward social reform that saw in books and reading a means to promote morality, stability, and the teaching of useful skills. These skills in particular would ensure the survival of the colony.

Ironically, as circulation evidence shows, most of the reading from the Hughes Public Library was for pleasure. Readers came to be entertained rather than instructed or morally strengthened. The first librarian, Eduard Bertz, German socialist and exile, reflected Hughes's didactic approach to the library. He felt that there was too much fiction in it and not enough literature of more practical value. But the novels kept coming, mostly received in 1882, gathered through the good efforts of Dana Estes, Boston publisher and an early promoter of children's literature. It was he who in 1880 got the idea of collecting books for Rugby from American and British publishers as a token of respect for Thomas Hughes.

The Hughes Library reached its peak circulation in 1886 and declined with the colony thereafter. Interested as they were in the amenities of life rather than in the hard work of clearing trees, tilling soil, and manufacturing goods, the colonists failed in their idealistic Tennessee project. Most went away to other areas of the United States. Some went back to England. Only a few remained. The library today is unused but protected, a recollection of a dream and an era of books among the tall trees.

The following is a preliminary bibliographical listing of the books in the juvenile section of the Hughes Public Library. The information here comes from the books themselves. The numerals and letters in parenthesis at the end of each entry indicate exactly where the volume is located on its shelf as it was placed there by Eduard Bertz or his successor as librarian and cataloguer, Mary Percival. The numerals I, II, III designate the shelf sections in the far right hand corner of the rear of the library: I and II lead into the angle of the wall; III is to the immediate right. Ranging down from the topmost shelf, *a*, to the bottommost, *j*, the small letter tells on which shelf the book is located. The Arabic numerals—counting from left to right from one to forty and more—show in what place the volume is located on its particular shelf. (Thomas Hughes's *Tom Brown's Schooldays*—New York: John Wurtele Lovell, 1880—is shelved away from the other juvenile books. An autographed copy presented to the library by Hughes disappeared shortly thereafter.)

Abbott, Rev. Edwin A. *The Good Voices, a Child's Guide to the Bible.* Illus. N.Y.: E. P. Dutton & Co., 1873. 132 pp. (IId/11)

Abbott, Jacob. *The Alcove; Containing Some Further Account of Timboo, Mark, and Fanny.* Harper's Story Books. Illus. N.Y.: Harper & Bros., 1855. 160 pp. (IIIb/12)

————. *Aunt Margaret; or, How John True Kept His Resolutions.* Harper's Story Books. Illus. N.Y.: Harper & Bros., 1856. 160 pp. (IIIa/60)

————. *Beechnut. A Franconia Story.* Illus. N.Y.: Harper & Bros., 1850. 211 pp. (IIc/33)

————. *Bruno; or, Lessons of Fidelity, Patience, and Self-Denial. Taught by a Dog.* Harper's Story Books. Illus. N.Y.: Harper & Bros., 1854. 160 pp. (IIIa/50)

————.*Caleb in Town. A Story for Children.* The Jonas Stories. Illus. N.Y.: Clark & Maynard, 1839. 180 pp. (IIc/45)

————. *Carl and Jocko; or, The Adventures of the Little Italian Boy and His Monkey.* Harper's Story Books. Illus. N.Y.: Harper & Bros., 1857. 160 pp. (IIIa/54)

————. *Congo; or, Jasper's Experience in Command.* Harper's Story Books. Illus. N.Y.: Harper & Bros., 1855. 160 pp. (IIIb/4)

————. *Dialogues for the Amusement and Instruction of Young Persons.* Harper's Story Books. Illus. N.Y.: Harper & Bros., 1855. 160 pp. (IIIb/9)

————. *Elfred; or, The Blind Boy and His Pictures.* Harper's Story Books. Illus. N.Y.: Harper & Bros., 1856. 160 pp. (IIIa/58)

————. *The Engineer; or, How to Travel in the Woods.* Harper's Story Books. Illus. N.Y.: Harper & Bros., 1855. 160 pp. (IIIb/13)

————. *The English Channel.* The Florence Stories. Illus. N.Y.: Sheldon & Co., 1871. 252 pp. (IIIb/23)

————. *Franklin, The Apprentice Boy.* Harper's Story Books. Illus. N.Y.: Harper & Bros., 1855. 160 pp. (IIIa/51)

————. *The Gibraltar Gallery: Being an Account of Various Things Both Curious and Useful.* Harper's Story Books. Illus. N.Y.: Harper & Bros., 1855. 160 pp. (IIIb/17)

————. *The Great Elm; or, Robin Green and Josiah Lane at School.* Harper's Story Books. Illus. N.Y.: Harper & Bros., 1856. 160 pp. (IIIa/56)

————. *The Harper Establishment; or, How the Story Books Are Made.* Harper's Story Books. Illus. N.Y.: Harper & Bros., 1855. 160 pp. (IIIa/49)

————. *Jasper; or, The Spoiled Child Recovered.* Harper's Story Books. Illus. N.Y.: Harper & Bros., 1855. 160 pp. (IIIb/1)

————. *John True; or, The Christian Experience of an Honest Boy.* Harper's Story Books. Illus. N.Y.: Harper & Bros., 1855. 160 pp. (IIIb/6)

————. *Jonas a Judge; or, Law Among the Boys.* The Jonas Stories. Illus. N.Y.: Clark & Maynard, 1840. 179 pp. (IIc/44)

————. *Judge Justin; or, The Little Court of Morningdale.* Harper's Story Books. Illus. N.Y.: Harper & Bros., 1857. 160 pp. (IIIa/53)

————. *Lapstone; or, The Sailor Turned Shoemaker.* Harper's Story Books. Illus. N.Y.: Harper & Bros., 1857. 160 pp. (IIIa/57)

————. *The Little Louvre; or, The Boys' and Girls' Gallery of Pictures.* Harper's Story Books. Illus. N.Y.: Harper & Bros., 1855. 160 pp. (IIIb/16)

————. *Little Paul; or, How to be Patient in Sickness and Pain.* Harper's Story Books. Illus. N.Y.: Harper & Bros., 1855. 160 pp. (IIIb/5)

————. *Minigo; or, The Fairy of Carinstone Abbey.* Harper's Story Books. Illus. N.Y.: Harper & Bros., 1855. 160 pp. (IIIb/7)

————. *The Museum; or, Curiosities Explained.* Harper's Story Books. Illus. N.Y.: Harper & Bros., 1855. 160 pp. (IIIb/15)

————. *Orkney the Peacemaker; or, The Various Ways of Settling Disputes.* Harper's Story Books. Illus. N.Y.: Harper & Bros., 1857. 160 pp. (IIIa/52)

————. *Prank; or, The Philosophy of Tricks and Mischief.* Harper's Story Books. Illus. N.Y.: Harper & Bros., 1855. (IIIa/55)

————. *Rambles Among the Alps.* Harper's Story Books. Illus. N.Y.: Harper & Bros., 1855. 160 pp. (IIIb/8)

————. *Rollo's Correspondence.* The Rollo Series. Illus. N.Y.: Sheldon & Co., 1868. 189 pp. (IIc/46)

————. *Rollo's Experiments.* The Rollo Series. Illus. N.Y.: Sheldon & Co., 1869. 180 pp. (IIc/38)

————. *Rollo's Philosophy.* [*Air.*] The Rollo Series. Illus. N.Y.: Sheldon & Co., 1869. 192 pp. (IIc/41)

———. *Rollo's Philosophy.* [*Fire.*] The Rollo Series. Illus. N.Y.: Sheldon
& Co., 1869. 92 pp. (IIc/40)

———. *Rollo's Philosophy.* [*Sky.*] The Rollo Series. Illus. N.Y.: Sheldon
& Co., 1870. 192 pp. (IIc/42)

———. *Rollo's Philosophy.* [*Sky.*] The Rollo Series. Illus. N.Y.: Sheldon
& Co., 1870. 192 pp. (IIc/43)

———. *Rollo's Philosophy.* [*Water.*] The Rollo Series. Illus. N.Y.:
Sheldon & Co., 1869. 192 pp. (IIc/39)

———. *Stories of Rainbow and Lucky. Handie.* Illus. N.Y.: Harper &
Bros., 1860. 187 pp. (IIc/34)

———. *Stories of Rainbow and Lucky. Rainbow's Journey.* Illus. N.Y.:
Harper & Bros., 1860. 201 pp. (IIc/36)

———. *Stories of Rainbow and Lucky. Selling Lucky.* Illus. N.Y.: Harper
& Bros., 1860. 183 pp. (IIc/37)

———. *Stories of Rainbow and Lucky. Up the River.* Illus. N.Y.: Harper
& Bros., 1861. 192 pp. (IIc/35)

———. *The Story of American History, from the Earliest Settlement of
the Country to the Establishment of the Federal Constitution.*
Harper's Story Books. Illus. N.Y.: Harper & Bros., 1855. 160 pp.
(IIIb/21)

———. *The Story of Ancient History, from the Earliest Periods to the
Fall of the Roman Empire.* Harper's Story Books. Illus. N.Y.: Harper
& Bros., 1855. 160 pp. (IIIb/18)

———. *The Story of English History, from the Earliest Periods to the
American Revolution.* Harper's Story Books. Illus. N.Y.: Harper &
Bros., 1855. 160 pp. (IIIb/20)

———. *The Strait Gate; or, The Rule of Exclusion from Heaven.* Harper's
Story Books. Illus. N.Y.: Harper & Bros., 1855. 160 pp. (IIIa/59)

———. *The Studio; or, Illustrations of the Theory and Practice of
Drawing, for Young Artists at Home.* Harper's Story Books. Illus.
N.Y.: Harper & Bros., 1855. 160 pp. (IIIb/14)

———. *The Three Gold Dollars; or, An Account of the Adventures of
Robin Green.* Harper's Story Books. Illus. N.Y.: Harper & Bros.,
1855. 160 pp. (IIIb/22)

———. *Timboo and Fanny; or, The Art of Self-Instruction.* Harper's
Story Books. Illus. N.Y.: Harper & Bros., 1855. (IIIb/11)

———. *Timboo and Joliba; or, The Art of Being Useful.* Harper's Story
Books. Illus. N.Y.: Harper & Bros., 1855. 160 pp. (IIIb/10)

———. *Vernon; or, Conversations About Old Times in England.* Harper's
Story Books. Illus. N.Y.: Harper & Bros., 1855. 160 pp. (IIIb/19)

———. *Viola and Her Little Brother Arno.* Harper's Story Books. Illus.
N.Y.: Harper & Bros., 1857. 160 pp. (IIIa/61)

———. *Virginia; or, A Little Light on a Very Dark Saying.* Harper's
Story Books. Illus. N.Y.: Harper & Bros., 1855. 160 pp. (IIIb/3)

———. *Willie and the Mortgage, Showing How Much May be
Accomplished by a Boy.* Harper's Story Books. Illus. N.Y.: Harper &
Bros., 1855. 160 pp. (IIIb/2)

About a Dog, and Other Stories. Illus. Philadelphia: J. B. Lippincott &
Co., n.d. 64 pp. (IIIa/13)

Adams, Emily. *Six Months at Mrs. Prior's*. Illus. Boston: D. Lothrop &
Co., 1879. 250 pp. (IIf/8)

Adams, Rev. H. C. *Hair-Breadth Escapes; or, The Adventures of Three
Boys in South Africa*. Illus. N.Y.: E. P. Dutton & Co., n.d. 366 pp.
(IIg/5)

Adams, Sarah B. *Amy and Marion's Voyage Around the World*. Illus.
Boston: D. Lothrop & Co., 1878. 390 pp. (Ie/33)

Adams, William T. (Oliver Optic). *Vine and Olive; or, Young America
in Spain and Portugal. A Story of Travel and Adventure*. Young
America Abroad—Second Series. Illus. frontis. Boston: Lee and
Shepard, Publishers, 1876. (IIb/1)

Aesop. *Aesop's Fables. The People's Edition*. Illus. N.Y.: S. R. Wells,
1880. 72 pp. (Id/18)

―――. *The Fables of Aesop With a Life of the Author*. Illus. Boston:
Houghton, Mifflin & Co., 1880. 311 pp. (Id/16)

Dr. Aikin, and Mrs. Barbauld. *Evenings at Home; or, The Juvenile
Budget Opened*. Illus. London and N.Y.: George Routledge and Sons,
n.d. 446 pp. (IIIe/3)

Alcott, Louisa M. *Aunt Jo's Scrap-Bag. Jimmy's Cruise in the Pinafore,
Etc*. Illus. frontis. Boston: Roberts Brothers, 1879. 208 pp. (IIf/3)

―――. *Aunt Jo's Scrap-Bag. My Boys, Etc*. Louisa M. Alcott's Famous
Books. Illus. frontis. Boston: Roberts Brothers, 1879. 215 pp. (IIf/2)

―――. *Jack and Jill: A Village Story*. Illus. Boston: Roberts Brothers,
1880. 325 pp. (IIf/4)

―――. *Jo's Boys, and How They Turned Out. A Sequel to "Little Men"*.
Boston: Roberts Brothers, 1886. 365 pp. (Ia/3)

Alden, Ellen Tracy. *Stories and Ballads for Young Folks*. Illus. N.Y.:
American Book Exchange, 1880. 250 pp. (Ia/2)

Aldrich, Thomas Bailey. *The Story of a Bad Boy*. Illus. Boston:
Houghton, Mifflin & Co., 1869. 261 pp. (If/1)

Alger, Horatio, Jr. *Ben, the Luggage Boy; or, Among the Warves*.
Ragged Dick Series. Illus. Philadelphia: Porter & Coates, n.d. 290 pp.
(IIe/15)

―――. *Julius; or, The Street Boy Out West*. Tattered Tom Series. Boston:
Loring, 1874. 276 pp. (IIe/18)

―――. *Mark, the Match Boy; or, Richard Hunter's Ward*. Ragged Dick
Series. Illus. Boston: Loring, 1869.

―――. *Sam's Chance; and How He Improved It*. Tattered Tom Series.
Boston: Loring, 1876. 271 pp. (IIe/20)

―――, and O. Augusta Cheney. *Seeking His Fortune, and Other
Dialogues*. Boston: Loring, 1875. 270 pp. (IIe/16)

―――. *Seeking His Fortune, and Other Dialogues*. Boston: Loring, 1875.
270 pp. (IIe/17)

A. M. W. *Patty Williams's Voyage*. The Silver Penny Series. Illus. N.Y.:
Sheldon & Co., 1869. 104 pp. (IIa/35)

Andersen, Hans Christian. *Andersen's Fairy Tales*. Illus. Philadelphia:
J. B. Lippincott & Co., n.d. 380 pp. (IIg/16)

———. *Andersen's Wonder Stories.* Illus. Boston: Houghton, Mifflin &
Co. 555 pp. Title page missing. (IIg/9)
———. *A Christmas Greeting: A Series of Stories.* Story Teller Series.
Hans Andersen's Library. Illus. N.Y.: Leavitt & Allen Bros., n.d. 165
pp. (IIc/18)
———. *Little Ellie, and Other Tales.* Story Teller Series. Hans Andersen's
Library. Illus. frontis. N.Y.: Leavitt & Allen Bros., n.d. 156 pp.
(IIc/20)
———. *Little Rudy and Other Tales.* Little Rudy Story Books. Hans
Andersen's Library. Illus. N.Y.: Leavitt & Allen Bros., n.d. 166 pp.
(IIc/21)
———. *A Picture Book Without Pictures. And Other Stories.* Little Rudy
Story Books. Hans Andersen's Library. N.Y.: Leavitt & Allen Bros.,
n.d. 154 pp. (IIc/19)
Arthur Morland. A Tale for Boys. Illus. Philadelphia: Alfred Martien,
1873. 108 pp. (Ia/30)
Arthur, T. S. *All's for the Best.* Arthur's Juvenile Library. Illus.
Philadelphia: J. B. Lippincott & Co., 1877. 219 pp. (IIIc/3)
———. *Cedardale; or, The Peacemakers. A Story of Village Life.* Arthur's
Juvenile Library. Illus. Philadelphia: J. B. Lippincott & Co., 1875.
153 pp. (IIIc/6)
———. *Heroes of the Household.* Arthur's Juvenile Library. Illus.
Philadelphia: J. B. Lippincott & Co., 1877. 192 pp. (IIIc/4)
———. *The Last Penny, and Other Stories.* Arthur's Juvenile Library.
Illus. Philadelphia: J. B. Lippincott & Co., 1875. 150 pp. (IIIc/9)
———. *The Poor Woodcutter, and Other Stories.* Arthur's Juvenile
Library. Illus. Philadelphia: J. B. Lippincott & Co., 1875. 153 pp.
(IIIc/8)
———. *The Seen and the Unseen.* Arthur's Juvenile Library. Illus.
Philadelphia: J. B. Lippincott & Co., 1877. 205 pp. (IIIc/2)
———. *Tired of Housekeeping.* Happy Child's Library. N.Y.: D.
Appleton & Co., 1873. 167 pp. (IIIa/37)
———. *Who Is Greatest? and Other Stories.* Arthur's Juvenile Library.
Illus. Philadelphia: J. B. Lippincott & Co., 1875. 154 pp. (IIIc/5)
———. *The Wonderful Boy, and Other Stories.* Arthur's Juvenile Library.
Illus. Philadelphia: J. B. Lippincott & Co., 1875. 154 pp. (IIIc/7)
Aunt Fanny. *Take Heed and Other Stories.* Illus. N.Y.: E. P. Dutton &
Co., 1878. 147 pp. (Ic/38)
———. *Take Heed and Other Stories.* Illus. N.Y.: E. P. Dutton & Co.,
1878. 147 pp. (Ic/39)
Aunt Hattie. *Fleda's Childhood.* The Happy Home Stories. Illus. frontis.
Boston: Henry A. Young & Co., 1871. 105 pp. (IIa/37)
———. *Lying Jim.* Aunt Hattie's Library. Illus. Boston: Henry A. Young
& Co., 1867. 104 pp. (IIa/40)
Aunt Mary's Illustrated Reading Book. Illus. London and N.Y.: George
Routledge and Sons, n.d. N.p. (IIh/32)
Auntie Bee. *More Dolls.* Illus. London: George Routledge and Sons,
1879. 139 pp. (IIb/9)

————. *Rosabella. A Doll's Christmas Story*. Illus. London and N.Y.: George Routledge and Sons, 1878. 127 pp. (IIb/10)

Bache, Mrs. Anna. *Legends of Fairy Land*. Illus. frontis. Philadelphia: Claxton, Remsen & Haffelfinger, 1869. 172 pp. (IIa/10)

Baker, Ella M. *Christmas Pie*. Illus. Boston: D. Lothrop & Co., 1879. 322 pp. (IIe/3)

Baker, Sir Samuel W. *Cast Up by the Sea*. Illus. Philadelphia: J. B. Lippincott & Co., 1881. 410 pp. (IIIe/18)

Ballantyne, R. M. *Away in the Wilderness; or, Life Among the Red Indians and Fur-Traders of North America*. Boys' Miscellany of Travel and Adventure. Illus. Philadelphia: Porter & Coates, 1869. 144 pp. (IIa/14)

————. *Black Ivory, A Tale of Adventure Among the Slaves of East Africa*. Illus. London: James Nisbet & Co., 1880. 416 pp. (IIIg/6)

————. *Black Ivory, A Tale of Adventure Among the Slaves of East Africa*. Illus. London: James Nisbet & Co., 1880. 416 pp. (IIIg/7)

————. *The Coral Island: A Tale of the Pacific Ocean*. The Boy's Own Library. Illus. London, Edinburgh and N.Y.: Thomas Nelson and Sons, 1881. 438 pp. (IIIh/23)

————. *The Coral Island: A Tale of the Pacific Ocean*. The Boy's Own Library. Illus. London, Edinburgh and N.Y.: Thomas Nelson and Sons, 1881. 438 pp. (IIIh/24)

————. *Deep Down. A Tale of the Cornish Mines*. Illus. Philadelphia: J. B. Lippincott & Co., 1880. 420 pp. (IIIh/14)

————. *The Dog Crusoe and His Master. A Story of Adventure in the Western Prairies*. The Boy's Own Library. Illus. London, Edinburgh and N.Y.: T. Nelson and Sons, 1880. 356 pp. (IIIg/22)

————. *The Dog Crusoe and His Master. A Story of Adventure in the Western Prairies*. The Boy's Own Library. Illus. London, Edinburgh and N.Y.: T. Nelson and Sons, 1880. 356 pp. (IIIg/23)

————. *Dusty Diamonds, Cut and Polished. A Tale of City-Arab Life and Adventure*. Illus. London: James Nisbet & Co., 1884. 430 pp. (IIIg/27)

————. *Erling the Bold. A Tale of the Norse Sea Kings*. Illus. Philadelphia: J. B. Lippincott & Co., 1880. 437 pp. (IIIh/13)

————. *Erling the Bold. A Tale of the Norse Sea-Kings*. Illus. London: James Nisbet and Sons, 1880. 437 pp. (IIIf/9)

————. *Erling the Bold. A Tale of the Norse Sea-Kings*. Illus. London: James Nisbet & Sons, 1880. 437 pp. (IIIf/10)

————. *Fighting the Flames. A Tale of the London Fire Brigade*. Illus. London: James Nisbet & Co., 1880. 420 pp. (IIIf/5)

————. *Fighting the Flames. A Tale of the London Fire Brigade*. Illus. London: James Nisbet & Co., 1880. 420 pp. (IIIf/6)

————. *The Fire Brigade; or, Fighting the Flames. A Tale*. Illus. Philadelphia: J. B. Lippincott & Co., 1880. 420 pp. (IIIh/16)

————. *The Floating Light of the Goodwin Sands. A Tale*. Illus. London: James Nisbet & Co., 1880. 403 pp. (IIIf/1)

————. *The Floating Light of the Goodwin Sands. A Tale.* Illus. London: James Nisbet & Co., 1880. 403 pp. (IIIf/2)

————. *Gascoyne, the Sandal-Wood Trader: A Tale of the Pacific.* Illus. London: James Nisbet & Co., 1880. 440 pp. (IIIg/1)

————. *Gascoyne, the Sandal-Wood Trader: A Tale of the Pacific.* Illus. London: James Nisbet & Co., 1880. 440 pp. (IIIh/17)

————. *Gascoyne, the Sandal-Wood Trader: A Tale of the Pacific.* Illus. Boston: Roberts Brothers, n.d. 356 pp. (IIIh/18)

————. *Gascoyne, the Sandal-Wood Trader: A Tale of the Pacific.* Illus. Philadelphia: Porter & Coates, n.d. 356 pp. (IIIh/19)

————. *The Gorilla Hunters. A Tale of the Wilds of Africa.* The Boys' Own Library. Illus. London, Edinburgh and N.Y.: T. Nelson and Sons, 1880. 442 pp. (IIIg/18)

————. *The Gorilla Hunters. A Tale of the Wilds of Africa.* The Boys' Own Library. Illus. London, Edinburgh and N.Y.: T. Nelson and Sons, 1880. 422 pp. (IIIg/19)

————. *Hudson Bay; or, Everyday Life in the Wilds of North America.* Illus. London, Edinburgh and N.Y.: T. Nelson and Sons, 1882. 367 pp. (IIIg/16)

————. *Hudson Bay; or, Everyday Life in the Wilds of North America.* Illus. London, Edinburgh and N.Y.: T. Nelson and Sons, 1881. 367 pp. (IIIg/17)

————. *The Iron Horse; or, Life on the Line. A Tale of the Grand National Trunk Railway.* Illus. London: James Nisbet & Co., 1879. 407 pp. (IIIg/4)

————. *The Iron Horse; or, Life on the Line. A Tale of the Grand National Trunk Railway.* Illus. London: James Nisbet & Co., 1879. 407 pp. (IIIg/5)

————. *The Lifeboat. A Tale of Our Coast Heroes.* Illus. London: James Nisbet & Co., 1880. 392 pp. (IIIf/17)

————. *The Lifeboat. A Tale of Our Coast Heroes.* Illus. London: James Nisbet & Co., 1880. 392 pp. (IIIf/18)

————. *The Lighthouse, Being the Story of a Great Fight Between Man and the Sea.* Illus. London: James Nisbet & Co., 1880. 405 pp. (IIIg/2)

————. *The Lighthouse, Being the Story of a Great Fight Between Man and the Sea.* Illus. London: James Nisbet & Co., 1880. 405 pp. (IIIg/3)

————. *The Lonely Island; or, The Refuge of the Mutineers. A Tale Founded on Fact.* Illus. London: James Nisbet & Co., 1880. 413 pp. (IIIf/15)

————. *The Lonely Island; or, The Refuge of the Mutineers. A Tale Founded on Fact.* Illus. London: James Nisbet & Co., 1880. 413 pp. (IIIf/16)

————. *Martin Rattler; or, A Boy's Adventures in the Forests of Brazil.* Illus. London, Edinburgh and N.Y.: T. Nelson and Sons, 1876. 330 pp. (IIIh/20)

————. *Martin Rattler; or, A Boy's Adventures in the Forests of Brazil.*
The Boy's Own Library. Illus. London, Edinburgh and N.Y.: T.
Nelson and Sons, 1881. 330 pp. (IIIh/21)

————. *My Doggie and I.* Illus. N.Y.: Thomas Nelson and Sons, 1882.
205 pp. (IIIg/8)

————. *My Doggie and I.* Illus. N.Y.: Thomas Nelson and Sons, 1882.
205 pp. (IIIg/9)

————. *The Norsemen in the West; or, America Before Columbus. A
Tale.* Illus. London: James Nisbet & Co., 1880. 406 pp. (IIIf/13)

————. *The Norsemen in the West; or, America Before Columbus. A
Tale.* Illus. London: James Nisbet & Co., 1880. 406 pp. (IIIf/14)

————. *Philosopher Jack. A Tale of the Southern Seas.* Illus. London:
James Nisbet & Co., 1880. 246 pp. (IIIg/12)

————. *Philosopher Jack. A Tale of the Southern Seas.* Illus. London:
James Nisbet & Co., 1880. 246 pp. (IIIg/13)

————. *The Pirate City. An Algerine Tale.* Illus. London: James Nisbet &
Co., 1880. 400 pp. (IIIf/11)

————. *The Pirate City. An Algerine Tale.* Illus. London: James Nisbet &
Co., 1880. 400 pp. (IIIf/12)

————. *Post Haste. A Tale of Her Majesty's Mails.* Illus. London: James
Nisbet & Co., 1880. 424 pp. (IIIf/7)

————. *Post Haste. A Tale of Her Majesty's Mails.* Illus. London: James
Nisbet & Co., 1880. 424 pp. (IIIf/8)

————. *The Red Eric; or, The Whaler's Last Cruise. A Tale.* Illus.
Philadelphia: J. B. Lippincott & Co., 1877. 420 pp. (IIIh/15)

————. *The Red Man's Revenge. A Tale of the Red River Flood.* Illus.
N.Y.: Thomas Nelson and Sons, 1881. 264 pp. (IIIg/14)

————. *The Red Man's Revenge. A Tale of the Red River Flood.* Illus.
N.Y.: Thomas Nelson and Sons, 1881. 264 pp. (IIIg/15)

————. *Rivers of Ice. A Tale Illustrative of Alpine Adventure and Glacier
Action.* Illus. London: James Nisbet & Co., 1880. 430 pp. (IIIf/19)

————. *Rivers of Ice. A Tale Illustrative of Alpine Adventure and Glacier
Action.* Illus. London: James Nisbet & Co., 1880. 430 pp. (IIIf/20)

————. *Shifting Winds. A Tough Yarn.* Illus. London: James Nisbet &
Co., 1880. 406 pp. (IIIf/3)

————. *Shifting Winds. A Tough Yarn.* Illus. London: James Nisbet &
Co., 1880. 406 pp. (IIIf/4)

————. *Six Months at the Cape; or, Letters to Periwinkle from South
Africa.* Illus. London: James Nisbet & Co., 1880. 256 pp. (IIIg/10)

————. *Six Months at the Cape; or, Letters to Periwinkle from South
Africa.* Illus. London: James Nisbet & Co., 1880. 256 pp. (IIIg/11)

————. *Under the Waves; or, Diving in Deep Waters. A Tale.* Illus.
London: James Nisbet & Co., 1880. 414 pp. (IIIf/21)

————. *Under the Waves; or, Diving in Deep Waters. A Tale.* Illus.
London: James Nisbet & Co., 1880. 414 pp. (IIIf/22)

————. *Ungava: A Tale of Esquimaux-Land.* The Boy's Own Library.
Illus. London, Edinburgh and N.Y.: Thomas Nelson and Sons, n.d.
509 pp. (IIIg/24)

_____. *Ungava: A Tale of Esquimaux-Land.* The Boy's Own Library. Illus. London, Edinburgh and N.Y.: Thomas Nelson and Sons, n.d. 509 pp. (IIIg/25)

_____. *The World of Ice; or, The Whaling Cruise of "The Dolphin,"* *and the Adventures of Her Crew in the Polar Regions.* The Boy's Own Library. Illus. London, Edinburgh and N.Y.: Thomas Nelson and Sons, n.d. 315 pp. (IIIh/22)

_____. *The World of Ice; or, The Whaling Cruise of "The Dolphin,"* *and the Adventures of Her Crew in the Polar Regions.* The Boy's Own Library. Illus. London, Edinburgh and N.Y.: Thomas Nelson and Sons, n.d. 315 pp. (IIIg/26)

_____. *The Young Fur-Traders; or, Snowflakes and Sunbeams from the* *Far North.* The Boy's Own Library. Illus. London, Edinburgh and N.Y.: T. Nelson and Sons, 1881. 429 pp. (IIIg/20)

_____. *The Young Fur-Traders; or, Snowflakes and Sunbeams from the* *Far North.* The Boy's Own Library. Illus. London, Edinburgh and N.Y.: T. Nelson and Sons, 1881. 429 pp. (IIIg/21)

Banyard, Joseph. *The Novelties of the New World.* Illus. Boston: D. Lothrop & Co., n.d. 324 pp. (IIc/7)

Barbara. Illus. Boston: D. Lothrop & Co., 1875. 361 pp. (IIIc/27)

Lady Barker. *A Christmas Cake in Four Quarters.* Illus. N.Y.: Anson D. F. Randolph, 1872. 304 pp. (Id/31)

Barker, Mrs. Sale. *Memoirs of a Poodle.* Illus. London and N.Y.: George Routledge and Sons, 1877. 128 pp. (Ig/15)

_____. *The Picture-Story Album for Girls.* Illus. London and N.Y.: George Routledge and Sons, n.d. 189 pp. (Ig/13)

Dr. Barnardo, ed. *Our Darlings.* Illus. London: J. F. Shaw. 426 pp. Title page missing. (Ih/8)

Barrett, Philip. *The Deaf Shoemaker.* Illus. N.Y.: Dodd, Mead & Co., 1859. 216 pp. (Ib/8)

Bates, Clara Doty. *Heart's Content, and They Who Lived There.* Illus. Boston: D. Lothrop & Co., 1880. 252 pp. (If/4)

Bates, L. *That Boy of Newkirk's.* Illus. Boston: D. Lothrop & Co., 1878. 247 pp. (IId/18)

Battles Worth Fighting. Illus. N.Y.: General Protestant Episcopal Sunday School Union and Church Book Society, n.d. 306 pp. (Ib/10)

Bell, Mrs. Lucia Chase. *"True Blue." A Story of the Great North-West.* Illus. Boston: D. Lothrop & Co., 1878. 271 pp. (IId/20)

Bessie at Stony Lonesome; or, Charlie's Mission. Illus. N.Y.: General Protestant Episcopal Sunday School Union and Church Book Society, 1866. 316 pp. (Ia/16)

Bettison, Rev. W. J. *Basil Grey; or, Tried and True.* Illus. N.Y.: Thomas Nelson and Sons, n.d. 184 pp. (Ic/30)

_____. *Basil Grey; or, Tried and True.* Illus. N.Y.: Thomas Nelson and Sons, n.d. 184 pp. (Ic/30)

Bible Stories, and Sunday Tales. Illus. London and N.Y.: George Routledge and Sons, n.d. 230 pp. (Ig/4)

Bickersteth, Edward Henry. *The Reef, and Other Parables.* Illus. N.Y.: General Protestant Episcopal Sunday School Union and Church Book Society, n.d. 322 pp (Ib/3)

Bird, Robert Montgomery. *Nick of the Woods; or, The Jibbernainosay. A Tale of Kentucky.* Illus. frontis. N.Y.: A. C. Armstrong, 1881. 392 pp. (Ie/8)

The Bird-Catcher, and Other Tales. Illus. Philadelphia: J. B. Lippincott & Co., n.d. 64 pp. (IIIa/6)

The Blackberry-Girl, and Other Poems. Illus. frontis. Philadelphia: J. B. Lippincott & Co., n.d. 64 pp. (Ib/47)

Mrs. Blackford. *The Scottish Orphans: Founded on a Historical Fact; —and Arthur Monteith: A Sequel to "The Scottish Orphans:" and The Young West Indian.* Illus. Philadelphia: J. B. Lippincott & Co., 1874. 255 pp. (IId/23)

Blake, The Rev. J. L. *The Juvenile Companion and Fireside Reader, Consisting of Historical and Biographical Anecdotes, and Selections in Poetry.* Harper's Select Library. Harper & Bros., 1864. 252 pp. (IIb/34)

Bliss, Mrs. J. Worthington. *Every Inch a King; or, The Adventures of Rex and His Friends.* Illus. N.Y.: E. P. Dutton & Co., n.d. 160 pp. (Ic/4)

Mr. Bodley Abroad. Illus. Boston: Houghton, Mifflin & Co., 1881. 210 pp. (IId/5)

The Bodleys Afoot. Illus. Boston: Houghton, Mifflin & Co., 1882. 202 pp. (IId/4)

The Bodleys Telling Stories. Illus. Boston: Houghton, Mifflin & Co., 1882. 236 pp. (IId/2)

The Bodleys on Wheels. Illus. Boston: Houghton, Mifflin & Co., 1882. 222 pp. (IId/3)

Bond, A. L. *The Child's Natural History. In Words of Four Letters.* Illus. London and N.Y.: George Routledge and Sons, n.d. 100 pp. (Ib/31)

A Book of Golden Deeds of All Times and All Lands. London: Macmillan & Co., 1881. 450 pp. (IIf/18)

Bourne, Benjamin F. *The Captive in Patagonia; or, Life Among the Giants. A Personal Narrative.* Illus. Boston: D. Lothrop & Co., 1853. 233 pp. (IIIh/12)

Bourne, H. R. Fox. *Famous London Merchants. A Book for Boys.* Harper's Select Library. Illus. N.Y.: Harper & Bros., 1869. 295 pp. (IIb/33)

Bowman, Ann. *The Boy Voyagers; or, The Pirates of the East.* Every Boy's Library. London: George Routledge and Sons, n.d. 400 pp. Some pages probably missing. (IIa/7)

Bradley, Mrs. Mary E. *The Story of a Summer; or, What do ye More Than Others.* Sunny Dell Series. Illus. Boston: D. Lothrop & Co., 1869. 121 pp. (IIIa/48)

Brenda. *"Especially Those." A Story on the Prayer "For All Conditions of Men."* Illus. N.Y.: E. P. Dutton & Co., n.d. 110 pp. (Ig/43)

————. *"Especially Those." A Story on the Prayer "For All Conditions of Men."* Illus. N.Y.: E. P. Dutton & Co., n.d. 110 pp. (Ig/47)

————. *Lotty's Visit to Grandmama. A Story for the Little Ones.* Illus. N.Y.: E. P. Dutton & Co., n.d. 162 pp. (Ig/44)

Bright Rays for Dull Days. Illus. London, Paris & N.Y.: Cassell, Petter, Galpin & Co., n.d. 183 pp. (Ig/46)

Bright Sundays. The Cosy Corner Series. Illus. London, Paris & N.Y.: Cassell, Petter, Galpin & Co., n.d. 183 pp. (IIe/32)

Bristol, Mrs. Mary C. *Alice Sutherland; or, Life in My Uncle's Family.* Illus. Boston: D. Lothrop & Co., n.d. 267 pp. (IIf/10)

Broderip, Francis Freeling. *My Grandmother's Budget of Stories and Songs.* Illus. N.Y.: E. P. Dutton & Co., n.d. 183 pp. (IIh/33)

Brown, Emma E. *Child Toilers of Boston Streets.* Illus. Boston: D. Lothrop & Co., 1879. 149 pp. (Ig/49)

————. *The Children's Hour at the Old South.* Illus. Boston: D. Lothrop & Co., 1881. N.p. (IIc/8)

Brownjohn, John. *The Exploits of Miltiades Peterkin Paul, as Traveller, Adventurer, Knight, Astronomer, Politician.* Illus. Boston: D. Lothrop & Co., n.d. N.p. (Ih/27)

Buds and Flowers of Childish Life. Illus. London and N.Y.: George Routledge and Sons, n.d. 94 pp. (Ig/33)

Bulfinch, Maria H. *Margie: A Christmas Story.* N.Y.: General Protestant Episcopal Sunday School Union and Church Book Society, 1864. 136 pp. (IIa/48)

Burdett, Charles. *Never Too Late.* Happy Child's Library. N.Y.: D. Appleton & Co., 1873. 180 pp. (IIIa/31)

Burnham, Anna F. *Stories and Pictures of Wild Animals.* Illus. Boston: D. Lothrop & Co., 1879. N.p. (Ih/12)

Buttercups and Daisies for Little Children. Illus. London and N.Y.: George Routledge and Sons, n.d. 94 pp. (Ig/36)

Caballero, Fernan. *Spanish Fairy Tales.* Illus. Philadelphia: J. B. Lippincott & Co., n.d. 241 pp. (IIg/13)

Cahun, Léon. *The Adventures of Captain Mago; or, A Phoenician Expedition, B.C. 1000.* Illus. N.Y.: Charles Scribner's Sons, n.d. 344 pp. (IIIe/8)

Camden, Charles. *Hoity Toity the Good Little Fellow.* Illus. London: Strahan & Co., n.d. 195 pp. (IIb/31)

Mrs. Cameron. *The Farmer's Daughter.* Happy Child's Library. Illus. N.Y.: D. Appleton & Co., 1873. 180 pp. (IIIa/33)

Campbell, Helen. *Ainslee and His Friends.* The Ainslee Series. Illus. N.Y.: E. P. Dutton & Co., 1879. 411 pp. (Ie/11)

————. *Four and What They Did.* The Ainslee Series. Illus. N.Y.: E. P. Dutton & Co., 1879. 315 pp. (Ie/13)

————. *Grandpa's House.* The Ainslee Series. Illus. N.Y.: E. P. Dutton & Co., 1879. 239 pp. (Ie/12)

————. *Harry's Winter With the Indians; or White and Red.* The Ainslee Series. Illus. N.Y.: E. P. Dutton & Co., 1879. 266 pp. (Ie/14)

Carey, Annie. *School-Girls; or, Life at Montagu Hall.* Illus. London,
　　Paris & N.Y.: Cassell, Petter, Galpin & Co., n.d. 292 pp. (IIe/6)
――――. *School-Girls; or, Life at Montagu Hall.* Illus. London, Paris &
　　N.Y.: Cassell, Petter, Galpin & Co., n.d. 292 pp. (IIf/1)
*Caroline Westerly; or The Young Traveller from Ohio, Containing the
　　Letters of a Young Lady of Seventeen, Written to Her Sister.* Illus.
　　frontis. N.Y.: Harper & Bros., 1870. 228 pp. (IIa/28)
Carroll, Lewis. *Alice's Adventures in Wonderland.* Illus. N.Y.: Macmillan
　　& Co., 1861. 192 pp. (Id/15)
――――. *Through the Looking Glass, and What Alice Found There.* Illus.
　　London: Macmillan & Co., 1881. 224 pp. (Id/14)
Castlemon, Harry. *Frank at Don Carlos' Rancho.* The Rocky Mountain
　　Series. Illus. Philadelphia: Porter & Coates, [1871]. 280 pp. (IIb/3)
Catherwood, Mary Hartwell. *The Dogberry Bunch.* Illus. Boston: D.
　　Lothrop & Co., 1879. 310 pp. (IId/19)
Chaney, George L. *F. Grant & Co.; or, Partnerships. A Story for Boys
　　Who "Mean Business."* Illus. Boston: Roberts Brothers, 1875. 281 pp.
　　(IIc/17)
――――. *Tom. A Home Story.* Illus. frontis. Boston: Roberts Brothers,
　　1877. 279 pp. (IIc/16)
Channing, Barbara H. *Sunny Skies; or, Adventures in Italy.* Illus.
　　Boston: D. Lothrop & Co., n.d. 261 pp. (Ie/18)
Chase, Mary Granger. *Worth and Riches.* Illus. frontis. N.Y.: General
　　Protestant Episcopal Sunday School Union and Church Book Society,
　　1876, 206 pp. (Ia/8)
Chats for Small Chatters. The Cosy Corner Series. Illus. London, Paris
　　& N.Y.: Cassell, Petter, Galpin & Co., n.d. 183 pp. (IIe/25)
Cheesbro, Caroline. *Amy Carr; or, The Fortune-Teller.* Illus. N.Y.:
　　Dodd, Mead & Co., 1868. 196 pp. (IIIb/28)
The Children of Blessing. Golden Rule Library. Illus. London and N.Y.:
　　George Routledge and Sons, n.d. 402 pp. (Ia/51)
The Children of the Parsonage. Illus. N.Y.: E. P. Dutton & Co., 1874.
　　136 pp. (Ib/2)
The Children of the Parsonage. Illus. N.Y.: E. P. Dutton & Co., n.d.
　　159 pp. (Ib/33)
Children's Songs and Hymns. Illus. Philadelphia: J. B. Lippincott & Co.,
　　n.d. 64 pp. (IIIa/14)
Chimes and Rhymes for Youthful Times! Illus. London and N.Y.:
　　George Routledge and Sons, n.d. N.p. (Ig/34)
*The Chip Boy; or, Grandpapa's Story about a Plumcake. And Other
　　Stories.* Illus. London, Paris & N.Y.: Cassell, Petter, Galpin & Co.,
　　n.d. 149 pp. (IIe/36)
Chubbs, Jr. A Story for Boys. Illus. N.Y.: Dodd, Mead & Co., 1870. 406
　　pp. (IIIb/37)
Church, Ella Rodman. *Borrowed Plumes.* Illus. Boston: D. Lothrop &
　　Co., 1881. N.p. (IIc/12)
――――. *The Golden Days.* Illus. frontis. N.Y.: General Protestant
　　Episcopal Sunday School Union and Church Book Society, 1878. 409
　　pp. (IIc/13)

Clark, Mrs. S. R. G. *Our Street*. Illus. Boston: D. Lothrop & Co., 1880. 343 pp. (IIId/9)

——. *Yensie Walton*. Illus. Boston: D. Lothrop & Co., 1879. 391 pp. (IIId/8)

Clarke, J. Erskine, ed. *Chatterbox*. Illus. Boston: Estes and Lauriat, 1879. 408 pp. (Ih/30)

——. *Chatterbox*. Illus. Boston: Estes and Lauriat, 1881. 412 pp. (Ih/26)

——. *Chatterbox*. Illus. Boston: Estes & Lauriat, n.d. 411 pp. (Ih/25)

Cock Robin's Picture Book. Illus. London and N.Y.: George Routledge and Sons, n.d. N.p. (Ig/2)

Coffin, Charles Carleton. *Winning His Way*. Boston: Estes and Lauriat, 1881. 258 pp. (IIe/21)

Coleridge, Sara. *Phantasmion, a Fairy Tale*. Boston: Roberts Brothers, 1874. 348 pp. (Ie/9)

Colter, Mrs. J. J. *One Quiet Life*. Illus. Boston: D. Lothrop & Co., 1876. 108 pp. (IIf/7)

Comfort, Lucy Randall. *Folks and Fairies. Stories for Little Children*. Illus. N.Y.: Harper & Bros., 1868. 259 pp. (Ic/44)

Coolidge, Susan. *Nine Little Goslings*. Illus. Boston: Roberts Brothers, 1875. 289 pp. (IIg/12)

——. *What Katy Did at School*. Illus. 278 pp. Title page missing. (IIf/5)

——. *What Katy Did. A Story*. Illus. Boston: Roberts Brothers, 1881. 274 pp. (IIf/6)

Cooper, James F. *"Leather-Stocking" Tales, Comprising The Deer Slayer, The Pathfinder, The Last of the Mohicans, The Pioneers, The Prairie*. Illus. frontis. London: George Routledge and Sons, n.d. 938 pp. (IIg/1)

——. *Stories of the Prairie, and Other Adventures of the Border*. Illus. N.Y.: Hurd and Houghton, 1876. 339 pp. (IIg/2)

——. *Stories of the Sea: Being Narratives of Adventure*. Illus. N.Y.: Hurd and Houghton, 1872. 360 pp. (IIg/4)

——. *Stories of the Woods; or, Adventures of Leather-Stocking*. Illus. N.Y.: Hurd and Houghton, 1874. 345 pp. (IIg/3)

Corbet, Robert St. John. *The Holiday Camp; or, Three Days' Picnic*. Illus. London and N.Y.: George Routledge and Sons, n.d. 375 pp. (Id/32)

Countess Kate. Illus. frontis. Boston: Loring, n.d. 224 pp. (IIf/16)

Cousin Virginia. *The Christmas Stocking*. Illus. N.Y.: Thomas O'Kane, 1870. 155 pp. (IIc/23)

Cousin Zilpha. *Sunnydell; or, Leaves from Miss Caro's Green Book*. Sunny Dell Series. Illus. Boston: D. Lothrop & Co., n.d. 167 pp. (IIIa/45)

——. *Katy's Christmas*. The Doll's Club. Philadelphia: Claxton, Remson & Haffelfinger, 1871. 123 pp. (IIc/24)

Coxon, Ethel, Mrs. M. Douglas, and others. *A Brave Boy's Trials; or, Say Well Is a Good Word, but Do Well Is a Better. The Quiet Daughter; or, When the Sun Has Set, the Little Stars May Shine. A*

Dazzling Acquaintance; or, Fair Words Butter No Parsnips. The 'Golden Acorn' Series. Illus. Philadelphia: J. B. Lippincott & Co., 1881. 128 pp. (Ic/8)

————. *A Brave Boy's Trials; or, Say Well Is a Good Word, but Do Well Is a Better. The Quiet Daughter; or, When the Sun Has Set the Little Stars May Shine. A Dazzling Acquaintance; or, Fair Words Butter No Parsnips.* The 'Golden Acorn' Series. Illus. Philadelphia: J. B. Lippincott & Co., 1881. 128 pp. (Ic/9)

Crampton, T. *Aunt Effie's Rhymes for Children.* Illus. London and N.Y.: George Routledge and Sons, n.d. 91 pp. (Ih/29)

Miss Crompton. *Tales in Short Words. Written for the Use of Sunday Schools.* Illus. frontis. London: George Routledge and Sons, n.d. 124 pp. (IIa/18)

Dalton, William. *The Tiger Prince; or, Adventures in the Wilds of Abyssinia.* Illus. Boston: Roberts Brothers, n.d. 311 pp. (IIIe/14)

————. *The Tiger Prince; or, Adventures in the Wilds of Abyssinia.* Illus. Philadelphia: J. B. Lippincott & Co., 1877. 311 pp. (IIIe/15)

————. *The War Tiger; or, Adventures and Wonderful Fortunes of the Young Sea Chief and His Lad Chow: A Tale of the Conquest of China.* Illus. Philadelphia: J. B. Lippincott & Co., 1879. 337 pp. (IIIe/12)

————. *The Wolf Boy of China.* Illus: Philadelphia: J. B. Lippincott & Co., 1879. 339 pp. (IIIe/13)

Dana, Charles A., trans. *German Fairy Tales.* Illus. Philadelphia: J. B. Lippincott & Co., 1881. 299 pp. (IIg/11)

Davenport, Emma. *The Happy Holidays; or, Brothers and Sisters at Home.* Illus. frontis. N.Y.: E. P. Dutton & Co., n.d. 210 pp. (IIh/34)

Davenport, Capt. Henry E. *Rovings on Land and Sea.* Illus. Boston: Estes and Lauriat, 1880. 316 pp. (IIIh/7)

Davis, Mrs. C. E. K. *Holidays at Home. For Boys and Girls.* Illus. Boston: D. Lothrop & Co., 1878. 184 pp. (Ig/38)

Day, G. T., ed. *African Adventure and Adventurers.* Illus. Boston: D. Lothrop & Co., n.d. 393 pp. (IIIh/9)

Day, Thomas. *History of Sandford and Merton.* Illus. Philadelphia: Published for the Trade, n.d. 538 pp. (If/10)

————. *The History of Sandford and Merton.* Illus. London: Ward, Lock & Co., n.d. 388 pp. (If/12)

————. *The History of Sandford and Merton.* Illus. Boston: Roberts Brothers, n.d. 380 pp. (If/13)

————. *The History of Sandford and Merton.* Illus. London and N.Y.: George Routledge and Sons, n.d. 462 pp. (If/14)

De Bonnechose, Emile. *The Hero of Brittany: The Story of Bertrand du Guesclin, Constable of France and of Castile.* Trans. Margaret S. Jeune. Illus. frontis. N.Y.: E. P. Dutton & Co., n.d. 158 pp. (Ib/32)

Deering, Mary S. *An Average Boy's Vacation.* Forest City Series. Illus. Portland, Maine: Dresser, McLellan & Co., 1876. 166 pp. (Id/34)

————. *An Average Boy's Vacation.* Forest City Series. Illus. Portland, Maine: Dresser, McLellan & Co., 1876. 166 pp. (Id/35)

———. *Phil, Rob, and Louis; or, Haps and Mishaps.* Forest City Series. Illus. Portland, Maine: Dresser, McLellan & Co., 1878. 182 pp. (Id/36)

Defoe, Daniel. *The Life and Adventures of Robinson Crusoe, of York, Mariner.* Illus. N.Y.: G. W. Carleton & Co., 1880. 432 pp. (IIId/19)

———. *The Life and Strange Surprising Adventures of Robinson Crusoe, of York, Mariner.* Illus. N.Y.: Hurd and Houghton, 1868. 356 pp. (IIId/20)

———. *The Life and Strange Surprising Adventures of Robinson Crusoe, of York, Mariner.* Illus. London: Thomas Nelson and Sons, n.d. 648 pp. (IIId/21)

———. *The Life and Strange Surprising Adventures of Robinson Crusoe, of York, Mariner.* Illus. London: Thomas Nelson and Sons, n.d. 648 pp. (IIId/22)

———. *The Life and Adventures of Robinson Crusoe, of York, Mariner.* Illus. Philadelphia: J. B. Lippincott & Co., n.d. 312 pp. (IIId/23)

———. *Robinson Crusoe.* London: Macmillan & Co., 1873. 607 pp. (IIIe/1)

———. *Life and Adventures of Robinson Crusoe.* Illus. London: George Routledge and Sons, n.d. 589 pp. (IIIe/2)

———. *The Life and Adventures of Robinson Crusoe, Who Lived Twenty Seven Years in an Uninhabited Island, with an Account of His Deliverance.* Illus. Philadelphia: Claxton, Remsen & Haffelfinger, 1874. 251 pp. (Ia/12)

———. *The Life and Adventures of Robinson Crusoe.* Illus. London: Frederick Warne & Co., n.d. 284 pp. (Ia/13)

De Joinville, and Froisart. *Stories of the Olden Time.* Arranged by M. Jones. Illus. frontis. London and N.Y.: Cassell, Petter, Galpin & Co., n.d. 159 pp. (IIe/35)

De Morgan, Mary. *The Necklace of Princess Fiorimonde; and Other Stories.* Illus. London: Macmillan & Co., 1880. 184 pp. (Ib/1)

Denison, Mary A. *Anne's Saturday Afternoons.* Illus. Philadelphia: Alfred Martien, 1873. 119 pp. (Ia/36)

Densel, Mary. *Goldy and Goldy's Friends.* Illus. N.Y.: E. P. Dutton & Co., 1880. 139 pp. (Ib/19)

———. *Lloyd Dolan.* Illus. N.Y.: E. P. Dutton & Co., 1874. 284 pp. (Ib/18)

———. *Tel Tyler at School.* Illus. N.Y.: E. P. Dutton & Co., 1872. 186 pp. (Ib/21)

———. *Tel Tyler at School.* Illus. N.Y.: E. P. Dutton & Co., 1880. 186 pp. (Ib/22)

———. *Tel Tyler at School.* Illus. N.Y.: E. P. Dutton & Co., 1880. 186 pp. (Ib/23)

———. *Three Little Tylers.* Illus. N.Y.: E. P. Dutton & Co., 1880. 162 pp. (Ib/20)

The Dew-Drop, a Pure Gift for the Little Ones. Illus. Philadelphia: J. B. Lippincott & Co., n.d. 64 pp. (IIIa/20)

Diaz, Mrs. A. M. *Christmas Morning. Little Stories for Little Folks.*
Illus. Boston: D. Lothrop & Co., n.d. N.p. (If/5)
———. *King Grimalkum and Pussyanita; or, The Cat's Arabian Nights.*
Illus. Boston: D. Lothrop & Co., 1881. 227 pp. (Ih/11)
———. *Polly Cologne.* Illus. Boston: D. Lothrop & Co., 1881. 192 pp.
(If/7)
———. *William Henry and His Friends.* Illus. Boston: James R. Osgood,
1881. 265 pp. (If/9)
———. *The William Henry Letters.* Illus. Boston: Jamse R. Osgood,
1881. 257 pp. (If/8)
Didley Dumps; or, John Ellard the Newsboy. Illus. Philadelphia: Alfred
Martien, 1873. 216 pp. (Ia/33)
The Doctor's Ward; A Tale for Girls. Illus. London and N.Y.: George
Routledge and Sons, 1868. 396 pp. (Ib/14)
The Doctor's Ward; A Tale for Girls. Illus. London and N.Y.: George
Routledge and Sons, 1868. 396 pp. (Ib/15)
Doings of the Bodley Family in Town and Country. Illus. Boston:
Houghton, Mifflin & Co., 1882. 250 pp. (IId/1)
Dot's Story Book. The Cosy Corner Series. Illus. London, Paris & N.Y.:
Cassell, Petter, Galpin & Co., n.d. 183 pp. (IIe/28)
Dotey, Clara. *Blind Jakey.* Sunny Dell Series. Illus. Boston: D. Lothrop &
Co., 1869. 144 pp. (IIIa/47)
The Dream Chintz, Etc. Sunbeam Stories. Illus. N.Y.: George Routledge
and Sons, 1875. 344 pp. (Ia/48)
Drifting Goodward. Boston: Gould and Lincoln, 1872. 224 pp. (Ia/38)
Dame Durden. *Mabel Howard.* Illus. Boston: D. Lothrop & Co., 1877.
212 pp. (IIf/11)
Dyer, Rev. Sidney. *The Beautiful Ladder; or, The Two Students.* Illus.
Boston: D. Lothrop & Co., 1881. 348 pp. (IIIc/19)
———. *Boys and Birds; or, Miss Truant's Mission.* Illus. Boston: D.
Lothrop & Co., 1880. 414 pp. (IIIc/16)
———. *Elmdale Lyceum; or, God's Mighty Workers.* Illus. Boston: D.
Lothrop & Co., 1877. 320 pp. (IIIc/17)
———. *Hoofs and Claws; or, Mrs. Burton's Policy.* Illus. Boston: D
Lothrop & Co., 1880. 363 pp. (IIIc/15)
———. *Ocean Gardens and Palaces; or, The Tent on the Beach.* Illus.
Boston: D. Lothrop & Co., 1880. 304 pp. (IIIc/18)

E. A. J. *The Christmas Tapers, and Other Stories.* Illus. frontis. General
Protestant Episcopal Sunday School Union and Church Book Society,
1870. 79 pp. (Ig/28)
Early Friendships. Happy Child's Library. N.Y.: D. Appleton & Co. 174
pp. Title page missing. (IIIa/24)
Eastern Fairy Legends. Enchanting Fairy Tales. Illus. Philadelphia: J. B.
Lippincott & Co. 331 pp. Title page missing. (IIg/14)
Edgeworth, Maria. *Moral Tales.* Illus. Philadelphia: J. B. Lippincott &
Co., 1880. 180 pp. (If/24)
———. *Parent's Assistant.* Illus. Routledge. 472 pp. Title page missing.
(If/22)

———. *Popular Tales*. Illus. London and New York: George Routledge and Sons, n.d. 413 pp. (If/21)

———. *Popular Tales*. Illus. Philadelphia: J. B. Lippincott & Co., 1880. 446 pp. (If/23)

Edson, N. I. *Silent Tom*. Illus. Boston: D. Lothrop & Co., 1872. 377 pp. (IIId/5)

E. L. F. *Our House in the Marsh Land; or, Days of Auld Lang Syne*. Illus. N.Y.: E. P. Dutton & Co., n.d. 191 pp. (IIf/28)

Eliot, Samuel, ed. *Six Stories from the Arabian Nights*. Illus. Boston: George A. Smith, 1880. 210 pp. (Id/19)

Elliott, J. W., and J. M. Bentley. *The "Little Folks" Album of Music. A Collection of Songs and Rhymes*. Illus. London, Paris & N.Y.: Cassell, Petter, Galpin & Co., n.d. 128 pp. (Ih/4)

Mrs. Ellis. *The Dangers of Dining Out; or, Hints to Those Who Would Make Home Happy*. Happy Child's Library. Illus. frontis. N.Y.: D. Appleton & Co., 1873. 174 pp. (IIIa/29)

———. *First Impressions; or, Hints to Those Who Would Make Home Happy*. Happy Child's Library. N.Y.: D. Appleton & Co., 1873. 174 pp. (IIIa/30)

———. *The Minister's Family; or, Hints to Those Who Would Make Home Happy*. Happy Child's Library. N.Y.: D. Appleton & Co., 1873. 174 pp. (IIIa/27)

———. *The Minister's Family; or, Hints to Those Who Would Make Home Happy*. Happy Child's Library. N.Y.: D. Appleton & Co., 1873. 174 pp. (IIIa/28)

———. *Somerville Hall; or, Hints to Those Who Would Make Home Happy*. Happy Child's Library. Illus. frontis. N.Y.: D. Appleton & Co., 1873. 174 pp. (IIIa/26)

Elson, Louis C. *Home and School. An Illustrated Song Book for Children*. Illus. Boston: D. Lothrop & Co., 1881. N.p. (Ih/6)

Elwes, Alfred. *Surprising Adventures of Paul Blake; or, The Story of a Boy's Peril in the Islands of Corsica and Monte Cristo*. Illus. Philadelphia: J. B. Lippincott & Co., 1879. 383 pp. (IIId/17)

Embury, Emma C. *The Blind Girl. With Other Tales*. N.Y.: Harper & Bros., 1860. 222 pp. (Ia/22)

———. *Pictures of Early Life; or, Sketches of Youth*. N.Y.: Harper & Bros., 1867. 310 pp. (Ia/21)

The Emigrant Children; or, Learning to Follow Jesus. Illus. Boston: D. Lothrop & Co., n.d. 276 pp. (IIIc/26)

Evelyn Hope; and the Game of Life. Illus. frontis. Boston: Massachusetts Sabbath-School Society, 1865. 79 pp. (IIa/51)

Ewing, Juliana Horatia. *A Great Emergency, and Other Tales*. Illus. frontis. Boston: Roberts Brothers, 1877. 284 pp. (IId/27)

———. *Six to Sixteen. A Story for Girls*. Illus. Boston: Roberts Brothers, 1881. 296 pp. (IId/28)

———. *The Story of a Short Life*. Illus. London: Society for Promoting Christian Knowledge; N.Y.: E. & J. B. Young, n.d. 82 pp. (IId/30)

———. *We and the World. A Book for Boys*. Illus. Boston: Roberts Brothers, 1880. 310 pp. (IId/29)

The Fairy Book: The Best Popular Fairy Stories Selected and Rendered Anew. London: Macmillan & Co., 1878. 368 pp. (Ia/28)

The Faithful Dog, and Other Stories. Illus. Philadelphia: J. B. Lippincott & Co., n.d. 64 pp. (IIIa/18)

Faithful Fido and Other Tales. Illus. Philadelphia: J. B. Lippincott & Co., n.d. 64 pp. (IIIa/2)

Famous Islands and Memorable Voyages. Illus. Boston: D. Lothrop & Co., n.d. 217 pp. (Ie/22)

Fanfan. *The Old Church in the Corner.* N.Y.: General Protestant Episcopal Sunday School Union and Church Book Society, 1869. 196 pp. (Ia/5)

Farley, Harriet. *Fancy's Frolics: or, Christmas Stories Told in a Happy Home (Hazelnook) in New England.* Illus. N.Y.: R. Worthington, 1880. 256 pp. (IIg/8)

Farquharson, Martha. *Our Fred; or, Seminary Life at Thurston.* Illus. N.Y.: Dodd, Mead & Co., 1871. 335 pp. (IIIb/38)

The Favorite Album of Fun and Fancy. N.Y.: Cassell, Petter, Galpin & Co. 192 pp. Title page missing. (Ih/18)

Fell, Archie. *Maybee's Stepping-Stones.* Illus. Boston: D. Lothrop & Co., 1880. 347 pp. (IIIc/21)

Fickle Flora; or, The Trial of Friendship. E. P. Dutton. 156 pp. Title page missing. (Ib/36)

Finley, Martha (Martha Farquharson). *Elsie's Girlhood: A Sequel to "Elsie Dinsmore," and "Elsie's Holidays at Roselands".* Illus. frontis. N.Y.: Dodd, Mead & Co., 1872. 422 pp. (IIc/25)

Fisler, Mrs. Annie. *Stories of a Governess.* Illus. N.Y.: Protestant Episcopal Sunday-School Union and Church Book Depository, 1870. 178 pp. (Ia/10)

Foolish Zoe. Illus. Boston: Roberts Brothers, 1868. N.p. (Id/13)

Forest, Neil. *Mice at Play. When the Cat's Away, the Mice Will Play. A Story for the Whole Family.* Illus. Boston: Roberts Brothers, 1876. 271 pp. (Ic/15)

Forster, The Rev. Edward, trans. *Select Tales from the Arabian Nights Entertainments.* Illus. N.Y.: Geo. A. Leavitt, n.d. 142 pp. (Ib/40)

Foster, Emile. *The Haven Children; or, Frolics at the Funny Old House on Funny Street.* Illus. N.Y.: E. P. Dutton & Co., 1876. 270 pp. (IIb/2)

Four Years Old. Illus. N.Y.: Dodd, Mead & Co., n.d. 201 pp. (IIa/29)

Frank. *Fourteen Pet Goslings, and Other Pretty Stories of My Childhood.* Illus. Boston: J. E. Tilton & Co., 1858. 102 pp. (IIa/13)

Friendly Hands, Kindly Words: Stories Illustrative of the Law of Kindness, the Power of Perseverence, and the Advantages of Little Helps. Friendly Hand Series. Illus. Philadelphia: Porter & Coates, n.d. N.p. (Ib/30)

From Darkness to Light; or, A Christmas Carol, and What Came of It. Sunny Dell Series. Illus. Boston: D. Lothrop & Co., n.d. 103 pp. (IIIa/44)

Garrett, Edward. *The Magic Flower-Pot, and Other Stories.* Illus. frontis.
London, Paris & N.Y.: Cassell, Petter, Galpin & Co., n.d. 284 pp.
(IIg/28)

Gaskoin, Mrs. Herman. *Children's Treasury of Bible Stories. Part I—
Old Testament.* London: Macmillan & Co., 1879. 182 pp. (Ib/44)

––––––. *Children's Treasury of Bible Stories. Part II—New Testament.*
London: Macmillan & Co., 1879. 126 pp. (Ib/45)

––––––. *Children's Treasury of Bible Stories. Part III—The Apostles.*
London: Macmillan & Co., 1880. 126 pp. (Ib/46)

Geddie, John. *Beyond the Himalayas. A Story of Travel and Adventure
in the Wilds of Thibet.* Illus. London, Edinburgh and N.Y.: T. Nelson
and Sons, 1882. 256 pp. (IIId/13)

Gerstaecker, Frederick. *Frank Wildman's Adventures on Land and
Water.* Trans. Lascelles Wraxall. Illus. Philadelphia: J. B. Lippincott
& Co., 1878. 312 pp. (IIIe/16)

Giberne, Agnes. *The Hillside Children.* Illus. frontis. N.Y.: E. P. Dutton,
n.d. 259 pp. (IIe/4)

A Gift for the Little Ones at Home. Illus. Philadelphia: J. B. Lippincott
& Co., n.d. 64 pp. (IIIa/19)

Girls' Playtime Book. Illus. 502 pp. Title page missing. (Ih/7)

Glyndon, Howard. *Brother and Sister; or, A Little Boy's Story.* Illus.
Philadelphia: J. B. Lippincott & Co., 1879. 306 pp. (IIh/13)

––––––. *Brother and Sister; or, A Little Boy's Story.* Illus. Philadelphia:
J. B. Lippincott & Co., 1879. 306 pp. (IIh/14)

Grandfather's Visit, and Other Stories. Illus. Philadelphia: J. B.
Lippincott & Co., n.d. 64 pp. (IIIa/5)

Grant, James. *The Adventures of Rob Roy.* Illus. Philadelphia: J. B.
Lippincott & Co., 1880. 387 pp. (IIIe/10)

––––––. *Dick Rodney; or, The Adventures of an Eton Boy.* Illus.
Philadelphia: J. B. Lippincott & Co., 1878. 424 pp. (IIIe/11)

––––––. *Dick Rodney; or, The Adventures of an Eton Boy.* Every Boy's
Library. London and New York: George Routledge and Sons, n.d.
434 pp. Final pages possibly missing. (IIa/6)

Gray, Louisa M. *Ada and Gerty; or, Hand in Hand Heavenward.* Illus.
London, Edinburgh and N.Y.: Thomas Nelson and Sons, 1882. 336
pp. (IIf/21)

––––––. *Ada and Gerty; or, Hand in Hand Heavenward.* Illus. London,
Edinburgh and N.Y.: Thomas Nelson and Sons, 1882. 336 pp.
(IIf/22)

––––––. *Nelly's Teachers and What They Learned.* Illus. frontis. London,
Edinburgh and N.Y.: T. Nelson and Sons, 1882. 448 pp.
(IIf/19)

––––––. *Nelly's Teachers and What They Learned.* Illus. frontis. London,
Edinburgh and N.Y.: T. Nelson and Sons, 1882. 448 pp. (IIf/20)

Greene, The Honorable Mrs. *Jubilee Hall; or, "There's No Place Like
Home." A Story for the Young.* Illus. frontis. London, Edinburgh and
N.Y.: T. Nelson and Sons, 1881. 220 pp. (Ie/5)

———. *Jubilee Hall; or, "There's No Place Like Home." A Story for the Young*. Illus. frontis. London, Edinburgh and N.Y.: T. Nelson and Sons, 1881. 220 pp. (Ie/6)

Greenwood, James. *The Adventures of Reuben Davidger; Seventeen Years and Four Months Captive Among the Dyaks of Borneo*. Illus. N.Y.: Harper & Bros., 1866. 344 pp. (If/32)

Hughes Public Library, Rugby, Tennessee

Griffis, William Elliot. *Japanese Fairy World. Stories from the Wonder-Lore of Japan*. Illus. Schenectady, N.Y.: James H. Barhyte, 1880. 304 pp. (Ia/4)

The Brothers Grimm. *The Almond-Tree and Other Tales*. Illus. London and N.Y.: George Routledge and Sons, n.d. 128 pp. (Ic/19)

———. *The Brave Little Tailor and Other Fairy Tales*. Illus. N.Y.: James Miller, 1876. 158 pp. (Ic/27)

———. *Clever Alice and Other Tales*. Illus. London and N.Y.: George Routledge and Sons, n.d. 128 pp. (Ic/20)

———. *The Donkey Cabbages and Other Tales*. Illus. London and N.Y.: George Routledge and Sons, n.d. 126 pp. (Ic/23)

———. *The Golden Bird and Other Fairy Tales*. Illus. N.Y.: James Miller, 1877. 180 pp. (Ic/28)

———. *Grimm's Fairy Tales*. Illus. Philadelphia: J. B. Lippincott & Co. 543 pp. Title page missing. (IIg/15)

————. *The Old Woman in the Wood and Other Tales.* Illus. London and N.Y.: George Routledge and Sons, n.d. 128 pp. (Ic/21)

————. *Snow-White and Rose-Red and Other Tales.* Illus. London and N.Y.: George Routledge and Sons, n.d. 128 pp. (Ic/22)

————. *Snow-White and Rose-Red and Other Tales.* Illus. London and N.Y.: George Routledge and Sons, n.d. 128 pp. (Ic/26)

————. *The Three Brothers and Other Tales.* Illus. London and N.Y.: George Routledge and Sons, n.d. 128 pp. (Ic/18)

————. *The Three Brothers and Other Tales.* Illus. London and N.Y.: George Routledge and Sons, n.d. 128 pp. (Ic/24)

————. *The Three Brothers and Other Tales.* Illus. London and N.Y.: George Routledge and Sons, n.d. 128 pp. (Ic/25)

Godolphin, Mary. *Sandford and Merton, in Words of One Syllable.* Illus. frontis. London, Paris & N.Y.: Cassell, Petter, Galpin & Co., n.d. 288 pp. (If/15)

Guernsey, Clara F. *A Mere Piece of Mischief: or, Amiel's Troubles.* Illus. Philadelphia: Alfred Martien, 1874. 238 pp. (Ia/34)

Habberton, John. *The Worst Boy in Town.* Illus. N.Y.: G. P. Putnam's Sons, 1880. 214 pp. (IIb/29)

Hackländer. *Enchanting and Enchanted.* Trans. Mrs. A. L. Wister. Illus. Philadelphia: J. B. Lippincott & Co., 1879. 226 pp. (IIg/17)

Haile, Ellen. *Hazel-Nut and Her Brothers.* Illus. N.Y., London and Paris: Cassell, Petter, Galpin & Co., 1881. 253 pp. (Ih/14)

Hale, Edward E. *Stories of Adventure Told by Adventurers.* Illus. frontis. Boston: Roberts Brothers, 1881. 310 pp. (IIb/16)

————. *Stories of the Sea Told by Sailors.* Illus. frontis. Boston: Roberts Brothers, 1880. 300 pp. (IIb/17)

Hall, Mrs. S. C. *The Whisperer.* Illus. frontis. N.Y.: Dodd & Mead, n.d. 149 pp. (Ib/27)

Hamilton's Cottagers of Glenburnie. Illus. Philadelphia: Perkinpine & Higgins, n.d. 137 pp. (IIa/12)

The Happy Land; or, "Willie the Orphan". Illus. N.Y.: Dodd & Mead, n.d. 131 pp. (IIc/22)

Harcourt, Major Alfred F. P. *The Royal Umbrella.* Illus. N.Y.: E. P. Dutton & Co., 1880. 128 pp. (IId/16)

Harnard, Lois. *Velvet-Coat, the Cat. A Story for Children.* Illus. frontis. Philadelphia: Claxton, Remsen & Haffelfinger, 1870. 125 pp. (Ic/35)

Harris, Miriam C. *Marguerite's Journal. A Story for Girls.* N.Y.: G. W. Carleton & Co., 1875. 328 pp. (IIg/6)

Harris, William T., Andrew J. Rickoff, and Mark Bailey, eds. *Appleton's Fifth Reader.* Illus. N.Y.: D. Appleton & Co., 1880. 471 pp. (Ia/1)

Harrison, Jennie. *The Old Back Room.* Illus. frontis. N.Y.: Dodd, Mead & Co., 1871. 392 pp. (IIIb/39)

Harry Lee; or, Hope for the Poor. Illus. N.Y.: Harper & Bros., 1859. 381 pp. (IId/9)

Harry's Summer in Ashcroft. Illus. N.Y.: Harper & Bros., 1860. 204 pp. (Ic/45)

Hatheway, Mary E. N. *Johnny's Vacations, and Other Stories.* Illus.
Boston: D. Lothrop & Co., 1878. 250 pp. (IId/17)

Haweis, Rev. H. R. *Pet; or, Pastimes and Penalties.* Illus. N.Y.: Harper
& Bros., 1874. 314 pp. (Ie/24)

Hawthorne, Nathaniel. *The Snow-Image: A Childish Miracle.* Illus.
N.Y.: Hurd and Houghton, 1866. 31 pp. (Ic/1)

––––––. *Tanglewood Tales, for Girls and Boys.* Boston: Houghton, Mifflin
& Co., 1881. 243 pp. (IIb/6)

––––––. *True Stories.* Boston: Houghton, Mifflin & Co., 1880. 389 pp.
(IIb/7)

––––––. *A Wonder-Book for Girls and Boys.* Illus. Boston: Houghton
Mifflin & Co., 1881. 256 pp. (IIb/5)

Hazen, Jacob A. *Five Years Before the Mast; or, Life in the Forecastle,
Aboard of a Whaler and Man-of-War.* Illus. Philadelphia: J. B.
Lippincott & Co., 1879. 444 pp. (IIIe/17)

Heaton, Mrs. Charles. *Happy Child Life.* Illus. London and N.Y.:
George Routledge and Sons, 1875. 78 pp. (Ig/32)

––––––. *Routledge's Album for Children.* Illus. London and N.Y.: George
Routledge and Sons, n.d. 368 pp. Final pages probably missing.
(IIh/10)

––––––. *Routledge's Sunday Album for Children.* Illus. London and N.Y.:
George Routledge and Sons, n.d. 309 pp. (IIh/8)

Henry's Holiday, and Other Stories. Illus. Philadelphia: J. B. Lippincott
& Co., n.d. 64 pp. (IIIa/12)

Henry Willard: or, The Value of Right Principles. Illus. N.Y.: Dodd,
Mead & Co., 1858. 318 pp. (IIIb/35)

Henty, G. A. *The Cornet of Horse. A Tale of Marlborough's Wars.* Illus.
Philadelphia: J. B. Lippincott & Co., 1881. 278 pp. (IIIe/19)

––––––. *The Young Franc-Tireurs and Their Adventures in the Franco-
Prussian War.* Illus. N.Y.: E. P. Dutton & Co., n.d. 376 pp. (IIIe/20)

Hering, Jeanie. *Golden Days. A Tale of Girls' School Life in Germany.*
Illus. frontis. London, Paris & N.Y.: Cassell, Petter, Galpin & Co., n.d.
311 pp. (IIe/5)

Heroic Life; or, Pictures of Heroes. With Lessons from Their Lives.
Illus. Philadelphia: J. B. Lippincott & Co., 1879. 247 pp. (If/28)

H. H. *Bits of Talk, in Verse and Prose, for Young Talkers.* Illus. Boston:
Roberts Brothers, 1879. 244 pp. (Ig/10)

––––––. *Mammy Tittleback and Her Family. A True Story of Seventeen
Cats.* Illus. Boston: Roberts Brothers, 1881. 101 pp. (Ig/6)

H. H. H. *Mrs. Linden's Teachings.* N.Y.: Protestant Episcopal Sunday
School Union and Church Book Society, n.d. 251 pp. (Ia/6)

Hildebrand, C. *Winter in Spitzbergen. A Tale of the Northland.* Illus.
N.Y.: Dodd & Mead, 1870. 300 pp. (Ib/7)

H. K. P. *The Orphans' Triumphs; or, The Story of Lily and Harry Grant.*
Illus. frontis. N.Y.: Dodd, Mead & Co., 1868. 295 pp. (IIIb/26)

––––––. *Paul and Margaret, the Inebriate's Children.* Illus. frontis. N.Y.:
Dodd, Mead & Co., 1869. 178 pp. (IIIb/25)

––––––. *Robert, the Cabin Boy.* Illus. frontis. N.Y. Dodd, Mead & Co.,
1868. 227 pp. (IIIb/27)

H. N. W. B. *Sophia and the Gipsies*. Sunshine Series. Illus. frontis.
 Boston: Andrew F. Graves, 1870. 171 pp. (Ia/37)
Hodder, Edwin. *Old Merry's Travels on the Continent*. Illus.
 Philadelphia: J. B. Lippincott & Co., 1873. 198 pp. (Id/11)
_____. *Tom Heriot: His Adventures and Misadventures*. Illus. London,
 Paris & N.Y.: Cassell, Petter, Galpin & Co., n.d. 212 pp. (Id/10)
Hofer, the Tyrolese. Illus. N.Y.: E. P. Dutton, n.d. 159 pp. (Ib/39)
Hoffman, Franz. *The Hartz Boys; or, As a Man Sows, So Must He Reap*.
 Illus. Boston: D. Lothrop & Co., n.d. 101 pp. (IIIc/20)
Mrs. Hofland. *The Good Grandmother and Her Offspring*. Illus. frontis.
 Philadelphia: Porter & Coates, n.d. 150 pp. (IIa/39)
_____. *The Merchant's Widow and Her Family*. Illus. frontis.
 Philadelphia: Porter & Coates, n.d. 178 pp. (IIa/42)
_____. *The Son of a Genius. A Tale, for the Use of Youth*. Boys' and
 Girls' Library. N.Y.: Harper & Bros., n.d. 213 pp. (Ia/23)
_____. *The Son of a Genius*. Illus. frontis. Philadelphia: Porter & Coates,
 n.d. 210 pp. (IIa/43)
Holmes, Mrs. Mary J. *Red-Bird. A Brown Cottage Story*. Illus. N.Y.:
 G. W. Carleton & Co., 1880. 107 pp. (Ia/43)
Holt, M. H. *Fern Glen; or, Lilian's Prayer*. Illus. N.Y.: Dodd, Mead &
 Co., n.d. 368 pp. (IIIb/36)
The Home Story Book. Illus. Philadelphia: J. B. Lippincott & Co., n.d.
 64 pp. (IIIa/1)
Homespun, Sophia. *Blue-Eyed Jimmy; or The Good Boy*. Illus. Boston:
 D. Lothrop & Co., 1870. 246 pp. (IIIc/12)
_____. *Johnny Jones; or The Bad Boy*. Illus. Boston: D. Lothrop & Co.,
 1870. 243 pp. (IIIc/11)
_____. *Much Fruit*. Illus. Boston: D. Lothrop & Co., n.d. 272 pp.
 (IIIc/10)
_____. *Nattie Nesmith; or, The Bad Girl*. Boston: D. Lothrop & Co.,
 1870. 280 pp. (IIIc/13)
_____. *Ruthie Shaw: or, The Good Girl*. Illus. Boston: D. Lothrop &
 Co., 1870. 294 pp. (IIIc/14)
Hood, Rev. Paxton. *Bye-Path Meadow*. Illus. frontis. Boston: D. Lothrop
 & Co., 1870. 464 pp. (IId/32)
_____. *Bye-Path Meadow*. Illus. frontis. Boston: D. Lothrop & Co., 1870.
 464 pp. (IId/33)
Hood, Thomas and Jane. *Fairy Land or Recreation for the Rising
 Generation*. Illus. N.Y.: E. P. Dutton & Co., n.d. 173 pp. (IIf/23)
Hope, Ascott R. *My Schoolboy Friends: A Story of Whitminster
 Grammar School*. N.Y.: R. Worthington, 1880. 354 pp. (IId/8)
Hope, F. T. L. *The Three Homes: A Tale for Fathers and Sons*. Illus.
 N.Y.: E. P. Dutton & Co., n.d. 389 pp. (IId/10)
Hosmer, Mrs. Margaret. *Juliet the Heiress*. Illus. frontis. Philadelphia:
 James A. Moore, 1869. 230 pp. (IIa/32)
_____. *Little Rosie's Christmas Times*. Little Rosie Series. Illus. frontis.
 Philadelphia: Porter & Coates, 1869. 175 pp. (IIa/31)
_____ *Little Rosie in the Country*. Little Rosie Series. Illus. frontis.
 Philadelphia: Porter & Coates, 1869. 168 pp. (IIa/30)

———. *Three Times Lost; or, Patty Norris*. Illus. frontis. Philadelphia:
James A. Moore, 1870. 233 pp. (IIa/33)

Howitt, Mary. *Mabel on Midsummer Day. A Story of the Olden Time*.
Illus. Boston: James R. Osgood, 1881. N.p. (Ih/1)

———. *Tales in Prose: For the Young*. Illus. frontis. N.Y.: Harper &
Bros., 1885. 183 pp. (Ia/27)

Howitt, William. *The Boy's Country-Book*. Illus. London, Edinburgh and
N.Y.: T. Nelson and Sons, 1880. 355 pp. (Ie/29)

———. *The Boy's Country-Book*. Illus. London, Edinburgh and N.Y.:
T. Nelson and Sons, 1880. 355 pp. (Ie/30)

Hunt, Madeline Bonavia. *Aunt Tabitha's Waifs*. Illus. London, Paris &
N.Y.: Cassell, Petter, Galpin & Co., n.d. 214 pp. (Id/9)

———. *Brave Little Heart*. Illus. London and N.Y.: George Routledge
and Sons, 1878. 316 pp. (Id/6)

———. *Brave Little Heart*. Illus. London and N.Y.: George Routledge
and Sons, 1878. 316 pp. (Id/7)

———. *Little Empress Joan*. Illus. London, Paris & N.Y.: Cassell, Petter,
Galpin & Co., n.d. 276 pp. (Id/5)

———. *Little Hinges*. Illus. London, Paris & N.Y.: Cassell, Petter &
Galpin, n.d. 287 pp. (Id/4)

Hutton, Barbara. *Castles and Their Heroes*. Illus. N.Y.: E. P. Dutton,
n.d. 306 pp. (If/30)

Ingelow, Jean. *Stories Told to a Child*. Illus. Boston: Roberts Brothers,
1880. 227 pp. (IIb/32)

In Mischief Again. Illus. London, Paris & N.Y.: Cassell, Petter, Galpin &
Co., n.d. 224 pp. (Ic/5)

Isabel; or, The Trials of the Heart. A Tale for the Young. N.Y.: Harper
& Bros., 1845. 182 pp. (Ia/25)

*Jack in the Forecastle; or, Incidents in the Early Life of Hawser
Martingale*. Illus. Boston: Estes and Lauriat, 1880. 452 pp. (IIIh/5)

James, Rev. Thomas. *Aesop's Fables: A New Version. Chiefly from
Original Sources*. Illus. Philadelphia: Porter & Coates, n.d. 215 pp.
(Id/17)

Jefferies, Richard. *Wood Magic; A Fable*. London, Paris & N.Y.: Cassell,
Petter, Galpin & Co., 1881. 263 pp. (IIg/7)

Jenness, Mrs. Theodora. *Two Young Homesteaders*. Illus. Boston: D.
Lothrop & Co., 1880. 238 pp. Final pages missing. (Ie/28)

Jewett, Sarah O. *Play Days. A Book of Stories for Children*. Boston:
Houghton, Mifflin & Co., 1881. 213 pp. (Id/28)

Johnson, M. O. *Carrie Ellsworth; or, Seed-Sowing*. Illus. Boston: D.
Lothrop & Co., 1878. 225 pp. (Ie/26)

———. *Carrie Ellsworth; or, Seed-Sowing*. Illus. Boston: D. Lothrop &
Co., 1878. 225 pp. (IIf/9)

Johnson, Rossiter. *Two Fortune-Seekers; and Other Stories*. Illus. Boston:
D. Lothrop & Co., 1875. 345 pp. (Ie/27)

Jones, J. B. *The War-Path: A Narrative of Adventures in the Wilderness:
With Minute Details of the Capitivity of Sundry Persons, Etc.* Wild

Western Scenes—Second Series. Illus. Philadelphia: J. B. Lippincott & Co., 1881. 335 pp. (IIId/14)
———. *Wild Western Scenes: A Narrative of Adventures in the Western Wilderness, Wherein the Exploits of Daniel Boone, the Great American Pioneer Are Particularly Described, Etc.* Illus. Philadelphia: J. B. Lippincott & Co., 1881. 263 pp. (IIId/15)
J. O. Y. *Rambling Chats and Chatty Rambles.* Illus. N.Y.: E. P. Dutton & Co., 1873. 210 pp. (IIb/35)
———. *Rambling Chats and Chatty Rambles.* Illus. N.Y.: E. P. Dutton & Co., 1873. 210 pp. (IIb/36)

Kampe, J. H. *The Swiss Family Robinson; or, Adventures in a Desert Island.* Illus. Philadelphia: J. B. Lippincott & Co., 1881. 383 pp. (IIIe/6)
———. *The Swiss Family Robinson; or, Adventures of a Father, Mother, and Four Sons, in a Desert Island.* Illus. N.Y.: G. W. Carleton & Co., 1880. 450 pp. (IIIe/7)
———. *The Swiss Family Robinson; or, Adventures of a Shipwrecked Family on a Desolate Island.* Illus. London, Edinburgh and N.Y.: T. Nelson and Sons, 1878. 690 pp. (IIIe/5)
———. *The Swiss Family Robinson.* Illus. 284 pp. Title page missing. Final pages missing. (IIIe/4)
Keary, E. *The Magic Valley; or, Patient Antoine.* Illus. London: Macmillan & Co., 1877. 176 pp. (IIg/29)
Keeping On, and Other Stories. Keeping On Series. Illus. N.Y.: T. Y. Crowell & Co., n.d. 112 pp. (Ig/22)
Kennedy, Grace. *Anna Ross the Orphan of Waterloo.* Illus. London and N.Y.: George Routledge and Sons, n.d. 123 pp. (Ib/4)
Kingsley, Rev. Charles. *The Water Babies. A Fairy Tale for a Land Baby.* Illus. London: Macmillan & Co., 1876. 388 pp. (IIe/10)
———. *The Water-Babies: A Fairy Tale for a Land-Baby.* Illus. frontis. N.Y.: Macmillan & Co., 1881. 310 pp. (IIe/24)
Kingsley, Henry. *Valentin. A French Boy's Story of Sedan.* Illus. London and N.Y.: George Routledge and Sons, n.d. 310 pp. (Ie/10)
Kingston, W. H. G. *Charley Laurel: A Story of Adventure by Sea and Land.* Illus. Boston: D. Lothrop & Co., n.d. 329 pp. (IIIi/22)
———. *Dick Cheveley: His Adventures and Misadventures.* Illus. Philadelphia: J. B. Lippincott & Co., 1881. 396 pp. (IIIj/18)
———. *The Fisher Boy; or, Michael Penguyne.* Illus. Boston: D. Lothrop & Co., n.d. 200 pp. (IIIh/2)
———. *Fred Markham in Russia; or, The Boy Travellers in the Land of the Czar.* Illus. N.Y.: E. P. Dutton & Co., n.d. 320 pp. (IIIi/1)
———. *Fred Markham in Russia; or, The Boy Travelers in the Land of the Czar.* Illus. N.Y.: Harper & Bros., 1858. 315 pp. (IIb/18)
———. *Hendricks the Hunter; or, The Border Farm: A Tale of Zululand.* Illus. N.Y.: A. C. Armstrong and Sons, 1881. 313 pp. (IIIj/21)
———. *In the Eastern Seas; or, The Regions of the Bird of Paradise. A Tale for Boys.* Illus. London, Edinburgh and N.Y.: T. Nelson and Sons, 1881. 608 pp. (IIIj/1)

————. *In the Eastern Seas; or, The Regions of the Bird of Paradise. A Tale for Boys.* Illus. London, Edinburgh and N.Y.: T. Nelson and Sons, 1881. 608 pp. (IIIj/2)

————. *In the Forest. A Tale of Settler-Life in North America.* Illus. London, Edinburgh and N.Y.: T. Nelson and Sons, 1880. 393 pp. (IIIj/8)

————. *In New Granada; or, Heroes and Patriots. A Tale for Boys.* Illus. London, Edinburgh and N.Y.: Thomas Nelson and Sons, 1879. 368 pp. (IIIj/7)

————. *In New Granada; or, Heroes and Patriots. A Tale for Boys.* Illus. London, Edinburgh and N.Y.: Thomas Nelson and Sons, 1879. 368 pp. (IIIj/9)

————. *In the Rocky Mountains. A Tale of Adventure.* Illus. London, Edinburgh and N.Y.: T. Nelson and Sons, 1882. 334 pp. (IIIj/10)

————. *In the Rocky Mountains. A Tale of Adventure.* Illus. London, Edinburgh and N.Y.: T. Nelson and Sons, 1882. 334 pp. (IIIj/11)

————. *In the Wilds of Africa. A Tale for Boys.* Illus. London, Edinburgh and N.Y.: T. Nelson and Sons, 1881. 558 pp. (IIIj/5)

————. *In the Wilds of Africa. A Tale for Boys.* Illus. London, Edinburgh and N.Y.: T. Nelson and Sons, 1881. 558 pp. (IIIj/6)

————. *In the Wilds of Florida. A Tale of Warfare and Hunting.* Illus. London, Edinburgh and N.Y.: T. Nelson and Sons, 1880. 461 pp. (IIIj/3)

————. *In the Wilds of Florida. A Tale of Warfare and Hunting.* Illus. London, Edinburgh and N.Y.: T. Nelson and Sons, 1880. 461 pp. (IIIj/4)

————. *Little Ben Hadden; or, Do Right, Whatever Comes of It.* Illus. Boston: D. Lothrop & Co., n.d. 267 pp. (IIIi/23)

————. *Mark Seaworth. A Tale of the Indian Ocean.* Illus. Philadelphia: J. B. Lippincott & Co., 1877. 401 pp. (IIIj/17)

————. *The Midshipman Marmaduke Merry; or, My Early Days at Sea.* Illus. Philadelphia: J. B. Lippincott & Co., 1880. 400 pp. (IIIj/13)

————. *The Missing Ship; or, Notes from the Log of the "Ouzel" Galley.* Illus. London: Griffith, Farran, Okeden and Welsh, n.d. 444 pp. (IIIj/24)

————. *My First Voyage to Southern Seas. A Book for Boys.* Illus. London, Edinburgh and N.Y.: T. Nelson and Sons, 1880. 448 pp. (IIIi/18)

————. *My First Voyage to Southern Seas. A Book for Boys.* Illus. London, Edinburgh and N.Y.: T. Nelson and Sons, 1880, 448 pp. (IIIi/19)

————. *Old Jack. A Tale for Boys.* Illus. London, Edinburgh and N.Y.: T. Nelson and Sons, 1881. 507 pp. (IIIi/20)

————. *Old Jack. A Tale for Boys.* Illus. London, Edinburgh and N.Y.: T. Nelson and Sons, 1881. 507 pp. (IIIi/21)

————. *Peter, the Ship-Boy.* Illus. Boston: D. Lothrop & Co., n.d. 212 pp. (IIIh/4)

————. *Peter Trawl; or, The Adventures of a Whaler.* Illus. N.Y.: A. C. Armstrong and Son, 1882. 350 pp. (IIIj/22)

_____. *Peter the Whaler; His Early Life and Adventures in the Arctic Regions and Other Parts of the World.* Illus. Philadelphia: J. B. Lippincott & Co., 1880. 389 pp. (IIIj/12)
_____. *Ralph and Dick; or, The Two Shipmates.* Illus. Boston: D. Lothrop & Co., n.d. 215 pp. (IIIh/1)
_____. *Roger Willoughby; or, The Times of Benbow.* Illus. London: James Nisbet & Co., 1881. 402 pp. (IIIi/6)
_____. *Roger Willoughby; or, The Times of Benbow.* Illus. London: James Nisbet & Co., 1881. 402 pp. (IIIi/7)

Hughes Library as seen from the librarian's desk

_____. *Round the World. A Tale.* Illus. Philadelphia: J. B. Lippincott & Co., 1880. 444 pp. (IIIj/16)
_____. *Salt Water; or, The Sea Life and Adventures of Neil D'Arcy, the Midshipman.* Illus. Philadelphia: J. B. Lippincott & Co., 1877. 388 pp. (IIIj/15)
_____. *Salt Water; or, The Sea Life and Adventures of Neil D'Arcy, the Midshipman.* Illus. Philadelphia: J. B. Lippincott & Co., 1877. 388 pp. (IIIj/20)
_____. *Saved from the Sea; or, The Loss of the "Viper," and the Adventures of Her Crew in the Great Sahara.* Illus. London, Edinburgh and N.Y.: T. Nelson and Sons, 1878. 379 pp. (IIIi/8)
_____. *Saved from the Sea; or, The Loss of the "Viper," and the Adventures of Her Crew in the Great Sahara.* Illus. London, Edinburgh and N.Y.: T. Nelson and Sons, 1878. 379 pp. (IIIi/9)
_____. *The School Friends and Other Tales.* Illus. frontis. London and N.Y.: George Routledge and Sons, n.d. 192 pp. (Ic/41)
_____. *The Seven Champions of Christendom.* Illus. London and N.Y.: George Routledge and Sons, 1879. 250 pp. (IIe/11)
_____. *Shore and Ocean; or, The Heir of Kilfinnan.* Illus. N.Y.: A. C. Armstrong and Son, 1881. 331 pp. (IIIj/23)

————. *The South Sea Whaler: A Story of the Loss of the "Champion,"* *and the Adventures of Her Crew.* Illus. London, Edinburgh and N.Y.: T. Nelson and Sons, 1879. 363 pp. (IIIi/12)

————. *The South Sea Whaler: A Story of the Loss of the "Champion,"* *and the Adventures of Her Crew.* Illus. London, Edinburgh and N.Y.: T. Nelson and Sons, 1879. 363 pp. (IIIi/13)

————. *The Three Commanders; or, Active Service Afloat in Modern* *Days.* Illus. N.Y.: E. P. Dutton & Co., n.d. 464 pp. (IIIj/19)

————. *Twice Lost. A Story of Shipwreck, and of Adventure in the Wilds* *of Australia.* Illus. London, Edinburgh and N.Y.: T. Nelson and Sons, 1881. 473 pp. (IIIi/2)

————. *Twice Lost. A Story of Shipwreck, and of Adventure in the Wilds* *of Australia.* Illus. London, Edinburgh and N.Y.: T. Nelson and Sons, 1881. 473 pp. (IIIi/3)

————. *A Voyage Round the World. A Book for Boys.* Illus. London, Edinburgh and N.Y.: T. Nelson and Sons, 1880. 460 pp. (IIIi/16)

————. *A Voyage Round the World. A Book for Boys.* Illus. London, Edinburgh and N.Y.: T. Nelson and Sons, 1880. 460 pp. (IIIi/17)

————. *Voyage of the Steadfast.* Illus. Boston: D. Lothrop & Co., 1877. 180 pp. (IIIi/24)

————. *The Wanderers; or, Adventures in the Wilds of Trinidad and Up* *the Orinoco.* Illus. London, Edinburgh and N.Y.: T. Nelson and Sons, 1879. 392 pp. (IIIi/14)

————. *The Wanderers; or, Adventures in the Wilds of Trinidad and Up* *the Orinoco.* Illus. London, Edinburgh and N.Y.: T. Nelson and Sons, 1879. 392 pp. (IIIi/15)

————. *Washed Ashore; or, The Tower of Stormount Bay.* Incident and Adventure Library. Illus. London: Frederick Warne, n.d. 213 pp. (Ic/42)

————. *The Young Foresters, and Other Tales.* Illus. Philadelphia: J. B. Lippincott & Co., 1880. 323 pp. (IIIj/14)

————. *The Young Llanero. A Story of War and Wild Life in Venezuela.* Illus. London, Edinburgh and N.Y.: T. Nelson and Sons, 1877. 454 pp. (IIIi/4)

————. *The Young Llanero. A Story of War and Wild Life in Venezuela.* Illus. London, Edinburgh and N.Y.: T. Nelson and Sons, 1877. 454 pp. (IIIi/5)

————. *The Young Rajah. A Story of Indian Life and Adventure.* Illus. London, Edinburgh and N.Y.: T. Nelson and Sons, 1878. 379 pp. (IIIi/10)

————. *The Young Rajah. A Story of Indian Life and Adventure.* Illus. London, Edinburgh and N.Y.: T. Nelson and Sons, 1878. 379 pp. (IIIi/11)

————. *The Young Whaler; or, Adventures of Archibald Hughson.* Illus. Boston: D. Lothrop & Co., n.d. 178 pp. (IIIh/3)

Kirby, Mary and Elizabeth. *The Discontented Children and How They* *Were Cured.* Illus. N.Y.: E. P. Dutton & Co., n.d. 149 pp. (Ib/37)

_____. *Julia Maitland; or, Pride Goes Before a Fall.* Illus. N.Y.: E. P. Dutton & Co., n.d. 160 pp. (Ib/38)

_____. *The World at Home; or, Pictures and Scenes from Far-Off Lands.* Illus. London, Edinburgh and N.Y.: T. Nelson and Sons, 1880. 296 pp. (Ih/16)

Kitty Bourne. Illus. N.Y.: Dodd & Mead, 1875. N.p. (IIIc/1)

Knatchbull-Hugessen, E. H. (Lord Brabourne). *Crackers for Christmas.* Illus. London: Macmillan & Co., 1877. 309 pp. (IIg/25)

_____. *Higgledy-Piggledy; or, Stories for Everybody and Everybody's Children.* Illus. N.Y.: D. Appleton & Co., 1876. 377 pp. (IIg/19)

_____. *Moonshine. Fairy Stories.* Illus. London: Macmillan & Co., 1875. 338 pp. (IIg/18)

_____. *Moonshine. Fairy Stories.* Illus. London and N.Y.: George Routledge and Sons, 1882. 338 pp. (IIg/20)

_____. *Queer Folk. Seven Stories.* Illus. London: Macmillan & Co., 1874. 357 pp. (IIg/21)

_____. *Stories for My Children.* Illus. Macmillan. 373 pp. Title page missing. (IIg/23)

_____. *Tales at Tea-Time. Fairy Stories.* Illus. London: Macmillan & Co., 1874. 357 pp. (IIg/22)

_____. *Tales at Tea Time. Fairy Stories.* Illus. London and N.Y.: George Routledge and Sons, 1882. 357 pp. (IIf/31)

_____. *Whispers from Fairyland.* Illus. N.Y.: D. Appleton & Co., 1875. 345 pp. (IIg/24)

Knox, Kathleen. *Cornertown Chronicles: New Legends of Old Lore.* Illus. N.Y.: E. P. Dutton & Co., 1880. 256 pp. (IIf/25)

_____. *Cornertown Chronicles: New Legends of Old Lore.* Illus. N.Y.: E. P. Dutton & Co., 1880. 256 pp. (IIf/26)

_____. *Fairy Gifts; or, A Wallet of Wonders.* Illus. N.Y.: E. P. Dutton, n.d. 128 pp. (IIf/24)

_____. *Father Time's Story Book. For the Little Ones.* Illus. N.Y.: E. P. Dutton & Co., n.d. 192 pp. (IIf/27)

La Blanche, Fanny. *Starlight Stories Told to Bright Eyes and Listening Ears.* Illus. London: Griffith and Farran, n.d. 212 pp. (IIg/10)

Lamb, Charles and Mary. *Mrs. Leicester's School.* Illus. frontis. N.Y.: Dodd & Mead, n.d. 151 pp. (Ib/26)

_____. *Tales from Shakespeare.* Ed. rev. Alfred Ainger. London: Macmillan & Co., 1881. 368 pp. (Ib/24)

_____. *Tales from Shakespeare.* Boston: Houghton, Mifflin & Co., n.d. 365 pp. (Ib/25)

Mrs. Lamb (Ruth Buck). *Captain Christie's Granddaughter.* Illus. N.Y.: Dodd, Mead & Co., n.d. 317 pp. (IIIb/40)

Lawford, Louisa. *Every Girl's Book. A Compendium of Entertaining Amusements, for Recreation in Home Circles.* Illus. frontis. London and N.Y.: George Routledge and Sons, n.d. 392 pp. (Id/29)

Lear, Edward. *Nonsense Songs, Stories, Botany, and Alphabets.* Illus. Boston: Roberts Brothers, 1877. N.p. (Ic/3)

Ledyard, Laura W. *Very Young Americans*. Illus. Boston: Roberts
  Brothers, 1873. 83 pp. (Ig/7)
Mrs. Lee. *Redesdale*. Illus. frontis. N.Y.: E. P. Dutton & Co., 1877. 147
  pp. (Ic/33)
——. *Redesdale*. Illus. frontis. N.Y.: E. P. Dutton & Co., 1877. 147 pp.
  (Ic/34)
Lee, Mrs. R. *Adventures in Australia: The Wanderings of Captain
  Spencer in the Bush and the Wilds*. Illus. N.Y.: E. P. Dutton & Co.,
  n.d. 336 pp. (If/31)
The Lent Jewels, and Other Tales. Illus. London and N.Y.: George
  Routledge and Sons, n.d. 148 pp. (Ig/9)
Leslie, Mrs. Eliza. *The American Girl's Book; or, Occupation for Play
  Hours*. Illus. N.Y.: Allen Brothers, 1870. 383 pp. (IIb/39)
Leslie, Mrs. Madeline (A. R. Baker). *Little Frankie and His Cousin*.
  Robin Redbreast Series. The Little Frankie Series. Illus. frontis.
  Boston: Woolworth, Ainsworth & Co., 1860. 104 pp. (IIa/24)
——. *Little Frankie and His Mother*. Robin Redbreast Series. The Little
  Frankie Series. Illus. frontis. Boston: Woolworth, Ainsworth & Co.,
  1860. 112 pp. (IIa/22)
——. *Little Frankie on a Journey*. Robin Redbreast Series. The Little
  Frankie Series. Illus. frontis. Boston: Woolworth, Ainsworth & Co.,
  1860. 112 pp. (IIa/23)
——. *Little Robins' Friends*. The Robin Redbreast Series. Illus. frontis.
  Boston: Woolworth, Ainsworth & Co., 1860. 104 pp. (IIa/20)
——. *Little Robins Learning to Fly*. The Robin Redbreast Series. Illus.
  Boston: Woolworth, Ainsworth & Co., 1860. 104 pp. (IIa/21)
——. *The Pearl of Contentment. Or, Flory and Her Nurse*. Mrs.
  Leslie's Bible Pearls. Illus. frontis. Boston: A. F. Graves, 1868. 109 pp.
  (IIa/26)
——. *The Pearl of Diligence. Or, The Basket-Makers*. Mrs. Leslie's
  Bible Pearls. Illus. frontis. Boston: A. F. Graves, 1868. 111 pp.
  (IIa/27)
——. *The Pearl of Peace: or, The Little Peace-Maker*. Mrs. Leslie's
  Bible Pearls. Illus. frontis. Boston: Graves and Ellis, 1868. 117 pp.
  (IIa/25)
Liesching, L. F. *Through Peril to Fortune: A Story of Sport and
  Adventure by Land and Sea*. Illus. London, Paris & N.Y.: Cassell,
  Petter, Galpin & Co., n.d. 224 pp. (Id/1)
Life and Adventure in the South Pacific. Illus. N.Y.: Harper & Bros.,
  1861. 361 pp. (Ie/7)
Lilliput Lectures. Illus. London: Strahan & Co., 1871. 155 pp. (Ic/16)
The Lily. A Love Token. Illus. Philadelphia: J. B. Lippincott & Co., n.d.
  64 pp. (IIIa/10)
Little Chimes for All Times. The Cosy Corner Series. Illus. London,
  Paris & N.Y.: Cassell, Petter, Galpin & Co., n.d. 183 pp. (IIe/26)
The Little Duke; Richard the Fearless. Illus. N.Y.: Macmillan & Co.,
  1880. 231 pp. (IIf/12)

Little Folks' Reader. Illus. Boston: D. Lothrop. 96 pp. Title page missing.
Final pages probably missing. (Ih/22)

Little Frank's Story Book. In Simple Words. Illus. N.Y.: E. P. Dutton &
Co., 1873. 78 pp. (Ig/20)

The Little Guardians, and Other Tales. Illus. Philadelphia: J. B.
Lippincott & Co., n.d. 64 pp. (IIIa/7)

Little Hazel, the King's Messenger. Illus. frontis. London, Edinburgh
and N.Y.: T. Nelson and Sons, 1881. 144 pp. (Ig/48)

Little Humpy, and Other Stories. Snow Drop Library. Illus. Philadelphia:
Perkinpine & Higgins, 1870. 116 pp. (Ig/25)

Little Lily's Travels Through France to Switzerland. Illus. frontis.
Boston: D. Lothrop & Co., n.d. 186 pp. (Ie/19)

Little Merry-Makers. Illus. N.Y., London, & Paris: Cassell & Co., 1881.
96 pp. (Ih/24)

The Little Messmates and Other Stories. Illus. N.Y.: E. P. Dutton & Co.,
1876. 154 pp. (Ic/40)

Little Nell's Story Book. Illus. E. P. Dutton. 81 pp. Title page missing.
(Ig/27)

Little Pet's Book. Illus. Philadelphia: J. B. Lippincott & Co., n.d. 64 pp.
(IIIa/16)

Little Primrose's Picture Book. Illus. London and N.Y.: George
Routledge and Sons, n.d. 96 pp. (IIh/29)

Little Snowdrop's Picture Book. Illus. London and N.Y.: George
Routledge and Sons, n.d. 64 pp. Final pages probably missing.
(IIh/31)

Little Talks With Little People. The Cosy Corner Series. Illus. London,
Paris & N.Y.: Cassell, Petter, Galpin & Co., n.d. 183 pp. (IIe/30)

Little Violet's Picture Book. Illus. London and N.Y.: George Routledge
and Sons, n.d. 64 pp. Final pages probably missing. (IIh/30)

Locker, Arthur (J. H. Forbes). *On a Coral Reef: The Story of a
Runaway Trip to Sea*. Illus. London, Paris & N.Y.: Cassell, Petter, &
Galpin, n.d. 220 pp. (Ig/50)

Looking Upwards; or, The Story of Wilhelm Deremann. Trans. Helen
G. Blythe. Illus. Boston: Henry A. Young & Co., 1875. 156 pp.
(IIa/41)

Loring, Laurie. *Children's Picture Story-Book*. Illus. Boston: D. Lothrop
& Co., 1874. 357 pp. (Ig/39)

The Lost Chamois-Hunter. A Tale of the Matterhorn. Illus. London and
N.Y.: George Routledge and Sons, n.d. 147 pp. (IIa/19)

Lost in the Woods, and Other Stories. Illus. Philadelphia: J. B.
Lippincott & Co., n.d. 64 pp. (IIIa/9)

Lowell, Robert. *Antony Brade*. Boston: Roberts Brothers, 1875. 416 pp.
(IId/22)

Lullabies Ditties and Poetic Tales for Children. Illus. N.Y.: American
Tract Society, 1865. 221 pp. (Ia/39)

Lushington, Henrietta. *The Happy Home; or, The Children at the Red
House*. Illus. N.Y.: E. P. Dutton & Co., n.d. 186 pp. (IIh/35)

Lyttle, Byrd. *Mary Austin; or, The New Home.* Illus. frontis.
Philadelphia: Alfred Martien, 1873. 216 pp. (Ia/29)

M. A. C. *Auntie's Christmas-Trees. The Child's Gift-Book for the
Christmas Holidays.* Illus. N.Y.: General Protestant Episcopal Sunday
School Union and Church Book Society, 1875. 308 pp. (Ia/15)

_____. *Bessie Melville; or, Prayer Book Instructions Carried Out into
Life.* Illus. frontis. N.Y.: General Protestant Episcopal Sunday School
Union and Church Book Society, 1870. 354 pp. (Ia/14)

McCabe, James D. *Our Young Folks Abroad. The Adventures of Four
American Boys and Girls in a Journey Through Europe to
Constantinople.* Illus. Philadelphia: J. B. Lippincott & Co., 1882. 344
pp. (Ih/10)

Macallan, Emma. *Tales for the Whitsun Season.* Illus. frontis. N.Y.:
General Protestant Episcopal Sunday School Union and Church Book
Society, n.d. 129 pp. (Ia/19)

MacDonald, George. *A Double Story.* Illus. N.Y.: Dodd, Mead & Co.,
n.d. 238 pp. (IIIf/24)

_____. ed. *Good Works for the Young for 1872.* Illus. London: Strahan
& Co., n.d. 572 pp. (IIh/1)

_____. *The Princess and the Goblin.* Illus. Philadelphia: J. B. Lippincott
& Co., 1881. 203 pp. (IIg/27)

McIntosh, M. J. *Grace and Clara; or, Be Just as Well as Generous.* Illus.
frontis. N.Y.: D. Appleton & Co., 1878. 124 pp. (Ia/47)

_____. *Jessie Graham; or, Friends Dear, but Truth Dearer.* N.Y.:
D. Appleton & Co., 1869. 140 pp. (Ia/46)

McKeen, Phebe F. *The Little Mother and Her Christmas.* Illus. Boston:
D. Lothrop & Co., 1876. 74 pp. (Ie/23)

McLain, Mary W. *Keeping Open House.* Illus. N.Y.: E. P. Dutton & Co.,
1874. 104 pp. (Ig/45)

_____. *Keeping Open House.* Illus. N.Y.: E. P. Dutton & Co., 1874. 104
pp. (Ig/42)

Maclaren, Archibald. *The Fairy Family. A Series of Ballads and Metrical
Tales Illustrating the Fairy Mythology of Europe.* London:
Macmillan & Co., 1874. 247 pp. (IIg/26)

Mannering, May. *The Cruise of the Dashaway; or, Katie Putnam's
Voyage.* Helping-Hand Series. Illus. Boston: Lee and Shepard, 1869.
221 pp. (IIc/14)

_____. *The Little Maid of Oxbow.* Helping-Hand Series. Illus. Boston:
Lee and Shepard, 1871. 207 pp. (IIc/15)

Maguire, Adelaide A. *Lizzie's Secret. A Story for Little Children.* Illus.
N.Y.: E. P. Dutton & Co., 1872. 126 pp. (Ic/43)

Mark Churchill. Illus. Boston: D. Lothrop & Co., n.d. 237 pp. (IIIc/23)

Marshall, Emma. *Matthew Frost, Carrier; or, Little Snowdrop's Mission.*
Illus. N.Y.: General Protestant Episcopal Sunday School Union and
Church Book Society, n.d. 214 pp. (Ib/9)

Martin, Mrs. A. H. *Roses from Thorns; or, The Old Manor House.* Illus.
London, Paris & N.Y.: Cassell, Petter, Galpin & Co., n.d. 151 pp.
(IIe/38)

Martin, William. *Noble Boys. Their Deeds of Love and Duty.* Illus.
London: Daldy, Isbister & Co., 1877. 284 pp. (Id/30)

Martineau, Harriet. *The Peasant and the Prince.* Happy Child's Library.
Illus. frontis. N.Y.: D. Appleton & Co., 1873. 180 pp. (IIIa/36)

Massey, L. *The Children of the Holy Scripture.* Illus. London, Paris &
N.Y.: Cassell, Petter, Galpin & Co., n.d. 179 pp. (Ig/1)

Mateaux, Clara. *Raggles, Baggles, and the Emperor.* Illus. London, Paris
& N.Y.: Cassell, Petter, Galpin & Co., n.d. 160 pp. (IIe/34)

_____. *Wee Willie Winkie: the Story of a Boy Who Was Found.* Illus.
London, Paris & N.Y.: Cassell, Petter, Galpin & Co., n.d. 177 pp.
(IIe/33)

Mathews, Joanna H. *Breakfast for Two.* Illus. Boston: D. Lothrop &
Co., 1881. 296 pp. (If/2)

Mathews, Margaret Harriet. *Dr. Gilbert's Daughters: A Story for Girls.*
Illus. Philadelphia: Porter & Coates, 1881. 375 pp. (If/29)

May, E. J. *Dashwood Priory; or, Mortimer's College Life.* Illus. London
and N.Y.: George Routledge and Sons, n.d. 433 pp. (IIc/32)

_____. *Louis' School Days.* Every Boy's Library. London and N.Y.:
George Routledge and Sons, n.d. 351 pp. (IIa/8)

_____. *Saxelford; A Story for the Young.* Illus. London and N.Y.:
George Routledge and Sons, n.d. 375 pp. (If/27)

May, Katharine E. *Alfred and His Mother; or, Seeking the Kingdom.*
Illus. Boston: Henry A. Young & Co., n.d. 153 pp. (IIa/38)

M. E. M. *Philip Brantley's Life Work and How He Found It.* Illus.
frontis. N.Y.: Dodd, Mead & Co., 1869. 262 pp. (IIIb/29)

Merrill, George E. *Battles Lost and Won.* Illus. Boston: D. Lothrop &
Co., 1872. 487 pp. (IIIc/22)

M. E. W. S. *Henrietta's Heroism.* Illus. Boston: D. Lothrop & Co., 1881.
N.p. (IIc/9)

M. H. S. *Mollie's Christmas Stocking, and Other Stories.* Illus. frontis.
N.Y.: E. P. Dutton & Co., 1877. 126 pp. (Ia/18)

Minnie's Love, Etc. Sunbeam Stories. Illus. N.Y.: George Routledge and
Sons, 1875. 340 pp. (Ia/49)

Miriam and Rosette; or, Trials of Faith. A Jewish Narrative. Illus. frontis.
London and N.Y.: George Routledge and Sons, n.d. 158 pp. (Ic/36)

Miss Matty; or, Our Youngest Passenger. A Tale of the Sea. Illus. frontis.
N.Y.: E. P. Dutton & Co., 1877. 106 pp. (Ig/17)

Miss Matty; or, Our Youngest Passenger. A Tale of the Sea. Illus. frontis.
N.Y.: E. P. Dutton & Co., 1877. 106 pp. (Ig/18)

M. L. B. *Bertha Weisser's Wish. A Christmas Story.* N.Y.: E. P. Dutton
& Co., 1882. 133 pp. (Ic/50)

Molesworth, Mrs. *A Christmas Child. A Sketch of a Boy-Life.* Illus.
London: Macmillan & Co., 1880. 223 pp. (Ie/31)

_____. *Hermy. The Story of a Little Girl.* Illus. London and N.Y.:
George Routledge and Sons, 1881. 216 pp. (Ie/32)

Moncrieff, A. R. Hope. *The Exiles of France.* Illus. N.Y.: Thomas
Nelson & Sons, 1871. 159 pp. (IIa/9)

Montgomery, Florence. *Thwarted; or, Duck's Eggs in a Hen's Nest.*
Philadelphia: J. B. Lippincott & Co., 1874. 164 pp. (Ic/2)

More, Hannah. *Rural Tales; Portraying Social Life.* Happy Child's Library. N.Y.: D. Appleton & Co., 1873. 180 pp. (IIa/32)

Mother Goose. Boston: Houghton, Mifflin & Co. 186 pp. Title page missing. (Ih/13)

Mother's Boys and Girls. Illus. Boston: D. Lothrop. N.p. Title page missing. First pages of text missing. (IIh/15)

Moulton, Louise Chandler. *New Bed-Time Stories.* Illus. Boston: Roberts Brothers, 1880. 230 pp. (IIa/1)

M. T. W. *Connor Magan's Luck.* Illus. Boston: D. Lothrop & Co., 1881. N.p. (IIc/10)

The Murmuring Fountain, and Other Tales. Illus. Philadelphia: J. B. Lippincott & Co., n.d. 64 pp. (IIIa/11)

"My Best Frock," and Other Tales. Illus. London and N.Y.: George Routledge and Sons, n.d. 308 pp. (Ig/35)

My Little Gentlemen, and Other Stories. Illus. Boston: D. Lothrop & Co., 1877. 324 pp. (If/16)

My Primer. Illus. Philadelphia: J. B. Lippincott & Co., 1877. N.p. (Ig/11)

Nanny's Christmas. Illus. frontis. Philadelphia: Claxton, Remsen & Haffelfinger, 1870. 130 pp. (IIa/11)

Nauman, Mary D. *Eva's Adventures in Shadow-Land.* Illus. Philadelphia: J. B. Lippincott & Co., 1872. 169 pp. (IIa/19)

Nichols, Laura. *Underfoot; or, What Harry and Nelly Learned of the Earth's Treasures.* Illus. Boston: D. Lothrop & Co., 1881. 234 pp. (Ih/17)

Nobody's Child and Other Stories. The Silver Penny Series. Illus. N.Y.: Sheldon & Co., 1869. 111 pp. (IIa/34)

Norah, the Flower Girl. Sunny Dell Series. Illus. Boston: D. Lothrop & Co., n.d. 101 pp. (IIIa/46)

The North Pole, and How Charlie Wilson Discovered It. Illus. N.Y.: E. P. Dutton & Co., n.d. 284 pp. (IIId/12)

Northrop, Mrs. E. L. *Aunt Charity.* N.Y.: General Protestant Episcopal Sunday School Union, and Church Book Society, 1858. 332 pp. (IIb/40)

Nursery Songs and Hymns, New and Old. Illus. Philadelphia: J. B. Lippincott & Co., n.d. 64 pp. (IIIa/3)

Old-Fashioned Fairy Tales. First Series. Illus. Boston: Roberts Brothers, n.d. 358 pp. (Ib/16)

Old Fashioned Fairy Tales. Second Series. Illus. Boston: Roberts Brothers, n.d. 407 pp. (Ib/17)

Old Ned, and Other Stories. Illus. Philadelphia: J. B. Lippincott & Co., n.d. 64 pp. (IIIa/15)

Oliver, Marie. *Ruby Hamilton; or, Lights in the Windows.* Illus. Boston: D. Lothrop & Co., 1880. 376 pp. (IIId/7)

Only a Dog. Illus. N.Y.: E. P. Dutton & Co., 1877. 217 pp. (Id/25)

Only a Dog. Illus. N.Y.: E. P. Dutton & Co., 1877. 217 pp. (Id/26)

O'Reilly, Mrs. Robert. *Daisy's Companions; or, Scenes from Child Life.* Illus. Philadelphia: J. B. Lippincott & Co., 1881. 240 pp. (IIb/25)

_____. *Deborah's Drawer.* Illus. Philadelphia: J. B. Lippincott & Co., 1881. 293 pp. (IIb/26)

_____. *Doll World; or, May and Earnest.* Illus. N.Y.: E. P. Dutton & Co., 1875. 256 pp. (IIb/20)

_____. *Doll World; or, May and Earnest.* Illus. N.Y.: E. P. Dutton & Co., 1875. 256 pp. (IIb/21)

_____. *Giles's Minority; or, Scenes at the Red House.* Illus. Philadelphia: J. B. Lippincott & Co., 1881. 275 pp. (IIb/22)

_____. *Gile's Minority; or, Scenes at the Red House.* Illus. N.Y.: E. P. Dutton & Co., 1877. 275 pp. (IIb/23)

_____. *Gile's Minority; or, Scenes at the Red House.* Illus. N.Y.: E. P. Dutton & Co., 1877. 275 pp. (IIb/24)

_____. *The Stories They Tell Me; or, Sue and I.* Illus. N.Y.: E. P. Dutton & Co., 1874. 254 pp. (Id/27)

Osborn, Yotty. *Two Little Turks; or, Getting into Mischief.* Illus. London, Edinburgh and N.Y.: T. Nelson and Sons, n.d. 191 pp. (Ig/40)

_____. *Two Little Turks; or, Getting into Mischief.* Illus. London, Edinburgh and N.Y.: T. Nelson and Sons, n.d. 191 pp. (Ig/41)

Our Boys and Girls. One Hundred Original Stories. Illus. Boston: D. Lothrop & Co., n.d. N.p. (Ih/23)

Our White Violet. Illus. N.Y.: E. P. Dutton & Co., n.d. 160 pp. (Ib/35)

Our Year: A Child's Book, in Prose and Verse. Illus. N.Y.: Harper & Bros., 1860. 297 pp. (Ic/46)

Our Young Folks at Home. Illustrated Prose Stories. Illus. Boston: D. Lothrop & Co., 1881. N.p. (Ih/21)

Over Seas; or, Here, There and Everywhere. Illus. Boston: D. Lothrop & Co., 1881. 253 pp. (Ia/50)

Pansie's Flour-Bin. Illus. London: Macmillan & Co., 1880. 177 pp. (Ic/11)

Pansy. *Bernie's White Chicken.* Illus. Boston: D. Lothrop & Co., 1866. 178 pp. (IIh/28)

_____. *Cunning Workmen.* Illus. frontis. Boston: D. Lothrop & Co., 1875. 349 pp. (IIh/20)

_____. *Daisy and Grandpa; and Other Stories.* Illus. Boston: D. Lothrop & Co., n.d. 190 pp. (IIh/18)

_____. *Docia's Journal; or, God Is Love.* Illus. frontis. Boston: D Lothrop & Co., 1866. 189 pp. (IIh/25)

_____. *Five Friends.* Illus. Boston: D. Lothrop & Co., 1882. 254 pp. (IIh/24)

_____. *Helen Lester.* Illus. frontis. Boston: D. Lothrop & Co., 1866. 170 pp. (IIh/26)

_____. *Jessie Wells.* Boston: D. Lothrop. 219 pp. Title page missing. (IIh/27)

_____. *Little Minnie; and Other Stories.* Illus. Boston: D. Lothrop & Co., 1877. 374 pp. (IIh/16)

_____. *Mother's Boys and Girls.* Illus. Boston: D. Lothrop & Co., n.d. N.p. (Ih/33)

————. *Pictures from Bobby's Life; and Other Stories*. Illus. Boston:
D. Lothrop & Co., 1877. 98 pp. (IIh/19)

————. *Robbie and the Stars: and Other Stories*. Illus. Boston: D. Lothrop
& Co., 1877. 282 pp. Final pages probably missing.

————. *Sidney Martin's Christmas*. Illus. Boston: D. Lothrop & Co., 1878.
610 pp. (IIh/22)

————. *Sidney Martin's Christmas*. Illus. Boston: D. Lothrop & Co., 1878.
610 pp. (IIh/23)

————. *Tip Lewis, and His Lamp*. Illus. frontis. Boston: D. Lothrop &
Co., 1867. 360 pp. (IIh/21)

The Pansy. For Sunday Reading. Illus. Boston: D. Lothrop & Co., n.d.
N.p. (Ia/52)

Parker, Mrs. C. E. R. *Work and Play. A Lesson for Little Children*. Illus.
frontis. N.Y.: General Protestant Episcopal Sunday School Union and
Church Book Society, 1872. 96 pp. (Ia/20)

Parley, Peter. *The Wanderers by Sea and Land, With Other Tales*. Illus.
N.Y.: D. Appleton & Co., 1873. 316 pp. (If/19)

Parrish, Mrs. Emma K. *The Dot's Inheritance*. Illus. Boston: D. Lothrop
& Co., 1881. N.p. (IIc/11)

Parrott, M. A. *Harry's Mistakes and Where They Led Him*. Illus.
Philadelphia: Alfred Martien, 1873. 176 pp. (Ia/35)

Paull, Mrs. Henry H. B. *Knowing and Doing; and Other Stories Founded
on Bible Precepts*. Illus. N.Y.: Thomas Y. Crowell & Co., n.d. 278 pp.
(IId/12)

————. *"Only a Cat"; or, The Autobiography of Tom Blackman*. Illus.
London and N.Y.: George Routledge and Sons, n.d. 299 pp. (IId/13)

Mrs. Perring. *Ellen and Frank*. London and New York: George
Routledge and Sons, n.d. 158 pp. (IIa/16)

————. *Lillian Seacroft*. Illus. frontis. London and New York: George
Routledge and Sons, n.d. 128 pp. (IIa/17)

————. *Sybil Grey*. London and New York: George Routledge and Sons,
n.d. 160 pp. (IIa/15)

The Pet Lamb, and Other Stories. Illus. Philadelphia: J. B. Lippincott
& Co., n.d. 64 pp. (IIIa/17)

The Pet Squirrel, and Other Stories. Illus. Philadelphia: J. B. Lippincott
& Co., n.d. 64 pp. (IIIa/21)

Pet's Posy of Pictures and Stories. The Cosy Corner Series. Illus. London,
Paris & N.Y.: Cassell, Petter, Galpin & Co., n.d. 183 pp. (IIe/31)

Peter Parley's Annual for 1882. Illus. London, Paris & N.Y.: Cassell,
Petter, Galpin & Co., n.d. 279 pp. (If/18)

Phelps, Elizabeth Stuart. *The Gates Ajar*. Boston: Fields, Osgood & Co.,
1869. 248 pp. (If/6)

A Picture Book of Animals and Birds. Illus. London and N.Y.: George
Routledge and Sons, n.d. 180 pp. (Ic/37)

Pictures for Happy Hours. The Cosy Corner Series. Illus. London, Paris
& N.Y.: Cassell, Petter & Galpin, n.d. 183 pp. (IIe/27)

Pictures on the Lord's Prayer. Picture Books for Little Children (No.
17). Illus. London: The Religious Tract Society, n.d. 64 pp. (IIa/52)

Pindar, Susan Cooper. *The Wentworths; Their Home and Friends.* Illus. Boston: D. Lothrop & Co., 1876. 238 pp. (IId/21)

Pitt, Sarah. *Dick's Hero, and Other Stories.* Illus. London, Paris & N.Y.: Cassell, Petter, Galpin & Co., n.d. 147 pp. (IIe/37)

Pleasant Pages and Bible Pictures for Young People. Illus. Boston: Estes & Lauriat, 1881. 94 pp. (Ih/19)

Plunket, The Hon. Zoe. *The Girl With the Golden Locks.* Illus. London, Paris & N.Y.: Cassell, Petter, Galpin & Co., n.d. 154 pp. (IIe/39)

Plympton, A. G. *The Glad Year Round. For Boys and Girls.* Illus. Boston: James R. Osgood, 1882. 60 pp. Final pages possibly missing. (Ih/5)

Poor Nelly; and Polly and Joe. Illus. London, Paris & N.Y.: Cassell, Petter, Galpin & Co., n.d. 222 pp. (Id/3)

Poplar Grove. Happy Child's Library, N.Y.: D. Appleton & Co., 178 pp. Title page missing. (IIIa/23)

Porter, Mrs. A. E. *This One Thing I Do.* Illus. Boston: D. Lothrop & Co., 1871. 344 pp. (IId/34)

Porter, Mary W. *Five Little Southerners.* Illus. Boston: D. Lothrop & Co., 1880. 321 pp. (IIe/13)

———. *Poor Papa.* Illus. Boston: D. Lothrop & Co., 1879. 218 pp. (IIe/14)

A Present for the Little Ones. Illus. Philadelphia: J. B. Lippincott & Co., n.d. 64 pp. (IIIa/22)

Preston, Paul. *Voyages, Travels, and Remarkable Adventures of Paul Preston.* Illus. Boston: Roberts Brothers, n.d. 336 pp. (IIb/38)

The Prince and the Page. A Story of the Last Crusade. Illus. N.Y.: Macmillan & Co., 1880. 256 pp. (IIf/13)

Ramsey, Mrs. V. G. *Evenings With the Children; or, Travels in South America.* Illus. Boston: D. Lothrop & Co., 1871. 234 pp. (Ie/17)

———. *Evenings With the Children; or, Travels in South America.* Illus. Boston: D. Lothrop & Co., 1871. 234 pp. (IIIc/25)

Ray, Rena. *Dainty Maurice; or, Lost in the Woods.* Illus. frontis. Philadelphia: James A. Moore, 1870. 106 pp. (IIa/46)

Reid, Captain Mayne. *Sounding the Signal; or, The Headless Horseman.* Illus. frontis. N.Y.: G. W. Carleton & Co., 1881. 408 pp. (If/25)

Richard the Fearless; or, The Little Duke. Illus. N.Y.: D. Appleton & Co., 1865. 208 pp. (IIf/17)

Richards, Laura E. *Babyhood: Rhymes and Stories, Pictures and Silhouettes, for Our Little Ones.* Illus. Boston: Estes and Lauriat, 1878. 192 pp. Final pages possibly missing. (Ih/32)

———. *Five Mice in a Mouse-Trap, by the Man in the Moon.* Illus. Boston: Estes and Lauriat, 1881. 102 pp. Final pages possibly missing. (Ih/18)

Richardson, Abby Sage. *Stories from Old English Poetry.* Illus. Boston: Houghton, Mifflin & Co., 1881. 281 pp. (Ie/31)

Richardson, Robert. *Almost a Hero; or, School-Days at Ashcombe.* Illus. London, Edinburgh and N.Y.: T. Nelson and Sons, 1880. 236 pp. (IIf/29)

―――. *Almost a Hero; or, School-Days at Ashcombe*. Illus. London, Edinburgh and N.Y.: T. Nelson and Sons, 1880. 236 pp. (IIf/30)

―――. *Ralph's Year in Russia. A Story of Travel and Adventure in Eastern Europe*. Illus. London, Edinburgh and N.Y.: T. Nelson and Sons, 1882. 351 pp. (IIf/32)

―――. *Ralph's Year in Russia. A Story of Travel and Adventure in Eastern Europe*. Illus. London, Edinburgh and N.Y.: T. Nelson and Sons, 1882. 351 pp. (IIf/33)

Riddell, Mrs. J. H., Mrs. M. Douglas, Maria J. Greer, and others. *The Curate of Lowood; or Every Man Has His Golden Chance. Lady Madalena; or, Never Make a Mountain of a Molehill. The Young Engineer; or, Sometimes Words Wound More Than Swords. The Romance of the Terrace; or, Never Wade in Unknown Waters*. The 'Golden Acorn' Series. Illus. Philadelphia: J. B. Lippincott & Co., 1881. 128 pp. (Ic/10)

The Rivals: A Tale of the Anglo-Saxon Church. Illus. frontis. N.Y.: General Protestant Episcopal Sunday School Union and Church Book Society, 1861. 153 pp. (Ia/26)

Roberts, Sarah. *My Childhood; or, The Good Grandmother*. Illus. N.Y.: General Protestant Episcopal Sunday School Union, 1869. 144 pp. (IIa/47)

Romaunt, Christopher, ed. *The Island Home; or, The Young Cast-Aways*. Illus. Boston: D. Lothrop & Co., 1851. 461 pp. (IIIh/8)

Ross, Mrs. Ellen. *Dora's Boy*. Illus. N.Y.: Thomas Y. Crowell & Co., n.d. 308 pp. (IId/26)

Rousselet, Louis. *The Two Cabin Boys*. Illus. Boston: Roberts Brothers, 1881. 361 pp. (IIe/12)

Routledge's Illustrated Reading Book. Illus. London and N.Y.: George Routledge and Sons, n.d. 158 pp. (Ig/3)

Ruth and Her Friends. A Story for Girls. Illus. London: Macmillan & Co., 1880. 348 pp. (Ic/14)

Sage, Rufus B. *Rocky Mountain Life; or, Startling Scenes and Perilous Adventures in the Far West*. Illus. Boston: Estes and Lauriat, 1880. 363 pp. (IIIh/6)

Saintine, X. B. *Dame Nature and Her Three Daughters. A Grandpapa's Talks and Stories about Natural History, and Things of Daily Use*. Illus. N.Y.: Hurd and Houghton, 1872. 268 pp. (IIb/8)

―――. *Grandpapa's Stories; or, Dame Nature. Being Talks and Stories about Natural History, and Things of Daily Use*. Illus. Philadelphia; J. B. Lippincott & Co., 1869, 268 pp. (If/11)

Samuels, Miss Adelaide F. *Palm Land; or, Dick Travers in the Chagos Islands*. Dick Travers Abroad Series. Illus. Boston and N.Y.: Lee, Shepard, and Dillingham, 1873. 98 pp. (IIa/49)

Samuels, Mrs. S. B. C. *Adele*. Springdale Stories. Illus. Boston & N.Y.: Lee and Shepard, 1871. 208 pp. (IIc/28)

―――. *Ennisfellen*. Springdale Stories. Illus. Boston & N.Y.: Lee and Shepard, 1871. 176 pp. (IIc/30)

———. *Eric.* Springdale Stories. Illus. Boston & N.Y.: Lee and Shepard, 1971. 178 pp. (IIc/29)

———. *Herbert.* Springdale Stories. Illus. frontis. Boston & N.Y.: Lee and Shepard, 1871. 180 pp. (IIc/26)

———. *Johnstone's Farm.* Springdale Stories. Illus. Boston & N.Y.: Lee and Shepard, 1871. 163 pp. (IIc/31)

———. *Nettie's Trial.* Springdale Stories. Illus. Boston & N.Y.: Lee and Shepard, 1871. 174 pp. (IIc/27)

Mrs. Sandham. *The Twin Sisters; A Tale for Youth.* The Happy Child's Library. N.Y.: D. Appleton & Co., 1873. 176 pp. (IIIa/35)

Sands, F. *Frank Powderhorn. A Story of Adventure in the Pampas of Buenos Ayres and in the Wilds of Patogonia. A Book for Boys.* Illus. London, Edinburgh and N.Y.: T. Nelson and Sons, 1881. 231 pp. (Ie/3)

———. *Frank Powderhorn. A Story of Adventure in the Pampas of Buenos Ayres and in the Wilds of Patogonia. A Book for Boys.* Illus. London, Edinburgh and N.Y.: T. Nelson and Sons, 1881. 231 pp. (Ie/4)

Sanford, Mrs. D. P. *Ida and Baby Dell.* Second of the Rose Dale Books. Illus. N.Y.: E. P. Dutton & Co., 1872. 261 pp. (Ig/24)

———. *Mark the Fisher-Boy and Other Stories.* Illus. N.Y.: E. P. Dutton & Co., 1880. 150 pp. (Ig/19)

———. *Mark the Fisher-Boy and Other Stories.* Illus. N.Y.: E. P. Dutton & Co., 1880. 150 pp. (Ig/29)

———. *Rose, Tom, and Ned.* First of the Rose Dale Books. Illus. N.Y.: E. P. Dutton & Co., 1872. 246 pp. (Ig/23)

———. *The Young Laymen: or, The Boy-Workers of Wiltham Parish.* Illus. N.Y.: E. P. Dutton & Co., 1877. 190 pp. (Ig/26)

Sanford, Mrs. E. B. *Names and Their Meanings.* Illus. N.Y.: E. P. Dutton & Co., 1874. 168 pp. (Ia/40)

Saunders, John. *Israel Mort, Overman. A Story of the Mine.* Illus. Philadelphia: J. B. Lippincott & Co., 1872. 291 pp. (IId/24)

Sauvage, Élie. *The Little Gypsy.* Illus. Boston: Roberts Brothers, 1868. 133 pp. (Ic/6)

Sauveur, L. *Chats With the Little Ones.* Illus. Boston: Estes and Lauriat, 1876. 172 pp. (IId/7)

Schnick Schnack. Trifles for the Little-Ones. Illus. London & N.Y.: George Routledge and Sons, n.d. N.p. (Ig/37)

Scudder, Horace E., ed. *The Children's Book.* Illus. N.Y.: Houghton, Mifflin & Co. 444 pp. Title page missing. (Ih/2)

Seamer, Mary. *Shakespeare's Stories Simply Told.* Illus. London, Edinburgh and N.Y.: Thomas Nelson and Sons, n.d. 312 pp. (IIe/22)

———. *Shakespeare's Stories Simply Told.* Illus. London, Edinburgh and N.Y.: Thomas Nelson and Sons, n.d. 312 pp. (IIe/23)

Searle, Edis. *Hymn Stories.* Illus. N.Y.: E. P. Dutton & Co., 1873. 165 pp. (IIb/13)

———. *Hymn Stories.* Illus. N.Y.: E. P. Dutton & Co., 1873. 165 pp. (IIb/41)

Sedgwick. *A Love Token for Children.* N.Y.: Harper & Bros., 1871. 142
pp. (IIa/45)
———. *The Poor Rich Man, and the Rich Poor Man.* N.Y.: Harper &
Bros., 1876. 186 pp. (IIa/44)
Seven Little People and Their Friends. Illus. N.Y.: Hurd and Houghton,
1878. 240 pp. (IId/6)
Seymour, Mary H. *Posy Vinton's Picnic and Other Stories.* Illus. frontis.
N.Y.: E. P. Dutton & Co., 1877. 150 pp. (Ig/12)
———. *Posy Vinton's Picnic and Other Stories.* Illus. frontis. N.Y.: E. P.
Dutton & Co., 1877. 150 pp. (Ig/14)
Shell Cove: A Story of the Sea-Shore and of the Sea. Illus. Boston: D.
Lothrop & Co., 1871. 350 pp. (IId/31)
Mrs. Sherwood. *The History of the Fairchild Family: or, The Child's
Manual; Being a Collection of Stories Calculated to Shew the
Importance and Effects of a Religious Education.* London: Ward, Lock
& Co., n.d. 297 pp. (If/20)
———. *The History of Susan Gray.* Illus. frontis. London and N.Y.:
George Routledge and Sons, n.d. 157 pp. (Ia/44)
Sidney, Margaret. *Five Little Peppers and How They Grew.* Illus.
Boston: D. Lothrop & Co., 1880. 410 pp. (If/17)
Silver Wings and Golden Scales. Illus. London, Paris & N.Y.: Cassell,
Petter, Galpin & Co., n.d. 192 pp. (Ih/34)
Slade, Mrs. Mary B. C. *Exhibition Days. Containing Dialogues,
Recitations, Charades, Tableaux, Original Blackboard Exercises,
Pantomimes, and Plays.* Boston: Henry A. Young, 1880. 128 pp.
(Ic/32)
Small Beginnings; or, The Way to Get on. Short Biographies for Youth.
Friendly Hand Series. Illus. Philadelphia: Porter & Coates, n.d. N.p.
(Ib/28)
Smith, Mrs. F. B. *Clem and Joyce; or, The Prairie School.* Illus. Boston:
. Lothrop & Co., 1870. 159 pp. (IIIa/42)
———. *Jimmy Don; or, Judy and Her Baby.* Sunny Dell Series. Illus.
Boston: D. Lothrop & Co., 1869. 128 pp. (IIIa/43)
———. *Tom, the Sailor-Boy.* Illus. Boston: D. Lothrop & Co., 1869. 165
pp. (IIIa/38)
———. *Tom, the Sailor-Boy.* Illus. Boston: D. Lothrop & Co., 1869. 165
pp. (IIIa/39)
———. *Tom, the Sailor-Boy.* Illus. Boston: D. Lothrop & Co., 1869. 165
pp. (IIIa/40)
———. *Tom, the Sailor-Boy.* Illus. Boston: D. Lothrop & Co., 1869. 165
pp. (IIIa/41)
Smith, Mary P. W. *The Browns.* Illus. frontis. Boston: Roberts Brothers,
1885. 264 pp. Final pages missing. (Ig/51)
Smith, Rev. S. F., ed. *Knights and Sea-Kings; or, The Middle Ages.* Illus.
Boston: D. Lothrop & Co., n.d. 330 pp. (IIIh/11)
———, ed. *Myths and Heroes; or, The Childhood of the World.* Illus.
Boston: D. Lothrop & Co., 1873. 324 pp. (IIIh/10)
Songs and Stories, for Mother's Darling. Illus. Philadelphia: J. B.
Lippincott & Co., n.d. 64 pp. (IIIa/4)

S. T. C. *The Little Fox: The Story of Captain Sir F. L. M'Clintock's Arctic Expedition.* Illus. N.Y.: Dodd, Mead & Co., n.d. 198 pp. (Ig/8)

Stewart, Louisa. *The Wave and the Battle-Field.* Illus. London: Strahan & Co., 1873. 283 pp. (Ic/7)

Stories for Children by Eleven Sophomores. Boston: Roberts Brothers, 1875. 118 pp. (Ig/16)

Stories for Young Persons. N.Y.: Harper & Bros., 1878. 185 pp. (Ia/24)

Stories on the Eight Beatitudes. Illus. N.Y.: General Protestant Episcopal Sunday School Union and Church Book Society, n.d. 175 pp. (IIa/36)

The Story of Joseph and His Brethren. Illus. N.Y.: General Protestant Episcopal Sunday School Union and Church Book Society, 1870. 106 pp. (Ia/7)

A Story of A Wooden Horse. Illus. London and N.Y.: George Routledge and Sons, 1878. 94 pp. (Ic/29)

Stretton, Hesba. *Cassy.* Illus. N.Y.: Dodd, Mead & Co., n.d. 236 pp. (IIIb/33)

————. *Lost Gip and Michel Lorio's Cross.* Illus. N.Y.: Dodd, Mead & Co., n.d. 245 pp. (IIIb/34)

————. *Nelly's Dark Days.* Illus. frontis. N.Y.: Dodd, Mead & Co., n.d. 180 pp. (IIIb/32)

Strickland, Miss Jane. *Christmas Holidays; or, A New Way of Spending Them.* Illus. frontis. London and N.Y.: George Routledge and Sons, n.d. 168 pp. (IIb/37)

Strong, Rev. J. D. *Child Life in Many Lands.* Illus. Boston: D. Lothrop & Co., 1870. 210 pp. (Ie/21)

Stuart, Esmè. *The Little Brown Girl.* N.Y.: Dodd, Mead & Co., n.d. 314 pp. (IIIb/41)

Studley, Mrs. S. C. *What Do I Want Most! A Story for the Children of the Church.* Illus. N.Y.: General Protestant Episcopal Sunday School Union and Church Book Society, 1850. 117 pp. (Ia/17)

Stwin, Adam. *Eyes Right!* Illus. Boston: D. Lothrop & Co. N.p. Title page missing. (Ih/15)

Sunday. Illus. 410 pp. Front cover and title page missing. (Ih/20)

Sunday. Illus. 452 pp. Title page missing. (Ih/31)

Sunday Evenings; or, An Easy Introduction to the Reading of the Bible. Part I. Illus. N.Y.: Harper & Bros., n.d. 199 pp. (Ib/41)

Sunday Evenings; or, An Easy Introduction to the Reading of the Bible. Part II. N.Y.: Harper & Bros., n.d. 207 pp. (Ib/42)

Sunday Evenings; or, An Easy Introduction to the Reading of the Bible. Part III. Illus. frontis. N.Y.: Harper & Bros., n.d. 227 pp. (Ib/43)

Sunlight Through the Mist; or, Lessons from the Lives of Great and Good Men. Illus. N.Y.: Dodd, Mead & Co., n.d. 213 pp. (IIIb/31)

Sunny Days; or, A Month at the Great Stowe. Illus. N.Y.: E. P. Dutton & Co., n.d. 160 pp. (Ib/34)

Dean Swift. *Gulliver's Travels into Several Remote Nations of the World.* Illus. Philadelphia: J. B. Lippincott & Co., 1880. 431 pp. (IIId/18)

Swift, Maggie. *Pro and Con. A Story for Boys and Girls.* Illus. Boston: D. Lothrop & Co., 1871. 288 pp. (Id/33)

Symington, Maggie. *Working to Win: A Story for Girls.* Illus. frontis.

London, Paris & N.Y.: Cassell, Petter, Galpin & Co., n.d. 445 pp.
(IIe/7)

————. *Working to Win: A Story for Girls.* Illus. frontis. London, Paris &
N.Y.: Cassell, Petter, Galpin & Co., n.d. 445 pp. (IIe/8)

A Tale of a Nest. Illus. N.Y.: E. P. Dutton & Co., 1872. 192 pp. (IIe/1)
A Tale of a Nest. Illus. N.Y.: E. P. Dutton & Co., 1872. 192 pp. (IIe/2)
Taylor, Jefferys. *The Young Islanders; or, The School-Boy Crusoes. A
Tale of the Last Century.* Illus. Philadelphia: J. B. Lippincott & Co.,
1878. 820 pp. (IIIe/9)
Temple, Crona. *Little Wavie, the Foundling of Glenderg.* Illus. Boston:
D. Lothrop & Co., n.d. 249 pp. (IIIc/24)
Thayer, Rev. William M. *Stories of the Creation.* The Pioneer Series.
Illus. Philadelphia: Perkinpine & Higgins, 1865. 262 pp. (Ib/5)
The Thousand and One Nights; or, The Arabian Nights' Entertainment.
Illus. Philadelphia: J. B. Lippincott & Co., 1881. 450 pp. (IId/14)
The Thousand and One Nights; or, The Arabian Nights' Entertainment.
Illus. Boston: Estes and Lauriat, n.d. 468 pp. (IId/15)
The Three Cripples. Illus. London: Society for Promoting Christian
Knowledge, n.d. 144 pp. (Ia/45)
Three Years at Wolverton. A School Story. Illus. Philadelphia: J. B.
Lippincott & Co., 1881. 330 pp. (IIId/16)
A Treasury of Pleasure Books for Young People. Illus. N.Y.: Hurd and
Houghton, n.d. N.p. (Ig/5)
The Treasury of Fairy Stories. Illus. N.Y.: Hurd and Houghton: n.d. 125
pp. (Ie/25)
Mrs. Trimmer. *The Story of the Robins.* Illus. London and N.Y.: George
Routledge and Sons, n.d. 192 pp. (Ic/17)
*The Triumphs of Steam. Stories from the Lives of Watt, Arkwright,
and Stephenson.* Illus. N.Y.: E. P. Dutton & Co., n.d. 248 pp. (Id/8)
Trowbridge, Miss C. M. *Emma Marble and Her Cousin.* Illus.
Philadelphia: Alfred Martien, 1874. 204 pp. (Ia/32)
————. *Frank and Rufus; or, Obedience and Disobedience.* Illus.
Philadelphia: Alfred Martien, 1873. 284 pp. (Ia/31)
Trowdridge, J. T. *Ironthorpe, the Pioneer Preacher.* Bright Hope Series.
N.Y.: Sheldon & Co., 1870. 300 pp. (Ia/41)
Twice Found. Illus. N.Y.: Dodd, Mead & Co., n.d. 131 pp. (IIIb/30)
The Twin Brothers. N.Y.: Harper & Bros., 1843. 243 pp. (Ia/42)
Two Fourpenny Boys. Illus. London, Paris & N.Y.: Cassell, Petter,
Galpin & Co., n.d. 224 pp. (Id/2)
The Two School-Girls, and Other Stories. Illus. Philadelphia: J. B.
Lippincott & Co., n.d. 64 pp. (Ib/48)
Tytler, Sarah. *Papers for Thoughtful Girls.* Illus. Boston: Estes and
Lauriat, 1880. 344 pp. (IIc/1)

Uncle Hardy. *Notable Shipwrecks: Being Tales of Disaster and Heroism
at Sea.* Illus. frontis. London, Paris & N.Y.: Cassell, Petter, Galpin &
Co., n.d. 278 pp. (IIh/12)
Uncle Harry's Lesson, and Other Stories. Keeping On Series. Illus. N.Y.:
T. Y. Crowell & Co., n.d. 112 pp. (Ig/21)

Uncle Herbert, ed. *The Boys' and Girls' Treasury. A Picture and Story Book for Young People.* Illus. Philadelphia: J. B. Lippincott & Co., 1879. 320 pp. (IIh/7)
_____. *The Budget. A Picture and Story Book for Boys and Girls.* Illus. Philadelphia: J. B. Lippincott & Co., 1877. 368 pp. (IIh/6)
_____. *Feet and Wings; or, Among the Beasts and Birds.* Illus. Philadelphia: J. B. Lippincott & Co., 1880. 176 pp. (IIh/2)
_____. *The My Books. Containing My Primer, My Pet Book, My Own Book.* Three Volumes in One. Illus. Philadelphia: J. B. Lippincott & Co., 1877. 288 pp. (IIh/5)
_____. *The Playmate. A Picture and Story Book for Boys and Girls.* Illus. Philadelphia: J. B. Lippincott & Co., 1878. 336 pp. (IIh/3)
_____. *The Playmate. A Picture and Story Book for Boys and Girls.* Illus. Philadelphia: J. B. Lippincott & Co., 1878. 336 pp. (IIh/4)
_____. *The Racoon, and Other Stories for Boys and Girls.* Illus. Philadelphia: J. B. Lippincott & Co., 1880. 192 pp. (IIh/11)
Uncle John. *Evenings at Home, in Words of One Syllable.* Illus. London, Paris & N.Y.: Cassell, Petter & Galpin, n.d. 224 pp. (IIb/30)
_____. *The Wonders of the World. As Related to His Young Friends.* Illus. London: Ward, Lock & Co., n.d. 315 pp. (Ie/16)
Uncle Ned. *The Tropics.* Illus. Boston: D. Lothrop & Co., n.d. 207 pp. (Ie/20)
Uncle Rod's Pet. Illus. N.Y.: General Protestant Episcopal Sunday School Union and Church Book Society, 1869. 135 pp. (Ib/11)
Uncle Rod's Pet. Illus. frontis. N.Y.: E. P. Dutton & Co., 1876. 135 pp. (Ib/12)
Under the Holly. A Book for Girls. By "A Pair of Hands". Presentation Series. Illus. Philadelphia: Porter & Coates, 1869. 403 pp. (IIb/27)
Ups and Downs of a Donkey's Life. The Cosy Corner Series. Illus. London, Paris & N.Y.: Cassell, Petter, Galpin & Co., n.d. 183 pp. (IIe/29)
Vance, Clara. *Andy Luttrell.* Illus. Boston: D. Lothrop & Co., 1869. 384 pp. (IIId/1)
_____. *Hidden Treasure.* Illus. Boston: D. Lothrop & Co., 1877. 301 pp. (IIId/2)
_____. *Strawberry Hill.* Illus. Boston: D. Lothrop & Co., 1870. 432 pp. (IIId/3)
_____. *The Talbury Girls.* Illus. Boston: D. Lothrop & Co., n.d. 487 pp. (IIId/4)
Verne, Jules. *The English at the North Pole.* Every Boy's Library. Illus. London and N.Y.: George Routledge and Sons, 1876. 254 pp. (IIa/5)
_____. *The Field of Ice.* Every Boy's Library. Illus. London and N.Y.: George Routledge and Sons, 1876. 190 pp. (IIa/4)
_____. *Five Weeks in a Balloon; or, Journeys and Discoveries in Africa by Three Englishmen.* Illus. Philadelphia: J. B. Lippincott & Co., 1881. 345 pp. (Ie/1)
_____. *A Floating City and The Blockade Runners.* Trans. Henry Frith. Every Boy's Library. London and N.Y.: George Routledge and Sons, 1876. 270 pp. (IIa/2)

————. *Journey to the Centre of the Earth.* Every Boy's Library. London and N.Y.: George Routledge and Sons. 254 pp. Front cover and title page missing. (IIa/3)

————. *Round the World in Eighty Days.* Illus. frontis. London and N.Y.: George Routledge and Sons, 1879. 254 pp. (Ie/2)

Vernor, Annie Fisler. *A Summer at Marley.* N.Y.: General Protestant Episcopal Sunday School Union and Church Book Society, 1866. 241 pp. (Ia/9)

A Very Young Couple. Illus. N.Y.: Scribner, Armstrong & Co., 1874. 268 pp. (IIb/4)

Mrs. Ward. *Hardy and Hunter. A Boy's Own Story.* Illus. London and N.Y.: George Routledge and Sons, n.d. 464 pp. (Ib/13)

Waring, Susie M. *Diamonds and Rubies; or, The Home of Santa Claus.* Illus. N.Y.: E. P. Dutton & Co., 1870. 49 pp. (Ig/31)

————. *Little Mirabel's Fair.* Illus. N.Y.: E. P. Dutton & Co., 1870. 55 pp. (Ig/30)

Warner, Charles Dudley. *Being a Boy.* Illus. Boston: Houghton, Osgood & Co., 1880. 244 pp. (IIb/28)

We Boys. Written by One of Us for the Amusement of Pa's and Ma's in General, Aunt Louisa in Particular. Boston: Roberts Brothers, 1879. 245 pp. (Ib/6)

Weeks, Helen. *Grandpa's House.* The Ainslee Series. Illus. N.Y.: Hurd and Houghton, 1876. 239 pp. (Ie/15)

Whitney, Mrs. A. D. T. *Boys at Chequasset; or, "A Little Leaven".* Illus. Boston: Houghton, Mifflin & Co., 1882. 258 pp. (If/3)

———— and others. *The New England Story-Book.* Illus. Boston: D. Lothrop & Co., 1880. N.p. (Ih/9)

Wide Awake Pleasure Book. Illus. Boston: D. Lothrop & Co. 392 pp. Title page missing. Final pages probably missing. (Ih/3)

Wide Awake Pleasure Book. Illus. Boston: D. Lothrop & Co., 1881. 569 pp. (IIh/9)

The Widow's Cottage, and Other Stories. Illus. Philadelphia: J. B. Lippincott & Co., n.d. 64 pp. (IIIa/8)

Wildermuth, Madame Ottalie. *Frau Luna, and Her Voyages.* Trans. Anna B. Cooke. Ottalie's Stories for the Little Folks. Illus. Boston: E. P. Dutton & Co., 1867. 120 pp. (IIb/14)

————. *Frau Luna, and Her Voyages.* Trans. Anna B. Cooke. Ottalie's Stories for the Little Folks. Illus. Boston: E. P. Dutton & Co., 1867. 120 pp. (IIb/15)

————. *A Queen. A Story for Girls.* Trans. Anna B. Cooke. Illus. N.Y.: E. P. Dutton & Co., 1874. 129 pp. (Ic/49)

Willie and Robert: A Narrative of the Pious Lives and Early Deaths of Two Christian Children. N.Y.: General Protestant Episcopal Sunday School Union and Church Book Society, 1870. 43 pp. (IIa/50)

Willie's Money-Box. Illus. Boston: D. Lothrop & Co., n.d. 316 pp. (IIc/6)

Willson, Marcius. *The First Reader of the Popular Series.* Illus. Philadelphia: J. B. Lippincott & Co., 1881. 96 pp. (Id/20)

––––––. *The Second Reader of the Popular Series.* Illus. Philadelphia:
J. B. Lippincott & Co., 1881. 160 pp. (Id:21)

––––––. *The Third Reader of the Popular Series.* Illus. Philadelphia: J. B.
Lippincott & Co., 1881. 228 pp. (Id/22)

––––––. *The Fourth Reader of the Popular Series.* Illus. Philadelphia:
J. B. Lippincott & Co., 1881. 334 pp. (Id/23)

––––––. *The Fifth Reader of the Popular Series.* Illus. Philadelphia: J. B.
Lippincott & Co., 1881. 479 pp. (Id/24)

Wilson, T. P. *Amos Huntingdon.* Illus. London: T. Nelson and Sons,
1881. 422 pp. (IIc/2)

––––––. *Amos Huntingdon.* Illus. London: T. Nelson and Sons, 1881. 422
pp. (IIc/3)

––––––. *Great Heights Gained by Steady Efforts; or, Perserverance and
Faithfulness Triumphant.* Illus. frontis. London: T. Nelson and Sons,
1882. 272 pp. (IIc/4)

––––––. *Great Heights Gained by Steady Efforts; or, Perserverance and
Faithfulness Triumphant.* Illus. frontis. London: T. Nelson and Sons,
1882. 272 pp. (IIc/5)

Wister, Mrs. A. L., trans. *Seaside and Fireside Fairies.* Illus.
Philadelphia: J. B. Lippincott & Co., 1880. 292 pp. (Id/12)

*Wonderful Adventures. A Series of Narratives of Personal Experiences
Among the Native Tribes of America.* Illus. Philadelphia: J. B.
Lippincott & Co., 1874. 313 pp. (IId/25)

Woods, Kate Tannatt. *Doctor Dick.* Illus. Boston: D. Lothrop & Co.,
1881. 420 pp. (IIe/9)

––––––. *Six Little Rebels.* Illus. Boston: D. Lothrop & Co., 1879. 412 pp.
(IIId/6)

*Wrecked on a Reef; or, Twenty Months in the Auckland Isles. A True
Story of Shipwreck, Adventure, and Suffering.* Illus. London,
Edinburgh and N.Y.: T. Nelson and Sons, 1880. 350 pp. (IIId/10)

*Wrecked on a Reef; or, Twenty Months in the Auckland Isles. A True
Story of Shipwreck, Adventure, and Suffering.* Illus. London,
Edinburgh and N.Y.: T. Nelson and Sons, 1880. 350 pp. (IIId/11)

Wright, J. Hall. *Ocean-Work, Ancient and Modern: or, Evenings on Sea
and Land.* Happy Child's Library. N.Y.: D. Appleton & Co., 1873.
168 pp. (IIIa/25)

Wright, O. W., ed. *Adventures of Telemachus, by Fenelon.* Boston:
Houghton, Osgood & Co., 1879. 559 pp. (If/26)

Wynne, Faith. *Flossy Lee.* Illus. Philadelphia: James A. Moore, 1869,
209 pp. (Ia/11)

A Year With the Everards. Illus. frontis. N.Y.: E. P. Dutton & Co.,
1874. 211 pp. (IIb/11)

A Year With the Everards. Illus. frontis. N.Y.: E. P. Dutton & Co.,
1874. 211 pp. (IIb/12)

Yonge, Charlotte M. *Bye-Words. A Collection of Tales New and Old.*
London: Macmillan & Co., 1880. 351 pp. (IIf/14)

––––––. *The Pigeon Pie. A Tale of Roundhead Times.* Illus. Boston:
Roberts Brothers, 1869. 172 pp. (IIf/15)

————, ed. *A Storehouse of Stories. Storehouse the First.* Illus. frontis. London: Macmillan & Co., 1880. 437 pp. (Ic/12)

————, ed. *A Storehouse of Stories. Storehouse the Second.* Illus. frontis. London: Macmillan & Co., 1880. 403 pp. (Ic/13)

Yvonne. *The General's Grandchildren; or, "Worth a Threepenny Bit".* Illus. N.Y.: E. P. Dutton & Co., n.d. 190 pp. (Ic/47)

————. *The General's Grandchildren; or, "Worth a Threepenny Bit".* Illus. N.Y.: E. P. Dutton & Co., n.d. 190 pp. (Ic/48)

Zschokke, H. *The Goldmaker's Village.* Happy Child's Library. N.Y.: D. Appleton & Co., 1873. 180 pp. (IIIa/34)

Reviews

Scholarship in New Disciplines

Thomas J. Roberts

Extrapolation: A Journal of Science Fiction and Fantasy, Vol. 16, no. 2 (May 1975). Edited by Thomas D. Clareson, Department of English, College of Wooster, Wooster, Ohio.

Within the past decade four new disciplines have emerged nationally in academic literary studies: children's literature, black literature, women's literature, science fiction. Others are knocking briskly at the door: the film, gay literature, the detective story, radical literature. Each of these has its journal, its bibliographies, its full-length studies, its conventions, and a growing number of recruits. Today, men and women are applying for position primarily as experts in science fiction and not merely as specialists in American literature who can also put a science fiction course together.

Extrapolation is one of the earliest journals in these new areas to receive Modern Language Association recognition and has now been appearing for sixteen years. Students of children's literature—even those with no interest in science fiction—might well cast an interested eye on this journal, then. What it is now may tell them something about what they will be when they have had sixteen years to get themselves established, to find writers, to raise their standards, to establish a focus. Or they might study it to discover pitfalls they would like to avoid.

It must be said right off that it is disappointing in many respects to find what one does find in this most recent issue. Consider merely this: not one of the essays comes from a major academic address. Apparently the older universities have yet to accept an interest in science fiction as respectable. There are recognized scholars studying science fiction—Robert Scholes and Leslie Fiedler—but apparently they are exceptions. Work on science fiction is pursued by teachers in the smaller colleges—by teachers, that is, who have twelve- and fifteen-hour teaching loads rather than six- or nine-, who have the most trouble getting money to free them for research, and who must work with very small libraries. There is evidence that this is true of children's literature—and of women's literature and black literature, too, even though these too draw strength from deeply powerful movements within our society. One wonders how long it will be before the older universities will be giving more than token recognition to any of these new lines of investigation. While some ambitious and talented young scholars and critics are entering these fields, most are still working in the older disciplines. Since it is from their ranks that the academic establishment of the next few decades will come, we may well wonder whether these disciplines still will be knocking at the door sixteen years from now.

Before we salve our frustration with an image of an academic establishment too tradition-oriented to entertain valid new inquiries, we ought, perhaps, to consider what it is we are doing. An examination of the contents of this May 1975 issue of *Extrapolation* is instructive.

There are eight essays in the issue. The *MLA Style Sheet* is honored to a fault. The "grammar" is impeccable: punctuation is accurate freshman-English punctuation, spelling is precise, diction is unadventurous and exact, sentences are always complete and can never be marked AWKWARD, paragraphs have topic sentences. The surface structure (if one might extend the linguists' metaphor) is superbly academic.

It is the deep structures that disturb one. Here are two matters of significant concern. The first is that of simple scholarship: it is demonstrably uncertain.

1. Janice Neuleib's essay compares Lewis's *Out of the Silent Planet* with Wells's *First Men on the Moon*. An incautious reader of her essay could certainly be exclused for supposing that C. S. Lewis had accepted H. G. Wells's fable as a matrix for showing something quite different than Wells had proposed—as Joyce did *The Odyssey*. But in Lin Carter's history of fantasy, *Imaginary Worlds*, Lewis is quoted as follows: "The real father of my planet books is David Lindsay's *A Voyage to Arcturus*—it was Lindsay who first gave me the idea that the 'scientifiction' appeal could be combined with the 'supernatural' appeal." Whatever the connections may be between the novels of Wells and Lewis, this sentence is a datum of fundamental importance. If Ms. Neuleib did not know of it, that is an error in scholarship; but if she did know of it, it is still an error in scholarship, for she owed it to fellow scholars less deep in Lewis studies than she is to warn them against simplistic assumptions of indebtedness.

2. Thomas Wymer describes a change in science fiction since the 1930s as a shift from Enlightenment to Romantic epistemologies. Clearly, there has been a change. The stories John Campbell wanted for *Astounding* in its most influential period (1937–49) were differ-

ent from those Harlan Ellison sought for *Dangerous Visions* (1967).
Yet to suggest that this change can be explained by citing an intellectual reorientation that occurred two hundred years earlier in Europe
is risky. If Goethe's *Faust* is Romantic, then one certainly might
argue that Campbell's own "Twilight" and Clarke's *Childhood's End*
are Romantic. In both there is a Faustian celebration of growth
through metamorphosis. This is quite plain in *Childhood's End*: the
human race will change into the Overmind. But it is evident in "Twilight" too. The human race will metamorphose into machines with
curiosity; Campbell was fully capable of imagining that as an improvement on the human species as it is today. This concern for
growth is certainly not emphasized in the classic Enlightenment texts.
In any case, "knowing" has never been given more than lip service
in science fiction. Its heroes have been engineer-adventurers who
would never have been satisfied with pure knowledge. It has been
"winning" and "losing" that has been science fiction's preoccupation
—winning with the help of technological magic, losing because of
inherent human limitations.

It seems a little cheap to carp at these essays in this way—for
what issue of any respected literary journal is not equally vulnerable
to complaint?—yet a disappointment in the scholarship of science
fiction studies is hard to subdue. The writers of the essays in this
issue share some of that disappointment, for they cite incredible
errors in reading from the books which are still the central studies
of the genre. Wymer correctly challenges Mark Hillegas's surprising
misreading of *Childhood's End*, and Dennis E. Showalter should not
have found it necessary to defend Heinlein's *Starship Trooper* against
the absurd charge of fascism. The new disciplines in literary study
manifest a slackness of standards that would be entertained in no
other areas. Indeed, *Extrapolation* has done splendid service in raising the standards. Apparently we who write about science fiction (or
about the detective story or children's literature or the film) feel that
the kinds of care we would take in our other essays can gratefully
be let slip: if we have read the book and own a typewriter we are
qualified to write. This must be one of the most exasperating problems editors of journals like *Extrapolation* and *Children's Literature*
face.

What is more disturbing than these more obvious lapses in scholarship is the fact that the essays in this issue leave one with the So what?
feeling. "Granted everything you have said is true, so what? Why
should I care?" This, too, is a failure in scholarship.

Too often these essays leave us suspecting that their writers really did not know why they wrote them. Or, to put it in another way, that they wrote their essays because they wanted (or had) to write *some* essay on literature and because this is the kind of essay people have been writing about other kinds of literature for decades. People did source-studies of "Kubla Kahn"; therefore I shall do a source-study of *Out of the Silent Planet*. People have shown the critics to be wrong in their characterizations of *The Turn of the Screw*; therefore I shall show people have been publicly wrong about Heinlein's *Starship Trooper*.

Consider this last matter. Dennis E. Showalter has an absolutely definitive refutation of the characterization of *Starship Trooper* as fascist. Fine. Job done. But, really, who cares? It was simply not worth the research and energy and time and intelligence that Showalter has devoted to proving that some of the people who wrote hastily have inaccurately used the word *fascist* when they wanted to express their distaste for Heinlein's value-system. They were wrong to say it is fascistic, but not every mistake is worth taking the time to correct—not when the same energy and intelligence (both very impressive) might have been given to a more serious matter. (I recognize that it is inconsistent of me to complain about the low standards of scholarship in this discipline and then turn around and complain when someone does something which will help raise those standards. I am unrepentant: Mr. Showalter's abilities should have been given to more serious matters.)

Compare, for contrast, Robert Plank's essay on the presidency in science fiction in this same issue. Let me admit at the outset that this essay told me all kinds of things I did not want to know and will soon forget. Yet Plank has a larger reason for his inquiry. He is interested in that old question of the genre's being able to prepare us for the future, and he concludes that it is actually not very good at doing that. Now, if it could be shown that science fiction *is* very good at guessing the future, that would be an important discovery for any reader of books—for any politician, investor, teacher, parent, child. But futurologists have been claiming precisely that: the question has some human weight, then, that the essays on *Out of the Silent Planet* and *Starship Trooper* lack.

The sorrowful truth is that the most lively and stimulating observations made on science fiction are not to be found in the academic science fiction journals but in the letters and reviews and essays which appear in the underground press devoted to the genre—in, for instance, the remarks of John Pierce in his fanzine *Renaissance*, in the writings of Mark Purcell and Paul Walker in *Luna*, in the talks reprinted in the British *Vector*, in the Australian *SF Commentary*, and elsewhere. The amateur criticism of the genre offers more than the professional criticism of scholars with years of training in literary studies.

As a reader and student of science fiction, then, I must admit that the intellectual character of science fiction studies in the academic world is not yet impressive. Most disturbing is that lack of a sense of larger purpose—the conviction not only that science fiction is important but that studies of the genre have their own importance, however indirect, to the Miltonist and the students of Ruskin and historians of the ode and the drama and the novel.

No doubt there is a *Wilkie Collins Newsletter* somewhere, a *Journal of Jones Very Scholarship*, and several score other academic fan-clubs (a T. E. Lawrence journal has just been announced). What are the rest of us to think of the groups that issue those journals? What are traditional students of literature to think of us?

This seems plain: a specialized activity like the investigation into science fiction or children's literature or gay literature is accepted as a full partner in literary studies only after it has managed to make some contribution to a general poetics upon which all other students of literature can draw. If science fiction studies have nothing more to say than that *Dune* and *Left Hand of Darkness* and *Foundation* deserve attention *too*, they will never attract the respect and support of students who happen not to take an interest in that genre as readers. This is a test every other discipline in literary studies has had to pass: each has had to convince people who have different tastes in their reading that even though they do not turn eagerly to, for instance, the minor eighteenth-century poets, the studies done of those poets contribute nevertheless to their understanding of the literature to which their tastes do draw them. Studies of modernist poetry evolved techniques of explication now being used everywhere; studies of seventeenth-century literature explored the connections between religion and literature which have been extended into other eras; studies of the eighteenth-century novel taught us fundamental lessons about the relations between a society and its literature. What has science fiction studies taught us about literature that we have not already learned in our studies of Milton or medieval literature? I do not find that it has taught us very much at all. The earlier studies of H. Bruce Franklin have subtly changed the ways in which we read

Hawthorne's "Artist of the Beautiful" and Twain's *Connecticut Yankee in King Arthur's Court*: we can now see that they are previously unrecognized outgrowths of this genre. But there is little else that would interest the person who does not read science fiction.

The more one learns about science fiction, the more surprising it should be that its students have been content to imitate earlier methods and goals and subjects. The genre is an aboriginal growth inside Western culture which developed in spite of the disapproval of that culture's institutions: there are no foundations to give fellowships for the writing of a science fiction novel and not until recently has it been studied in the schools. Yet it has continued to flourish. That in itself is a fact worth investigation.

Or consider this fact: science fiction is unique in the quality of the interest it has shown in technology. Those who do not read it suppose it has given itself over wholly to the worship of the false god of the machine, but that is wildly inaccurate. Science fiction is the only imaginative genre that has intuitively explored the full range of man/machine relationships today. Ellison's "I Have No Mouth and I Must Scream" gives dramatic expression to the humanist's horror of the machine, but there is much more to our feelings about machines than that—as those humanists who express their horror at man's worship of technology in essays written on typewriters might occasionally stop to recognize. Del Rey's "Helen O'Loy" recognizes that men fall in love with machines—a fact one can easily verify by watching the eyes of the people who visit boat shows or by remembering how he felt about his first bicycle. Bester's "Fondly Faherenheit" goes beyond both stories in describing a psychosis which first develops within a machine (an android, actually), is passed on to its human owner, and is then passed on from him to another machine. One could make a good—if somewhat theatrical—case for arguing that our planet has already been invaded, not by flying octopi from Venus but by machines from inside our own brains. There are more tractors than tigers today, more cars than horses, more ships than whales: our animal companions of as little as two centuries ago are rapidly being replaced by the devices we have created—the canary by the radio, the watchdog by the burglar alarm, sheep by lawnmowers. One aspect of the human condition today is this increase in our emotional involvement with machines. The writers of serious fiction have yet to recognize how complex the situation actually is. Can they really feel that those machines in the hospitals which will later keep them alive are *all* bad? Only science fiction offers a genuinely humanistic consideration of this frightening but fascinating situation in which we find ourselves.

Here, then, are two features of science fiction that have some bearing on matters that interest all readers: an aspect of the sociology of literature which its students are not exploring, a feature of the human condition today which this genre alone is prepared to help us understand. But there are other ways in which this genre might usefully be studied. I shall cite one and finish.

Science fiction remains interesting to its readers even while it is failing to produce any text that compares favorably with the greatest works of the past. I would put Stapleton's *Last and First Men* on a shelf with *Don Quixote* and *Faust* and *Moby-Dick* and *Ulysses* and *King Lear* and the other twenty or fifty texts accepted everywhere as masterpieces and feel confident that the library has been enriched —but I cannot say that of any other book in science fiction, and I am sure other readers of this genre feel just the way I do. Now, let us take stock for a moment. Experienced readers in this genre continue reading in it even though they know there are other books available which are more satisfying than any this genre produces. Why is that?

We tell ourselves this is a special category of reading and we call it "escapist," yet if this pattern is a symptom of escapist reading, what are we to say of our reading of contemporary poetry? Was every seriously intended poem published in 1975 a masterpiece? Were any? Does the knowledge that none we read last year or this year bears comparison with *Paradise Lost* or *The Rape of the Lock* or Meredith's *Modern Love* or Steven's *The Comedian as the Letter C* deter us from following the vagaries of that genre? It does not—and we do not call it escapist.

In both cases, the interest we are taking in the books is an interest in the life of a genre in a conveniently pure and unambiguous form. As it happens, there is very little known about this kind of reading. Genre-theory is still in a very primitive state—in part, I suggest, because of the difficulties students have in distinguishing genre-appeals from those made by the masterpieces that genres like the epic and Elizabethan revenge tragedy managed to produce. Students of science fiction might be making contributions which would help us understand why it is we can read minor novelists of the past as well as major novelists, the lesser Wordsworth as well as the major, and so forth; for the reader of Wordsworth who goes beyond the major poems is in the condition in which the science fiction reader finds himself: he knows that there are better poems available than the poems he will be reading, but he reads the poems nevertheless.

These are features of the reading of this genre and of its history and of its subject matter that happen to interest me greatly. No doubt there are dozens of other ways in which its students might investigate this genre and in the process throw light into corners still left dark in literary studies. Until they have accepted for themselves that battle-cry we inherited from the poets earlier in this century—"Make it *new!*"—the discipline will continue to be regarded outside its coterie as imitation scholarship.

I read and teach science fiction and learn from the essays in *Extrapolation* and such other scholarship as does appear. I am also fully confident that science fiction studies can become important even to people with no interest in the genre—but that has not happened yet. Let those of us who work in these new disciplines take warning: we could all of us *still* be knocking at the door sixteen years from now.

History of Childhood

Julius A. Elias

The History of Childhood, edited by Lloyd deMause. New York: The Psychohistory Press, 1974. $12.50.

This fascinating collection of chronologically ordered essays offers some extraordinary facts about the history of childhood, afflicted by a theory. The "psychogenic" theory of history, largely shaped by Mr. deMause in his introductory material and the first essay (and largely ignored by the other contributors), is explained (pp. 3, 51–54) and pictured (p. 53) in a graph reminiscent of Condorcet's philosophy of history. It suggests a steady improvement in the attitude toward children from utter beastliness in Roman times (the "abandoning" mode) to enlightenment in 1974 ("helping"). Vestiges of the earlier modes survive to account for battered and starving children in 1974; but there is no provision (despite a good deal of evidence to the contrary) for anyone to have been nice to children in earlier days— it's all Astyanax dashed upon the rocks, unless not so fortunate and preserved for a fate worse than death.

It is hard to know how much to fuss about deMause's insistence on his historiographic principles. Many examples, internal to the book, come to mind. One of them is found in his own treatment. He cites Giovanni Dominici (1405) in opposition to sexual abuse of children, requiring that children be so clothed as to inhibit abuse (p. 48). But Dominici, as quoted, himself finds authority in antiquity for these restraints; deMause passes in silence over the implication that antiquity was more enlightened than the fifteenth century. Of course, Dominici's may merely be a rival Renaissance view that looked to antiquity as a Golden Age and model for imitation superior to current practices. The historiographer, however, should be as critical of Golden Age as of millennial preconceptions.

It is left to some of the other essayists to provide correctives based on more modest historical objectives. Richard B. Lyman, Jr., for example, in a word on method (pp. 76–80) warns against the use of "isolated sources," "rare and bestial attitudes," on the one hand, and against "idealized patterns" on the other. Mary Martin McLaughlin notes the specialized audience and ideology which some of her materials served (p. 109). But these and other reasonable cautions are recklessly disregarded by the editor.

Another major objection is the misnomer "*The* History of Child-hood"; it's not even *A* History. Selected Aspects of Western Child-hood would more accurately describe the book. There is nothing on Asia, Africa, nor even a systematic treatment of classical antiquity (where is Werner Jaeger? where is Pauly-Wissowa?); no examina-tion of contemporary child-rearing practices in India, China, or Latin America; no use of the considerable body of work on children in kibbutzim, such as that by Bettelheim, little on developmental the-ories, say, of Erik Erikson (some use is made by Patrick Dunn, but another Erikson is confused with Erik by the indexer in n. 121 on p. 348). There is no reference to Dickens, nor, if that should seem tendentious, to the Sadler Report (1832) with its grueling accounts of child labor: children have been vulnerable economically as well as in the ways deMause chooses to dwell on.

The editorial hand rests all too lightly in some ways. The apparatus of scholarly literature is formidable for most of the essays, but what is merely a collection of journal articles has scarcely been welded into a book. There is no systematic bibliography and the index is far from comprehensive. Among several others McLaughlin is surely right to find wet-nursing pretty much limited to the noble and pros-perous (p. 115), while the editor apparently expands the practice to most mothers, depending how far one goes back (p. 34). DeMause believes "the further back in history one goes, the more filicidal im-pulses are acted out by parents," and implies that this is due to a brutal spirit that condones such atrocities (pp. 25ff.). Yet Lyman cites legislation of Theodosius around A.D. 320 the tone of which stronglyy suggests horror at infanticide, even if on account of extreme poverty (p. 84). At page 90 he cites an "admonition of Barnabas (ca. 130)" against infanticide.

The editor treats Héroard's account of the childhood of Louis XIII as typifying some horrifying and widespread practices in support of his theory (pp. 21ff.), while Elizabeth Wirth Marvick, drawing on the same material, finds it pathological and "unrepresentative of pat-terns of child care of the time" (p. 263). Readers must judge for themselves; the reviewer's money is on Marvick.

The contributions are of quite uneven merit. Lyman's piece on late Roman and early medieval times is spotty and anecdotal; he records the slow impact of Christianity as a moderating influence, and finds the barbarians in many ways more humane than the Ro-mans. McLaughlin's article is among the best in the book. She has shaped the necessarily fragmentary material from the ninth to the thirteenth centuries into a well-structured piece with an invaluable critical apparatus. (Thus it is odd, since she mentions at page 102 essays on the "cult" of childhood, that she does not refer to George Boas's brilliant collection under that title.) Her own title, "Survivors and Surrogates," evokes the pathos of appallingly high mortality rates both among mothers and infants (pp. 112ff.). Despite some deplorable exceptions, she is under the impression that everybody loves babies, a view gladly shared by this reviewer and St. Hugh of Lincoln (p. 118).

James Bruce Ross draws attention to the sex bias favoring boys over girls, drawing materials from some unpublished *ricordi* of Italian fourteenth- through sixteenth-century mercantile families. M. J. Tucker moves uncertainly between the innocence and imperfection of children as viewed in England of the fifteenth and sixteenth centuries, without noticing the simultaneous presence of both theories, or what consequences this might have for historiographical premises. There is some delightful material about that gentle soul Sir Thomas More, who "beat" his children with a peacock feather—was it to warn them against spiritual pride?

Marvick's essay, "Nature versus Nurture," is exceptionally fine, eliciting variations in child rearing keyed to class and educational theory in seventeenth-century France. Very direct and succinct on wet-nursing: "With a high rate of infant mortality in all classes the affluent could count on a supply of women ready to nurse their children" (p. 281). She movingly documents the treatment of abandoned infants that led St. Vincent de Paul to found his order. She comes closest of all the authors to realizing a broad-based historiographic approach to the material (cf. p. 292). Joseph E. Illick repeats familiar tales from seventeenth-century England and America. His précis of Locke's humane theories, as physician and educator, is accurate and refreshing. Most of the U.S. material is drawn from touching accounts of the self-control and religious resignation needed to face high mortality. But it is curious that he does not deliver on a promise to explain changes in English practices (p. 323); the article ends lamely with a concluding paragraph for which the groundwork has not been laid. Perhaps the piece was cut.

John F. Walzer is disappointing on eighteenth-century America, adding little to a heavily documented period. Is it true, as he says (pp. 365–66) that there is no information on the child-rearing practices of the 20 percent of the American population who were black? Even from ideologues of extreme persuasions there is a great deal of material to be garnered about the impact of slavery on black families. More can be gathered from Dumas Malone on Jefferson than Walzer has to offer. At least he might have explained what "twert yourself" (p. 358) means. The OED doesn't know, which makes it all the more intriguing.

Imperial Russia, or more specifically 1760–1860, is the area explored by Patrick Dunn: a most disconcerting account, showing Russia to have been much more primitive than other European countries, whose practices began to be introduced under Catherine II. That swaddling "persisted" well into the twentieth century (p. 384) need not be put in the past tense. A recent picture book of Moscow from the early 1960s shows rows of cocoons in a maternity hospital. The marvel is that anybody survived. Dunn cites vivid accounts of subfreezing baptismal immersions and boiling steambaths. The dominant thesis, that repression of children was a reflection of the society as a whole (p. 399), is nowhere better exemplified than in Maxim Gorky's *My Childhood*, to which Dunn does not refer. But he has made use of many original and untranslated sources to document a pretty ghastly picture—Mother Russia, indeed!

Priscilla Robertson's paper on "Home as a Nest" covers middle-class childhood in nineteenth-century Europe, when it might cost 15 pounds to deliver a girl, but 20 pounds for a boy. Is the humor, unique in the book, a ray of optimism as the twentieth century dawns, or are the wry asides all Ms. Robertson's own?

Several of the authors treat selections from the factors that might make a coherent thesis, but none draws together the materials that would need to be treated conjointly to do justice to the theme. Among them, but by no means an exhaustive list:

1. The Ariès thesis that there was no "concept of childhood" until the early modern period (i.e., that children were merely little adults). This, as several of the authors are able to show, simply flies in the face of evidence available in all the cultures studied (deMause, pp. 5–6; Lyman, pp. 80ff.; McLaughlin, p. 102).

2. The whole constellation of psycho-social elements which deal with (*a*) self-fulfillment in parenthood (Tucker, pp. 248–49); (*b*) dynastic impulses, intimately connected with the quest for immortality through one's children, including property and inheritance considerations (Lyman, pp. 76–77; McLaughlin, p. 129; Ross and Tucker, *passim*; Marvick, pp. 281ff.; Illick, p. 311; Robertson, p. 426); (*c*) the continuity of the ethos or social fabric, whether dictated by ethical, racial, religious, or other cultural motives, with or

without particularist or xenophobic overtones (Lyman, p. 83; Walzer, pp. 360, 363–64); (*d*) sentimental concerns focusing about the as-yet-unrealized potential of the child to attain goals denied the parents (McLaughlin, *passim*; Illick, p. 317); (*e*) the impact of political and economic insecurity on the more vulnerable segments of the population, among whom children would surely have to be counted (McLaughlin, p. 111; Tucker, pp. 233ff; Dunn, p. 399); (*f*) the relationship of more enlightened modes of child-rearing as a function of the spread of literacy, science, and systemic codes of law effectively disseminated across ever-widening geographical areas (Lyman, p. 90; McLaughlin, p. 140; Marvick, p. 260 and *passim*); (*g*) more particularly, advances in medical science that have taken much of the terror, pain, and mystery out of childbirth, both for children and for parents (Robertson, p. 408); (*h*) educational theories based on any of the foregoing (McLaughlin, pp. 125, 136ff.; Ross, p. 211, Illick, pp. 318ff.).

3. A comparative appraisal of historiographic approaches, rather than the simplistic method of the editor already sufficiently denounced. Among these the phenomenon of cultural primitivism so thoroughly explored by Lovejoy and Boas comes sharply to mind, though virtually ignored by all the authors (only Robertson makes substantial reference to Rousseau). The iconography of childhood surely includes some of the idealized versions mentioned in the essays (Lyman, pp. 78–80, McLaughlin, pp. 103ff., Ross, pp. 204–5, Tucker, p. 231), but the essays pay little attention to the ideological motives for the idealizations: the child as simple, pure, innocent, close to nature, unencumbered by the several curses of intellect, civilization, hyper-specialization, and thus more distinctly human. They have, however, made much more of the imperfection and incompleteness of the child as a rival hypothesis calling for compulsory, often violent, education (Tucker, p. 230; Illick, *passim*; Walzer, p. 364; Robertson, pp. 421–22). Play theory, with all its complexities, is dealt with seriously only in one place (Tucker, pp. 251–52) and in reliance only on J. H. Plumb, who is at odds with most of the literature of the field.

One could go on; but what would emerge is another book, taking most of the material of this work and slicing it in other ways. Shouldn't the authors be left to take their own tacks, and be exempted from attack for not writing the book the reviewer would prefer to see? Yes and no. No, because the claim that this book is a history provokes the demand for thematic analysis, the shaping of a comprehensive theory by articulation of the logical structure of the subject.

This certainly has not been done; and again one returns to the book, still fascinated by a wealth of material, hitherto much neglected, that despite its anecdotal character rebuffs some of the crude generalizations of the past, and sets the record straight in so many useful ways.

Children's Literature as Historical Evidence

Ruth Barnes Moynihan

Mother Was a Lady: Self and Society in Selected American Children's Periodicals, 1865–1890, by R. Gordon Kelly. Westport, Conn.: Greenwood Press, 1974. $12.50.

Guardians of Tradition: American Schoolbooks of the Nineteenth Century, by Ruth Miller Elson. Lincoln, Neb.: Univ. of Nebraska Press, 1964. Paper 1972, $3.25.

The Child and the Republic: The Dawn of Modern American Child Nurture, by Bernard Wishy. Philadelphia: U. of Pa. Press, 1972. $8.00.

The study of children's literature as a basis for social and cultural history is a relatively recent phenomenon in historical scholarship. But it is a welcome phenomenon, and one with great possibilities. If what people do and think as children often influences the future of a society in numerous ways, then knowing what a particular generation of children read, and what adults intended to teach them, can provide many insights into their society.

Mother Was a Lady: Self and Society in Selected American Children's Periodicals, 1865–1890 by R. Gordon Kelly is the most recent of several studies of nineteenth-century children's literature in America. Concentrating on post–Civil War fiction in such leading children's magazines as *St. Nicholas, Our Young Folks,* and *Youth's Companion,* the book is a valuable addition to American cultural history as well as to the study of children's literature. Kelly provides substantial evidence about the "body of beliefs, values, attitudes and practices" which the "gentry" adult community of the time wished to transmit to younger generations. The themes of the stories and the format of their presentation are especially indicative, he says, of the increasing anxiety about immigration, urbanization, and industrialization among the adults of the "gilded age."

Before analyzing the fiction itself, Kelly describes the publication histories of the magazines, the editorial requirements, and the personal backgrounds of the editors. He finds that both editors and contributors, including many of the leading authors of the time, constituted a New England coterie of "gentry" intelligentsia within, but distinct from, the more general American middle class. On the other hand, such magazines as *Leslie's Boy's and Girl's Weekly,*

253

published in New York by a wealthy entrepreneur who was also
known for his fashionable and conspicuous lifestyle, featured dime-
novel-type fiction, full of violence, exciting adventure, and "lurid
illustrations keyed to the more sensational episodes in the stories."
And the well-known Horatio Alger novels featured virtuous hardworking poor boys who achieve success in the big-city business world.

The gentry magazines had distinctly different values. They were
pervasively and deliberately family- and rural-oriented, while their
emphasis was on the development of character and the spirit of
service and duty in a dangerous and threatening society. For their
fictional heroes, the pursuit of wealth or adventure was immoral.
Only personal integrity, domestic devotion, and rural harmony constituted true success and achievement.

Children in these stories, says Kelly, were always either innocent
or only inadvertently guilty, subject to change of heart or heroism in
adversity through strength of will, virtue, courage, and character.
Often lonely and isolated, the child protagonist may discover his
own inappropriate or immoral behavior and make a dramatic change,
or through his own strength and gentility bring about a change in
others merely by his presence or example. Plots range from a boy
deciding not to eat a doughnut without his mother's permission, to a
little girl saving a train from a flood-wrecked bridge, to an old man's
nobility leading the men of a dissolute mining camp to develop order,
cooperation, and community harmony.

Kelly's analysis reveals that the New England gentry tradition
contrasted sharply with the code of raw competition and economic
success epitomized by the Alger stories. The gentry ideal "stressed
a necessary reciprocity between freedom and responsibility" and the
importance of "self-discipline, conscience, and character." Personal
integrity through adherence to a strict moral code and loyalty to rural
rather than urban communities determined one's value, not money
or fashion. In fact, "the fashionable elite of the large seaboard cities
. . . were at once a threat to the gentry ideal and a useful foil to
children's writers," who often showed their standards to be "effete,
devitalized, and superficial," if not even, sometimes, a disguise for
criminality. "The gentleman was both a social and an aesthetic ideal,"
committed to culture and social order through personal discipline.

And it was the family that constituted the paradigm of such social
order, especially the mother, whose relationship to her children was
seen as the basis of all genteel values. The child was innocent, adventure and sensationalism dangerous and potentially immoral, and "the

city . . . no place for children growing up." The stories in these maga-zines, says Kelly, are "decisively shaped by the spaciousness, the rhythms, and the manners of rural and village life," partly because of the authors' own predominantly rural childhood experiences. Kelly's perceptive discussion of gentry nostalgia and anti-urban fears is one of the best in his book.

Other values taught by this literature included fearful suspicion of labor, strikes, and foreigners and a general assumption that vir-tuous capitalism involved "producing the requisite goods or services to fill a particular social need" from which wealth flowed only as a reward for virtue. Mothers tended to be much more in evidence than fathers, who were almost always away on business. Charity meant smiling kindly rather than giving money, while the poor could always improve their lot through virtuous effort. Unfortunately, Kelly does not pursue these issues in depth. He also avoids making any judg-ments about the effects of this gentry literature on the generations that reached maturity from the 1890s on (though he does point out that Theodore Roosevelt was an avid reader of *Our Young Folks*). Kelly's concern is with intentions and form, a more strictly literary type of analysis. The extensive methodological discussion which was appropriate to a dissertation could have been trimmed in the book, as well as a tendency toward repetitiveness, but as a monograph the work is successful and valuable. The bibliography should also be useful to other investigators.

The concluding chapter of *Mother Was a Lady* relates Kelly's findings to other discussions, like John Tomsich's, of the genteel tradition. Kelly points in particular to the continuing influence of gentry standards on children's librarians, editors, and educators throughout the twentieth century which "may help to explain why twentieth-century writers considered most significant by modern criti-cal standards have contributed so little to children's literature and why, institutionally, the teaching of children's literature is largely divorced from, or barely tolerated in, departments of English."

Ruth Miller Elson's *Guardians of Tradition: American School-books of the Nineteenth Century* uses different material and different methodology for a much larger and more detailed study of American values. By analyzing one thousand nineteenth-century textbooks in-tended for use in grades one through eight, she attempts to learn about the ideas of "ordinary man" by examining what he might have read during his crucial childhood years. Since, for most nineteenth-century children, such textbooks had no competition from other

books or from TV or radio or films as they do today, and since the
primary method of instruction was memorization, Elson makes a
good case that "the authors of schoolbooks both created and solidi-
fied American traditions" during this period. Though a large proportion of children had no access to schools in the early part of the
century, basic readers and spellers were often passed from family to
family or carried in wagons across the Oregon trail, while public
elementary schools became ubiquitous by the later part of the century.
And though everyday experience might modify some ideas taught in
schoolbooks, attitudes toward remote nations and peoples, Negro
slavery, or American economic development as presented in such
books were particularly influential.

Elson shows that New England was indeed the "schoolmaster of
the nation" throughout the nineteenth century. Even Southerners
read Northern textbooks, sometimes with offending pages clipped
together, though in most cases any anti-slavery sentiments were so
carefully muted that clipping was not necessary. New England
"printers, journalists, teachers, ministers, and future lawyers," with
now and then someone from New York or Pennsylvania, were the
authors—many of them also among the "gentry" Kelly describes.
And it is clear that "the premise of the founders of New England
themselves—that New England was the New Zion and they the New
Hebrews—is thoroughly accepted in these schoolbooks for the entire
United States." America had been guided and blessed by Providence,
and "love of the American nation is a correlative of love of God."

The central concern of nineteenth-century schools and texts, says
Elson, was the moral development of the child. The emphasis was
on "the formation of character and sound principles rather than the
pursuit of truth," even at the college level, and usefulness was the
criterion of worthy knowledge. In the textbooks, "the fact that we
have not produced scholars is mentioned with pride as a sign that
knowledge is democratically diffused," while European learning and
fine arts were evidences of effete decadence and decline. Children
were even admonished not to read too much and to value direct
experience more highly than thought. As Elson puts it, "anti-intellec-
tualism . . . is thoroughly embedded in the schoolbooks that have
been read by generations of pupils since the beginning of the Republic."

Specific values taught by these textbooks—spellers, arithmetics,
readers, geographies, histories—receive detailed discussion with pertinent quotations and perceptive analysis. For example, the concepts

of man and nature based on the biblical account of creation and Romanticism taught that "the world was created for man, and man for God," with everything harmonious and purposeful. The only change in post-Darwinian textbooks after 1859 was to see evolution as part of God's plan for that still-harmonious universe. Elson speculates that few Americans were really prepared for Darwinian assumptions since even the discovery of fossil dinosaurs in 1800 was not mentioned in textbooks until 1870.

Admiration for rural life and for agriculture as the "solid basis of all prosperity" remained pervasive long after widespread industrialization. By the later part of the century the nostalgia which Kelly describes also appeared in the textbooks, along with some pride in industrial progress, but it was unquestionably "the city for wealth, the country for health," "the town for manners, the country for morals." The small, independent farmer was the true patriot, the trader loved only money, and the Southern plantation owner was indolent and self-indulgent. Virtue was always rewarded and vice punished in immediate and material ways, while affluence was an adjunct of virtue, not an end in itself. "Getting ahead is a moral duty enjoined on man by God," but not for mere enjoyment or pleasure, only for the "sense of achievement and the surety of virtue." There was a fear of excessive industrialization, but also a celebration of the machine as a product of American talent and the factory as an opportunity for the poor. In all but one book, says Elson, labor unions were equated with violence, agitators with subversion, and strike leaders with idle, selfish, vicious, lazy characters. Industry and frugality were crucial virtues, while poverty was the fruit of idleness or immorality in such a land of opportunity. The word "millionaire" first appeared in an 1859 speller, along with an increasing emphasis on the idea that, though unearned wealth and luxury were evil, a rich man who "contributes to the national economy and busies himself in community affairs" was admirable. In these textbooks "the law of history is one of steady and inevitable progress toward greater material wealth and comfort as well as toward greater virtue and freedom"—and America was uniquely prosperous and therefore uniquely chosen.

Elson's analysis of the development of an American "mythology" about the Revolution is particularly interesting. Children were taught that ours was a rational, conservative Revolution, not violent and radical like the French. And though most of the books preached the importance of peace, their format and content actually glorified war with minute and exciting descriptions of battles and martial heroes. Americans always fought for liberty, "but for the child to find out from these books what this liberty is would be astonishing." Therefore, rebellion against tyrants is good, but rebellion against anything American is criminal since America and her Constitution equals liberty.

Stereotypes of various "national characters" appear in all these textbooks, though there was a shift from religious and moral to racial criteria after the 1870s. Such stereotypes awaited new immigrants long before they arrived in America. Before the Civil War there was general concern about the evil of slavery, though descriptions of slave conditions became more conciliatory by mid-century and were seldom mentioned after the Civil War. In fact, there was a "lack of consciousness of the Negro after his emancipation, either as an individual or as a component part of the American population." Though girls attended elementary schools, the books were all directed to boys and took for granted that women had all the equality they needed. The ideal woman had no interests or ambitions, only self-abnegation for the sake of husband and children. She must never engage in masculine activities like building carts or talking politics, and "symbolic emasculation awaits boys who admit girls into their activities."

In general, says Elson, despite slight shifts in emphasis, children's textbooks throughout the nineteenth century showed a fundamentally conservative orientation toward life as a moral struggle in an ethical universe and America as "an ideal world, peopled by ideal villains as well as ideal heroes." The books also revealed an ambiguity which is still evident today: "The American is not clear on who he is, and he tends to wear his Americanness like a cloak he puts on rather than a skin that grows with him."

Bernard Wishy's *The Child and the Republic: The Dawn of Modern American Child Nurture* is an interesting correlative to both the Kelly and Elson books. By studying child nurture material as well as representative children's books throughout the nineteenth century, Wishy shows that there was, in fact, a change after the Civil War, but that the beliefs in "realism" and "experience" as modes of child nurture—both in literature and in education—had roots in early nineteenth-century popularizers, long before John Dewey and Freud expounded their ideas at the turn of the twentieth century.

Neo-orthodoxy after the American Revolution was a response to the sense of instability in the new republican society. But along with moral rectitude children needed flexibility to deal with "a culture in which everything in life was a problem and a gamble." The result was an increasing emphasis on loving family relationships, the mother's role in education, gentler methods of discipline based on guilt and repentance rather than physical punishment, and didactically realistic children's literature emphasizing the development of character. The "great and constant lesson," says Wishy, was that "merit lies in moral fitness and righteousness. Be good and all will be granted; be bad and you lose both the world and heaven." He refers to "Federalist-Whig rhetoric; all working people and employers, being Americans, have their mutual interests at heart; the rich man is wealthy because he has 'character' which also makes him the exemplar and best friend of the laborer."

Wishy points to the conflict inevitable in such an emphasis on the relentless will and demanding law; the child and future adult would be torn between achievement and guilt, between the "will for righteousness and will for success." Or, as Elson put it, the poor man in America would tend to "develop a strong feeling of his own inadequacy, not just in business but in moral character as well," even though the poor were portrayed as much more happy and blessed than the rich.

Wishy agrees with Kelly in his description of the change after the Civil War. There was a new malaise and anxiety, nostalgia for lost innocence and rural virtue, and a sense of the purity of childhood in a dangerous and difficult world. Contrasting the pre–Civil War Rollo series by Jacob Abbott with the post–Civil War Alger books, Wishy finds that the child was now not merely good and redeemable, but might even be the redeemer of adult failures. "Above all, although the notion endured that only the pure and innocent could save the world, it was increasingly feared that the world might be too much for the pure and innocent." The golden age of children's books, says Wishy, began around 1880 with Stevenson, Pyle, Baum, and others, their greatest literary achievement being "the modern adventure story for children." These had "one unifying theme"; the child confronted with a situation must find his true self, test his character, or explore the possibilities of his world. Childhood, however, had become the garden of Eden, and a return to mother, home, and rural innocence was the only acceptable denouement.

Books and stories for children provide particularly clear indices of the basic conflicts and continuities within American culture. Despite differences in emphasis and in sources as well as approaches to the subject, all three of these books make a valuable contribution to our understanding of nineteenth-century America and its twentieth-century residue. It is not only that men like Theodore Roosevelt read *Our Young Folks*, but also that thousands of other children were equally avid readers. For example, in 1899, *Youth's Companion* had a subscription list of 500,000, comparable to that of the *Saturday Evening Post* a few years later. Kelly's *Mother Was a Lady* documents the distinctness of a particular segment of children's literature from 1865 to 1890, thus showing differences within the genre which Wishy's much broader *Child and the Republic* had overlooked. But Wishy's breadth of material and time span covered enables him to show continuities and changes which narrower studies cannot reveal. Elson's extraordinarily detailed analysis of the whole body of nineteenth-century elementary textbooks in *Guardians of Tradition* not only supports and enriches Kelly's and Wishy's findings, but also provides basic and essential documentation for understanding the ideological content of American education and child formation through reading. These three books are excellent evidence of the value of studying children's literature as a source for cultural history.

American History for Young People at Bicentennial

Ruth Barnes Moynihan

So What About History? by Edmund S. Morgan, New York: Atheneum, 1971. $5.95.

Jamestown: The Beginning. by Elizabeth A. Campbell, Boston, Toronto: Little, Brown and Co., 1974. $5.95.

Billy Bartram and His Green World, by Marjory Bartlett Sanger, New York: Farrar, Straus & Giroux, 1972. $6.50.

Mr. Whittier: A Biography, by Elizabeth Gray Vining, New York: Viking, 1974. $7.95.

The Perfect Life: The Shakers in America, by Doris Faber, New York: Farrar, Straus & Giroux, 1974. $6.95.

The Education of Abraham Lincoln, by William H. Armstrong, New York: Coward, McCann & Geoghegan, 1974. $4.64.

The Fiery Trial: A Life of Lincoln, by Herbert Mitgang, New York: Viking, 1974. $7.95.

The Apprenticeship of Abraham Lincoln, by Olivia Coolidge, New York: Charles Scribner's Sons, 1974. $6.95.

Three for Revolution, by Burke Davis, New York and London: Harcourt Brace Jovanovich, 1975. $6.25.

The First American Revolution, by Milton Lomask, New York: Farrar, Straus and Giroux, 1974. $6.95.

Spies on the Devil's Belt, by Betsy Haynes, New York: Thomas Nelson, 1974. $5.50, paperback.

"History is junk," says distinguished historian Edmund Morgan, paraphrasing Henry Ford, in *So What About History?* He then leads young readers artfully from a junkyard to an abandoned Pueblo to the "junking" of the king in the American Revolution in order to show the many ways in which broken pieces of our past have provided foundations for the present. It is the admirable simplicity of this book, ideally suited to the mid-grammar-school level, coupled with the sophistication of its historiographical concepts, which makes it not only a distinguished book for children but also a distinctive piece of evidence about American society in the 1970s.

For, like so many other things, and people, children's books and children themselves have often been considered "junk"—precursors, of course, to great books and great men but hardly worth looking at for themselves alone. Yet ever since the advent of childhood literacy, the books that children have read and the way their history books have presented the past have helped to mold the adult behavior and ideology of each new generation. Judging from the caliber of most of the books here under review, publishers of children's history books in the 1970s are finally recognizing the importance of genuine historical expertise in their authors. With the exception of Coolidge, whose list of previous books shows the peripatetic nature of her scholarship, as her writing shows its shallowness, all these authors are specifically qualified to deal with their subjects. None of their books can be classified as junk.

First of all, there is Edmund Morgan, one of the nation's foremost historians. His contribution to the future adults who read *So What About History?* is not just factual knowledge. It is also a sense of equality, of curiosity, of skepticism—every piece of junk may have value, while every child can, and should, question the experts and look for new meanings in society's junk. "Historians are not always right," he says. Even using the idea of junk as the stuff of history indicates an egalitarianism and open-minded eclecticism which could not be found in American children's books of 150 years ago, or in Russian or Chinese children's books today. American values are not slighted—for example, there is no doubt that Morgan is praising the American Constitution—but American failures are also presented, like the prejudices retained from the institution of slavery. As Morgan puts it, "Sometimes we hang on to things that we should have sent to the junk pile long ago."

The dominant message is that pieces of the past are often worth investigating and saving, but they are always also subject to change —and human beings must decide what to save and what to change. This is, of course, profoundly different from nineteenth-century presentations. Then, in an age of change, the ideal was stability, continuity, and preservation of rural virtue. Today change and variety are taken for granted and virtue is self-defined within particular contexts.

Most history books for young people in this bicentennial era seem to share Morgan's open-minded egalitarianism. They also share with him another theme, one that psychoanalyst Erik Erikson has called a peculiarly American concern. This is the problem of identity. Morgan sounds its note when he claims that the most basic reason for studying history, aside from curiosity, is to know who we are today. "Since so much of what we are comes from the past, we cannot know what we are or who we are without knowing what we have been." It is the cry of the uprooted, the frontiersman, which remains in almost all Americans, children of immigrants, of slaves, of pioneers, of an ever-moving society and an ever-changing world. Perhaps only in America can that search for identity take such varied forms. As the variety of books in this review suggests, it is the uniqueness of the individual and the integrity of his contribution to society which defines American identity in the later twentieth century. There is no one formula for achievement or integrity, nor is there any hero without faults and failures. The American is his own man—and America has room for all types of heroes.

To begin at the beginning—*Jamestown* by Elizabeth Campbell is a beautifully illustrated and sensitively written book, based on original accounts and maintaining the flavor of those originals for both the English and the Indian point of view. Describing the Atlantic voyage and the first year in America in detail, the book succeeds in showing (but not preaching) the sad misunderstanding and lack of communication between English and Indian at every step of the exploration and settlement process, as well as English determination, adventurousness, and idealism in regard to the new country. When the English unwittingly chose to build their town on the Indians' prime hunting ground, an island particularly valuable to Indian economy though it looked empty to the English, young readers can see for themselves why the Indians were resentful. So also when English explorers finished up a shellfish feast, while the Indians who had cooked it were hiding in fear in the nearby forest. *Jamestown* is an excellent corrective to old legends of Indian savagery and treachery, while it also gives full credit to the good intentions among the English. A fine example of modern history for children at its best.

Three of the most interesting new books are about little-known heroes, people who "marched to a different drummer," as Thoreau once put it, and left a different heritage for the future as well. *Billy Bartram and His Green World* by Marjory Bartlett Sanger is particularly interesting, not only for its factual portrayal of an early American naturalist, but also for its sensitive insights into the life of a "different" child. Billy Bartram could not succeed either in school or in business, but he had a genius for drawing and for scientific observation which enabled him to "succeed" in a very different way. Though a close and respected friend of such men as Benjamin Franklin and Thomas Jefferson, Bartram took no part in the great public events of his day. In fact, throughout the first year of the Revolution he was alone in the wilderness drawing and writing. But his work laid important foundations for American science, and his writing influenced many great European poets like Coleridge and Wordsworth as well as Americans. Furthermore, he befriended and described Indians with a perception and intelligence which others of his time often lacked. In every community or school there is undoubtedly at least one child who could find inspiration and hope from reading this book. Teachers and parents could also benefit from its lesson about the importance of encouragement and forbearance to such gifted children.

John Greenleaf Whittier was a nineteenth-century Quaker poet and abolitionist. He has been best known for his great narrative poem *Snowbound*, written when he was sixty, after the Civil War, but prize-winning author Elizabeth Gray Vining, in *Mr. Whittier*, gives us a picture of his whole life and many other notable accomplishments. A shy, sensitive pacifist, this strong-minded New Englander moved nineteenth-century Americans by the force of his words and character, especially in regard to abolitionism. Though he was too poor to afford a college education, and not healthy enough to be a successful farmer, Whittier's writing talent was recognized early and might have led to a far more successful life (in worldly terms) if he had not chosen to write a significant abolitionist tract, *Justice and Expediency*, in 1833, when he was twenty-five. Mrs. Vining's words in this regard give a classic statement about youthful identity choice:

> It sometimes happens to a young person that he cannot see clearly what his life should be. He is distracted by many possibilities and influences. He wavers and changes course many times. Then something happens: he makes a decision to do one perhaps simple thing, and after that all doors close except that one which opens upon the single path that is his own destiny to follow. His personality becomes integrated, the meaning of his life clear. This is what happened to Whittier. For the next thirty years, until slavery was finally abolished, he gave himself to the cause of emancipation. He put aside his dreams of success and fame to enter upon this difficult, demanding, and occasionally dangerous course. As Professor Edward Wagenknecht has said, "He took his place with the outcasts, and he knew exactly what he was doing."

Whittier's interest in justice for blacks, women, workers, and in disarmament, non-violence, and human rights make him a particularly appropriate subject for today's young readers. And from Mrs. Vining they will also learn a great deal about the facts of life in the nineteenth century, from twelve-hour work days for mill workers to the heart-breaking difficulties of genteel romance. (Whittier never married.)

Doris Faber's *The Perfect Life* is another example of the sophistication of modern literature for young people. To describe the history of the Shakers, an ascetic, celibate religious group now mainly remembered for strength and simplicity in architecture and furnishings, could have been a dull process. Instead Faber's skill as a former *New York Times* reporter and her awareness of today's culture—including communes, idealistic hippies, and the *Whole Earth Catalog*—enable her to treat both her subject and her readers with dignity, sympathy, and respect. Starting with a refreshing description of her visit to interview the last remaining elderly Shaker women in Maine, Faber moves easily and gradually back to Shaker beginnings shortly before the Revolution and traces their intervening history. But, aside from the book's value to student term-paper writers (which Faber admits), it also shows a welcome clarity and honesty about such complicated problems as freedom versus security, perfection versus sin, authority versus disorder, individuality versus group harmony. Such intellectual integrity cannot fail to make young readers think. In fact, not the least of its merits is that it assumes that today's young people are very capable of thinking.

The three books on Lincoln aspire toward the same goals. But William H. Armstrong's *The Education of Abraham Lincoln* can be called a small masterpiece. It belongs on the shelves of serious historians as well as of children, both for its superb and unobtrusive scholarship about frontier life and for its equally superb writing style. Perhaps this is to be expected from a distinguished educator and the prize-winning author of *Sounder* (recently made into a prize-winning movie), but it is nevertheless a joy to discover.

Basing his work on a personal library about Lincoln of over four hundred volumes, as well as the fifteen volumes of Lincoln's own writing, Armstrong has traced every book Lincoln read and the name, training, teaching methods, and personality of every teacher with whom he studied. Though the time of Lincoln's schooling was short, it was by no means slipshod, nor was father Tom Lincoln opposed to schooling as later legends have so often repeated. In fact, he was among the first subscribers to local schools for his children in both Kentucky and Indiana. And Lincoln's teachers, contrary to many others on the frontier, were particularly well-educated, gifted, and sensitive individuals. Frontier schoolroom methods of oral recitation and extensive memorization were crucial to Lincoln's intellectual development and greatness, as Armstrong amply documents. The silences and deprivations of the frontier also provided an environment for intuitive learning and creative listening upon which a mind like Lincoln's thrived. Lincoln's mother testified to his constant questions as a child, and Lincoln's copybooks show his understanding of some things like mathematics which he was later supposedly taught by others. Interspersing his narrative with appropriate frontier dialogue, folk wisdom, superstitions, and events, Armstrong brings to life a period of history and a mode of life as well as the childhood of a great man. The book is a marvelous example of the way good historical scholarship can make reality far more exciting and inspiring than the legends it replaces. The bibliography is intelligently chosen for young readers.

Olivia Coolidge's *Apprenticeship of Abraham Lincoln* and Herbert Mitgang's *The Fiery Trial* are also bent on debunking old legends. But the differences in presentation and style are significant. Mitgang relies almost entirely on Lincoln's own writings, thus sometimes conveying a rather fragmentary sense of the man. But he makes a valuable effort to come to terms with various Lincoln controversies, especially the recent charge that Lincoln was a white supremacist. Describing the context and presenting Lincoln's actual words and actions, Mitgang quite successfully confronts a problem of which other writers—Coolidge, for example—are unaware. There is also a perceptive chapter on Mary Todd Lincoln.

Coolidge is another doubter of legends. But despite overtones of skepticism about any idealistic motives among her characters—she invariably finds a good economic or pleasure-oriented reason for anything that appears altruistic—Coolidge accepts old shibboleths like "all abolitionists were fanatics" without question. (One has only to read Vining's *Mr. Whittier* as well as recent historical studies like Aileen Kraditor's *Means and Ends in American Abolitionism* to see the mistake.) Lincoln was an upholder of the Constitution, not an opponent of slavery, says Coolidge (contradicting Mitgang and oversimplifying a complex issue), but when she details Lincoln's principles and tactics they turn out to be substantially the same as those advocated by an abolitionist like Whittier. The emphasis on peaceable solutions and the containment of slavery in hopes of its natural attrition, the opposition to slavery's extension into northern and western territories, and so on, were all part of a sincere effort to achieve justice without bloodshed. Mitgang does a fine job of showing this; Coolidge reduces all issues to political expediency.

The style and content of Coolidge's book are at least a generation out of date—and such a weakness must also appear to today's students as positive bias. How else can one explain the apology on page 96 for Lincoln's opposition to the Mexican War and the explanation that he must have been merely following the Whig Party line "because he did not have deep convictions" about it? Coolidge also calls an Illinois legislative discussion condemning abolitionist propaganda "intelligent and informed," refers to "extremists . . . brought up in Europe [who] put freedom ahead of any constitution," and mentions slave breeding and slave shortages as if such callousness was just another normal historical fact.

There, perhaps, is the rub. The "objective and unobtrusive scholarship" is neither objective enough nor sufficiently informed. Coolidge follows the mid-century "consensus" historians who, at their worst, saw no significant ideological conflicts in the American past, and only power and expediency as the guiding motives of action. The portrayal of Lincoln as just another party politician is disturbingly inadequate in 1970s America. Though Mitgang's book is less detailed and comprehensive, it conveys a richer awareness of the complexity of Lincoln as both politician and great man.

New books about the American Revolution confront their subject with refreshing honesty and vitality. Although Betsy Haynes' *Spies on the Devil's Belt* is actually a novel based on a factual episode, it rings true in both historical and human terms. The moral sophistication and intellectual honesty in all the best new books for children is found here too. "But being free and independent meant making decisions on his own," says Haynes' hero, "and he had found out firsthand that it was not always easy to know what was the right thing to do. I suppose that if this country gets her independence, she'll have that problem too, he mused." The Devil's Belt is Long Island Sound, which a small rowboat of patriots crossed regularly in order to take information about the British on Long Island to the American commanders. Haynes' young hero has his flaws and fears and mistakes, but he makes his decisions and does the right thing in a crisis for a most enjoyable and exciting story. Unfortunately, the book is a bit over-priced for a paperback.

Milton Lomask's *The First American Revolution* is an excellent work of history in every respect. Lomask's bibliography as well as his presentation indicates a solid knowledge of all the standard sources. He writes with admirable simplicity and wit, making complex ideas comprehensible to beginning historians. For example, of mercantilism he says, "According to these notions colonies were 'cows to be milked'; they existed for the purpose of enriching the parent country." The book covers the Revolutionary era from about 1763 to 1783 with abundant detail and careful delineation of time, place, and general environment. The concluding chapter is a fine short historiographical discussion of the meaning of the Revolution as it has been variously interpreted. The creation of a more perfect society involves a continuing revolution which has not yet ended, says Lomask. His book is a must for any young student of the Revolution.

Burke Davis' *Three for Revolution* is best compared to *The Education of Abraham Lincoln* because it deals with the childhood and youth of Patrick Henry, Thomas Jefferson, and George Washington. Davis is a historian with the Colonial Williamsburg Foundation, and his book's details reflect quality scholarship. The three heroes were very different sorts of boys—in background, education, talent, and experience—and very different too from the one-dimensional figures of popular legend. The book tends to be somewhat repetitive, but that may be just as well for its potential audience of younger readers.

All these new books share the lack of prudishness which is another hallmark of our times. Davis mentions Washington's sixteen-year-old passion for his neighbor's eighteen-year-old wife. Lomask tells of "Champagne Charley" Townshend and the bawdy houses of colonial Philadelphia. Coolidge remarks that Lincoln's mother was "probably illegitimate." And Faber perceptively discusses the causes of Shaker Mother Ann Lee's negative attitudes toward sexuality. The difficulties in love of Whittier, Bartram, and Lincoln are handled frankly by their authors.

In most of these books the role of blacks in American history is no longer slighted. Lomask includes the black soldiers at Bunker Hill and Lexington as well as those who fought for the Loyalists in order to gain their freedom. Faber mentions the equality they held among the Shakers. Only Coolidge seems unaware of American blacks either in history or as modern readers.

Indians do not fare as well. The stereotype remains of the ignorant savage and natural enemy in several books. But the exceptions provided by Armstrong, Sanger, and Campbell are notably refreshing.

Children reading any or all of these books should develop new interest in the "junk" of their own past. Despite the corruption and pessimism of our times, a new generation brought up with the spirit of equality, open-mindedness, and individual potential represented by these books should be able to carry that abundantly American ideal far into the future. Perhaps, in fact, this bicentennial generation, lacking ideological rigidity and conformity but imbued with concern for human rights, intellectual curiosity, and personal integrity, will be closer to the spirit of that great generation of the Revolutionary era than most of the generations in between. At least these books seem to point in that direction.

A Novel of Children's Liberation

Virginia L. Wolf

Nobody's Family Is Going to Change, by Louise Fitzhugh. 221 pp.
New York: Farrar, Straus & Giroux, Inc., 1974. $6.95.

In her last novel, Louise Fitzhugh (October 5, 1928–November 21,
1974) uses techniques in many ways reminiscent of her masterpiece,
Harriet the Spy. Emancipation (Emma) Sheridan, the heroine of
Nobody's Family Is Going to Change, is, like Harriet, an eleven-
year-old, very bright child of an upper-middle-class family who re-
side in Manhattan. She, too, has already chosen her profession: she
wants to be a lawyer like her father. Unlike Harriet, Emma is black,
overweight, an advocate of Women's Liberation, and the older sister
of Willie, who wishes to be a dancer. These differences are suggestive
of a new note, or of a note more firmly sounded, in this last novel.
Social criticism is implicit in *Harriet the Spy*, but here it is overt.
This novel is an angry evocation of the need for children's liberation
and a bitter denunciation of parenting which over-protects, over-
controls, and forces children into set social roles. The difference in
tones is the result of the differences in the heroines. For this novel,
like *Harriet*, is told from the heroine's perspective. A few sections
give us Willie's point of view but the story is mainly Emma's, and
she is angry and bitter.

Emma and Willie are the children of traditional parents. Mr. Sheridan, a district attorney, is the successful breadwinner. Mrs. Sheridan
is a mother and wife. Mr. Sheridan, at the age of nine, was left with
the responsibility for supporting himself and his younger brother.
His wife and her younger brother were motherless and supported by
a father who danced when he was not drunk. Mr. Sheridan sees
himself as a rescuer, the strong man who by suffering, hard work, and
diligence saved his brother, his wife, and himself from the slums
and who is now saving his son from a similar fate by keeping him off
the stage. He intends that Willie be like him, a credit to the race and
a lawyer. His response to Emma is typically: "Women lawyers are
idiots! They're the laughing-stock of any group of lawyers. I think
any woman who tries to be a lawyer is a damned fool!" (p. 221).
Emma is to marry and become the mother of two lovely children.
Usually, Mrs. Sheridan weakly and fearfully acquiesces in all this.

270

Eventually, she supports her son's right to dance in a Broadway musical, but she never takes Emma's aspirations seriously.

This portrait of the Sheridans is psychologically acute and full. Emma's parents are not villains. They do not physically abuse or consciously inflict emotional pain on their children. They are simply people who are driven by unconscious compulsions instilled in them by their past experiences. The reader sees this, as it were, over Emma's shoulder. But Emma also eventually sees this herself, in her own terms.

The process whereby Emma does this structures the novel. Dissatisfied with herself and her family, she joins the Children's Army, whose creed is that if "the decision makers were forced to make decisions that would be good for children, there would only be good decisions made" (p. 75). As a result, she sees her father's treatment of her brother (and her) as unjust and takes Willie's side against her father. But after her father is defeated, Emma recognizes that she is the loser. "She thought of all the times he had beaten her. . . . She let the humiliation of those moments fall into her. She felt the frustration, the helplessness, the rage. She wanted to cry, feeling it. She felt like a nothing" (pp. 193–94). She concludes that she loses because it pleases her father, because she wants him to love her and he won't.

I endorse the validity of this perception. We see that Mr. Sheridan must control. His investment in his family is for the sake of proving his strength and rightness. He cannot love either of his children for what they are. They must be what he wants. Emma, unable to be what he wants, overeats, isolates herself, and fantasizes to compensate for her need for approval and to express her anger because she fails to get it. But this anger is turned inward in fear and denial of the rejection which she daily experiences. Such a response to her family is self-destructive. She is a loser. Emma's final realization— "they're not going to change, I have to change" (p. 221)—holds out the only hope.

There is some distortion caused by limiting us to Emma's perspective. Families do change; her parents might be forced to change in response to her change. Furthermore, an adult might be more sympathetic toward the Sheridans, recognizing the source of their present mistakes in their painful childhoods. But if Emma's perception is not whole, it is nevertheless valid.

Louise Fitzhugh's great strength as a novelist is her remarkable insight into the psychodynamics of human relationships and their

effects upon children. What Emma learns is what Harriet learns from
Ole Golly: a person must find out who she is, be herself, and not
just live like her family. Indeed Ms. Fitzhugh's exploration of the
necessity for self-love and self-determination is a most fascinating
aspect of all her work. She doesn't pull any punches in this novel.
Emma's truth is a harsh one, but I am convinced it is the only one
worth offering a child in Emma's position, and I believe there are
many children similarly enmeshed in hopeless and self-destructive
struggles to change their parents.

However, I am not convinced that Emma is capable of perceiving
this truth. I am not convinced that the novel establishes that she has
sufficient ego strength for doing so. Harriet has Ole Golly's support
and guidance over a considerable number of years. I can believe that
Harriet can insist upon and verbalize her need for self-discovery and
self-determination. For this is what Ole Golly taught her. Ole Golly,
like a good parent, gave Harriet permission, gave her loving approval
for her essentially selfish preoccupation with herself. We can believe
that Harriet, without guilt or anger, would be able to be honest with
herself. There is no Ole Golly in Emma's life and no similar source
of approval and support. From where has she gained sufficient faith
in herself to be able to love herself in the face of her parents' failure
to do so? Her contacts with her peers are new and only tentatively
supportive. She, in fact, is more supportive of them than they are
of her.

The capacity for psychological insight in this novel is hers and
hers alone. Where did she get it? How did she break through her
anger and guilt to acceptance and change? She is not only alone;
she is also only eleven years old. Coming from homes such as hers,
many adults are still unable to achieve her insight without psychiatric
help. I can believe that Emma would recognize that her parents do
not love her. The incidents of the novel force this recognition. But
I cannot believe that she would quit trying to change them and see
that the solution for her is to change herself. Harriet faced with total
rejection resorts to physical violence. She needs Ole Golly's understanding before she can change.

Emma's insight is valid, but, in my opinion, it is not hers. It is
Louise Fitzhugh's. In *Nobody's Family Is Going to Change*, message
dominates at the expense of the heroine's credibility. It is an important and worthwhile message, but the novel is flawed. Fascinating
and vivid, *Nobody's Family Is Going to Change* is not the literary
triumph of *Harriet the Spy*.

From Shakespeare to Brooklyn

New Trends in Children's Poetry

Marilyn Apseloff

Miracles: Poems by Children of the English-Speaking World, collected by Richard Lewis. New York: Simon and Schuster, 1966.

Overhead the Sun, by Walt Whitman. Edited and illustrated by Antonio Frasconi. New York: Farrar, Straus and Giroux, 1969.

Emily Dickinson: Poems for Youth, edited by Alfred Leete Hampson. Boston: Little, Brown, 1918.

The Me Nobody Knows, edited by Stephen M. Joseph. New York: Avon, 1969.

Somebody Real, edited by Nicholas Anthony Duva. Rockaway: American Faculty Press, 1972.

Wishes, Lies, and Dreams, by Kenneth Koch. New York: Chelsea House, 1970.

Green Is Like a Meadow of Grass, edited by Nancy Larrick. Illustrated by Kelly Oeschli. Champaign: Garrard, 1968.

For many generations children have delighted in poetry as a natural extension of the beloved Mother Goose rhymes (rhymes that, when first published in *Mother Goose's Melody*, were accompanied by sixteen songs of Shakespeare), from the early gentle moralizing of Isaac Watts and Ann and Jane Taylor, through the lyricism of Christina Rossetti and Sara Teasdale and the nonsense of Edward Lear, Lewis Carroll, and Laura Richards, to poets like Robert Louis Stevenson and A. A. Milne, who speak to children directly of their own world. For about the last decade children have had an extremely wide range of poetry to choose from, not all of it originally written for them: in addition to the works of Harry Behn, Elizabeth Coatsworth, David McCord, and others there are editions out for children now containing selected poems of Shakespeare, W. B. Yeats, Walt Whitman, and D. H. Lawrence, to name only a few. In addition to this new trend there is another that bears upon it: the publication of books of poetry written by children. There can be remarkable values in such writing for both children and adults, as a study of some of the books will reveal. Certainly some adult misconceptions about children's poetry should be dispelled, as well as the belief that certain poets should be left for the more mature, experienced older reader or adult.

One of the first books to appear containing poems by children was *Miracles*, collected by Richard Lewis and published in 1966. In the Introductory Note he explains how the book came about:

My desire to collect the poems of children began in 1961, when
I started teaching literature and creative writing in an elementary
school in New York City. I organized these classes because I felt
that children would respond to literature by expressing themselves
in their own stories and poems. In time, my belief was supported
by some remarkable work. (p. 7)

Lewis also makes clear his intention in presenting such a book: "It
is . . . to be read as poetry, not as a sampling of precociousness"
(p. 7). It is his hope

that this book will demonstrate the artistry of which children are
capable when they are given the opportunity; that it will serve as
a testament to the power and value of the poetic vision that is
an integral part of childhood; and finally that, as all real poetry
does, it will give delight. (p. 8)

A look at a few of the poems will disclose the range of that poetic
vision. Often the poetry is brief, capturing all that needs to be said
in a few lines:

TREES

The trees share their shade with
all who pass by,
But their leaves whisper secrets
only to the wind.

Nelda Dishman, age 12, United States

WAR

Not bad, but miserable
Drenched in gray sadness
Lonely grief handed out to all.

Sarah Mason, age 10, United States

THE DOORS

The doors in my house
Are used every day
For closing rooms
And locking children away.

Brian Andrews, age 10, Australia

Here a common misconception that adults have about poetry for
children, that it has to have rhyme to have any appeal, is dispelled
by what the children themselves have written: in these examples,
except for lines two and four in "The Doors," there isn't any. The
sensitivity of the authors should be apparent to all. The child's ability

to create images from familiar objects is revealed in the following two selections:

CANDLES

The candle screamed with fury,
Hot tears trickled down her face.
With figure slumped,
She slowly dwindled into shadows
Darkness!

Susan Heitler, age 11, United States

Silent logs floating
Statue still—
Sly vicious animal, a sinister monster.
Regiments of scaly armored troops
Drifting down the river.
Hot, damp, steamy jungles.
A brute of a creature
Flesh-eater, killer.
Icicle teeth, in a huge dark abyss.
A crocodile.

Michael Goodson, age 9, New Zealand

Again rhyme was not used. The image in the first poem may bring to mind the death of the Wicked Witch of the West in L. Frank Baum's *The Wizard of Oz*; in the second the tone is established through effective use of alliteration and word choice. For example, the selection of "icicle teeth" in the "Hot, damp, steamy jungles" setting makes that image even more pronounced because of the contrast: substituting "ivory teeth" wouldn't give quite the same chilling effect.

In just these few selections one can see the need to discard another false notion adults have about poetry for children: that it should be written down to them, be childish so that they will enjoy it. On the contrary,

> it has been often demonstrated . . . that children do not need to have poetry written down to their intellectual level. . . . The clear-eyed children go straight to the heart of the mystery, and recognize in the music of words, in the enduring charm of metrical quality, an element of never-ending delight . . . and one lifelong source of happiness is gained. But it is never through infantine or juvenile verses that the end is reached.[1]

Perhaps that is why we are now seeing a profusion of books containing the poetry of prominent literary figures: adults are finally beginning to realize that "restricting children to poems supposed to be on their age- or grade-level deprives them of too many good things. They get more out of genuinely good poems than out of mediocre ones, even if the better ones are difficult in some ways."[2] Furthermore, if children are properly introduced to such writers for the sheer pleasure of the sound and imagery of the poetry, "they could go on enjoying it and learning from it for a long time."[3] The fear that adults have, that children won't understand all the words and the meaning, does not appear to be valid, either; as Kenneth Koch discovered in working with children using poets such as Shakespeare, Whitman, Lawrence, "in the excitement of reading the poems, the children were glad to learn the meanings of strange words, of old forms like *thee* and *thine*, and of strange conceptions like symmetry and sublunary."[4] An additional benefit of becoming familiar with such poets early is evident later: when children encounter them in high school they are not poets to be dreaded as their peers may try to tell them, but old friends.

Now even young children are being offered books such as *Overhead the Sun: Lines from Walt Whitman* chosen and illustrated in woodcuts by Antonio Frasconi. The following passages are brief but appropriately suited to the wondering nature of a child:

> To me the sea is a continual miracle,
> The fishes that swim—the rocks—the motion of the waves
>   —the ships with men in them,
> What stranger miracles are there?

Or the following three lines:

> Long and long has the grass been growing,
> Long and long has the rain been falling,
> Long has the globe been rolling round.

And finally:

> I have not so much emulated the birds that musically sing,
> I have abandon'd myself to flights, broad circles.
> The hawk, the seagull, have far more possess'd me than
>   the canary or the mocking-bird,
> I have not felt to warble and trill, however sweetly,
> I have felt to soar in freedom and in the fullness of power,
>   joy, volition.

This Whitman book has no introduction because it needs none: it is for a young child to listen to, look at, and enjoy. Several other books intended for the youngest readers follow a similar format. *Hand in Hand We'll Go: Ten Poems by Robert Burns*, illustrated in woodcuts by Nonny Hogrogian (Crowell, 1965), has a glossary to help the reader with the unfamiliar words but again has no introduction to some of Burns' best-loved poems ("A Red, Red Rose," "The Dusty Miller," "My Heart's in the Highlands") because they can speak for themselves. Even Shakespeare, in *Seeds of Time*, compiled by Bernice Grohskopf and illustrated by Kelly Oechsli (Atheneum, 1964), is presented without preamble, with selections from twenty-four of his plays including the tragedies ("Song of the Witches" from *Macbeth* is included, for example, with an appropriate illustration to delight the reader). Some of the excerpts are only three or four lines long, others five or six times that. All, despite some unfamiliar language, are on subjects children can understand: fairies, nature, even war. All are meant to be heard, not studied, to be taken into the mind and heart for perpetual enjoyment.

It is interesting to note that when editors or compilers begin to make selections of such poetry for middle-grade readers and above, introductions to the poet's life and the main themes of the poetry (with examples) are usually included. Lloyd Frankenberg, in his two books *Poems of William Shakespeare* (Crowell, 1966; illustrated by Nonny Hogrogian) and *Poems of Robert Burns* (Crowell, 1967; illustrated by Joseph Low), has sixteen pages of such material in the former, eight in the latter. Certainly for the child who is curious about the life of the poet, such information can be fascinating, especially since humanistic details are often included that bring the poet to life. But at the same time too much explaining of a thematic nature can be overdone: after all, it is the poetry that we want the children to have first—meaning and understanding can come later. It is often best to leave excessive introductory material until after the child has become familiar with several of the poems, has been caught up in the power of the language and imagery. For example,

> In Blake's more mature poems, there is something to which children will answer, even without asking for a meaning which so often and so humbly they refrain from doing. "Tiger, Tiger burning bright in the forests of the night" is a picture which remains long in any child's inward eye.[5]

And so another false notion, that adult poetry was intended for and thus should only be given to adults, has fallen by the wayside. Lillian Smith tried to point that out over twenty years ago:

In giving poetry to children it is well to remember that they understand far more than they can express. Children apprehend by intuition and imagination that which is far beyond their limited experience. . . . There is no dividing line between poetry children like and poetry liked by adults, except that the very freshness and eagerness of their approach gives children the advantage. Children respond to the best and deserve the best.[6]

But how do books like *D. H. Lawrence: Poems Selected for Young People* by William Cole (Viking, 1967; illustrated by Ellen Raskin) or *Running to Paradise: Poems by W. B. Yeats* selected by Kevin Crossley-Holland (Macmillan, 1967; illustrated by Judith Valpy) relate to the poetry being turned out by the children themselves? Actually, they do so in a profound way, for unless children are made aware of what the very best poetry can do with their language, can make them feel and imagine, their own efforts will be stunted. If they are constantly exposed to vapid, sentimental verse, we should not be too surprised at what they themselves will try to write: children are marvelous imitators. And although imitation is not desired in children's own writing, if that is the springboard to original creations I would much rather see a poem resembling one of Shakespeare's than of Edgar Guest's. The great writers should be able to instill in children the importance of finding the right word that not only gives the meaning of what they are trying to say but the sound and feeling as well, demonstrating the musicality, rhythm, and feeling of language in addition to its semantics.

The next question might well be, then, why should children be encouraged to write poetry at all? That has already been partly answered: it teaches them the concrete use of their language, enlarging their understanding of what words can do and their own vocabularies at the same time. And because poetry is a condensed form, it encourages the writer to get directly to the point, to say what needs to be said in the briefest but most telling manner: it necessitates organization of thought and direction. May Lamberton Becker, in her introduction to *Emily Dickinson: Poems for Youth*, repeats a point she had made elsewhere: "poetry is the most direct way of saying anything. It deals with the very nature of things and goes straight to it . . . and while we are arguing through pages of prose, a poem has given us the essence of the idea in two perfect lines" (p. 3 of Foreword).

Still another reason why children should be encouraged to write poetry is that by so doing they gain a better understanding of what the creative process is, what other poets go through, and are more appreciative of poetry as a result. As Kenneth Koch discovered after he had gotten children to write poetry for a while, "this was a great help to them in reading what other poets had written. They were close to poetry because it was something they had created themselves. Adult poetry wasn't so strange to them; they could come to it in some degree as equals" (*Rose*, p. 26). So it is to the advantage of those who love poetry and want to kindle that same affection for it in children to take very seriously children's writing of poetry. Fortunately, that writing is finally getting the attention it deserves.

As was previously mentioned, *Miracles* was one of the first such books to become popular, and it was soon followed by several others. Interestingly, many of the volumes that were published contain the poetry of city children, as in *The Me Nobody Knows: Children's Voices from the Ghetto*, edited by Stephen M. Joseph. In his introduction he explains: "My intention, in this book, is to diminish the stigma of this word [slum] by showing that these children of the ghetto, if given the chance and an open climate to write, have a tremendous amount to say and are anxious to speak" (p. 9). The book is divided into five sections: "How I See Myself," "How I See My Neighborhood," "The World Outside," "Things I Can't See or Touch," and "And Now . . ." Each section contains both poetry and prose by children who are trying to "write what they feel" (p. 18). The following examples demonstrate the range of their feelings:

BLACK

Black we die
Black you cry
Black I cry
Does White they cry
Cause Black we die?
Why they kill me?
What crime you and me?
Oh, yes! Now I see.
Black is our skin and
We want to be free.
Yes black we be
That they can see
Of you and me
But what of the soul
That yearns to be free?
This they do not see in
You or I

But this is that
This cannot die.

                                                        R. C., age 16

Spring turns into
Summer my hate into like
And Fall comes once again.

                                                        C. S., age 14

WHO LOOKS

Beneath the sidewalks
    to tunnels—
    merging
    separating—
    searching out the
      earthy blackness;
Behind the neons
    proving
    camouflage
    for purple-veined faces;
Past the faces—
    hiding
    selves.

                                                        Nell Moore, age 14

For those interested in working with children and getting them to write, Stephen Joseph's indispensable introduction points out all the pitfalls to be avoided in addition to giving helpful positive suggestions.

Other books containing city children's poetry are *I Heard a Scream in the Streets: Poems by Young People in the City*, edited by Nancy Larrick (Evans, 1970; illustrated with photographs by students); *The Children: Poems and Prose from Bedford-Stuyvesant*, edited by Irving Benig (Grove, 1971); and *Somebody Real: Voices of City Children*, edited by Nicholas Anthony Duva. Mr. Duva's comments in his introduction apply to all the books:

> out of the tenements, onto the glass-strewn streets, past the fences decorated with the curse words and the peace signs, past the tires and the sticks, and the sneakers dangling from the telephone wire, the children of the city walk to school.
>
> These are the writings of those children. They are sometimes joyous, sometimes sad; sometimes angry, and often very, very quiet. But they are all strong, all reflective, all potent and real. The children tell us about themselves, and all they ask is our attention. (p. vii)

One of the children in Mr. Duva's class apparently thought highly enough of a poem by Langston Hughes that she turned a similar version in as one of her own, a practice which certainly should not be encouraged. Here are the two poems for comparison:

LOVE

I loved my friend,
he went away from me.
So this poem ends,
as soft as it began.
I loved my friend.

Olga

POEM

I loved my friend.
He went away from me.
There's nothing more to say.
The poem ends,
Soft as it began—
I loved my friend.

Langston Hughes[7]

Of course all the poetry contained in these books is not of equal merit: one wouldn't expect to find a consistently high quality in any book by beginning writers. But it is a start on what could be a lifelong love of writing and of literature, and for that reason it should not be treated lightly.

One man who has paid a great deal of attention to the writing of children is Kenneth Koch, mentioned earlier. One of his best-known books on the subject is *Wishes, Lies, and Dreams*, which should be of great value for anyone wishing to work with children, for there is a long section on "Teaching Children to Write Poetry." He breaks down the old inhibitions about the poetic atmosphere (hushed tones) in favor of a noisy classroom, and builds confidence in the children through class collaborations, where each student contributes something.

> No one had to worry about failing to write a good poem because everyone was only writing one line; and I specifically asked the children not to put their names on their line. Everyone was to write the line on a sheet of paper and turn it in; then I would read them all as a poem. (p. 5)

In order to get the children started on their individual lines, Koch and the children made up a few rules to follow: "every line should contain a color, a comic-strip character, and a city or country; also the line should begin with the words "I wish" (p. 5). Although such an approach may be frowned upon by some as being too regimented, certainly presenting children with an idea such as "I wish" to begin with almost guarantees some kind of result:

> it gave them something to write about which really interested them: the private world of their wishes. One of the main problems children have as writers is not knowing what to write about. Once they have a subject they like . . . they find a great deal to say. (pp. 7–8)

Koch discovered an advantage in having the children collaborate at first: "These collaborations almost always made the children want to make up, and usually to write, poems of their own" (p. 48). Further on he elaborates:

> The educational advantages of a creative intellectual and emotional activity which children enjoy are clear. Writing poetry makes children feel happy, capable, and creative. It makes them feel more open to understanding and appreciating what others have written (literature). It even makes them want to know how to spell and say things correctly (grammar). (p. 53)

So although one might argue that the results of the class collaborations should not be called poetry, but, perhaps, versifying, the use of the technique to stimulate writing, to break down reticence and shyness, obviously has great benefits for all concerned. As Karla Kuskin points out, "Reading and writing encourage each other. Once you want to write, you read more."[8] And I doubt that anyone would dispute the advantages of extended reading.

Nancy Larrick has also discovered the values in getting children to write poetry:

> As the children wrote their own poetic images and listened to the rhythmic lines of published poetry, they became more sensitive to fresh and original ideas in both poetry and prose. Their pleasure in reading and writing expanded remarkably.[9]

The poems she selected for the book *Green Is Like a Meadow of Grass* came out of the 1967 Lehigh University Workshop in Poetry for Children. Two of the books used to stimulate the children to write were Mary O'Neill's *Hailstones and Halibut Bones* and Carmen Bernos de Gasztold's *Prayers from the Ark*. It is easy to see the influence of each:

Green is like a meadow of grass
Banana peels that are not ripe
And broccoli.

Beth Smith, age 8

Gray is a feeling
Like forgetting your lunch.

Cindy Peifly, age 8

THE SNAKE

I hiss while I am hunting down my prey.
Everyone runs any old way.
Lord! perhaps you can make them understand
I'm not made to sing like a bird.

Michael Kerecz, age 10

THE MOUSE

I would like to know why all the cats chase me.
And why people set a trap to catch me.
I want to thank you, Lord,
for making me smart enough
to miss some of the traps
so I can live a little while longer.

Robert Vargo, age 13

In a sense the poems are imitative, but at the same time they are highly original, expressing what the child thinks and feels about colors and animals. And this technique of giving children poetry that they can respond to and take off from, that will stimulate them to write, is being used more and more with children, even with poetry not originally intended for them. In his recent book *Rose, Where Did You Get That Red?* (1973) Koch explains:

> I was looking for themes and forms in the very best poems. "The Tiger," speaking to children's sense of strangeness and wonder, could heighten their awareness of nature and of their place in it. Herrick's "Argument" would help them to think about their poems in a new way, somewhat as they might think of places they had been or of specific things they had seen or done. . . . Whitman could encourage them to trust their secret feelings about the world and how they were connected to it—it told them these feelings were more important than what they found in books. (p. 9)

Notice here and in the following Koch's interest in the feelings of children:

> I didn't want a poetry idea which commanded a child to closely imitate an adult poem. That would be pointless. I wanted my students to find and to re-create in themselves the main feelings of the adult poems. (p. 16)[10]

In *Rose* Koch has a section entitled "Ten Lessons," each one dealing with a different poet not ordinarily thought of in connection with children (John Donne, William Carlos Williams, Wallace Stevens, and others). He explains how he used each poet in terms of ideas stressed and gave other suggestions, too. Some of the children's writing is then included. The next section is "Anthology" whose aim "is to suggest a number of fine poems . . . that children can enjoy reading. . . . Each poem is followed by a poetry idea and sometimes also by a few other notes on teaching it" (p. 209). He further points out that

> children aren't bothered by the same kinds of difficulties in poetry that adults are bothered by and aren't bothered in the same way. If children can get the main feelings of a poem, they won't be intimidated by some one thing they don't understand. . . . They have an advantage over some more educated readers whose fear of not understanding every detail of a poem can keep them from enjoying it at all. (p. 42)

Thus in Koch's book we have a combination of the two new trends in poetry: the great poets of the past and present are there to be read by and to inspire children to write, children who may become the great writers of tomorrow.

The new trends in children's poetry offer great rewards. Even if the children do not become our future published, respected poets, they have been given two valuable gifts, the gift of their own language and how to use it to express themselves, and the enjoyment of poetry that should endure throughout their lives, brightening and enriching their experiences.

NOTES

1. Agnes Repplier, "The Children's Poets," in *Children and Literature: Views and Reviews*, ed. Virginia Haviland (Glenview, Illinois: Scott, Foresman, 1973), p. 264.

2. Kenneth Koch, *Rose, Where Did You Get That Red?: Teaching Great Poetry to Children* (New York: Random House, 1973), p. 209.

3. Koch, p. 6.

4. Ibid., p. 10.

5. Cornelia Meigs et al., *A Critical History of Children's Literature* (New York: Macmillan, 1967), p. 159.

6. Lillian Smith, *The Unreluctant Years* (New York: Viking, 1953), p. 113.

7. Langston Hughes, *Don't You Turn Back*, ed. Lee Bennett Hopkins, ill. Ann Grifalconi (New York: Knopf, 1969), p. 24.

8. Karla Kuskin, " 'Talk to Mice and Fireplugs . . .' " in *Somebody Turned On a Tap in These Kids: Poetry and Young People Today*, ed. Nancy Larrick (New York: Delacorte, 1971), p. 48. The entire volume is valuable to those interested in children's writing.

9. *Green Is Like a Meadow of Grass*, p. 63.

10. Ted Hughes apparently disagrees with Koch about using great poetry as models for children's writing. See Ted Hughes, *Poetry Is* (New York: Doubleday, 1967), p. xvi.

Nonsense As Reality

K. Narayan Kutty

Poems of Lewis Carroll, selected by Myra Cohn Livingston. New York: Thomas Crowell Company, 1973. $4.95.

Carroll's poetry may be too sophisticated and witty to appeal to very young children. The children he knew best and adored belonged to the 8–11 age group. But not all children of this group will appreciate Carroll's riddles, puzzles, parodies, acrostics, and serious verse. This should not disturb anyone. After all, how many adults read Shakespeare? The children Carroll wrote for, like the adults Pope and Johnson wrote for, had cultivated tastes. For such children, whose number is not alarmingly large, thanks to the attention poetry receives in American schools, Myra Cohn Livingston's selections from Carroll is a book of unexpected delights. She offers them the best of Carroll's poetry: the poems of the *Alice* books, of *Sylvie and Bruno*, of *Sylvie and Bruno Concluded*, *The Hunting of the Snark*, and many more. The original illustrations of John Tenniel, Harry Furniss, Henry Holiday, Arthur B. Frost, and Carroll himself reproduced in the book enhance its value. The book also has an informative introduction and useful notes on the poems. The omission of *Phantasmagoria*, which has much to offer young readers and adults, is a lamentable one.

Carroll knew too much about life to limit the appeal of his works only to children. What W. H. Auden said, with *Alice* in mind, that "there are no good books which are only for children," may be said about all Carroll's major works. There is already encyclopaedic evidence for the adult world's fascination with Carroll's works. One particularly appealing feature of his career as a writer is his life-long interest in nonsense as a literary medium. Reading Carroll and about Carroll over a period of time, one comes to the conclusion that he seems to have resorted to nonsense not only because he enjoyed doing so but also because he found it to be the most appropriate medium for his version of reality. His response to reality seems to have been like Alice's response to the "Jabberwocky." Alice thought that the poem filled her mind with ideas but she could not say what they were. It is possible that it is the perception of reality as unknowable that inspired Carroll to play games with it in his novels and poems. Look at *The Hunting of the Snark*, for instance. Hunting for the snark is like searching for something unknowable. What is searched for is named arbitrarily, and what is found is not a snark but a boojum. And what a boojum is nobody knows. Consider "The Gardener's Song" in *Sylvie and Bruno*. The gardener is unable to see things right; nothing appears as it is to him. But this elusiveness of reality did not reduce Carroll to mystic silence. He decided to play games with it. The unknowability of reality had intriguing artistic possibilities for Carroll. All this is nothing new now but was a hundred years ago, when Beckett, Nabokov, Borges, and Barthelme had not been born.

Six Fantasies

Theme and Style

William H. Green

The Master Key, by L. Frank Baum. Illustrated by F. Y. Cory. Introduction by David L. Greene and Douglas G. Greene. Hyperion, Conn.: Hyperion Press, Inc., 1973. $3.75. Reprint of the 1901 Bowen-Merrill Company edition.

Sailing to Cythera, by Nancy Willard. Illustrated by David McPhail. New York: Harcourt Brace Jovanovich, 1974. $5.95.

Sweetwater, by Laurence Yep. Illustrated by Julia Noonan. New York: Avon Books, 1975. $1.25. Previously issued, New York: Harper & Row, 1973.

Mr. Death, by Anne Moody. Foreword by John Donovan. New York: Harper & Row, 1975. $5.95.

Into the Unknown. Edited by Terry Carr. Nashville, Tenn.: Thomas Nelson, Inc., 1900. $6.50.

Ladies of the Gothics. Edited by Seon Manley and Gogo Lewis. New York: Lothrop, Lee & Shepard Company, 1975. $6.95.

Critics of children's books are expected to be moralists. Probably this is inevitable. There are books which, regardless of one's politics, are evidently harmful to young readers—books which countenance cruelty, cowardice, or despair. But if morality becomes the chief concern of criticism, literature is degraded to propaganda, critics to would-be censors. Whatever harm immoral books may do to readers, poorly written books do greater harm to the practice of literature—especially if they are applauded for the mere moral correctness of their themes. The best children's books are unsurpassed in their precision of style and richness of imagination; and the best children's fantasies, in particular, evoke a miraculous sense of completeness, of word-magic raised to sacramental perfection. Magic is our birthright. If we disinherit ourselves for moral correctness or transitory social causes, we lose.

Happily, of the six fantasy books reviewed here, two exhibit the lucid style, smooth pacing, and imaginative completeness characteristic of classic fantasies such as the Alice books, *The Hobbit*, and the tales of Narnia and Oz. Not surprisingly, one is by the creator of Oz himself. *The Master Key*, subtitled "An Electrical Fairy Tale," is a reprint of L. Frank Baum's 1901 novel about a boy named Rob who accidentally invokes the Demon of Electricity and is given electrical marvels to show the world: a ray which induces unconsciousness, small tablets which contain one day's nourishment, and an anti-gravity device shaped like a wristwatch. With these devices, Rob flies foolishly to a cannibal island, barely returning in time to receive three more marvels. Turn-of-the-century American ambiance pervades the tale. Full of optimism and industry, Rob soars across the Atlantic wearing only walking clothes and a small anti-gravity device, later to return and conclude that there is no place like home. While abroad, Rob displays an American willingness to intervene in local politics. Of course, he always intervenes on the good side, but his notions of good and evil are frankly ethnocentric: "I believe it's about time I interfered with the politics of this Republic," he tells himself in Paris. "If I don't take a hand there probably won't be a Republic of France very long and, as a good American, I prefer a republic to a monarchy" (p. 136). Such lambent faith in Truth, Justice, and the American Way may seem passé, and Baum's stock characterizations of cannibals and Turks might draw charges of racism if he wrote today; but it would be ungracious to blame the author of such a lively and good-natured fable for occasionally reflecting the values of his age. And the ending of the story, where Rob returns the Demon's gifts because he has seen how unready men are to control such powers, transcends optimism and addresses a warning to our gadget-ridden nuclear age. Solid meals, it proposes, are more satisfying than energy pills—happy homes more important than transoceanic tours. Finally, however, it is not the moral which makes the tale successful, but rather the vividly evoked wonder, the eerie realism of Rob's soaring—almost the reader's soaring—asleep through night skies, with only the stars above and the sea beneath him. A reprint of the 1901 edition, with large print and strong illustrations, the book is at once a scholarly edition and an attractive children's book. Young readers may omit the critical introduction by David L. Greene and Douglas G. Greene, brothers and long-time students of Baum, but academic readers will welcome their insights into a neglected classic.

No less deserving of praise is Nancy Willard's *Sailing to Cythera*. This volume, beautifully printed on high-quality paper and charmingly illustrated by David McPhail, includes three stories, each a dream-vision of a little boy named Anatole. In "Gospel Train" he goes with his cat to the land of the dead and learns lessons about life and death; in "The Wise Soldier of Sellebak" he flies to Scandinavia, where he scales an Yggdrasil-like tree in search of the past; and in "Sailing to Cythera" he sails into the antique wallpaper at his grandmother's house, there facing and assimilating his fears of the house where the past hangs heavy, promising decay. Reading Willard, one is reminded both of Lewis Carroll and C. S. Lewis: the mythic settings and themes evoke Lewis, but the lucidly labyrinthine dream-plots move with the magic of Alice. Nevertheless, Willard has her own personal vision, a stunning blend of myth and reality. At the center of the land of the dead, Anatole's cat's deceased aunt rides an eternal merry-go-round; a T-shirt marked *Oxford, Michigan, Gravel Capital of the World* symbolizes worldly substance; nursery rhymes become magical incantations; and Van Houten's Cocoa is a sacramental drink at the home of the Sun. Death and mutability are the principal themes in these stories. A cat dies and a grandfather is paralyzed, but Anatole is gently led—along with the reader—down a path of reconciliation and wisdom, so that beneath the surfaces of Anatole's little visions the lines of spiritual allegory begin to emerge; and the effect is as wholesome as it is delightful. The writing itself leaves little to be desired, as Willard's sentences move with the lucid and inevitable rhythms that one expects in a fine children's story.

Laurence Yep's *Sweetwater* is an exciting story of the future. The hero, Tyree, belongs to an invented minority group called Silkies, descendants of space-ship crews which were long ago stranded on the planet Harmony and now inhabit the half-flooded ruins of a city by the sea. The novel traces simultaneously the boy's growing up and the destruction of the Silkies' communal life-style after the intrusion of a greedy capitalist and a vast sea dragon. The themes here are strong and contemporary—the rights of minorities, the necessity for courage, the utility of art, and the interdependence and sacredness of all life—themes woven into a unit of immediate socio-ecological thrust. And Yep evokes the warm and complex relationships between the members of Tyree's family. Why, then, is the book less successful than Baum's or Willard's? To some extent the very transparency of the themes may be blamed; but I think the principal difficulty lies in Yep's handling of point of view. The story is told by Tyree, and the narrator's boyish diction and frequent intrusions may account for the diffuseness and lack of immediacy in action sequences, for the fact that wonders such as the sea dragon are only partially re-alized in their enormity. Tyree is no Huck Finn. Nevertheless, the book is a rich piece of imagination and a well-constructed story. In its inexpensive paperback edition, *Sweetwater* may be recommended to anyone with an appetite for recent science fiction.

Mr. Death, however, is so negative in theme, so flawed in execution, that it can scarcely be recommended to anyone. It is a collection of four grim, mechanically plotted fables. Two involve lonely children who are cruelly neglected by faceless adults and die meaninglessly: the boy in "Mr. Death" kills himself, triggering his father's suicide; and the girl in "Bobo" is eaten by her own dog. In "All Burnt Up," wholesome human emotion is fitfully displayed between two families—even between two races—but then the principal source of wholesome emotion, one Old Lady Hudson, is arbitrarily carbonized in an accidental fire, as though death were the inevitable penalty for showing flashes of humanity in the livid haze of cruelty and despair which darkens Moody's fictive world. John Donovan's Foreword labors to exhume a positive theme from the morass of morbidity, suggesting that love is shown to transcend death and that the stories are tragedies. But they lack the elements of nobility essential to tragedy, and where significant love is shown in Moody's tales —for instance in "Mr. Death" and "Bobo"—the love itself becomes a destructive force. Moody's twisted little protagonists might be taken as sympathetic testaments of the conditions of the poor in rural Mississippi, indictments of an oppressive social system, were it not for the fact that visible oppressors are generally close relatives of the oppressed. Moody's people are abused and neglected by their parents, raped by their uncles, and shunned by their mothers-in-law in a murky circle of inhumanity which dulls more than it awakens sympathy.

Moreover, *Mr. Death* is not well written. The plots are mechanical and, although the catastrophes are dutifully foreshadowed, they are not persuasively caused. For instance, in the title story readers are made privy to a suppressed boy's morbid dream and then, without transition, are told that the boy has killed himself. The dream itself is lushly haunting, the realistic final scene grimly dull. Moody has strapped a richly imagined dream to a half-developed plot-frame about a double-suicide and a tape recorder. The dream and the plot-frame remain two things—distinct and at odds. Moody's style, too, is inconsistent. Her sentences, especially in "The Cow," lapse habitually into wordiness and anticlimax. Consider the following: "Then on his way home in the evening he'd stop and cut grass all the way along the twenty-five-mile stretch of road on his way back home" (pp. 34–35). Repetitive and vague, this sentence might be allowed if the narrative were consistently filtered through the mind of the protagonist, who is a naive and uneducated woman. But, if so, why in the next paragraph is she said to have "subconsciously wished" —bookish diction which her mind would surely have filtered out? The style veers wildly throughout this story: from "a lonesome old pain in the ass" to "contemplating the ripples," from "sweating up a storm" to "subsist on a diet of carbohydrates and fats." Moody's rendering of Mississippi dialect is also inconsistent. In one speech (p. 31), "dis" appears alongside "this," "tuh" alongside "to," and "nothin" alongside "horsing." And a number of ostensibly dialectical spellings, such as "jus take" and "whattaya," are actually phonetic representations of standard American pronunciation.

The two remaining books are serviceable anthologies of short fiction. *Into the Unknown* is a collection of eleven brief fantasy tales which, typically, present odd intrusions of the supernatural into ordinary lives and tease the reader into wondering if such things really happen—the sort of plots that fed the old "Twilight Zone." Some of the stories, such as those by Ray Bradbury and Robert Silverburg, are thin and themeless flourishes; others, particularly the contributions of Jorge Louis Borges and J. G. Ballard, are haunting little masterpieces; but all the stories in Terry Carr's anthology are entertaining and well written—excellent fare for teenage readers.

The stories in *Ladies of the Gothics* have, as the title implies, two things in common: they are gothic and they were written by women. The editors, Seon Manley and Gogo Lewis, have clearly endeavored to cover the field—yoking classic ladies such as Emily Brontë and Mary Shelley unchronologically to modern practitioners such as Celia Fremlin and Ruth Rendell—and the team does not pull well together. Beginning with stylistically simple modern short stories, the book moves abruptly into formidable gobbets of *Wuthering Heights* and *The Mysteries of Udolpho*, material which is widely available elsewhere and hardly benefits from being fragmented. The editors have stationed modern tales at the edges of the book, presumably as sugar coating for the nineteenth-century pill within, but this strategy hardly mitigates the inconsistency of the material; it rather sacrifices such coherence as chronological order would lend the book. There is, however, an apparent reason for all of this: the anthology, with its charming biographical introductions, is a girl's book, a feminist document intended to inspire pride in young women by praising the literary accomplishments of their gender. In this purpose, the anthology is quite successful; but it is doubtful that anyone, male or female, will read with enthusiasm all of the stories and snippets assembled by force between its covers.

The recovery of an eclipsed L. Frank Baum classic and the emergence of Nancy Willard's Anatole stories are happy events. And, though *Sweetwater*, *Into the Unknown*, and *Ladies of the Gothics* lack somewhat the richness and precision of great fantasy, they are generally entertaining and worth reading.

Recent Science Fiction and Science Fantasy

Craig Wallace Barrow

Matthew Looney and the Space Pirates, by Jerome Beatty, Jr. Illustrated by Gahan Wilson. New York: Camelot Books, 1974. $1.25.
Dragonfall 5 and the Royal Beast, by Brian Earnshaw. Illustrated by Simon Stern. New York: Lothrop, Lee & Shepard, 1975. $4.50.
Grinny: A Novel of Science Fiction, by Nicholas Fisk. Nashville: Thomas Nelson, 1974. $5.50.
A Wrinkle in Time, by Madeleine L'Engle. New York: Farrar, Straus and Giroux, 1962. $5.95.
Chains of the Sea: Three Original Novellas of Science Fiction, edited and with an introduction by Robert Silverberg. Nashville: Thomas Nelson, 1973. $6.50.

Unlike much science fiction of the past, where so-called adult books were sometimes taken over by adolescents and children, some recent science fiction and science fantasy works have been written for a youthful audience. Occasionally works of high quality are produced, such as the Newberry Award winner *A Wrinkle in Time,* but all too often censorship by the authors and sentimentality prevail. While one can appreciate Sylvia Engdahl's concern for her young readers when she says, "I feel that anyone who writes science fiction for young people has a responsibility to consider carefully whether the outlook of the story is truly one that he wants to foster,"[1] one can easily see how such a concern could be vulgarized to justify cheaper varieties of fantasy. While the experience of shifting taste in literature from the vulgar to the mature is common to most readers, I doubt that Professor Thomas J. Roberts is correct in seeing this "metamorphosis" as a justification for "sentimental lard" in children's science fiction and science fantasy.[2]

Matthew Looney and the Space Pirates is full of this self-same lard; no attempt is made to preserve verisimilitude even from children's questions and meager store of facts. Even though children know that the moon is not capable of supporting life, the plot involves moonsters who fear invasion from earth and are consequently planning to cultivate an uninhabited planet, Freeholy. Facts of space travel are violated by both text and illustrations, and even as entertainment, at best the comic adventure, which features Matthew Looney's being lost in space, his rescue by a chance encounter with a princess in a spaceship, his imprisonment on the waterlogged planet Bolunkus, and his clever plan to free himself and his friends using a potion remarkably like LSD, is a tired renewal of Peter Pan's conflict with Captain Hook. The values the book propagandizes are obnoxiously repeated. One can easily see liberal, anti-capitalist sentiment in the portrayal of Captain Morgus and anti-colonialism in the story as a whole; the drug culture is seen as innocuous and the police enforce puns instead of laws. While I do not consider myself conservative, I do not consider this book fair.

Dragonfall 5 and the Royal Beast is slightly better. There are fewer violations of verisimilitude and the language is less cliché ridden, but this story, like *Matthew Looney*, is too overtly propagandistic, dealing with racism and possibly even the Viet Nam war. The stealing of the Royal Beast by the Molok'hi, a society of cultivated bears, is similar to stealing a slave out of slavery. The actions by Tim and Sanchez taken against the bears, when they do not know the bears' intent except through the word of Patachari, a primitive chieftain, is racist. The threat by Tim to destroy the Molok'hi stronghold can easily be likened to American bombing in Viet Nam and the atrocities perpetrated on "gooks."

Some of the difficulty in exposing these books is contributed by an inadequate conception of fantasy. A dream has a logic of its own, and readers seem to know that Kafka's literary fantasies are of high quality, but we do not have a clear idea of the genre so that vain pretenders to the form can be easily discarded. Laurence Gagnon's "Philosophy and Fantasy"[3] is helpful in its discussion of the purpose of comparative worlds in literature and philosophy, but more work is needed.

Madeleine L'Engle's *A Wrinkle in Time* is a splendid fantasy; unlike *Dragonfall 5 and the Royal Beast* and *Matthew Looney and the Space Pirates*, it seldom violates reality. The Murry family relationships, Calvin's relationship to his parents, and Meg's relation to school authorities and the community, as well as the character portraits, are probable and realistic. Envy of the Murrys, gossip about the supposedly runaway father-husband, malice, selfishness, and even Charles Wallace's arrogance, are unflinchingly presented. Tesseracting, a seemingly instantaneous movement in time and/or place, is given a metamorphic fifth-dimension explanation. The witches who were formerly stars dying in the struggle against the evil shadow fight a symbolic battle steeped in classical and Gospel-of-John traditions, a battle that is psychically realistic even though symbolic. One can

even relate Mrs. Whatsit's, Mrs. Who's, and Mrs. Which's actions to
current theories of black holes in space and neutron stars; even the
life style on Camazotz has an affinity to entropy. The only weakness
in the novel is the confrontation with the It-brain by Mr. Murry and
the children; the shift from the symbolic to the actual confrontation
is a dramatic collapse of an antagonist from the infinite to the finite
much like the cannon battle in *Paradise Lost*.

Grinny: A Novel of Science Fiction is just what the title implies;
it is realistic science fiction, not fantasy. The book is scrupulously
probable, told in diary form by Tim, the central character. The story
unfolds the discovery by Tim, his sister, and their common friend,
Mac, that a woman known to them as Great-Aunt Emma is an alien
and shows their subsequent battle with "her." The use of the diary
form is reminiscent of Richardson's *Clarissa*; the drama of psychological warfare is acutely presented. There is just enough apparent
random information in the diary so that clues to Grinny's identity
are not obvious, and the author never violates the conditions he sets
for the children in their recognition and defeat of the alien. *Grinny*
is excellent science fiction, capable of appealing to children and adults.

Like *Grinny*, the three novellas in Silverberg's anthology are all
science fiction, not fantasy, which would mostly appeal to adult
readers rather than children. Geo. Alec Effinger's *And Us, Too, I
Guess* is a science fiction disaster story in which all plant or animal
genus members die off completely on single days. Story interest
centers on public reactions to the disaster, the gradual awareness of
the problem, and finally the panic. Using an unhappily married
couple and two scientists as point-of-view characters, Effinger delights in the selfish meanness of their lives; everyone is alienated
from everyone else in a way that suggests a cause of this disaster,
an inability to communicate, to feel a sense of community. In mood
the novella is similar to *Last Exit to Brooklyn*.

The title novella, *Chains of the Sea* by Gardner R. Dozois, poses
two possibilities: life forms on earth undetected by men and an
invasion by aliens who are in league with these life forms. While the
novella spends much time describing the world reactions at the places
of the aliens' arrival, the central story concerns a young boy's relation
to his parents' unhappy marriage, his father's anger, his mother's
fear, and his playmates and school authorities. Tommy, unlike the
adults, is aware of the life forms vaguely known and forgotten by the
adult world; the betrayal of him and all human beings by these life
forms is what finally draws the two story elements together. While

the novella is interesting, particularly in its characterization of Tommy and computer thinking, both story elements are so separated that the novella's unity is seriously challenged.

George Eklund's story, *The Shrine of Sebastian*, occurs after healthy men abandon the earth, leaving it to be run by robots and flawed men and women. Julian, the last pope, rides with Andrew, a robot, to bury Julian's mistress, who was formerly pope, at the shrine of Sebastian. World decay is similar to that seen in *A Canticle for Leibowitz*, but the effect Eklund appears to have felt most important is Julian's discovery that Maria was a robot. The tension of the novella concerns what is most alive and human; as in *2001 A Space Odyssey*, where Hal is more human than the people about him, so are the robots more human than the so-called people. The sexual liaison between Maria and Julian is, especially when one considers Maria's composition, a curiously intellectual pornography. While adolscents will surely read these novellas, all appeal primarily to an older reading audience. The psychological complexity of each novella, the absence of adventure and conflict with forces outside the self, and the determinism and lack of freedom in the novellas would turn off most young readers. Unlike the naturalism of a Zola with its surreptitious message of social reform, there often appears to be little that people can do to alter destiny in these science fiction writers' worlds.

Between the despair of the Silverberg anthology and the optimism of Brian Earnshaw and Jerome Beatty are two exceptional works of science fiction and science fantasy, *Grinny* and *A Wrinkle in Time*. Maybe needless distortions of the real are children's true enemy in science fiction and science fantasy, soupy optimism and will-less pessimism. Challenges that are met, no matter how great, only promote growth; optimism and pessimism only promote disease.

NOTES

1. Sylvia Engdahl, "The Changing Role of Science Fiction in Children's Literature," *Children and Literature: Views and Reviews*, ed. Virginia Haviland (Glenview, Ill.: Scott, Foresman, 1973), p. 253.

2. Thomas J. Roberts, "Science Fiction and the Adolescent," *Children's Literature: The Great Excluded*, II (1973), 90.

3. Laurence Gagnon, "Philosophy and Fantasy," *Children's Literature: The Great Excluded*, I (1972), 98–103.

Six Females

A Mixed Bookbag

Rebecca Lukens

Mia Alone, by Gunnel Beckman. New York: Viking Press, Inc., 1975. $5.95.

Ramona the Brave, by Beverly Cleary. New York: William Morrow, 1975. $5.50.

L.C. Is the Greatest, by Phyllis Krasilovsky. Nashville, Tenn.: Thomas Nelson, 1975. $5.95.

The Purple Mouse, by Elisabeth MacIntyre. Nashville, Tenn.: Thomas Nelson, 1975. $5.95.

The Real Me, by Betty Miles. New York: Camelot (imprint of Avon Books), 1975. $.95.

The Girl Who Would Rather Climb Trees, by Miriam Schlein. New York: Harcourt, Brace Jovanovich, 1975. $4.95.

Six new books, all with girls as protagonists. Is The Movement making an impact on the publishing world? Will the day finally come when girls will read books about girls—maybe even before they read books about boys?

Betty Miles has created in *The Real Me* an unwitting Fem-libber. Until Barbara finds that tennis is only for boys at Jefferson Middle School, until she finds she's stuck with slimnastics because girls need pretty figures, she's just an ordinary girl. When Barbara circulates a petition, she hears all the traditional female responses, all the chauvinistic one-liners. But only when she is refused a newspaper route does the prejudice really get to Barbara: "It's never been done." "There are rules, you know." "Girls don't go out in bad weather." Satisfied customers carry news of Barbara's success to the *Journal*, but it takes the governor's signature on a new law to win for Barbara the paper carrier job. Frankly, that's disappointing. How much more satisfying to let Barbara earn the job by sheer human competence.

Ramona the Brave is no crusader, but she is a truly individualized girl, and that is news enough. Beverly Cleary once again captures the real human mixture, for first-grader Ramona is indignant and loving, resentful and thoughtful, ornery and kind. We are finally delighted when she can handle a scary new bedroom with an elevator-doored closet, when she can lose a shoe on the way to school and have the courage to wear a paper-towel slipper. Ramona makes us all feel good about ourselves; we like mixtures of good and bad—like us.

No one wants to be an idealized little paperdoll. We'd rather be Ramona.

Mia Alone (translated from the Swedish novel by Gunnel Beckman) can't decide what to do about her life. For four long days while she awaits results of a pregnancy test, Mia considers what it would be like to marry at seventeen, to be a single parent, to have an abortion. Mia needs someone to talk to, and, for a refreshing change, Mia's confidante is not her friend nor her mother but her father. As he sadly confides news of his separation from her mother, he tells Mia what too-early marriage, marriage-on-demand, may do to a woman's life. As Mia sees her mother's difficulty in picking up her interrupted education in her middle age, she realizes some of what she may face. With the help of a librarian who finds for Mia all kinds of opinions on abortion—from church leaders' to ardent feminists'—Mia concludes that she can listen to no one. Although the book seems at times to be more a vehicle for theme than a real story, it is effective in its way. The seeming climax is an unusual one: a trickle of menstrual blood running down Mia's leg. The real climax in the internal conflict is Mia's discovery that since the life most dramatically changed by a baby is Mia's, not that of the future father and/or husband, not those of parents or church leaders or legal advisers, she alone must decide about having or aborting the baby. In addition to clear theme, Beckman's story makes a sensitive use of point of view; the everyday events of eating and sleeping and talking acquire significance because everything is tinged with Mia's self-questioning.

On to two more ordinary stories, but not ordinary really, because the protagonists are girls. Louise of *L.C. Is the Greatest* doesn't like being singular, particularly when she isn't exactly sure what being Jewish is supposed to mean. At twelve she feels left out, and having parents unhappy with one another doesn't help. But worst of all are two boys in the brownstone neighborhood who take a sudden interest in Louise; they want to kiss and feel. But Louise's change from being troubled and inadequate to feeling sure and competent seems too sudden and unaccountable. (Louise, however, is a far cry from Krasilovsky's *Very Little Girl*, who may never sort out her individuality, never feel competent.)

The story *The Purple Mouse* comes to us from the Australian writer Elisabeth MacIntyre. Hatty is deaf; she feels left out even when she screws up courage and tries to be part of a group. When she accidentally drops the pet mouse in purple dye, Hatty finds that gray mice do not accept purple ones. Nor does Emily the cat for that matter. Any different creature is affected by its singularity. A thoroughly competent mother is trying to show her children that their lives are what they make them, but to Hatty she seems indifferent. Only when Hatty's need for a mouse-cage for the ostracized rodent sends her to work in the gift shop does Hatty recognize her own abilities. No feminist or anti-feminist point is being made. Hatty switches from jeans to ruffles, it's true, but the more important change is Hatty's acceptance of herself.

Perhaps the book most clearly inspired by rejection of sexual stereotypes is *The Girl Who Would Rather Climb Trees*, a picture book written by Miriam Schlein and illustrated by Judith Brown. If a girl is a real girl, she should know how to play with a doll. But Melissa tries holding her gift doll in several ways—like a baseball bat, and like a roll of carpet. What do you *do* with a doll? Melissa finds that unlike her baby brother, a doll is so predictable. What would it do next? What it's doing now—nothing. So Melissa goes out to climb a tree. Passive toys and passive roles are not fun. That is, not for everyone.

What can we expect from a bag of books, all of them about girls? Just what we found, it seems. Some girls are traditionalists, some are compromisers, and some are crusaders. What matters is whether the girls are individuals, human and believable; whether we care enough about them to stay with the story and discover them; whether we find their problems relate to us, or help us to understand others. A good story can make a feminist point, or a good story can be a good story about a girl-type human being.

Recent Biographies of Women for Young Readers

Sheila M. Duram

Anna, by E. M. Almedingen. New York: Farrar, Straus and Giroux, 1972, $4.50.
Shelley's Mary: A Life of Mary Godwin Shelley, by Margaret Leighton. New York: Farrar, Straus and Giroux, 1973. $5.95.
Lady for the Defense: A Biography of Belva Lockwood, by Mary Virginia Fox. New York: Harcourt, Brace, Jovanovich, 1975. $6.50.

The choices made by a biographer in presenting the lives of women to young readers will affect their understanding of what a woman's life is, and what it can become. The writer who focuses upon the marriage of a woman remarkable in her own right implies that a woman's life is lived within the limits of men's. Each of these three biographies is about a woman who chooses to marry. The first, *Anna*, ends with her marriage at sixteen, although Anna Poltoratzky, in real life, lived to seventy years. The second, of Mary Godwin Shelley, is entitled *Shelley's Mary*, although she was married to Shelley for only six of her fifty-four years, and was an established writer herself. The third, a biography of Belva Lockwood, presents a woman whose marriage, although certainly an important part of her private life, did not limit her public existence.

E. M. (Marth Edith) Almedingen's 1972 award-winning *Anna*, the fourth of her historical biographies about her Russian ancestors, presents an engaging young woman of late-eighteenth-century Tsarist Russia. She is vital, curious, competent, and extremely intelligent. Her father, a prosperous seed merchant who passionately collects rare books, allows her to study foreign languages with her elder brother. She eventually masters eight, including Turkish and Arabic. When her brother becomes an expatriate, she is trained to become a knowledgeable heir to her father's vast estates. At sixteen, she falls in love and marries, and thus the book endeth. In the author's epilogue to Anna's "diary," we are told that her great-grandmother had "thirty-seven years of happiness with her husband," bearing him six daughters and a son. We are also told a lot about the son, whom Anna encouraged to pursue a literary career; of her six daughters, we learn only that Anna "saw three of [them] married to men she approved of. Two others died, unwed, in the 1820's." The diary

itself ends with the church bells ringing, and Anna deferentially telling her husband, as they ride off (literally) into the sunset, that he
has "not married a genius." But if he married the young woman to
whom we are introduced in the diary, it would appear that he did,
and because the diary itself is actually an imagined one, Anna's story
as the author thinks she "would have liked to have it told," the final
self-deprecating disclaimer is disturbing. The book is beautifully
written, however. It is full of detail which makes Anna's era, that of
Empress Catherine the Great, seem immediate. Almedingen does
succeed in relating one young life to history for young readers; both
the history and the life are interesting.

The title of Margaret Leighton's book, *Shelley's Mary*, puts one
off immediately. He did not buy the woman; he married her. *Mary
Godwin Shelley: Author of Frankenstein* would have attracted the
attention of more young readers, who probably know her story better
than her husband's poetry. Of her very famous mother, we learn only
that she made "an important impact on the thinking of her day,"
but nothing about with what issues she dealt in *The Vindication of
the Rights of Women*. Most young readers would be interested in
those ideas, and Mary Shelley's often tragic life would have been
perceived in a different light within the context of her intellectual
and literary legacy. Although Mary never knew her mother (who
died in childbirth), we know, from her daughter's journal, which is
the biographer's source, how deep the attachment was. She often ran
from her unhappy home to read by her mother's grave, where, we
are told, she sat reading her mother's book because Shelley praised
it. Leighton tells us young Mary knew the book by heart. It is hard
to believe she memorized it simply to please Shelley. If Shelley
himself had understood the book, he would not have fathered two
families simultaneously, causing both Mary and his wife Harriet
incalculable anguish. Harriet committed suicide. Shelley then proposed to Mary, simply to gain custody of Harriet's children. In the
last years of her life, Mary's journal as quoted by Leighton records
her deep sense of guilt about Harriet's death, suggesting that she
thought her own griefs were perhaps a punishment for having run off
to Italy with Shelley. She does not discuss, or seem to even consider,
Shelley's complicity.

The poet's life is given almost as much attention as his wife's.
Claire (Jane) Clairmont Godwin, Mary's stepsister and Byron's mistress, also takes up too many pages, as does Byron himself. Not that
they are uninteresting, but the result is a groupie biography, rather

than the story of one woman's life. Although the titles of her novels and of her travel book are mentioned, they are not given the consideration which her editing of Shelley's work is given. Her annotations and editing of Shelley's work are certainly an important part of *her* work, but it is that part which is least directly related to the woman herself. The major strength of this biography is the extent to which Leighton has quoted and assimilated material from Mary Shelley's journals, for it makes one anxious to read the journals themselves. The excerpts reveal a sensitive and gifted observer of human nature and of her times, quite different from both her famous parents and very different from her husband. Mary Shelley's contemporaries thought her abilities greater than her husband's; perhaps, as her work becomes more available, succeeding generations of readers will at least be able to consider the issue.

Mary Virginia Fox has written an excellent biography of Belva Lockwood, who in 1884 became the first woman to run for President. (Victoria Woodhull's earlier nomination, in 1872, never came before the electorate.) *Lady for the Defense: A Biography of Belva Lockwood* is so engagingly written that we enter into her story as if we were reading about a female Abe Lincoln (which, in fact, we are).

The book begins with young Belva's courageous rescue of her cat, stuck on the steep, icy roof of her family's log cabin in rural New York State around 1840. After marriage and widowhood, and a brief career as a New York school administrator, she remarried and returned to law school at the age of thirty-nine, becoming the first woman lawyer in the United States. She drafted and saw passed the first equal-pay-for-equal–work legislation, sponsored the first black male lawyer before the U.S. Supreme Court, drafted the first bill for a World Court for international peace, and was the U.S. Delegate to the first World Peace Conference. Perhaps her most remarkable achievement: she won, at seventy years of age, a several million dollar settlement for the Cherokee Indians against the U.S. government. The fact that most of us have never heard of her speaks for itself.

Throughout the telling of Lockwood's remarkable life, the author evokes a sense of excitement. As in *Anna*, we are given the homely underpinning which creates a credible character within the context of her notable accomplishments. But unlike *Anna*, the marriage of the heroine, as presented in her biography, is not the end of her story.

Isaac Bashevis Singer's Books for Young People

Thomas P. Riggio

Zlateh the Goat and Other Stories, by Isaac Bashevis Singer. Translated by the author and Elizabeth Shub. Pictures by Maurice Sendak. New York: Harper and Row, 1966. $4.50.

When Shlemiel Went to Warsaw and Other Stories, by Isaac Bashevis Singer. Translated by the author and Elizabeth Shub. Pictures by Margot Zemach. New York: Farrar, Straus and Giroux, 1969. $4.95.

A Day of Pleasure: Stories of a Boy Growing Up In Warsaw, by Isaac Bashevis Singer. Photographs by Roman Vishniac. New York: Farrar, Straus, and Giroux, 1969. $4.50.

Why Noah Chose the Dove, by Isaac Bashevis Singer. Translated by Elizabeth Shub. Pictures by Eric Carle. New York: Farrar, Straus, and Giroux, 1974. $5.95.

The Wicked City, by Isaac Bashevis Singer. Translated by the author and Elizabeth Shub. Pictures by Leonard Everett Fisher. New York: Farrar, Straus, and Giroux, 1972. $4.50.

"Who among our readers remembers such things?" lamented an editor at the *Jewish Daily Forward* when Isaac Singer began submitting stories about devils and ghosts. Forty years later Singer appears as much an anomaly. The phenomenon of children's literature translated from the Yiddish, grounded in the world of the *shtetl,* or East European Jewish village, and saturated with the arcana of Polish folklore suggests a formidable barrier even for the children of orthodox Jewish parents, not to mention the *goyim* among us. One anticipates the sort of cultural fence-straddling that Leonard R. Mendelsohn pointed out as the major pitfall for the writer of Jewish children's literature.[1] Singer's stories surmount the problem of the incompatibility of traditional Jewish materials and vernacular literatures, simply, by ignoring it. America—the twentieth century—might not have been discovered; no concessions are made to a pluralistic audience. The stories demand attention for what they are, good yarns, however populated by *shlemiels* and broken-down rabbis, devils and *dybbuks,* Hannukkah and Passover vigils, dreidel games, or *cheder* days.

The vocabulary and customs of the *shtetl* make exotic what in more modern dress would appear commonplace. Only a splinter of knowledge is necessary to make these collections accessible to most children over the age of four. A certain degree of culture shock is, of course, unavoidable. Not only is "sin" taken for granted, but some explanation will be due the youngster who first reads a story in which a grandmother-narrator begins, "A father had four sons and four daughters." The *shtetl* was a patriarchal world, and on the surface Singer offers little resistance to its conventions. Yet as anyone who recalls "Yentl the Yeshiva Boy" knows, Singer is not untouched by the many tragic dilemmas women face in such societies. Even in these stories the women of the *shtetl* most often emerge as the only sound guides to social order in a world ruled by male folly and incompetence. Behind such portraits lies the figure of the author's strong-willed mother as she appears in his memoirs, *A Day of Pleasure.*

Most young people will have little trouble dealing with the tales' pre-rational ambiance, which is Singer's heritage from his early study of the Cabbala, his father's Hasidism, and the materials of a native Yiddish folklore. True, these elements are "secularized" as Singer passes biblical stories and folklore through the alembic of his erratic sensibility. Like Singer's other fiction, these tales attract readers who shy away from dogmatic theology and yet maintain a need for a morality grounded on theological uncertainties. Here Singer translates this need into the child's world: the stories provide an elusive spectacle of primary values—good and evil—battling within the matrix of an imaginary world that is meaningful without being exclusive. Faith, in its aspect as a container of moral and cultural valuation, is a steady theme. A young boy can outwit the devil, and thereby rescue his parents, because he kept the Hannukkah candle lit; the fate of Lot and his family is sealed when they turn their backs on sacred traditions to enter "the wicked city"; a rabbi's magic is more potent than a witch's after he resists her seductions to power and wealth. In each case opposing forces fight for the possession of a human soul, and the microcosm of the story pushes the young reader to consider the larger order of which he is a part.

Despite the religious trappings, these narratives are not theocentric; instead they follow the moral curve of the traditional folktale. Even in the Bible stories, God performs only on the fringes of the miraculous. We know that He caused the flood because men sinned, and that He promised never to visit in such a way again; but in between Singer focuses our attention on the beasts gathered around the ark. Noah's story becomes an animal fable. (And Eric Carle's bold, pure-color illustrations complete the coup against the Almighty.) As they vie for a berth on the ark all but the dove display their human nature: the skunk boasts of his fine bouquet, the donkey of his intelligence, and so on. Singer, not Yahweh, provides the story's moral: "The truth is that there are in the world more doves than there are tigers, leopards, wolves, vultures, and other ferocious beasts. The dove lives happily without fighting. It is the bird of peace." Which is sound enough historically—for a children's book.

With all the magic, then, the imps, the devils, and mysterious charms, Singer forces the reader to contemplate this world, not the next. Often the action turns on the child's wonder at the incongruous and the grotesque. The grotesques are mainly demons or witches caught at a point of emergence from human forms. "The Grandmother's Tale" tells of a handsome young man who came out of a storm one Hannukkah evening. All proceeded merrily until someone noticed that the stranger did not cast a shadow. When the clock struck thirteen, there was no longer any doubt.

> The stranger saw by the children's frightened faces that his secret was out. He rose with a loud laugh, stuck his tongue out to his belly and grew twice as tall. Horns came from behind his ears, and there he stood a devil. Before anyone could say a word, he began to spin like a dreidel, round and round, and the house spun with him. The Hannukkah lamp swayed, plates clattered to the floor which shook like a ship on a stormy sea. The devil whistled. Mice appeared and goblins in red caps and green boots whirled around in a ring, laughing and screaming. Suddenly the devil sprouted wings, clapped them together, "Cock-a'doodle-do," and the whole company disappeared.

Such vivid portraits confirm the reality of evil and, in the process, awaken our modern, repressed feelings of awe for the irrational. Singer's grotesques are never gratuitous. They are minor figures in a tradition of Judeo-Christian allegory which includes Hieronymus Bosch, the author of *Piers Plowman*, Bunyan, and the traditional chassidic tales. Singer's modernism consists in his unwillingness to serve narrow dogmatic ends; but the precision of his creations and the seriousness with which he describes the supernatural communicates a sensibility highly skeptical of empirical reality. The very meticulousness of his treatment creates the illusion that there is something behind and beyond the prosaic sanities of our day-to-day existences. It is on this level especially that Singer charms the imagination of his younger readers.

Singer's animals, like his devils, share a pagan intimacy with the natural world. The stories work allegorically, and at times mythically. The title story in *Zlateh the Goat and Other Stories* tells of a young boy sent by his impoverished father to sell the family goat. Caught in a bizarre snowstorm, they seek refuge in a haystack within whose tomb-like confinement the goat nourishes the boy with her milk. On the third day they arise and go back to the father's house, where the deeds of the goat have saved her from slaughter. The archetypal resonances of such fables substantiate Singer's own account of his imaginative growth out of the provincial ethos of a Warsaw ghetto. *A Day of Pleasure* relates the tragedy felt by his rabbinical father and pious mother as he and his brother, Israel Joshua, indulged in "secular" books. It is to this achieved "worldliness" that we can trace Singer's panculturalism, his fascination with the mythic and cultural underpinnings of Western literature. It is what makes his children's books more than literature exclusively for Jewish children. The troubling aspects of Singer's other fiction—the reluctance to tamper with history and politics, the tendency to depersonalize character— are virtues in children's stories whose conventions, after all, give small play to history or "real" people.

There is a sense, of course, in which Singer's writing owes a great deal to the traditions of his ancestors. The Jews for many centuries had little to do with governments or national identities. The *shtetl* and the Warsaw ghetto were ethnic enclaves that existed outside the mainstream of European history. Like the *shtetl*, Singer's fiction walks a thin line between history and myth, the world and the imagination. In the ghetto, diplomacy and the destiny of rulers took second place to a messianic dream and a futuristic orientation based on a few books from the remote past. *A Day of Pleasure* reveals that for Singer's parents the relationship of a people to their God, not local or national politics, was primary. And Singer's stories, likewise, lie at a tangent to history. Though the God of his fathers is only a remote presence in these pages, still, he asserts the old moral precepts and the fact of immortality with the insistence of a true believer. To be sure, we are forced to translate a bit: the Messiah comes when man is in harmony with himself; immortality is "a song which is heard only by those who know that everything lives and nothing in time is ever lost." However understood, however sophisticated, Singer's key concerns are traceable to those early years he celebrates in his memoirs: "Although later in my life I read a great deal of philosophy, I never found more compelling arguments than those that came up in my own kitchen." These children's books and the memoirs, which draw both their materials and their point of view from the author's childhood memories, pay tribute to that heritage.

The second type of story in these collections, the "realistic" sketch, also communicates an aura of timelessness. It is the timelessness of the *shtetl*, the platonic form of which is Chelm. Chelm is a Polish town in the Jewish story-telling tradition remarkable for the large number of fools who live there. In this realm Singer's comic talent comes to the fore. The comedy centers largely on the figure of the *shlemiel*, or the eternal loser. The *shlemiel* fuels Singer's imagination as a symbol for a vital part of the identity imposed upon the Jew by history. In all his fumbling attempts to come to grips with the *shtetl*, the *shlemiel* represents in microcosm the Jew's sense of his own futility in the face of the world's logic. As such he achieves something of a sacred status in these pages.

Readers of "The Spinoza of Market Street" know that Singer rejects any acceptance of cosmic order that bypasses the world's absurdities. Rather, he chooses to embrace the foolishness of human disharmony. Ironically, the fool in this world is the only one who lives a social life consistent with man's phenomenological confusion. The ordinary run of mortals manufacture a false logic that deprives experience of its magical properties; the *shlemiel* accepts the world and takes its apparent illogic on faith. This awful ingenuousness is what the story-teller—and the child—finds most endearing in him. It is no coincidence that Singer's most famous fool, Gimpel, ends his life as a teller of tales.

If the *shlemiel* is beloved as an unselfconscious source of humor and a reminder that in the mind of God we are all *shlemiels*, Singer's skepticism fills these pages with another type of fool. The Elders, the traditional wisemen of the *shtetl*, are invariably more ridiculous in their pretended wisdom than the *shlemiel*. When a shortage of milk threatens to deprive the Pentecostal blintzes of sour cream, the people take counsel with the Elders. In their wisdom the old ones make a law that water is to be called sour cream and sour cream is to be called water. On Pentecost there is no lack of "sour cream," though some housekeepers complain of a "water" shortage. But that is another problem to be solved after the holidays with yet another law. Singer draws such Elders comically, though one wonders if any private rage lurks behind the picture of leaders unable to meet the exigencies of day-to-day existence in the *shtetl*. Unlike the *shlemiel*, who has only nature, biology, and the fates to blame for his state, the Elders are blinded by pride and sustained by a tradition that gives them power. The silliness of the insulated Talmudic scholar is comic in these stories, but, as *A Day of Pleasure* inadvertently tells us, the Elders seldom relieved any true suffering in the real ghetto. Yet Singer's memoirs everywhere make clear his unwillingness to grapple strenuously with the more painful parts of his own past. In this sense, the autobiographical pieces are basically another form of narrative for young people. They tell of life in the Warsaw ghetto as the child might have absorbed it—apolitically, asexually, and without any apparent scars carried into manhood. And Singer's way of remembering his youth, as a bemused observer absorbed in the spectacle, carries over into the fiction where he chooses to believe that all, even the Elders, have a place.

Such trust is finally a virtue of these books because Singer grounds himself not in a sentimental pluralism but in a belief in the value of communal bonds. The loyalties that result do not preclude moral imperatives: in "Utzel and His Daughter Poverty," a father learns that borrowing to satisfy his daughter's desire for shoes leads to a strange obesity on her part; as he grew poorer Poverty grew larger and uglier. "At last Utzel and Poverty understood that all a man possesses he gains through work." If Benjamin Franklin had written these stories, they could not contain a stronger work ethic. However, no final judgments are made, which is another way of saying that Singer's ethic is not a glorification of self via the profit motive but a child of necessity—the necessity of survival in the Warsaw ghetto. Poverty, if not a virtue, is not a source of guilt. The village finds room for the lazy and for the *shlemiel*, for whom all gain is by nature impossible; such exceptions soften Singer's perspective in ways the work ethic never does. Singer offers a *community* in which all, including the poor, find a place. *A Day of Pleasure* has as many saintly Gentiles as Jews. The death of a hardworking Gentile washwoman: "Her soul passed into those spheres where all holy souls meet, regardless of the roles they played on earth, in whatever tongue, of whatever creed. I cannot imagine paradise without this Gentile washerwoman." It is this record of human community, of shared values and customs, and of ritual communions which both partake of and transcend ethnic ties that makes these volumes so strange and so valuable for American children.

One final note. Singer is fortunate in sharing his text with a few of the finest illustrators of our time. Eric Carle's work for *Why Noah*

Chose the Dove would fascinate the child who had not yet learned to read the words. Margot Zemach and Maurice Sendak's drawings compete with the text for the reader's attention. Both capture with warmth the comic and grotesque side of Singer's version of the *shtetl*. Leonard Everett Fisher's pictures for *The Wicked City* are more static and severe than the others, but this is perhaps consistent with the nature of the story. Fourteen of the nineteen sketches in *A Day of Pleasure* can be found in *In My Father's Court*. The addition of Roman Vishniac's photographs of the Warsaw ghetto, however, is an important reason to get *A Day of Pleasure*. Vishniac's photographs were taken between the time the Nazis came to power and the invasion of Poland in 1939, that is, a generation after the period covered by the memoirs. Singer's note to the effect that the world portrayed in the photographs is essentially the same as the one in the stories dramatizes the timelessness of the ghetto.

NOTE

1. Leonard R. Mendelsohn, "The Travail of Jewish Children's Literature," *Children's Literature*, III (1974), 48–55.

Literature for and by Children

The Other Side of Elizabeth I's Character Never Before Revealed by Previous Historians

Judy Rosen (age 13)

She Was Nice to Mice, by Alexandra Sheedy. New York: McGraw-Hill Book Co., 1975. $5.95.

She Was Nice to Mice was written by Alexandra Sheedy (age 12), illustrated by Jessica Levy (age 13). The age doesn't really matter, because this book is written with a wit and style that would do credit to an author of any age.

She Was Nice to Mice is the story of a 16th century literary mouse, who lived at the court of Queen Elizabeth I, and grew to know and love her. The mouse's memoirs reveal to us the public and private life of the Queen (known to the mice as the Beautiful Nest Supplier, because her red hair was highly prized for purposes of decoration).

The author has written about life as a mouse and life as an Elizabethan. In both she uses a skillful mixture of fact and fantasy, which makes this book not only enjoyable, but informative. Through the mouse's observations, we learn about Elizabeth's royal rages, the secrets of her makeup, and her weakness for men, jewels, and dresses.

Not all the things in this book are true to fact. For instance, in this story Essex is without question the lover of the Queen. This enhances the story, but is historically unproven. Generally though, most things are accurate. The banquet scene is especially informative. We are told about the kinds of food the Elizabethans ate, how the table was set, and what kinds of entertainment followed the meal.

I would recommend this book for children between the ages of 8 and 12, as well as for any adults who enjoy good writing.

Of Note

Dissertations of Note: 1974–75

Bailis, Lawrence A. *The Concept of Death in Children's Literature on Death.* Case–Western Reserve University, 1974. 207 pp. 75-5050.
"The purpose of this study was to determine and classify the concepts of death that occur in children's literature on death for ages three through twelve." Includes a bibliography of children's books on death.

Green, Mary Lou Johnson. *The Image of Death as Portrayed in Fiction for Children.* Lehigh Unviersity, 1975. 126 pp. 75-23,992.
A statistical analysis of death imagery, vocabulary, and thematic approaches in ninety fictional books for children.

Hayden, Rose Lee. *The Children's Literature of José Bento Monteiro Lobato of Brazil: A Pedagogy for Progress.* Michigan State University, 1974. 333 pp. 74-27,421.
An analytical and historical survey of Lobato's thirty-nine works and seven adaptations.

Huthwaite, Motoko Fujishiro. *An Analysis of Contemporary Japanese Children's Literature with a Focus on Values.* Wayne State University, 1974. 151 pp. 74-29,815.
Explores a wide variety of types and themes in 500 Japanese children's books from 1968 to 1972.

Jennings, Coleman Alonzo. *The Dramatic Contributions of Aurand Harris to Children's Theatre in the United States.* New York University, 1974. 327 pp. 75-8577.
An overview as well as critical evaluation of the plays of the foremost writer for children's theatre in this country. Gives particular attention to *Once Upon a Clothesline, Pinocchio and the Indians, Buffalo Bill, Androcles and the Lion, Rags to Riches,* and *Punch and Judy.* "The bibliography, consisting of 223 entries, included thirty-one masters theses and sixteen doctoral dissertations related directly to playwriting for children's theatre."

Lamme, Linda Leonard. *A Longitudinal Study of the Relationships between Children's Reading Habits and Scores on* A Look at Literature. Syracuse University, 1974. 233 pp. 75-10,552.
Concerned primarily with the reading habits of 4th, 5th, and 6th graders over a three-year period. Correlates information with the NCTE's *A Look at Literature: An Assessment of Literary Sensitivity.* For comparison, one might consult Irma Lou Griggs, *The Development of an Instrument to Measure Literary Discrimination and Its Use with Other Tests to Judge Children's Literary Tastes* (University of Akron, 1974), 185 pp., 75-23,971.

MacKinnon, Theresa Lucina. *Theatre for Young Audiences in Canada*. New York University, 1974. 836 pp. 74-25,007.
Thorough analysis of the unprecedented growth in Canadian Children's Theatre from 1953 through 1973.

Muller, Alfred Peter. *The Currently Popular Adolescent Novel as Transitional Literature*. Florida State University, 1974. 336 pp. 74-18,038.
Concludes that "despite the growing sophistication of the adolescent novel, the genre conforms to traditional characteristics of traditional literature."

Orth, Michael Paul. *Tarzan's Revenge: A Literary Biography of Edgar Rice Burroughs*. Claremont Graduate School, 1974. 409 pp. 74-20,108.
Comments on Burroughs' early failures and ultimate success with the Tarzan series, then discusses reasons for its popular and literary appeal.

Rosenthal, Lynne Meryl. *The Child Informed: Attitudes towards the Socialization of the Child in Nineteenth Century English Children's Literature*. Columbia University, 1974. 340 pp. 74-7531.
Surveys the ideas of John Locke, David Hartley, and Rousseau, and focuses on *Sandford and Merton*, Edgeworth's *Early Lessons*, Sherwood's *The Fairchild Family*, Sinclair's *Holiday House*, and Montgomery's *Misunderstood*, as well as *Tom Brown's Schooldays, Eric, or Little by Little*, and *Stalky & Co.*

Schlager, Norma Marion. *Developmental Factors Influencing Children's Responses to Literature*. Claremont Graduate School, 1974. 154 pp. 75-2276.
Based on the Newberry Award Books, the dissertation tries to answer the question "Is there a relationship between the content of books widely read by children and the developmental aspects of growth characterized and displayed by characters within those books?"

Schon, Isabel. *A Descriptive Study of the Literature for Children and Adolescents of Mexico*. University of Colorado, 1974. 109 pp. 75-3832.
Studies the limited amount of literature published for children in Mexico during the nineteenth and twentieth centuries.

Sinanoglou, Leah Powell. *For Such Is the Kingdom of Heaven: Childhood in Seventeenth-Century English Literature*. Columbia University, 1971. 281 pp. 74-29,665.
"The study traces two separate currents—the Puritan concern for 'real' children and the poetic use of childhood as a symbol of lost ideals." Concentrates on a contrast between Calvinism, Puritanism, and Anglicanism.

Smith, Carolyn. *The Literary Image of Daniel Boone: A Changing Heroic Ideal in Nineteenth- and Twentieth-Century Popular Literature*. University of Utah, 1974. 184 pp. 74-20,485.
Treats juvenile biographies as well as adult biographies, comic strips, TV plays, dime novels of the 1800s, and historical novels of the 1900s.

Bibliographies of Note

Fordyce, Rachel. *Children's Theatre and Creative Dramatics: An Annotated Bibliography of Critical Works*. Boston: G. K. Hall and Company, 1975. viii, 275 pp.

An annotated bibliography of 2,267 critical sources related to Children's Theatre and Creative Dramatics. Includes lengthy sections on "Education in the Schools." Individual sections are cross-indexed and there is an extensive author index.

Gottlieb, Gerald. *A Descriptive Catalogue of an Exhibition at the Pierpont Morgan Library*. Available from the Pierpont Morgan Library, 29 East 36 Street, NYC 10016. xxx, 263 pp.

A compilation, by the Curator of Children's Books, of the extensive and spectacular Fall-Winter 1975 exhibition of rare children's books. Essays by Charles Ryscamp and J. H. Plumb round out the critical material.

Pugh, Michael, ed. *International Bibliography of Plays in Translation*. Available, biannually, from the editor at 10 Adamson Road, London NW3, England.

A comprehensive on-going bibliography compiled from recommendations of the ASSITEJ Centers (International Association of Theatre for Children and Young People). Lists all plays translated from their original language into English, plus production information.

Whalley, Joyce Irene. *Cobwebs to Catch Flies: Illustrated Books for the Nursery and Schoolroom, 1700–1900*. Berkeley: University of California Press, 1975. 163 pp.

A critical and bibliographical work related to illustrated instructional books for children over a 200-year period. The work also traces the history of illustration for a variety of types of books within the genre.

Of General Note

AB Bookman's Weekly for August 25 and November 17, 1975, are devoted exclusively to children's books at auction, primarily in Great Britain. The editors plan to extend their coverage to auctions in this country, and the "Special Children's Book Issue" will be annual.

—*Rachel Fordyce*

Suggested Topics for Research

Values

Social Values Expressed in Thornton Burgess's Books
Values of Dr. Seuss
Values in Children's Singing Games
Outdated Values in Children's Books
Values in Shirley Temple Movies
Moral Values in Andersen
Values in Louisa May Alcott's Books
Values in the "Peanuts" Comic Strip
Values in Children's Television

Fables, Folklore, Myth

Design in Children's Folktales
Fables of LaFontaine Compared to Stories of Marie de France
Origins of American Indian Myths
Folk Literature North of Quebec
Effect of West African Folklore on Black American Folklore
Nigerian Folklore (Interviews with Nigerians)
Lloyd Alexander: Moral Implications of His Fantasies
Economics in the *Blue Fairy Book*
Stereotypes in Children's Fairy Tales
Folk Music as Children's Literature
Wishes in Fairy Tales
Italian Folktales
A Comparative Study of Russian and Western Fairy Tales
Lithuanian Folk Tales
Evil in Fairy Tales
Japanese and Spanish Fairy Tales: A Comparison
Relevance of Aesop's Fables to Children Now
Clothes in Fairy Tales
Water Symbolism in Grimms' Tales

Emotional and Psychological Reactions

Fear of Animals in Children's Literature
Loneliness in Children's Poems and Stories
Peter Pan as a Nonconformist
Applying Piaget's Theories to "Winnie the Pooh"
Prejudice in Children's Literature
Reactions of Five-Year-Olds to Selected Fantasies
Achievement Ethics as Conveyed in Children's Literature
Masochism in Children's Literature
Negative Reaction to *Huckleberry Finn* of Some Children
Emotional Disturbances in the Stories of Hans Christian Andersen
Children's Literature from a Psychological Viewpoint
Adult Perceptions of Picture Books for Children
Correlation between Personality and a Person's Favorite Stories

Social Aspects

Children's Books about Physically Handicapped Children
Commercialism in Children's Literature
The Role of Women in Appalachian Folklore
Sex Roles in Arthur Ransome's Books
Children's Literature, 1812–14
Trends in the Treatment of Mothers in Contemporary Children's Books
Realism in *The Red Pony, The Yearling, Charlotte's Web*
Political Aspects of Children's Literature, 1929–70
Role of Athletics in Children's Literature

Presentation of Sick People in Children's Literature
Literature for Deaf Mutes
Children's Literature and the Maintenance of the Status Quo
Children's Literature of the Future
Sign Language as Symbolic Expression in Children's Literature
Differences between Children's Stories Now and Twenty Years Ago
Interviews in Prison: The Childhood Reading of Criminals

Art, Theatre, Music

Adult Considerations in Producing Children's Theatre
Illustrator's Depictions of Hands
Philosophy of Children's Theatre
Children's Literary Themes in Modern Music
Themes of Interest to Children in Black Music
Reader's Theatre for Children

Literary Criticism and General

Black Children's Poetry
Criteria for Choosing Children's Books
Literature on Biology for Children
Rainy-Day Literature for Children
Food Imagery in Children's Literature
Dogs in Children's Literature
The Miniature Adult as Portrayed in *Lord of the Flies*
Birth in Children's Literature
Contemporary Literature of Dual Interest to Children and Adults
Tom Swift Series
Virginia Hamilton's Books for Children
Poetry by and For Children
The Character of Jo in *Little Women*: Anti-feminist?
Relationship of Plants to Children's Literature
Bible Stories as Children's Literature
Pennsylvania Dutch Children's Cook Books and Rhymes
Bears in Children's Literature
"Legend of Sleepy Hollow" and "Rip Van Winkle" as Children's Literature
Death as Viewed in *Charlotte's Web* and *The Little Prince*
Evaluation of Zindel's *Pigman*
Poetry by Fourth-Grade Children
Comic Books as Children's Literature
Best Black Literature for Children
Role of Witches in Children's Literature
Analysis of *The Jungle Books*
Personification of Inanimate Objects in Children's Literature
"Black Sambo" and "Uncle Remus" Stories
Horses in Children's Literature
Character Study of Mary Poppins

CONTRIBUTORS AND EDITORS

JAN BAKKER teaches in the English Department of the University of Tennessee, Knoxville, Tennessee.

ANN BEATTIE is Writer in Residence at the University of Virginia. She has contributed articles to the *New Yorker*, the *Atlantic Monthly*, and other magazines and is also the author of a novel and a book of short stories.

CRAIG W. BARROWS is an Assistant Professor of English at the University of Tennessee, Chattanooga, Tennessee, and is interested in children's science fiction.

OSMOND BECKWITH is a poet who is interested in the land of Oz.

BENNETT A. BROCKMAN is at work on a book on the invention of children's literature. He is the author of a number of essays and articles on medieval and children's literature.

FRANCELIA BUTLER is Professor of English at the University of Connecticut. She is the author of forthcoming works on children's literature in the seventeenth century and a critical anthology of children's literature.

CHARITY CHANG is head of the Serials Department, University of Connecticut Library. She reviews children's books for various journals and for the *Hartford Courant*.

DANIEL A. COHEN is at Amherst College, Amherst, Massachusetts.

SHEILA M. DURAM is a Lecturer in English at Eastern Connecticut State College, Willimantic, Connecticut.

JULIUS A. ELIAS is Dean of the College of Arts and Sciences at the University of Connecticut and Secretary of the Board of Directors of the *Journal of the History of Ideas*.

FRED ERISMAN is Associate Professor of English and director of the Honors Program at Texas Christian University, Fort Worth, Texas.

CLIFTON FADIMAN is the noted author, critic, editor, and publisher, whose latest adventure in children's literature has been as Senior Editor of *Cricket* (since 1972). He was for ten years Book Editor of *The New Yorker*. He is also a board member of the Encyclopedia Britannica Corp.

RACHEL FORDYCE, Assistant Professor of English at Virginia Polytechnic and State University, Blacksburg, Virginia, is a specialist in children's theatre. She is the author of *Children's Theatre and Creative Dramatics: An Annotated Bibliography of Critical Works* (Boston: G. K. Hall, 1975).

MARTIN GARDNER, author of over a hundred scientific and critical works, is best known to students of children's literature for his *Annotated Alice* and his introductions to several of L. Frank Baum's *Oz* books. He has also contributed some eighty short stories to *Humpty Dumpty*.

WILLIAM H. GREEN is an Assistant Professor of English at Clayton Junior College, Atlanta, Georgia. The subject of his dissertation was

The Hobbit (Louisiana State University, 1969), and he has published articles on children's literature for various periodicals. He has also published numerous poems and stories for children, and is currently writing a children's novel.

JIM HASKINS is the author of more than thirty books for children and adults.

RAVENNA HELSON, Research Associate of the Institute of Personality Assessment and Research, University of California, Berkeley, has recently completed a study of critics and criticism in children's literature which was supported by the National Endowment for the Humanities.

JAMES T. HENKE is Associate Professor of English at Youngstown State University, Ohio.

ANNE DEVEREAUX JORDAN is Executive Secretary of the Children's Literature Association.

CAROL KAMMEN teaches at the Tompkins-Courtland Community College, Groton, New York.

NARAYAN KUTTY teaches children's literature and theater at Eastern Connecticut State College in Willimantic, Connecticut. A specialist in modern British literature, he has written essays for a forthcoming critical anthology of children's literature to be published by David McKay Company.

REBECCA LUKENS is a Senior Instructor in English at Miami University, Miami, Ohio. She is the author of numerous articles and reviews on children's literature. Her most recent book, *A Critical Handbook of Children's Literature*, was published in November 1975 by Scott-Foresman.

ALISON LURIE, novelist and critic, teaches, among other subjects, children's literature at Cornell University, Ithaca, New York. She reviews children's literature for the *New York Review of Books* and the *New York Times* and is co-editor, with Justin G. Schiller, of Classics of Children's Literature 1631–1932, published by Garland Publications.

JULIE CARLSON MCALPINE, Ph.D., Children's Literature, formerly of the University of Connecticut, is one of the founders of the Modern Language Association Seminar on Children's Literature.

ANNE S. MACLEOD is an Associate Professor in the College of Library and Information Services at the University of Maryland.

MERADITH T. MCMUNN is the co-author with William Robert McMunn of a forthcoming volume, *Children and Literature in the Middle Ages*, to be published by Stonehill-Chelsea Publications, New York. She is also chairman of the 1976 section on children in the Middle Ages at the Eleventh Annual Conference of the Medieval Institute, Western Michigan University, Kalamazoo.

RUTH BARNES MOYNIHAN is a doctoral candidate in American history at Yale University. She is a contributor to previous issues of *Children's Literature*.

WILLIAM T. MOYNIHAN is Chairman of the Department of English, University of Connecticut.

PETER F. NEUMEYER is Chairman of the Department of English, West Virginia University. He is the author of several children's books.

CARLA POESIO has translated and edited books, and written for Italian and foreign reviews. She is presently a reviewer of young people's literature for the Centro Didattico Nazionale, Florence, under the auspices of the Italian Ministry of Education. She has been a member of the jury for the Hans Christian Andersen Award.

THOMAS RIGGIO is an Assistant Professor of English at the University of Connecticut. He specializes in nineteenth- and twentieth-century American literature.

THOMAS J. ROBERTS is a Professor of English at the University of Connecticut who specializes in science fiction literature and literary critical theory.

JUDY ROSEN is a thirteen-year-old critic in residence at E. O. Smith High School, Storrs, Connecticut. Her areas of specialization include poetry and the Elizabethan Age.

WILLIAM ROSEN is the author of *Shakespeare and the Craft of Tragedy.*

GLENN W. SADLER, Ph.D., University of Aberdeen, Scotland, is the editor of the centennial edition of *George MacDonald's Fairytales and Stories, The Gifts of the Child Christ: Fairy Tales and Stories for All Ages* (Eerdman's, 1973). Mr. Sadler teaches children's literature at Point Loma College, San Diego, California.

ALVIN SCHWARTZ is writing a book on "the symbolism behind the major artifacts of our popular culture," of which his article in this volume is the first chapter. A resident of Quebec, he has received a grant from the Canada Council for this study.

WILLIAM E. SHEIDLEY has published articles on Elizabethan poetry in various journals and is presently at work on a book about Barnabe Googe.

JON C. STOTT is Secretary of the Board of Directors of the Children's Literature Association.

SUSAN WARD is Associate Professor of English at St. Lawrence University, New York.

VIRGINIA L. WOLF is a Lecturer in English at the University of Kansas, Lawrence, Kansas.

JACK ZIPES is Associate Professor of German at the University of Wisconsin, Milwaukee. He has written and translated books on German literature and is an editor of *New German Critique: An Interdisciplinary Journal of German Studies.*